LIFE IN THE
MIDDLE AGES

ROBERT DELORT

LIFE IN THE
MIDDLE AGES

TRANSLATED BY ROBERT ALLEN

Greenwich House

Distributed by Crown Publishers, Inc.
New York

Copyright © 1972 by Edita S.A. Lausanne and Robert Delort
Copyright © 1973 Translation by Edita S.A. Lausanne

All rights reserved.

This 1983 edition is published by Greenwich House, a division
of Arlington House, Inc., distributed by Crown Publishers, Inc.

Printed in Italy and bound in Switzerland.

Library of Congress Cataloging in Publication Data

Delort, Robert.
    Life in the Middle Ages.

Reprint. Originally published: Lausanne: Edita
Lausanne, 1972.
    Translation of: Le Moyen Age.
    Bibliography: p.
    Includes index.
    1. Civilization, Medieval.   2. Europe — Social
life and customs.   I. Title.
CB351.D4413   1983   940.1   82-24231

ISBN 0-517-40771X

hgfedcba

CONTENTS

FOREWORD

This book is intended for all those who, though not historians, are interested in medieval society and want to form an idea of the period when Western Europe with its civilization and its first divisions began to take shape. It is also intended for those who want to discover the traces of the Middle Ages that still remain in the technology, religion and mentality that make up our daily life at the present time, as well as that part of the vast heritage we have lost or forgotten.

These intentions have determined the themes I have dwelt on and the manner of their presentation. Till now all books on everyday life have concentrated on a certain period of time contained within narrow territorial limits. For example, Paris in the reign of Saint Louis, life in France during the fourteenth and fifteenth centuries, in England during the twelfth, at Florence during the fifteenth, and so on. Even Alwin Schulz's great pioneer works are devoted to life at court in the twelfth and thirteenth centuries and in Germany during the fourteenth and fifteenth.

Given these premises, an attempt to offer an over-all, though inevitably very superficial, vision of an area equal to three quarters of present-day Europe through ten centuries of its history would have been foredoomed to failure. Consequently, I have selected a certain number of themes—those that the reader expects to find—namely, the castle, the cathedral, court and monastic life, the corporation, the fair, the commune, the university, country life, the home, popular uprisings and festivities. I have also briefly sketched those of a more general nature that should be explored and meditated in connection with any type of civilization: What was Medieval Man like, physically, spiritually and mentally? What was the impact of the Christian ethic and religion on every-day life, love, the status of woman, children, adolescents, the warrior class and the clergy?

The proper procedure would have been to take examples from all the countries that made up the Western World during the Middle Ages—the Iberian Peninsula, Italy, France, England, Germany, the Scandinavian countries, Hungary, Poland, even Cyprus and the Holy Land. Actually, though intensely interested in the countries of the Mediterranean basin and the North-East, the author was forced to restrict his choice, preferring to take most of his documentary material from the quadrilateral bounded by the Rivers Ebro, Arno, Rhine and Severn. It was there that the majority of the inhabitants of the West lived—those who are credited, rightly or wrongly, with having known and distilled Western civilization in its purest and most quintessential form.

Historians may wish to consult this work for the wealth of splendid illustrations it contains. I would ask them to view with a lenient eye the liberty I have taken in my choice of themes. If they read a few passages of a text that can teach them nothing new, I trust that they will also bear with the few approximations aimed at making it easier for the general reader to grasp the essentials of a picture which historians know is extremely complex, diverse and changing.

THE PHYSICAL CONDITIONS OF EVERYDAY LIFE

The Middle Ages saw the shaping and development of the world we are familiar with today; a world that some consider to be on the point of vanishing, if it has not already done so. But, though the framework was laid by this period, the commonplace details of our daily life differ to a large degree from those that then prevailed. For example, as we drive smoothly along a motorway across levelled hills and filled-in valleys, the shapes of the mountain formations have very little effect on our progress; this, of course, is still more true of travel by aeroplane. The mountains, which for centuries dominated the landscape, have been so thoroughly settled upon and so deeply penetrated by man that they are now in need of protection against his ultimate assault. Today, agricultural science can make the most sterile soil yield as abundant a harvest as the most fertile virgin soil. The mightiest rivers of the West have been channelled for man's benefit and the sea itself is held in check by artificial dykes along the low-lying coasts. The natural flora and fauna are everywhere in jeopardy; even the primeval forest is threatened. The miserable fragments that still remain are confined in pitiful reserves, or exist only as fossils.

Modern man himself is protected from birth against disease, both epidemic and endemic, as well as against drought and nutritional deficiency. His average lifespan has increased threefold in a few centuries. Those who are free to follow the sun through the hemispheres are totally independent of climatic conditions; others on a less exalted level can adapt their clothing to suit the season and defy inclement weather in a heated motorcar or air-conditioned home. These truisms need to be stated in order to provide a firm basis for our study of life in the Middle Ages.

Nowadays, if man is still aware of the forces of nature, it is only because of a few intractable climatic and cosmic phenomena and his own physical condition. In all other respects he is cut off from the environment by a screen of technology that serves as an indispensable link while preventing all direct

This page from the *Evangéliaire de Godescal* (781-783) gives a picture at once idyllic and symbolical of nature and animals during the Middle Ages. Cocks, peacocks, pheasants, pigeons; a duck, a heron and a deer all drink at the Fountain of Life. Reality was very different—mankind had a hard struggle to feed and clothe himself.

contact. However, during the Middle Ages such direct contact, which hand-tools promote and machines impede, was the basic fact of life. The woodcutter felled the tree with his axe; the hunter transfixed the wild boar with his spear; the farmer furrowed the ground with his plough. Man was alone in his struggle against cold, hunger and sickness; his only hope lay in his strength and resistance. Consequently, before undertaking a detailed study of life in the Middle Ages we must investigate the material circumstances in which people lived and the environment which framed and conditioned their life. That environment was not quite identical with ours, either in itself or in its relationship to man. We must also discover what means people used to protect themselves against it and master it. Lastly we must consider what sort of people they were who were sometimes overwhelmed by the forest, famine or disease and forced to retreat, but who were never defeated, always returned more numerous, more vigorous and more dynamic than before, to defy nature, check its onslaughts, and finally make the first awkward but successful efforts to subdue it.

THE MEDIEVAL ENVIRONMENT

The daily life of an organism—or, if you prefer, its life pure and simple—is conditioned by that organism's nature and the environment in which it lives. The science of ecology has made great strides since the German biologist Ernst Heinrich Haeckel invented it, or laid down its aims, in 1866. More recently the environment has been defined as a sum of abiotic and biotic factors. The first may have their origin in the cosmos—solar radiation, gravity, etcetera—or be inherent in the earth itself—climate, mountain formations, the physical and chemical properties of soil and water. The second derive from other organisms, of the same or different species, which live in that environment; they are often dependent on the first and include the fauna, the flora and so on.

Many attempts have been made and are still being made, with varying success, to determine in greater detail the interactions of man and his environment. But so far the results have been unsatisfactory because a number of unknown or imponderable factors have been neglected. As if this human ecology were not sufficiently complicated, the historian adds another dimension. Not content to study man and his environment at the present time, he seeks to apply all the latest procedures to their study in a distant past for which much essential information is lacking.

It is extremely tempting to presume that neither man nor his environment has altered basically, at least in the short term, and that their interactions make up the entire warp and woof of history. Actually, this convenient postulate is only very approximately correct. It is certainly erroneous for such biotic factors as the number of individuals and the variations of the fauna and flora, perhaps for man himself, and very likely for the abiotic factors too.

No doubt, when we examine pictorial representations and written descriptions of landscapes or natural phenomena, a great many of them recall precisely those we are familiar with. We can hardly imagine, for instance, that the Matterhorn, the island of Crete, the English Channel, the Mediterranean rains—or the forest of Brocéliande—made famous by legend in Brittany—have changed perceptibly in the last thousand or fifteen hundred years, and therefore with stronger reason within the lifetime of people who seldom lived more than half a century. The fact is, however, that virtually all the infinitely complex factors of the geographical environment have been modified not only through the centuries but within very brief periods of time.

Sudden modifications of the landscape have been caused, for example, by earthquakes, volcanic eruptions (chiefly of Etna in Sicily and Vesuvius in Italy), landslides that carry away whole mountainsides, as in the Abîmes de Myans near Chambéry, and chasms that gape without warning in the karst lands of Southern France and Yugoslavia.

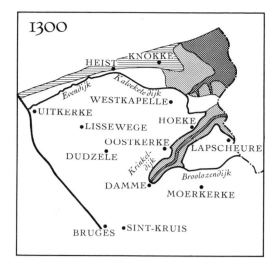

Dunes

Channels

Flooded areas

1150

Evendijk · Kalvekeledijk
• UITKERKE
WESTKAPELLE •
• LISSEWEGE
OOSTKERKE •
DUDZELE •
Krinkeldijk
BRUGES • SINT-KRUIS

1300

HEIST — KNOKKE
Evendijk Kalvekele dijk
• UITKERKE
WESTKAPELLE •
• LISSEWEGE   HOEKE
OOSTKERKE •
DUDZELE •   LAPSCHEURE •
Krinkel-
dijk
Broolozendijk
DAMME •   MOERKERKE
BRUGES   • SINT-KRUIS

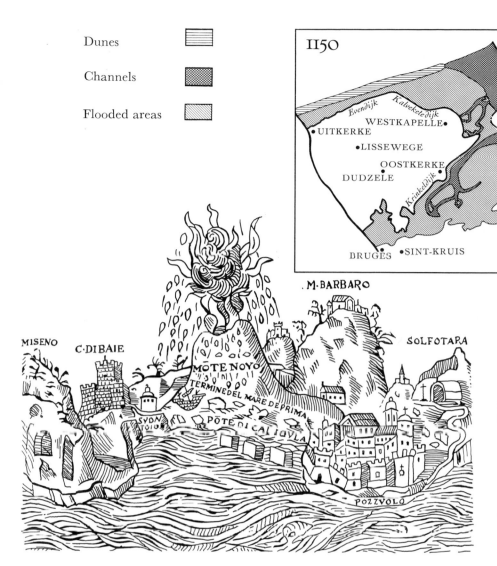

The level of the sea varied greatly during the Middle Ages. For instance, the Flemish plain was flooded for lengthy periods. The Gulf of Zwyn formed in the twelfth century made Bruges the first sea port of North-West Europe for 200 years.

The Bay of Naples was frequently modified by movements of its volcanic subsoil. The woodcut (left) shows how Monte Nuovo rose suddenly between Cape Miseno and Pozzuoli in 1538. The inscription 'TERMINE DEL MARE DE PRIMA' on the picture indicates the previous shore line.

Some European landscapes have changed little or not at all since the Middle Ages. Château-Gaillard, erected by Richard the Lion Heart in 1197, still towers above the River Seine, the township of Petit-Andely and a valley that continues green.

13

In November the peasants pastured their pigs in the oak forests. Here the swineherd is brandishing a stick to knock down the acorns on which they fed. In those days pigs were hairy and quite long in the leg.

Less rapid changes become noticeable within a few centuries. For instance, the region of Venice has subsided under the weight of the alluvia deposited by the Po, Adige, Brenta and Piave. In the vicinity of Naples volcanic activity has accelerated alternate submersions and emersions that form part of a general movement which has lifted the coast of the Tyrrhenian Sea dozens of feet in some places since Roman times. In Venice the ground is sinking steadily. The ancient port of Baiae is submerged and the columns of the nearby temples show traces of the molluscs that became attached to them before they emerged again in more recent times. The Scandinavian buckler, after being crushed 20,000 years ago under an ice cap up to 2 miles thick, is rising at the rate of 3 feet a century; this means that during the Middle Ages the area north of Stockholm rose some 30 feet. Though unaware of these phenomena, the local population must have felt their good or bad effects. We all know about the plight of Venice today.

The rock structure in the depths of the earth may vary little or not at all, but the composition of the top layer can be altered considerably by alluvial deposits, sedimentation, or the complex action of living organisms that settle on its surface.

Modifications of the scenery are sometimes speeded up drastically by the action of water. The sudden collapse of the head of a glacier can carry away a mountainside, as at Argentière. Or an extraordinary flood can completely alter an entire river basin. This occured to the Po valley in 587, when the Adige was driven back towards the north and forced to flow into the Adriatic, while its tributary the Mincio changed its course so that it flowed into the Po, whose mouth was shifted several miles to the south.

The vast amount of energy expended by oceans, rivers and glaciers makes an impact that can be observed in the course of a few generations, if not in a single lifetime. Meanders are cut, as in the valley of the Sava between Provo and Progar or of the Lot between Cahors and Duravel. Important alluvial deposits force rivers to change their course; thus Brisach is now on the right bank of the Rhine, and therefore in Germany, after having long been on the left bank and in France; the mouths of the Escaut continue to change, as do those of the Meuse and the Rhine; the Romanche was blocked by a flood in 1191, forming a lake that swallowed up Bourg d'Oisans, only to break through the bar twenty-eight years later.

The sea undermines cliffs, as in the region of Caux; engulfs whole forest like the Dol of Brittany in the eighth century, or villages and arable land, as on the coast of Flanders and Friesland in the eleventh and thirteenth. A sudden rise due to a storm or an exceptional flood tide can create enormous havoc. The coastline is incessantly modified. At the beginning of the Christian era, where we now see the Point de Grave and Soulac there was a large island separated from the rest of the Medoc by a branch of the Gironde that was blocked during the Middle Ages. A vast series of lagoons between the Isonzo and the Po were silted up within a few centuries, sounding the death-knell of towns like Aquileia, Grado, Comacchio, Concordia and Heracleia that had become uninhabitable or had lost their livelihood. This phenomenon can be observed at many points along the Mediterranean coast between Leghorn and Barcelona, for instance, at Ampurias in Catalonia and Ruscino near Perpignan. At Aigues-Mortes, Luni and Pisa the land has advanced, filling in the lagoons when not pushing back the sea itself. On the Baltic coast the 'Nehrungen' (alluvia) have caused the rapid silting up of the inland 'Haffen' (bays), notably between Danzig and Königsberg. Sand brought by the sea and sculptured by the wind has encroached upon the hinterland, barring rivers, creating lakes and inexorably destroying villages, as in the Landes of Western France.

These local actions are sometimes accentuated by very general phenomena at the level of our planet or even of the cosmos, most of them caused by the sun. As it travels through the Milky Way, the sun may pass through dark zones that temporarily attenuate its brilliance and diminish the heat and other radiations it emits. Moreover, every ten or eleven years the recrudescence of the sun-spots, combined with the emission of ultra-violet rays of extremely short wavelength, causes sudden changes of pressure in the earth's atmosphere at high altitude. High-energy particles, notably neutrons, produced by the sun or constituting the core of the cosmic radiation, could destroy all life on earth, were not most of them trapped by the magnetic field and forced to rotate; this is the origin of the Van Allen belts. The number of such particles that reach the surface of our planet depends on the intensity of the cosmic radiation and of the earth's magnetic field. Both factors are variable. The first is due in part to the solar radiation, the second to many different influences that affect the electromagnetic fields within the viscous mass of iron and nickel which forms the essential component of the earth's core. The intensity of our planet's magnetic field decreased about 12 per cent during the Middle Ages, which is far from negligible for a lapse of some ten centuries, but at the end of the period it was still about 22 per cent higher than it is today.

The maxima and minima of the sun's activity have been determined with rough approximation. They have always been more or less cyclic, except during the twelfth and thirteenth centuries. However, they were very different in the Middle Ages than they are at present. Without going into details, let us say that the population received fewer high-energy particles than we do today and that the sun is no longer quite the sun they knew. Hence the climate they knew was not quite the same as ours, at the same latitude, and did not remain constant all through the period we are dealing with.

On the one hand, the sun may have exerted a stronger attraction on the mass of warm equatorial water that forms the Gulf Stream and circulates above the colder water from the polar region, so that it reached a higher latitude. During the many centuries when that happened the polar ice extended less far towards the south. As a result the Vikings had no difficulty in sailing to Greenland, so named from its verdant vegetation at that time, and even Labrador, where they discovered salmon and grape-vines. Moreover, the prevailing winds in Western Europe, which blow in from the west, pass over the surface of that mass of water, absorbing warmth and moisture. This gave the British Isles and Scandinavia a milder climate than they have at the present time.

Another factor is the northern jet stream, an air current that flows in the opposite direction to the earth's rotation at medium altitude above the temperate zone and influences the climate of our regions by approximately establishing the polar front. It is very sensitive to sudden variations of pressure. When it accelerates, its centrifugal force shifts it towards the equator and its speed makes its path an almost perfect circle. As a result, the polar front advances towards a lower latitude, causing low temperatures in Western Europe and the passage of cyclones over the Mediterranean, increasing the humidity, and establishing weather conditions linked with the latitude. When the jet stream slows down, it is pushed back towards the north and its reduced speed gives it a sinuous path. Western Europe gets a warmer, moister climate; but the weather may differ in region situated on the same parallel owing to the sinuosity of the polar front and the consequent flux or reflux of cold or warm air.

The fundamental importance of these variations in climate is easy to grasp. For example, when the polar front and the Gulf Stream recede towards the north — they bring a rise in temperature that makes the glaciers melt; consequently, the level of the sea tends to rise and encroach upon the low-lying coasts. The periods during which this phenomenon occurred have been established with a certain precision by studying the glacier of Grindelwald and the peat-bog of Fernau, from which the glacier recedes when the temperature rises and to which it returns when the temperature falls. These movements still occur and therefore their causes and effects can be observed; they coincide with each other and, by and large, with those of the sea described above. At present we are living in a period of rising temperature: the glaciers are receding and the level of the sea rises one-twentieth of an inch a year.

There seems to have been a brief period of low temperature during the Merovingian epoch until about 750; a period of rising temperature from 750 to 1200, characterized by the flooding of the marsh of Dol and the Flemish plain; a slightly cooler period during the thirteenth century, still more marked about the middle of the fourteenth; and a slight rise in temperature from the fourteenth to the sixteenth. The warm spell may have been accompanied locally by drought, and there may have been some cold winters owing to the sinuosity of the polar front. When that happened the Seine was frequently frozen over; wheeled vehicles crossed the Rhine or Rhône on the ice; wine could be chopped with an axe and carried in a hat (1478); and the cold prevented access to the forest of Franconia (873). A clerk of the Paris Parliament recorded—and we can check the truth of his words on the manuscript—that his ink froze before it had time to touch the parchment. However, as a general rule, the climate tended to be milder than it is today.

In the last analysis climate is the major factor in the environment because it has a preponderant effect on the vegetation and therefore on all living creatures, including man. The form of vegetation that covered the greater part of the West during the Middle Ages was the forest. But that primeval forest

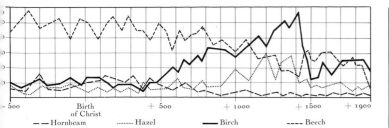

The forests of Western Europe comprised the same species then as now, but in different proportions. Researches on the pollen in the Rotes Moor peat bog (North Germany) proves that the beech predominated in that part of the world but was ousted progressively by the birch during the thirteenth, fourteenth and fifteenth centuries.

During the early Middle Ages the West was covered with forests. This map shows how extensive they were before AD 1000 from the Massif Central in France to Bohemia. A) major wooded areas; B) wooded areas of uncertain limits and compactness; C) limits of the inquiry. The species found in the major wooded areas were the following: 1. Weald: oak, birch; 2. Bavarian Vorland: beech, oak; 3. Bohemian forest: oak, beech; 4. Buchonia: beech; 5. Dreieich Forst: oak, beech, hornbeam; 6. Diepholz: oak, birch; 7. Lusatia: elm, hornbeam; 8. Ardennes: beech; 9. Othe: oak, beech; 10. Evrecin: oak, beech, maple; 11. Sologne: oak, birch; 12. Langres: oak, hornbeam, beech; 13. Jura: pine, fir, Norwegian pine; 14. Graves: oak; 15. Médoc: oak, pine; 16. Sylva Godesca: pine; 17. Sète: pine; 18. Abruzzi: oak, beech; 19. Cilento: pine; 20. Sila: pine; 21. Catalonia: oak, English oak, birch, pine; 22. Algarve: pine; 23. Serrania de Cuenca: pine; 24. Balearic Islands: pine.

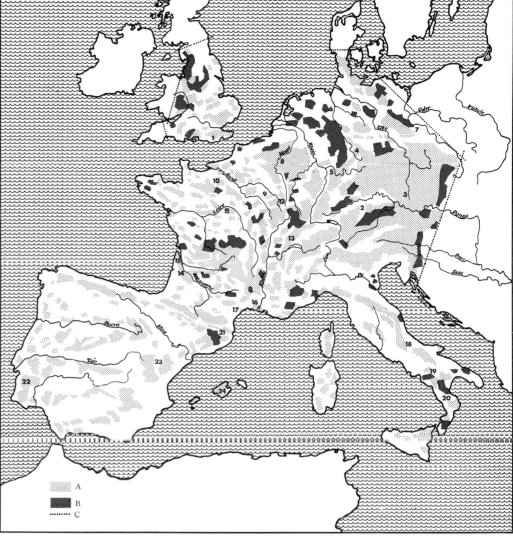

was not quite the same as the patches that still survive. It grew and spread during a cool, moist period in the days of the Merovingian kings, and its vast expanse modified the climatic trend. The rapid evaporation, due to the foliage, maintained a more constant humidity with abundant precipitations; this enabled the forest to flourish and multiply even when external conditions changed. On the other hand, when forests were destroyed by fire, clearance or grazing, they could grow again spontaneously in regions where conditions were still favourable, but not elsewhere. Those that lined the Mediterranean coast degenerated to scrub land except at a certain altitude as we can see in Corsica. In the Iberian Peninsula those laid waste by sheep during the Middle Ages have been replaced by steppe. The wholesale destruction of the forest of Orléans has caused the level of the streams to fall considerably. The slopes of Upper Provence, after losing their trees through disafforestation, were stripped of their soil by the heavy rains and deprived of the last shreds of vegetation, leaving the gaunt rock exposed in many places.

But even in the regions where the natural forest was strong enough to regenerate spontaneously it has not maintained its original composition. There is an incessant struggle among the different species, even where the soil is apparently the same, one or another being favoured by imperceptible differences of climate. These variations in the composition of the plant covering have been studied with the help of the pollens found in peat-bogs and of whole tree-trunks preserved in the glacier ice, as at Grindelwald, or in the ground (the *couérons* of the forest of Scisy at Dol). The hazel that predominated in the fifth millennium BC was first ousted by oak, elm and lime, and during the Middle Ages by beech, hornbeam, fir and pine. The peat-bog of Fernau shows how conifers gradually took over from the birches; in the Rotes Moor, in Germany, the beech and hornbeam that flourished until about 800 was gradually but completely displaced by birch and hazel by 1000. At the dawn of the Christian era the Flemish plain, before it was invaded by the sea, was stocked with alders and hazels which no longer grow there. The

SECURITAS

SENÇA PAVRA OGNVOM FRANCO CAMINI
ELAVORANDO SEMINI CIASCVNO ·
MENTRE CHE TAL COMVNO ·
MANTERRA QVESTA DONA TSIGNORIA ·
CHEL ALEVATA AREI OGNI BALIA ·

chestnuts of the forest of Orléans dwindled during the twelfth century. The plane tree was unknown before the Carolingian epoch and, like the poplar, remained extremely rare until deliberately planted by man.

Spontaneous variations in the preponderance of one element or another have extremely important effects. Certain trees extract certain minerals from the soil and thus alter its composition. More important still, the rapid decomposition of the dead leaves produces a layer of vegetable soil, called humus, that may attain a very substantial depth.

Humus is most abundant in forests of leafy trees; conifers produce a thinner, drier carpet of needles that are not only less fleshy but also less abundant; this is true even of larches and other types that shed their needles every winter. This obviously affects the conditions that prevail when the forest is cleared and the land tilled, as well as the livestock that can feed in the patches of forest that are preserved. Swine prefer acorns, beech nuts and chestnuts, they are repelled by resin-smeared pine-cones.

The undergrowth too differs with the species; the beech for example is intolerant of all underbrush, while the oak accepts many differents sort. This acts directly on the vegetarian fauna and indirectly on the carnivores that devour the vegetarians and the supercarnivores that prey in turn on the lesser ones. It is no exaggeration to say that the plant covering is the basic element of the landscape and chief among the biotic factors that affect man.

To view the Western World during the Middle Ages as an immense forest of oak and beech gradually giving way to pines and firs in the northern and mountainous regions is elemental to our study of how man lived during that period. But we must not forget that man in turn acted on the forest, destroying it entirely or selectively in some places and altering its composition deliberately or unknowingly in others by planting different species. This caused changes in the natural forest during and after the Middle Ages and in the fauna that inhabited it, independently of climatic trends and biological cycles.

As a result, the fauna of the Western World was slightly different in quality from what we find today, and very different as regards the relative proportions of the various species and the number of individuals of each. This may be ascribed to a wide range of natural causes. For example, insects, reptiles, batrachians and birds are closely linked with the environment, the climate and the vegetation, all of which were different from those of the present day. Some species emerged, while others declined or passed through biological cycles that still have not been explained. The clouds of locusts practically disappeared after the ninth century, but the destructive cockchafers were terribly active at the beginning of the fourteenth. The rabbit was unknown in the British Isles until about the twelfth century. The black rat multiplied, notably after the eleventh century, and was not seriously rivalled by the formidable grey variety until modern times. It is worth noting that the black rat was responsible for the dreadful pestilence known as the Black Death, which killed off one third of the population of Western Europe between 1348 and 1350. Periodic outbreaks of epizootic diseases decimated or contaminated some strains of wild or of domestic animals. We must also bear in mind the fundamental fact of human intervention. Man acted blindly against toads and owls; with more reason against birds of prey that killed off poultry, ruminants that destroyed the harvest, and edible game; and in self defence against wild beasts and venomous reptiles. He did his best, instead, for the flocks and herds of domestic animals.

We can judge the outcome for ourselves. The destruction of birds of prey led to the rapid multiplication of rodents and the proliferation of birds that batten on certain species of insects; as a result, some plants were favoured while others found it difficult to survive. Relentless action against the wolves, whether for offensive or defensive purposes, strengthened the packs of wild boar; the eradication of snakes allowed rats to multiply. Domestic cats had long been known but were quite rare until the end of the Middle Ages; their importation from

Until the early nineteenth century, the wolf was the beast most feared by man. Gaston Phoebus (d. 1391), in his *Livre de la Chasse*, shows how in the Middle Ages the peasants captured wolves with nets and finished them off with spears.

Africa was a mixed blessing, for some reverted to the wild state and helped to perpetuate and aggravate the damage done by natural felines like the lynx and wildcat. The decline of otter and mink, together with the improvement in fishing methods and the stocking of pools and lakes, led to a qualitative modification of the river population.

A number of species that were common in the West during the Middle Ages have disappeared or become extremely rare. The auroch *(Urus)* was the first to be eliminated; by the beginning of the sixteenth century only a few survived in Poland, but they were so rare that the Germans mistook them for bison. The last author to describe and make drawings of them was the ambassador Sigismund von Herberstein; he said they were like oxen 'except that they are all black and have a sort of whitish stripe on their back'. But since the late Middle Ages they had retreated to the Eastern Marches, mentioned seldom in either hunting or general literature.

Bears, however, were 'very common beasts'. In 1387 that great hunter Gaston Count of Foix, known as Phoebus, described in detail their habits, the places where they were found, and how to hunt them. Peasants, particularly those who lived in the uplands, were familiar with the big, strong, lumbering beasts that loved honey, could be terrible or playful, but were easy to fool even when enraged. Bears declined chiefly because they were exterminated by the great nobles—the only people who could keep packs of mastiffs for hunting them and who were trained in the sport of bear spearing. Their habit of hibernation, their very low fertility, their lack of

aggressiveness, their surly solitude, and their relative defencelessness put them in an inferior position.

Wolves were a very different matter. They made a deep impact on the Middle Ages by their numbers, their strength, their cunning, their pugnacity and their permanent contact with man. The western forest was an extension of the vast Eurasiatic taiga which provided an inexhaustible supply of those agile, swift, ubiquitous beasts. They travelled in packs, could cover hundreds of miles in a few days, and haunted the long, cold winters of the West. England, protected by the sea, was the only country that succeeded in exterminating the wolf during the Middle Ages.

Everywhere else terror of the wolf, who ruthlessly devoured women, children and the aged, became a part of the folklore like the werewolf. Hunting and popular literature abound in tales of Isengrim (the Wolf personified), who could be mocked at from a safe distance, while hunters extolled the beast's amazing strength, cunning and courage. Innumerable documents prove that the presence of the wolf was one of the dominant facts of life. Near Genoa, in the thirteenth century, no fewer than six cubs were found in a single day. Brittany, Auvergne, Sicily, the Cantabrian Cordillera, the Meseta and the mountains of the Harz were infested by wolves. In 1420 they invaded Paris and in 1438 its outskirts. The wolf population has been viewed as a symptom of the health of the Western World. Till the end of the eighteenth century, if not later, they took advantage of the briefest spell of weakness or inattention to settle, multiply and devour victims that came their

way. The other carnivores were contained with less difficulty or could not develop so long as the wolf was king. Thus the lynx *(Lupus cervarius)*, of which the northern strain was already relegated to Scandinavia and Russia, while the southern strain hardly ventured beyond Spain, Southern Italy and the Balkan Peninsula, though isolated individuals were occasionally found north of the Pyrenees, in Bearn and Savoy. This is also true of the wildcat. The wild boar, which Gaston Phoebus of Foix called the strongest of all beasts, was very common; but its expansion was limited by the wolves, which devoured its young, and by the frequent battues organized by the nobles, who were fond of braving a beast that could kill with a single blow of its snout armed with long tusks. Boar was also an important item in their diet. Alphonse de Poitiers (1220-71) had 2,000 killed and salted before starting out on the Crusade.

Less attention has been paid to the many other species equally familiar to lords and peasants because they were common until the beginning of the twentieth century. They ranged from foxes and badgers, pheasants, hares, deer and chamois, to ants and bees. The beaver was rare everywhere but in Germany after the Carolingian period.

We are left with the difficult problem of discovering whether animals were stronger, bigger and hardier during the Middle Ages than their descendants of the present day. Some ecological laws point in that direction for cold or humid periods. But the

Packs of wild boar were very common in the Western forests. For a single man to attack so strong and savage a beast armed only with a spear took both skill and courage. Other denizens of the Western forests during the Middle Ages: above, the stag, very common in those times, was hunted with hounds or shot with bow and arrow.

Below, the auroch *(Urus)*, a vigorous black bull, the last specimens of which survived in Poland till the sixteenth century. The lynx, wild cat, otter, mink and even the stag are now all but extinct.

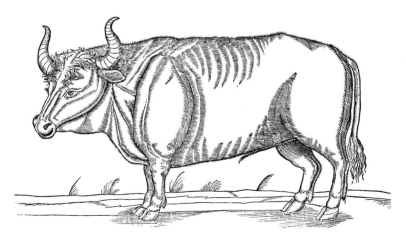

bone tissue examined in Poland and Russia does not permit it to be stated beyond question. Parchments were made from the pelts of domestic animals (sheep and, exceptionally, calves) and are no help to us in this context. But from the study of furs—the available texts enable their size to be calculated on the basis of hundreds of thousands of items—we can say with certainty that weasels, ermines, squirrels and so on were largely comparable with those we know, and that the difference in stature between some forest and some moorland animals was exactly the same as it is today.

On the whole, therefore, the environment in the Western World has changed very little from those days to ours. The average temperature may perhaps have been about one degree higher, but that did not prevent the winters from being sometimes very severe. The presence of forest on every side increased the humidity of the atmosphere while impeding sudden fluctuations. As far as flora and fauna are concerned, few species have disappeared but the forests were far more extensive. Yews, which poison livestock, and wolves, which devoured man and his flocks, were more numerous. Some species of conifers and leafy trees were more common.

The fundamental difference between the Middle Ages and modern times is that man had fewer means of acting on the environment, exploiting it or coping with it; also that he was far closer to and dependant on it. His daily life was largely spent in an incessant struggle against a powerful and little-known nature.

MAN AND HIS ENVIRONMENT

Actually, man was less at the mercy of the world around him during the Middle Ages than his primitive forbears had been, thanks to tools and techniques inherited from Graeco-Roman and German Antiquity. He improved some, invented others and lost track of a certain number. Not all of them were equally suited for their purpose, which explains why his efforts achieved results that varied so in quality.

Fire and iron were still man's chief resources, but the iron he now produced by Germanic procedures was far superior. We know from analyses carried out, on swords mainly, that during the Merovingian period blacksmiths were quite capable of making tempered steel with 0.4 to 0.6 per cent of carbon as well as very tough steel that could be welded to soft iron owing to its low carbon content — 0.32 per cent. Moreover, case hardening resulted in a much harder edge because nitrogen lowers from 723 to 590 degrees Centigrade the temperature at which carbon dissolves in iron.

On the other hand, output was increased to the point where the metal was no longer employed exclusively for weapons. From the eleventh century it was also used in tools for working wood and stone and, more important still, in agricultural equipment; harrows, ploughs, scythes, sickles and so on. The ore was still mined chiefly by the opencast method and only exceptionally in shafts, so the growth in production was not due to improved mining techniques. It must be ascribed to the spread of a new type of furnace. Before the end of the Carolingian period smelting was done in large pans supported on masonry above ground level, and ventilation, provided either by the prevailing wind or by water-driven bellows, was in common use. Ventilation had two advantages. First, it served to produce more metal of better quality; secondly, by increasing the intensity of the fire and so raising the temperature, it greatly improved the processes employed for making glass, bricks, ceramics and fire clays.

Better use of water power in floating mills—at Toulouse—tide mills—at Dover—and particularly by building dams and weirs was perhaps the most important technical advance achieved between the tenth century and the thirteenth. In a short time tilt-hammers, tanbark mills, oil mills, malt mills, brew-houses, paper mills, hemp mills, fulling mills, grinding mills and the like, were set up on all the rivers of the West after they had been suitably harnessed. Flour mills were always by far the most numerous, and from the eleventh century some of them began to be driven by the wind. Full exploitation of wind and water as sources of energy depended on the solution of a technical problem. In fact, the circular motion obtained at a first stage by means of horizontal or vertical wheels was merely a quantitative improvement on that obtained with turn-benches, foot-lathes or the primitive hand-mills. The camshaft that enabled a circular motion to be converted to an alternating motion was not a new invention for Hero of Alexandria had already known it in the third century BC, but it was rediscovered and generalized in the eleventh and twelfth centuries. The addition of a crank-and-rod system in the fourteenth century was a revolution whose impact is still felt today.

Where reduction gearing, cog wheels and wheel trains, presses, winches and hoisting tackle of various kinds were concerned, the Middle Ages were satisfied to take over the methods employed in Antiquity; at most their efficiency was increased by using stronger materials and more careful construction. The fourteenth century treadmill crane at Bruges was greatly admired, and improved types of presses led to the screw-jacks and capstans common in the thirteenth century, with which very heavy loads could be raised. It is unfortunate that lifting jacks, though their principle was known and utilized at least in the crossbow, required too large a quantity of metal for their use to become general.

Driving power was supplied mostly by men and animals because they were readily available everywhere. Examples of this at the elementary level are the blacksmith wielding his hammer, the woodcutter his axe, the peasant his mattock, the vine-grower shouldering his dosser, and the mason his stones. Teams of men worked capstans and treadmills, towed boats and hauled wagons. A number of inventions at once simple and revolutionary made this power more effective. The wheelbarrow first appeared in the thirteenth century and was generalized in the fourteenth and fifteenth; wheels were made with spokes and had iron-shod rims; the hooped felloe came later. Pack and draught animals were utilized

far more rationally due to still more far-reaching inventions. The shoeing of horses, mules and donkeys began in the early Middle Ages, making them more resistant to, and less easily fatigued by, stony ground. Oxen worked with their heads, through a yoke set on their horns; horses worked with their shoulders, pushing on a collar instead of being throttled by pulling on a halter; teams were harnessed in line instead of abreast. This had an even greater impact on agriculture than on transport because it enabled heavy ploughs to be employed on very hard, recently cleared land.

Actually, the greatest revolutions in transport took place on the water, notably on the sea or wide rivers, through the construction of new types of vessels. They were broad of beam and round of bow, and could carry large quantities of merchandise and sail fairly near the wind with their mixed rig and robust stern-post rudder. The ancient galleys and Scandinavian drakkars were gradually replaced by ocean-going ships, huge galleons, small hookers and white caravels, that sailed the seas with the assistance of compass, astrolabe, portulan and solar inclination tables.

Technical progress was very slow in the early Middle Ages when the Germanic innovations were adopted but the procedures of the ancients were forgotten. It developed faster from the eleventh century and still more from the thirteenth, when the idea of progress penetrated man's consciousness. Empirical recipes were gradually replaced by rational, if not scientific, thinking. This was enormously promoted and diffused by the capital invention of printing in the fifteenth century. But, then as now, too much effort was expended on the development of deadly weapons and methods of waging war. The crossbow, more powerful and accurate than the long bow but extremely slow-firing, could be used at a pinch against wild animals; but two gigantic catapults—the trebuchet, invented in the late ninth century, and the mangonel, introduced to the West in the eleventh—made more effective by the incorporation of winches, springs and counterweights, were

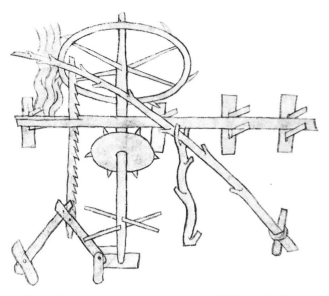

The thirteenth century architect Villard de Honnecourt drew many machines both real and imaginary in his sketchbooks. Above: a rudimentary water-powered system used to saw a tree-trunk lengthways for beams or planks.

Right: this winch-actioned catapult was employed in siege warfare before the cannon. Man's ingenuity and technological progress were exploited chiefly to improve war machines, which found buyers and users throughout the West.

This crane was greatly admired in Flanders in the fourteenth century. The tread-wheel supplied the power needed to hoist heavy loads in the port of Bruges.

employed exclusively for warlike purposes during the Middle Ages. This, with still more reason, may be said of the cannon, which first appeared in the early fourteenth century.

People in a position to invest large sums to promote advances in other fields felt no urge to do so or were opposed to all innovation. It is true that the nobles built mills and improved roads, but only to increase their feudal dues. They squandered their surplus on unproductive expenditures, keeping the peasantry at subsistence level and so preventing them from playing a part in the technological revival. Only the monks, who lived in an independent, self-governing economic system, helped to develop machines that relieved toil or made it more effective. As a result, medieval man was thrown back on his tools, the work of his hands and his personal struggle with nature, of whose force and power he had to bear the brunt. Small wonder that, with his preoccupations, his ignorance and the few instruments at his disposal, his action on nature produced uneven results.

No doubt he fought and exploited the natural fauna on a large scale. For fishing and hunting he possessed a whole arsenal of extremely effective equipment. Peasants employed nets, both fixed and mobile, to catch birds perched in trees and on the wing; hares, rabbits and other small rodents; fish, such as salmon, tench, trout, pike, lamprey and eel. They also used wicker pots, gins set along the runs, leather bags before the burrows, harpoons and fish-

The plate on the right shows how gold and silver ores were mined and sold in the fifteenth century near the town of Kutna Hora in Moravia. The mineral is raised to the surface while the miners prospect for new veins. Above ground men crush, wash and sort the mineral; others sell it under the supervision of royal controllers.

The miniature on the left illustrates glass and pottery making. The great heat of a brick oven is used to make glass for blowing and to fire ceramic cups. Viking blacksmiths also used fire to forge the tools reproduced below.

gigs, traps and snares that postulate the existence of strong, powerful springs made of thin supple wire. Hunting large or very swift game required crossbows and other missile weapons, pikes and other arms for in-fighting, as well as specially trained animals such as horses, hounds and falcons. This demanded an investment which was only within reach of the knightly class, although the peasants who could use the long bow were able to poach deer at great risk.

Domestic animals did their part in curtailing or destroying the natural fauna. Buffaloes, bulls and swine drove out wild beasts; poultry, sheep and goats, protected by the elimination of weasels, foxes and wolves, annexed a large portion of the food previously consumed by herbivorous wild animals and at the same time damaged the vegetation by destroying the young shoots; goats were the chief culprits in this respect.

The forest too was greatly encroached upon and exploited. Indeed it was a major factor in the peasant economy. Gathering was still an important activity that yielded wood, mushrooms, chestnuts, hazelnuts, pine kernels, acorns for mashes and beechnuts for oil. There was also the honey produced by wild bees, besides edible game. In addition to timber, the forest supplied fascines for roads, foundations, walls and huts, as well as faggots for heating and charcoal burning. Leafy boughs, after being used for bedding domestic animals, were buried in the ground and served to improve old soil, whose acidity was also modified by adding heathmould. New land obtained by clearing stands of trees had a thick layer of fertile humus; the deep soil of drained marshes, once it was weeded, harrowed and ploughed, provided excellent land for growing grain. The need for virgin land led to a wholesale attack on the forest as early as the seventh and eighth centuries; the population explosion from the eleventh to the thirteenth speeded up the process. It was then that heavy axes came into general use for felling trees and adzes for eradicating undergrowth and the brambles that sprang up again and again; saws for cutting the trunks into logs for transportation, at least to the nearest suitable stream;

and hatchets, hoisting gear, and heavy ploughs for chopping and removing roots and large stumps that could not easily be charred on the site.

Clearance work was restricted and finally brought to a standstill before the end of the thirteenth century for lack of adequate methods, not so much of doing the job itself as for increasing the yield of the land thus won. On the other hand, the great diminution of the area under forest endangered the balance of the local economy, which depended no less on gathering dead wood, feeding swine and hunting game than on an increased production of cereals. Much newly cleared land was left fallow in the fourteenth century as a result of the demographic crisis and was soon covered again by forest and brush. By that time people in Northern Italy, Upper Provence and other regions too had realized that the destruction of the trees entailed the irreversible erosion of the soil, and endeavoured to prevent peasants and their goats from continuing their ravages. In England, France and Poland a number of forests were preserved for hunting by kings and nobles.

But encroachment on and exploitation of the dominant vegetation had other consequences of fundamental importance, though in many cases that was not realized for a very long time. One was the accelerated modification of the species. The wholesale felling of the big trees that could be utilized immediately favoured the less robust specimens. The problem was already serious in the twelfth century. In fact, Abbot Suger of Saint-Denis recorded how, after his men had searched in vain, he himself discovered the few trunks absolutely necessary for the long beams for his minster. It is true that the destruction of the forest provided millions of acres of new arable land, but excessive clearance and unskilful exploitation did much to speed up the deterioration of the plant life and brought about a partial modification of the hydrographic situation, the microclimate, the profile of the terrain, and the soil itself.

Man also made conscious efforts to utilize or modify the facts of physical geography. His struggle against the rivers and the sea was responsible for the

Hunters used very strong nets of different shapes, into which they drove the game, aided by dogs. Here servants are finishing the nets with slip-knots.

most important projects carried out in the Middle Ages. The Loire was enclosed by huge embankments as early as the Carolingian period; the Po valley was systematically organized by changing the course of the Ticino between the twelfth century and the fourteenth and of the Adda in the thirteenth, in addition to regulating the Po itself. During the same period the Venetians deviated the Brenta and the Piave, curbed the Adige and saved the lagoon from being silted up. Enormous dykes were built in an attempt to save the coast of Flanders and Holland from the inroads of the sea; the recently formed Gulf of Zwyn was enclosed by walls and part of the flooded area was reclaimed, giving rise to the polders. Charlemagne attempted to link the Black Sea and the North Sea by connecting the basins of the Rhine and Danube with a canal whose traces are still visible; but the project failed and was not finally realized, at a more suitable site, until the nineteenth century. The Hanseatic towns were more fortunate for they succeded in 1398 in linking the rivers Trave and Elbe and consequently the Baltic with the North Sea through the Stecknitz Canal, predecessor of the Kiel Canal of our own day. But the most important, though less spectacular, achievements in this field were the draining of marshes and their reclamation and cultivation, the irrigation of parched areas like the Roussillon and parts of Sicily, and the harnessing of water power.

The development of the territory also raised the problem of building roads, causeways across marshes and bridges over watercourses, marking fords and equipping mountain passes. In the Middle Ages the highways often followed the lines of the old Roman roads, but the splendid bridges scattered through the West are sufficient proof of the vast effort produced by man during that period.

The scenery of the Western World as we know it today was unquestionably moulded by the untiring labour of the Middle Ages. The overall result was achieved in the course of many centuries. This means that the daily work of millions of individuals, using only the simplest tools, brought about modifications which are very considerable in the aggregate but were virtually imperceptible within the lifespan of each. What really counted for Western Man was not the certitude of victory but the impression of engaging in a daily struggle against a hostile or rebellious environment, the result of which always remained in doubt.

Like primitive man, he was preoccupied with defence rather than aggression and his major aims—to protect his life and ensure his subsistence—crystallized around the elemental problems of habitation, food and clothing.

The struggle against cold, wind, rain and excessive heat, as well as against wild beasts, the night, the evil eye and an alarming nature, led him to build a home and endow it with an artificial climate, as his forbears had done in bygone centuries. Given the prevalence of the forest, timber was naturally the basic building material. Castles over a long period were merely wooden towers erected on mounds; that of Hastings was still standing at the end of the twelfth century. The houses of the townspeople, or at least their studding, were made of wood; hence the frequent fires. In some countries peasants and villagers built their cabins mostly of branches and treetrunks. Churches too were often built of timber, notably in Norway, but also at Honfleur, in the Carpathians and in Venice. The same is true of the ramparts of the Polish grod, the framework of earthen embankments strengthened with stakes the palissades of strongholds. Wood was the material for the joists that supported floorboards and flagstones, the rafters and battens of roofs (some shingled, some thatched), pieces of furniture and many tools and domestic utensils. The means for providing an artificial climate were not very elaborate; wood fires and, exceptionally, turf fires raised the temperature slightly in the immediate vicinity of the nobleman's chimney-piece and the peasant's hearth.

The earth was the source of the few other building materials used; though the tar that was sometimes employed as a preservative came from wood. Clay mixed with chopped straw formed daub, which was

Two quite primitive implements were often used for clearing forests—a big felling axe for cutting down the trees and a type of long-handled bill-hook for lopping the branches. In the miniature on the right we can see the two operations being performed at the same time.

Clearings gradually eroded the forest unless it was protected as at Compiègne by hunt-loving kings. Here we see the hamlet of Saint-Jean-aux-Bois on land cleared by the monks from the forest of Compiègne.

31

often applied over a wooden frame. Clay was also dried in the sun or baked to make bricks and tiles, but they were in general use only at a late date and in a few countries like Denmark and Flanders, the Hanseatic towns and the Toulouse district. It was not till after the Middle Ages that bricks and tiles replaced timber on a large scale.

What little stone was employed was seldom dressed except for such grand buildings as churches, monasteries, castles, mansions and palaces. Where the forest had receded to the point where it could provide timber only for beams and roof trusses, stone was commonly used, embedded in clay or mortar. Water conduits were still made of stone, wood, terra cotta and even lead, but they were rare indeed.

The houses offered adequate shelter from rain and snow, the sun and visible nature in general. Their windows were exceedingly narrow, not only for architectural reasons.

Many of the peasant's dwellings had none at all, and even in the castles they were very small compared to the vast area of the rooms. Churches, cathedrals and other buildings in the Romanesque style were extremely sombre. It was not until the thirteenth century, or even later, that sunlight flooded the homes of the privileged classes and the house of God. When medieval man discovered the beauty of bright colours, the blue of the sky, the green of the leaves, love of nature began to replace, up to a point, the distrust it had previously inspired.

Houses built of wood, brick and stone, into which little light could penetrate, also afforded protection against excessive summer heat where that was necessary. In southern countries whitewashed walls reflected the sun's rays, and the narrow streets squeezed between the houses were no more than passageways and often very dark. On the other hand they did not keep out the damp and cold. The wind blew through the narrow, unglazed windows, which at best were spread with oilcloth, or through the chinks in the framework. There was little in the way of decorative fabrics to blunt the contact with the bare walls and the floors of chilly flags or beaten earth. Heating was, in general, far from adequate. Vast fireplaces that diffused their heat in all directions were invented, or their use became widespread, in the eleventh century. They were undoubtedly a great improvement on the braziers with which the Mediterranean population had made do, but a regression compared with the hypocaust of the wealthy Romans. Noblemen and peasants suffered the same discomfort: smoke was often inseparable from warmth and fires that drew well radiated little heat. It is tempting to believe that the thatched cottage which offered shelter to both man and beast was warmer than the huge castle with its twinned fireplaces. If we leave aside the greater comfort enjoyed by some few nobles, clerics and rich burghers at a late date, it is no exaggeration to say that, whatever his rank, medieval man's dwelling was both dark and cold.

Of course, cold is a relative notion: it varies with the time and the place. Many rich peasants at the end of the Middle Ages could have lived comfortably in better built homes but did not dream of doing so. It should be said, however, that medieval dress afforded very effective protection against fluctuations of temperature and that, even if our ancestors felt the cold as much as we do, life in their houses, was not a great hardship because of the type of clothes they wore.

Dress has different functions and defending the wearer against the weather was probably neither the first nor the principle one during the Middle Ages. But we cannot help noting that throughout that period, until the mid-fourteenth century or thereabouts, everybody—men, women, priests, nobles and peasants, rich and poor—dressed in long, flowing clothes. The few slight differences were due to practical reasons. Men in general wore breeches; workers and warriors wore shorter, less cumbersome costumes and carried special tools or weapons when they were at work or war; clerics wore a distinctive garb; nobles and rich burghers were, as a rule, clothed in more precious materials; thick, sumptuous woollen cloths, fine Reims linens and rich, supple

Clearance work began in the seventh century and increased during the great population boom of the twelfth. Man endeavoured to utilize nature or modify it to his advantage. The forest was replaced by pastureland and tilled fields, while roads were built across rivers to link towns.

Timber was the commonest building material and most of the iron implements—saws, axes, planes, gimlets, etc.—were used for working it. Many houses consisted merely of a strong framework of beams starting at ground level and supporting floors and roof; the inner and outer walls were made of planks.

Building involved the intervention of mason-architects and a clever system of pulleys and cranes operated by man or animal power. The methods illustrated in the miniature reproduced below seem rather rudimentary and ineffectual.

Walls of mud or pisé (with timber studwork), brick, tiles or stone were also employed, depending on the region and the owner's means. The photograph on the right shows the narrow Rue du Matelas at Rouen, which was preserved intact from the Middle Ages until the Second World War. The house walls were made of rough-cast and beams. Before the twelfth century many bridges and castles were built of timber because building in stone was extremely costly.

This old house at Ypres (below) is one of the rare examples of timber houses that have been preserved from the Middle Ages to our own day.

silken fabrics were reserved for them. The poor wore lindsey-wolsey, duffel and coarse linen. Headgear and footwear too varied with the period and the class of the wearer. Whatever the reason, the generalization of a single type of dress—ample, long and flowing—resulted in the whole body being covered and protected against the vagaries of the climate.

Furthermore, seasonal dress was unknown and the same clothes were worn in summer and winter. This leads us to suppose that in winter people must have worn various garments one over the other and the layers of air that separated them provided effective insulation even if those next to the skin were not always very close-fitting. Lastly, the outer garment was practically always lined with fur, a material at once light and thick, which more than any other has the property of preventing loss of heat and of being impervious to water and not to air. It has been calculated recently that pelts worn with the fur outside are twice as effective as the most compact woollen cloth. In the Middle Ages they were always worn with the fur inside and therefore the body was protected still better. We should not let ourselves be tempted to believe that fur-lined garments were the privilege of the rich and powerful. The skins of kids and sheep cost no more than the coarsest woven stuffs, while badgers, foxes and many other beasts of prey that were killed on sight supplied excellent pelts at no cost whatsoever. True, the sable, ermine and miniver worn by the great ones of the world were certainly more expensive and were considered 'finer'— another very relative concept—but were hardly more effective. In any case, the result was the same: medieval costume offered everyone outstanding protection against the cold. So much so that summer must have seemed very warm to those who could not lay aside their furs or were unwilling to do so. Bright, sun-drenched houses were perhaps not so greatly missed after all.

Long robes and furs were also connected with other functions of dress, chief among them to defend modesty and respect sexual taboos. It has become a commonplace to contrast antiquity, with its love of

The big fireplace was a medieval invention. The fire, which was kept up almost the whole year round, provided both heat and light. It could also be used to cook food in pots and coppers slung on chains or racks some distance from the hearth. Left: the great fireplace in Marksburg Castle.

sunlight and nakedness, to the sombre, gloved, fur-clad Middle Ages, when Christianity exerted a far stronger influence than the Germanic tradition. In fact, the contours of the body were broken and concealed by those thick, rigid draperies that reached down to the ground and clothed in the same fashion men and women, priests and kings, making them all members of the same universal family.

The mid-fourteenth century was marked by an utter change of mentality. The calamity of the Black Death was followed by an economic and social crisis whose effects were felt for a very long time. Dress too underwent a change. Short, tight-fitting clothes put in an appearance; masculine and feminine attire became progressively differentiated; the form of dress a person wore, and not only the material, grew to be a badge of his social and professional situation—as a preliminary to the development of national modes and costumes. The elaborate garb of the period took on entirely new functions, namely to adorn the body and distinguish the wearer; his wealth or rank should be obvious at a glance. Infinite pains were lavished on varying forms, colours, materials and accessories. This placed dress on a par with jewels in rare and precious metals, of exquisite shape, and studded with brilliant, coloured gems, created for an élite whose position on the social ladder was scrupulously established.

36

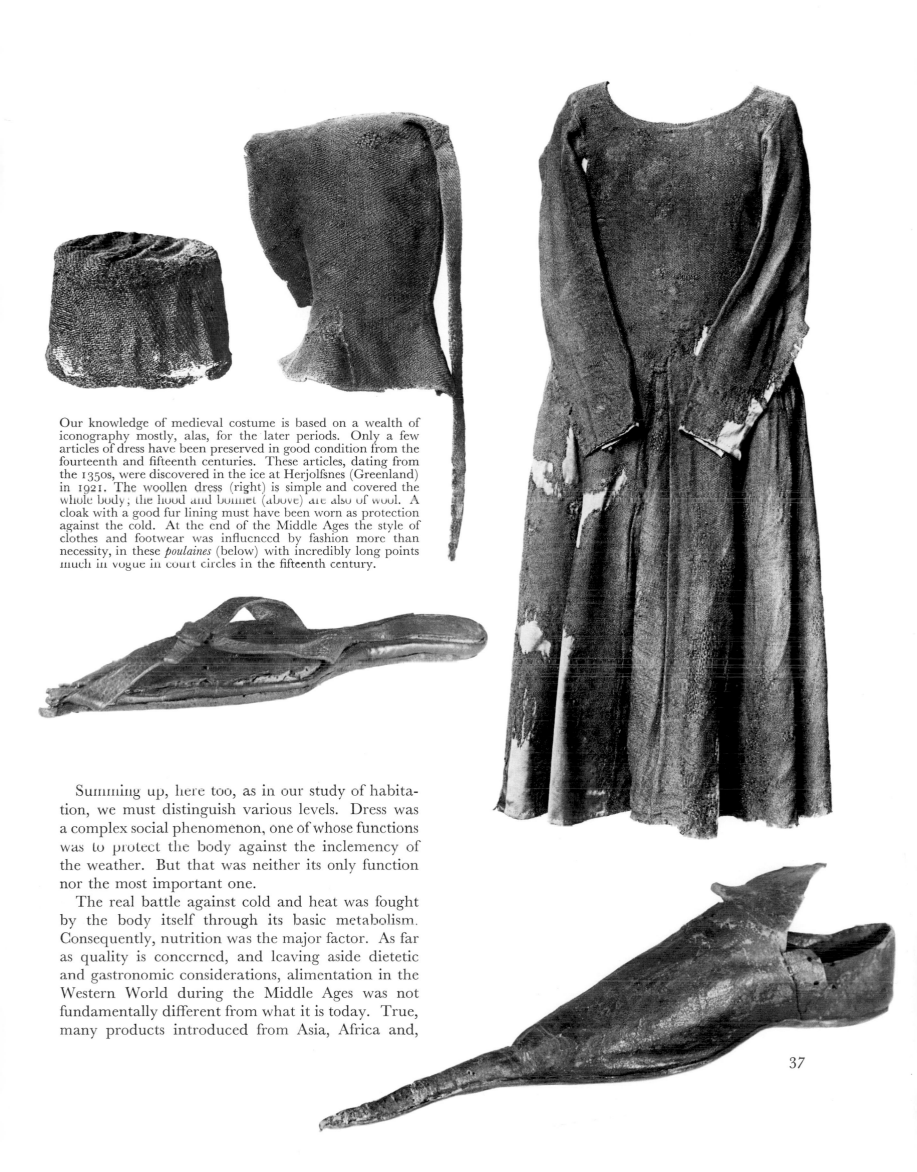

Our knowledge of medieval costume is based on a wealth of iconography mostly, alas, for the later periods. Only a few articles of dress have been preserved in good condition from the fourteenth and fifteenth centuries. These articles, dating from the 1350s, were discovered in the ice at Herjolfsnes (Greenland) in 1921. The woollen dress (right) is simple and covered the whole body; the hood and bonnet (above) are also of wool. A cloak with a good fur lining must have been worn as protection against the cold. At the end of the Middle Ages the style of clothes and footwear was influenced by fashion more than necessity, in these *poulaines* (below) with incredibly long points much in vogue in court circles in the fifteenth century.

Summing up, here too, as in our study of habitation, we must distinguish various levels. Dress was a complex social phenomenon, one of whose functions was to protect the body against the inclemency of the weather. But that was neither its only function nor the most important one.

The real battle against cold and heat was fought by the body itself through its basic metabolism. Consequently, nutrition was the major factor. As far as quality is concerned, and leaving aside dietetic and gastronomic considerations, alimentation in the Western World during the Middle Ages was not fundamentally different from what it is today. True, many products introduced from Asia, Africa and,

37

notably, America in modern times, such as coffee, tea, chocolate, tobacco, tomatoes, potatoes, maize and some species of beans, were unknown; but the range of generally available foodstuffs was extremely wide and varied.

Carbohydrates and starches were supplied chiefly by cereals like wheat—rice was very rare—of which there were many different species which varied with the latitude, the climate and the type of soil: spelt, rye, wheat, maslin—a mixture of wheat and rye—millet, oats, barley and buckwheat. The flour obtained from the grain was used to make porridges, pancakes and, with the addition of yeast, bread.

Fats and proteins were supplied by foods of vegetable and animal origin: rape, poppy-seed, linseed and olive oil; butter, lard, tallow and dripping; the meat of domestic animals—poultry, pork and mutton—and wild animals—boar, heron, teal, hare and rabbit—fresh-water fish—tench, trout, salmon—and sea fish—whiting, herring and cod. Fish, a prime necessity in Lent and on fast-days, was supplied by ponds and rivers in sufficient quantity to satisfy the demands of the rich. Dried or salt herring was eaten by all classes at the end of the Middle Ages. A number of foodstuffs, notably dry vegetables, lentils, beans, peas, hazlenuts, chestnuts and mushrooms, provided both fats and proteins, also eggs, which were consumed in large quantities except during Lent—Easter Eggs marked the end of that period of penitence—and dairy products such as cheese, made by peasants and praised by poets. This is how one poet described it:

> *Non mie blanc comme Hélène*
> *Non mie plourant comme Magdelaine*
> *Non Argos mais du tout avugle*
> *Et aussi pesant comme un bugle*
> *Contre le pouce soit rebelle*
> *Et qu'il ait tigneuse croutelle*
> *Sans yeux, sans plourer, non pas blanc*
> *Tigneux, rebelle, bien pesant.*

> Not at all white like Helen
> Not weeping like Magdalen
> Not Argo but completely blind
> And just as heavy as a bullock
> Be it rebellious against the thumb
> And have a scabby rind
> Without eyes, without tears, not white
> Scabby, rebellious, right heavy.

There was little cultivated fruit except for apples. The apple was the typical fruit of the Indo-European West, which explains why it is called *pomme* in French—from *pomum*, the Latin word for fruit in general. The German *Apfel*, the Russian *jabloko* and the Celtic *aballo*—the root of many place names—are identical with the English *apple*. But pears, quinces, walnuts, mulberries and even peaches were grown in orchards and had their place on the table alongside such woodland fruits as sorbs, medlars and sloes, and wild berries like strawberries, raspberries and red currants.

Few vegetables were eaten, though most species were already known: leeks, carrots, turnips, cardoons, chicory, cabbage, lettuce, cress, asparagus, parsley, onions, shallots. Rue, tansy, lovage, sage, savory, betony and other herbs were grown and used in cooking in the days of Charlemagne.

The rich improved their diet with exotic fruits, such as dates and pistachio nuts, particularly during the period of the Crusades. They also used highly spiced sauces based on pepper, ginger, cinnamon, nutmeg and cloves. The saffron flower, though native to Europe, notably Aragon, was also a favourite spice. The less moneyed made do with mustard and garlic. It is worth recalling that the consumption of salt was very high, perhaps twice what it is today, because of the many salt-cured meats and fish. For centuries honey was largely used in place of sugar. The latter, already known and produced in the Mediterranean lands half-way through the Middle Ages, was mostly employed for medicinal purposes.

Water was the principle beverage. It was often scarce in the towns, where water-carriers were a common sight right up to the nineteenth century and a great deal of labour and money was spent on aqueducts and fountains. Venice could never have survived without its complicated system of wells and cisterns. Castles were no better supplied and during sieges, when the cisterns often went dry or were poisoned, their inmates suffered cruelly from thirst. Some writers drew a distinction between the different sorts of water; the best were mineral water, rain water, river water, spring water, well water and, lastly, pond water. It was known that boiled water 'spoils' less quickly than untreated water and that water was less good pure than mixed with liquorice, honey or wine.

Alcoholic beverages were widely used, though not so much alcohol itself, or spirit, which was obtained reasonably pure by distillation and kept for medicinal purposes. More popular were cider—called *pomade* in France—which originated in the Basque country in the eleventh century and reached Normandy via the Auge between the thirteenth and the fifteenth; perry and the fermented juices of cherries, sloes and mulberries; mead (also called hydromel); and beer, which had been made from fermented cereals of all sorts since the early Indo-European cultures but was first flavoured with hops in some parts of Germany during the eleventh century. Wine, though hard to keep—the seven-year vintage mentioned by a thirteenth century monk named Joffroi must have been a rarity—and not easy to transport, since that made it sour still more quickly, was drunk everywhere. Wine and bread, the two elements of Holy Communion, were essentially the food of Christians. Wine was deemed to nourish the body, restore health, ward off sickness, help the digestion, intensify the natural warmth, clarify the ideas, open the arteries, refresh the brain, relieve congestion of the liver, cure melancholy and favour procreation.

The vine was cultivated wherever the climate permitted, even in England; but the Paris region was the most important wine-growing district. The quantity of wine produced and consumed in the West was very substantial but the quality often left much to be desired. Some wines were in great demand and therefore very expensive—for instance, Malmsey and Cyprian; Grenache, extolled by one thirteenth-century author as 'the periwinkle of all wines'; the vintages of Beaune, Auxerre and Saint-Pourçain; the white wines of the Rhineland, Alsace and Saint-Emilion; and the red of Orléans.

Actually the problem of quality concerned only the very small élite that could afford to build houses in dressed stone and wear luxurious apparel. They could indulge in a great variety of dishes: hare and young boar; tench and eel, bream pasty and boar's tails, and have the same meats and vegetables prepared according to different recipes. The peasantry does not seem to have gone in for such gastronomic refinement; their diet was made up locally of a limited number of nourishing dishes such as cabbage soup. The true connoisseurs were to be found among the rich burghers, nobles and princes. Cookery books from the late Middle Ages are still existent. One of the most famous, *Le Viandier* by Taillevent, chef to King Charles VI of France (1368-1422), contains recipes that were copied out again and again and give a good idea of how food was prepared and seasoned at that time. Attempts made in the last century and this to reproduce those dishes by following the instructions to the letter have had very disappointing results. Which goes to show that tastes have changed radically since those far-off days. Here, by way of example, is a recipe for jugged veal which a Parisian husband recommended to his young wife at the end of the fourteenth century:

'Jugged veal: not washed, not overboiled, half-cooked on the spit or grill, then cut it into pieces and fry in lard with a large quantity of pre-cooked onions; then take slightly browned bread or untoasted crumbs, because browned bread would be too dark for jugged veal (though it would make good jugged hare). Soak the bread in beef broth and a little wine or mashed peas, and while it is soaking crush ginger, cinnamon, clove, Guinea pepper and saffron in quantity to make it yellow and give it colour, and dilute with verjuice, wine and vinegar, then crush your bread and pass it through a sieve; and put in your spices, the softened bread, or caudle, and boil all together; and it should be rather yellow than brown, sharp for vinegar, and mixed with spices. And note that it can take a lot of saffron, and avoid putting in nutmeg or cinnamon because they brown.'

The same élite took pleasure in inordinately copious and complicated banquets with four, five or six courses, descriptions of which have also been preserved.

Let us take, for instance, the menu of a gentleman of the time of Richard II, found by T. Wright. This menu, of the end of the fourteenth century, consists, quite normally, of three courses:

First Course

Boar's head enarmed (larded), and 'bruce', for pottage.
Beef. Mutton. Pestles (legs) of Pork.
Swan. Roasted Rabbit. Tart.

Second Course

Drope and Rose, for pottage
Mallard. Pheasant. Chickens, 'farsed' and roasted.
'Malachis', baked.

Third Course

Conings (rabbits), in gravy, and hare, in 'brasé', for pottage.
Teals, roasted. Woodcocks. Snipes.
'Raffyolys', baked. 'Flampoyntes'.

A recipe book explains what 'bruce' is:

'Take the umbles of a swine, and parboil them (boil them slowly), and cut them small, and put them in a pot, with some good broth; then take the whites of leeks, and slit them, and cut them small, and put them in, with minced onions, and let it all boil; next take bread steeped in broth, and "draw it up" with blood and vinegar, and put it into a pot, with pepper and cloves, and let it boil; and serve all this together.'

The 'drope', or better the drose, is made like this:

'Take almonds, and blanch and grind them, and mix them with good meat broth, and seethe this in a pot; then mince onions, and fry them in fresh "grease", and put them to the almonds; take small birds, and parboil them, and throw them into the pottage, with cinnamon and cloves and a little "fair grease", and boil the whole.'

Rose and rabbit needed great care in preparation:

'Take powdered rice, and boil it in almond-milk till it be thick, and take the brawn of capons and hens, beat it in a mortar, and mix it with the preceding, and put the whole into a pot, with powdered cinnamon and cloves, and whole mace, and colour it with saunders (sandal-wood)... Take rabbits and parboil them, and chop them in "gobbets", and seethe them in a pot with good broth; then grind almonds, "dress them up" with beef broth, and boil this in a pot; and, after passing it through a strainer, put it to the rabbits, adding to the whole cloves, maces, pines (the kernels of the pine cone), and sugar; colour it with sandal-wood, saffron, bastard or other wine, and cinnamon powder mixed together, and add a little vinegar.'

It is possible to make a choice from amongst the other dishes. Some 'brasé', perhaps?

'Take the ribs of a boar, while they are fresh, and parboil them till they are half boiled; then roast them, and, when they are roasted, chop them and put them in a pot with good fresh beef broth and wine, and add cloves, maces, pines, currants, and powdered pepper; then put chopped onions in a pan, with fresh grease, fry them first and then boil them; next, take bread, steeped in broth, "draw it up" and put it to the onions, and colour it with sandal-wood and saffron, and as it settles, put a little vinegar mixed with powdered cinnamon to it; then take brawn, and cut it into slices two inches long, and throw it into the pot with the foregoing, and serve it all up together.'

For 'flampoynts'...

'Take good "interlarded" pork, seethe it, and chop it, and grind it small; put to it good fat cheese grated, and sugar and pepper; put this in raised paste like the preceding; then make a thin leaf of dough, out of which cut small "points", fry these in grease, and then stick them on the foregoing mixture after it has been put in the crust, and bake it.'

2

Foodstuffs and cultivated plants differed little from those of our own day. The twelfth-century *Tacuinum Sanitatis* is illustrated with dozens of examples. On this page we can recognize lettuce (1), sycamore or Pharaoh's figtree (2), garlic (3), melon (4), cauliflower (5), barley (6), wheat (7) and cheese (8). Of course, plants that originated in America, such as maize, potato or tobacco had yet to appear.

3

7

5

8

Perhaps some 'raffyolys'?

'Take swine's flesh, seethe it, chop it small, add to it yolks of eggs, and mix them well together; put to this a little minced lard, grated cheese, powdered ginger, and cinnamon; make of this balls of the size of an apple, and wrap them up in the cawl of the swine, each ball by itself; make a raised crust of dough, and put the ball in it, and bake it; when they are baked, take yolks of eggs well beaten, with sugar and pepper, coloured with saffron, and pour this mixture over them.'

The meal we have just seen was relatively simple. It would be easy to extend it in the following way:

First Course

Browet farsed, and charlet, for pottage.
Baked mallard. Teals. Small birds. Almond milk served with them.
Capon roasted with the syrup
Roasted veal. Pig roasted 'endored, and served with the yolk on his neck over gilt.' Herons.
A 'leche.' A tart of flesh.

Second Course

Browet of Almayne and Viaunde rial for pottage.
Mallard. Roasted rabbits. Pheasant. Venison.
Jelly. A leche. Urchynnes (hedgehogs).
Pome de orynge.

Third Course

Boar in egurdouce, and Mawmené, for pottage.
Cranes. Kid. Curlew. Partridge. (All roasted.)
A leche. A crustade.
A peacock endored and roasted, and served with the skin.
Cockagris. Flaumpoyntes. Daryoles.
Pears in syrup.

Banquets of this type were rare and they have a curiosity value for those who study the origin and progress of gastronomy. Preoccupation with diet is mirrored in works like *Le Secret des Secrets*, which were widely read in certain circles during the thirteenth century; but it concerned only a small number of heavy eaters. Yet liver attacks and stomach trouble were already common. The former were 'relieved'

Most people usually drank water. Wine (above), owing to its link with the Christian religion, ousted beer, which was the traditional beverage in many countries.

Drinking cups were made of wood, horn or metal. Glasses were used from the Frankish period.

with aloe wood, camphor, amber, myrtle, lettuce, chicory, lupin, birthwort, fenugreek, plantain, valerian, houseleek, the flesh of doe, venison, fowl, partridge and the 'mirobolans', wormwood, agaric, colocynth, senna and others.

Sufferers from stomach trouble were given acid or aromatic products, toast dipped in sour wine and cow or hare meat cooked over a slow fire. The strong meat of goat, ox and full-grown sheep suited only the robust stomachs of workers. Sucking pig and lamb were strongly disapproved of; pork and veal were considered nourishing; salt meat and wild boar were parching, and so on. Overeating was inadvisable because it made for corpulence.

The fundamental problem that faces those who study nutrition in the Middle Ages is not to discover the range of edible or even delectable products available at that time. It is to determine the quantities consumed and how they were apportioned, in other words the daily rations and the normal diet.

Cereals undoubtedly formed the staple of all nutrition. Even in the upper class, whose menus have been easier to come by, and in Sweden and other countries where game was extremely abundant, cereals constitued two-thirds or even three-quarters of the daily ration. Wheat was the chief, if not the only species. Bread was the stand-by of salaried workers and those liable for statute labour, which was payable in kind. Famines were preceded by a rise in the price of wheat, and we know from medieval literature that it was consumed universally and in vast quantities.

Unfortunately there is no way to establish with any precision what those quantities were. In 1328, France counted 3,200,000 homesteads spread over an area of some 162,000 square miles. Clearance had extended arable land to a maximum in a country with few high mountains; the Jura, the Vosges, the Alps and a large part of the Pyrenees, Roussillion and Navarre were not included in its boundaries. So over a quarter of those 162,000 square miles may well have been under wheat—that was the proportion at the beginning of the nineteenth century—with three-

IC:COQVI VR:CARO ET HIC: MINISTRAVERVNT MINISTRI HICFECERVN:PF

The Bayeux Tapestry shows how a banquet was served at William the Conqueror's court in the eleventh century. The embroidered Latin texts explain (from left to right): 'here meat is being cooked ... here servants served... here the bishop blesses the food and drink'. The whole tapestry relates the conquest of England by the Normans.

yearly rotation. We know from the works of Slicher van Bath that the average yield during that period was about 7 bushels an acre. Therefore 25 million acres supplied 175 million bushels or about 50 million quintals. This would seem to be a minimum, since in the eighteenth century, according to J. Toutain, French production amounted to 275 million bushels or 80 million quintals. France was then slightly larger in area but the increase was due chiefly to mountainous country unsuitable for growing wheat. If we allow for a three-yearly rotation, only two-thirds of those 25 million acres were sown. This would give a total output of barely 35 million quintals, or just 42 per cent of that achieved in the eighteenth century. From this minimal estimate 25 per cent must be deducted for seed. Presuming that losses and exports were negligible, there would remain about 25 million quintals for 3.2 million families, or slightly less than 8 quintals per family, a year. Under these conditions a peasant family would have had less than 4 acres under wheat, which seems

very little indeed. However, if we assume that a family consisted of four or five persons with a high proportion of children, our estimate would allow each adult more than 20 ounces of wheat a day at a time when France had far outgrown the demographic optimum.

At the present day the inhabitants of the developed countries receive 3,500 calories per head a day. If medieval man received the same amount—a most unlikely hypothesis—over half came from cereals. If we suppose the still acceptable figure of 2,800 to 3,000 calories a day and deduct the large number of infants and children not yet weaned, we find a far higher proportion: about 70 or 80 per cent. Calculations made along the same lines for England or certain regions of Italy would lead to similar results. In any case the paramount importance of carbohydrates in medieval nutrition cannot be too strongly stressed.

Should we infer that proteins played a minor, if not negligible, role? As matter of fact, compared

44

This Flemish painting of Job's dinner with his children shows that in the fifteenth century wealthy Flemish families used pewter ware and tablecloths, but they had neither forks nor spoons.

with the Islamic world and the Far East, the West seems to have eaten a great deal of meat and the trend was apparently intensified towards the end of the Middle Ages. The banning of meat in Lent, on Fridays and on all fast-days is an indication that it was a common food, though perhaps considered superfluous or even impure. Very thorough investigations into conditions in Germany during the fourteenth and fifteenth centuries, in England and in the Slav countries supply what in my opinion is sufficient proof of this. The men who worked for the Dominicans at Strasbourg received over 20 ounces of meat a day. In Frankfurt-on-Oder in 1307 beef consumption amounted to 220 pounds a year per head of the population. In 1397 the inhabitants of Berlin devoured almost 3 pounds a day each. It is worth recalling that a pound of not very fat meat, like beef or poultry, provides from 750 to 935 calories.

I should like to quote some more figures for the French towns before passing on to consider the peasantry, who ate pork, poultry and game. Paris is reported to have slaughtered 30,316 bullocks, 19,604 calves, 108,532 sheep and 30,794 pigs in 1394, and towards the middle of the fifteenth century 12,500 bullocks, 25,000 calves, 208,000 sheep and 31,500 pigs. These figures take no account of the poultry and pigs home-grown by a population of probably more than 150,000 people. A recent study of the urban population of Carpentras showed that in the fifteenth century meat consumption was at least 57 pounds per head a year, chiefly mutton, lamb and beef; home-grown pigs and other sources of protein were not taken into account. Other studies mention between 88 and 110 pounds for neighbouring districts. But the 57 pounds quoted as a minimum—more of it was eaten on the 52 Sundays than on the 313 weekdays—came to close on 90 pounds if poultry and pork products are included. This makes a total of well over 3 ounces a day, or about 200 calories.

Pigs supply about 1,700 calories a pound if moderately fat and 2,600 if very fat. Therefore if

45

The loaves of bread eaten in the Middle Ages differed little in shape from those baked in the French countryside today. Below: a rye loaf as made in the ninth century; lower: a fifteenth century loaf.

pork consumption is included in the reckoning one gets the impression that proteins formed a not unimportant part of the diet, which also comprised cheese, eggs and vegetables. Let us take as an example a peasant family that killed only one pig a year, though as a rule pictures in calendars and the like usually show two. It could count on 160-220 pounds of meat at 1,700 calories a pound, pork products at 1,900 and bacon at 4,100, plus small game, poultry and others. This gives a minimum of 400,000 calories a year, an average of 1,000 calories a day for four or five persons, many of them children, equal to 200 each. Adding 3 eggs, we obtain a further 480 calories.

We may leave out the vegetable oils, which were probably consumed in very small quantities. But we must not forget the large amount of energy provided, at least for adults, by alcoholic beverages. Nowadays wine is weak in alcohol and supplies about 665 calories a quart, so a workman who drinks 3 quarts absorbs about 2,000 calories. Beer too is very rich in calories: 600 a quart. There is reason to believe that it was lighter in the Middle Ages, providing perhaps between 225 and 400 calories a quart. Besides which, the grain it was made of was withdrawn from normal consumption. But cider, which contains 385 calories

Above: The inscription on this bronze measure preserved in St John's Hospital at Ghent says: 'Master Giles of Saint Peter made me in the year of grace 1281.' Measures of this sort were common before the introduction of the metric system, and many are preserved in museums.

Cereals were the staple diet, hence the importance of the grain market, which employed a quantity of measurers, grain-chandlers and scriveners (left hand page). After the ear was separated from the straw and the grain from the chaff (by threshing and winnowing), the wheat was shovelled into a basket and poured into a measure. It was measured (sometimes under the control of a royal official) and packed in sacks for transport to the town, the castle or the village to be made into bread (right).

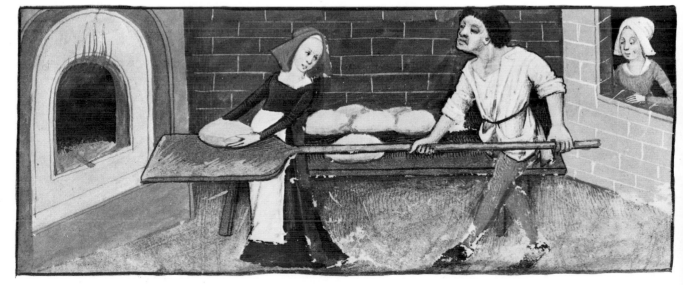

eln czoubern noch in troyme

gelouben ; Ir sult nicht scheib

lecht ewern schopf besneiden

noch den part bescheren · Auch

sult ir vbir die toten ewer v

fleisch zu sneiden noch keiner

narczeichen · noch geschaffen

Outside castles and monasteries and inside the walls of towns there were orchards that supplied cultivated fruits to supplement the wild fruits gathered in the woods and fields. This miniature in the Bible of King Wenceslaus shows labourers culling fruit. The commonest fruit trees were the plum, cherry, apple, pear and walnut. Peach and almond trees grew in warm countries and, after the Crusades, the apricot was introduced. Fruit was eaten fresh or dried, raw or cooked, or sometimes in the shape of fruit cheese.

a quart, perry and the like are made with orchard or forest fruit produced on land not used for cereals.

Summing up briefly, a rough calculation of the average ration in normal times gives between 2,000 and 3,000 calories. This is slightly less than the figure generally accepted for the developed countries at the present day. Leaving aside some few nobles, whose rations have been reckoned at 6-7,000 calories, a peasant who could count on 20-25 ounces of wheat plus about 3 ounces of ham, meat and poultry would receive 2,300 calories. Let us add 2 eggs (320 calories), a quart of rough wine (550 calories), and a little bacon for when the hens were not laying. The total is quite acceptable. I might add that, if this were not the case, there would be no explaining the great increase in population that continued for at least three centuries.

Let us consider a few examples for which comprehensive figures are available. In 1268 a married couple handed over their small estate to Beaumont le Roger in exchange for board and lodging. In addition to wood for heating and 30 sols a year for clothes, they received a daily ration of 1 convent loaf plus 2 other loaves, estimated at about 4 ½ pounds of whole-wheat bread or 5,000 calories; 6 eggs, equal to 960 calories; or, three times a week, a dish of meat equal to about 400 calories; or, in Lent, 4 herrings estimated at just under a pound or 400 calories; plus a gallon of cider, beer or other beverage, equal to about 1,300 calories or even 2,000 if the beer was strong. This gives a total of about 7,000 calories, or 3,500 each, not counting vegetables, wild fruit and such extras as honey and the like.

The men who worked for Montebourg Abbey in 1312 received 1 loaf (2,500 calories), 6 eggs (960 calories) or 3 eggs (480 calories) and a quarter pound of cheese (300 calories), plus an adequate quantity of light beer (minimum 700 calories). In Lent, 3 herrings (300 calories) and some walnuts (at 400 calories per quarter pound unshelled). Probably between 3,500 and 4,000 calories in all. Was theirs a normal diet, or did the Abbey give them an exceptional allowance to make them work harder? And what

should we make of the 3,915 calories a day supplied to Venetian sailors in 1310, of which 14.4 per cent came from proteins, 14.3 per cent from fats and 71.3 per cent from carbohydrates?

The situation in the cereal-growing regions was obviously more reassuring than in those which specialized in the production of wine, woad, wool-bearing animals etcetera owing to the increase in trade from the twelfth or thirteenth century. And still more compared with that in the towns, where home industry and the secondary sector began to develop at the end of the Middle Ages. No doubt, most peasants engaged in the production of a commodity that sold at a high price, either growing the little wheat which they needed for their own consumption or buying it; and many small craftsmen owned a garden which would help mitigate or nullify the effect of a sudden crisis. But the allowance received by urban workers and the poor was very likely balanced out by that of the noble and wealthy on either side of the average attained by the peasants. If that average lay between 2,500 and 3,000 calories, the 6 or 7,000 taken up by the rich must have reduced the poor people's pittance to 2,500, 2,000 or even less. In Paris at the end of the thirteenth century an adult is reckoned to have spent four Parisian deniers a day on food and drink. A pig cost 12 to 16 sols, a quintal of wheat between 7 and 20. There was no such thing as a minimum wage, but few workers were paid less than 48 sols a month; that left a man about twenty deniers a day for his keep. If his wife did not work—a less frequent occurrence than is generally believed—and he had several children, they could just manage spending 12 to 16 deniers a day on food. But if a slight climatic disturbance pushed up the price of cereals, they were reduced to penury and starvation.

On the whole, even though meat consumption was far greater in the West than in the Islamic world or the Far East, the excessive importance of cereals, the small proportion of fats, the lack of fresh vegetables and fruit, and consequently of certain vitamins, resulted in a dual imbalance. First, the diet was inadequate even when the energy balance was acceptable; secondly, it depended directly on the wheat crop and therefore on climatic conditions, the foresight of the authorities responsible for stocks, and the state of regional and even international transport. This was one of the main causes of crises in those early times. Wheat is sensitive to a number of factors closely linked with the latitude, such as cold in Scandinavia and drought in North Africa, the nature of the soil and a complex of local conditions. In England, on the estates of Winchester Abbey—whose exceptionally complete accounts from 1209 to 1350 were studied in detail by J. Titow—the danger lay in excessive humidity during autumn and winter; if the summer and autumn were dry, even a severe winter did not prevent a good harvest. In Scandinavia the enemy was a cold summer, because the wheat could not ripen; in Southern Italy it was summer drought, for that burned up the crop. Wholesale crises were rare in the West during phases of rising

temperature, for then the weather was variable and areas of shortfall and plenty were never far apart. Where trade in cereals was organized famine was limited or avoided entirely. For example, the Hanseatic fleets loaded with wheat from the German-Polish region saved the Norwegians time and again by supplying the relatively small quantity needed to bridge the gap before the new harvest was in. But vital convoys were slowed down and often brought to a standstill by speculation on wheat, by hazards of all sorts on delapidated roads and by plundering nobles. During phases of falling temperature, when the jet stream and the polar front were almost circular, the risk of a bad harvest over a vast area was far greater.

In any case, the urban population was always the first to feel the pinch because the price of wheat went up and the available quantity went down. In 1315-1317 Ypres and Bruges lost 10 per cent of their inhabitants, all of them poor people of the artisan class

50

through famine. Though not always lethal or permanent, famine helped to spread the terrible epidemics that killed off the weaker members of the undernourished population—women and children, the old and the poor—before attacking the strong, the rich and the powerful.

On the other hand, normal rations, though seemingly more or less adequate, were never far from the lowest admissible limit and the total dependance on wheat resulted in a very real danger of famine. No doubt, from the time of Charlemagne catastrophic destruction of the winter wheat by frost or damp could be made up by a good crop of spring wheat. But a shortfall of even a quarter of a pound a day in a worker's ration entailed a loss of 350 calories that he had no way of recovering and therefore resulted in an insufficient energy balance; the pernicious effects of this do not have to be stressed.

If, therefore, the mass of the population was adequately nourished in normal times, it was faced at frequent intervals with very tough problems of subsistence. To say that Western Man was 'haunted by the spectre of starvation' would presuppose foresight, an eye on the future and a way of life not entirely focused on the present. That would be presuming too much; but the fact is that he often went hungry. Land clearance and development and the rise in cereal production were both the cause and the effect of the population explosion. This latter was also influenced by physiological factors, the permanent presence of an unstable balance, and the uncertainty of ever definitively conquering cold, damp and hunger.

MAN IN THE MIDDLE AGES

A preliminary question of some importance deserves careful consideration: Was Western Man in the Middle Ages similar physically to his descendants

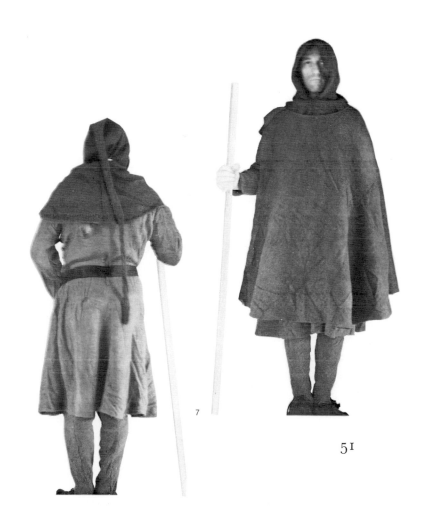

We know what our ancestors looked like from the works of painters and sculptors. Except for their costume, they seem to have been very like ourselves. Uta of Naumburg (5), who lived about 1260, and Lucrezia Borgia (1480–1519) painted by Pinturicchio (6), have lost nothing of their charm with the passage of the centuries. The same is true of the knight at Strasbourg (1), St Theodore at Chartres (thirteenth century) (2), or St Louis (early fourteenth) (3). Also worthy of note is the suit of armour made for the boy Claude de Vaudrey in 1500 (4), and still more the gigantic Dane (7) murdered about 1380, whose body was preserved virtually intact in a peat-bog.

51

of the present day or, at least, to the peasants of Western Europe before the First World War? Improved alimentary, sanitary and hygienic conditions have brought about striking changes in weight, stature, the age of puberty, and so on, in the course of the two or three generations since the beginning of the twentieth century. What then was the impact of the fifteen, twenty or fifty generations that separate us from the Middle Ages? May we presume that the changes they made were far more deep-seated? And that the ethnic characteristics that are now being rapidly diluted by intensive intermarriage were once far more marked?

Unfortunately, we are very poorly equipped to find this out. Blood serum studies based chiefly on contemporary data prove that many population mixtures stretch back to prehistoric times. The serological characteristics of a race are seemingly 'permanent' and transmitted by heredity. Actually, some factors of the blood have very little resistance to such serious infections as plague and smallpox, while others are altered by malaria. It is also hard to believe that groups A, B and O already existed when man first appeared on earth—another reason to doubt the permanence of those characteristics as a whole. If, therefore, changes have occurred in the long term, there seems to be no reason to exclude the possibility of their occurring in the course of scores of generations since the different groups appeared.

Populations in which the O group is preponderant may well be more sensitive to plague, and therefore have paid a heavier toll to the Black Death of 1348, than those in which the other two groups prevail. Populations in which the O group predominates still form the majority in many regions of the West, so they were probably even more numerous before 1348. The same train of reasoning could be used to explain how it is that the Hungarians, a large proportion of whom belong to the B group, have stood up to that sort of epidemic far better than the other peoples of Europe.

The study of recessive characteristics transmitted by heredity also lead one to suppose that people's eyes and hair were formerly lighter in colour.

There are other methods of working back from the present day population to their distant ancestors. By studying in the various districts of Languedoc the number of conscripts too short for military service in the nineteenth century, one can determine the places where small, dark men predominated and those where tall people, who had immigrated from or through Auvergne, settled during the Middle Ages.

Ancient descriptions tell us a great deal about the appearance of a population—for instance, those by Caesar and Tacitus of the Germans; so do pictures and sculptures. As soon as portrayal became more realistic it showed us people who seemingly differed from our contemporaries only in hairstyle and cos-

In 1348 the plague, after raging in many parts of Europe for a year, reached Tournai. The dreadful disease came from Asia by way of the Mongols. The miniature on the opposite page shows the people of Tournai burying the victims of the epidemic.

tume. Ulrich of Naumburg and Saint Louis King of France, Giovanna Cenami Arnolfini and Lucrezia Borgia have lost nothing of their strength, charm or beauty with the passage of time.

For the most obvious somatic characteristics—stature and cephalic index—there is no lack of documents which can be studied scientifically. The Germanic and Christian custom of interment, which rivalled or ousted cremation, has preserved millions of skeletons that supply a quantity of useful information, at least when they can be dated. That, indeed, is the major problem. For, in spite of survivals and revivals, the pagan custom of burying characteristic objects with a corpse disappeared during the Carolingian period. On the other hand, it is only in bones 2,000 years old or more that the increase in fluorine and the decrease in nitrogen can be established with any precision.

For the early Middle Ages, from the fifth to the ninth century, much is known about the spread of brachycephalism or dolichocephalism, the stature of the tall Germanic warriors and the small Mongoloid Huns, and also about cases of malnutrition, the high incidence of dental caries, the age of death, the proportions of the sexes and so on. But hardly any systematic research has been carried out for subsequent periods. In any case anthropological data are often limited to princes, saints and other very small élites, whose relics are not always authentic, or to the inhabitants of tiny rural units. Demographic data are more important. They are obtained in various ways: First by archaeological methods, which establish the area of a town or village, the number of its houses and the probable number of people who lived in each; secondly, by studying the plans of churches and presuming that, on the occasion of important ceremonies, they could hold the entire local population except for small children, young mothers and the very old. Other sources are texts of a fiscal character and, for the nobles and wealthy merchants, genealogies.

Marriage and procreation were promoted for religious and psychological reasons, though virginity was held in high regard and the number of clerics vowed to celibacy was very large. Girls were married either at a very tender age—those of the upper classes often when only 14 years old—or when quite adult; for instance, between 20 and 24 among the English aristocracy. As a rule the husband was considerably older and died when the wife was still capable of bearing children. But there were many obstacles in the way of a widow remarrying, and very few did so. Many widowers took a second wife, but there was slight risk of a 'baby boom' because of the relative scarcity of women of child-bearing age—so many died in childbed—and, in the towns, because there were so many bachelors too poor to found a family. Procreation outside wedlock was

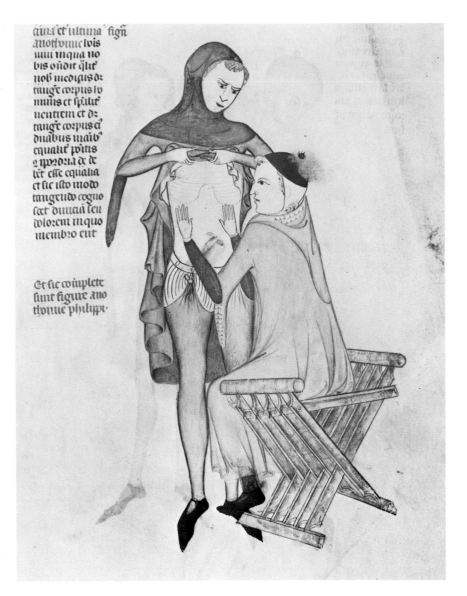

The major internal organs of the human body were known very approximately through the more or less secret dissection of corpses. The illustration on the opposite page, dated 1412, is taken from a handbook on surgery of the fourteenth century.

Surgeons were not quite helpless, particularly when it came to operating on a healthy man injured in an accident or wounded in a fight. Above right: extracting an arrowhead.

Auscultation made great progress in the fourteenth century (above left). The influence of Arab and Jewish science was preponderant for a very long time, notably along the Mediterranean coast.

severely punished and contraceptive practices were probably very widespread. I shall return later to these problems of a psychological nature, which were due to the prevailing mentality.

Lastly, a woman's period of fecundity was relatively brief and still further curtailed by death in childbed or widowhood, and also perhaps by the fact that puberty set in later than it does now. In Norway, for example, the age at which the first menstruation occurs has been lowered by four years from 17 to 13 in the course of the last century. There is no room here for a detailed study of medieval woman. But it is worth recalling that Blanche of Castille, who married when she was 12—true, the groom was only 13—did not give birth to the first of her twelve children until she was 18.

On the other hand, the interval between pregnancies was rather short, though lengthened by the periods of amenorrhoea due to breast-feeding. Many noble and working-class women put their children out at nurse (for different reasons), and a great many nurses were available owing to the dreadfully high level of infant mortality. The queens who preceded Blanche—one of them at least was widowed at the age of 39—bore their children at quite regular intervals of 16 to 19 months.

By and large natality seems to have been extremely high, about 35 per cent. But it was nowhere near some present-day rates—for instance, the 56 per cent recorded in· the rural districts of Persia; not to mention countries where women, wedded and fertile when very young, live—and their husbands too—at

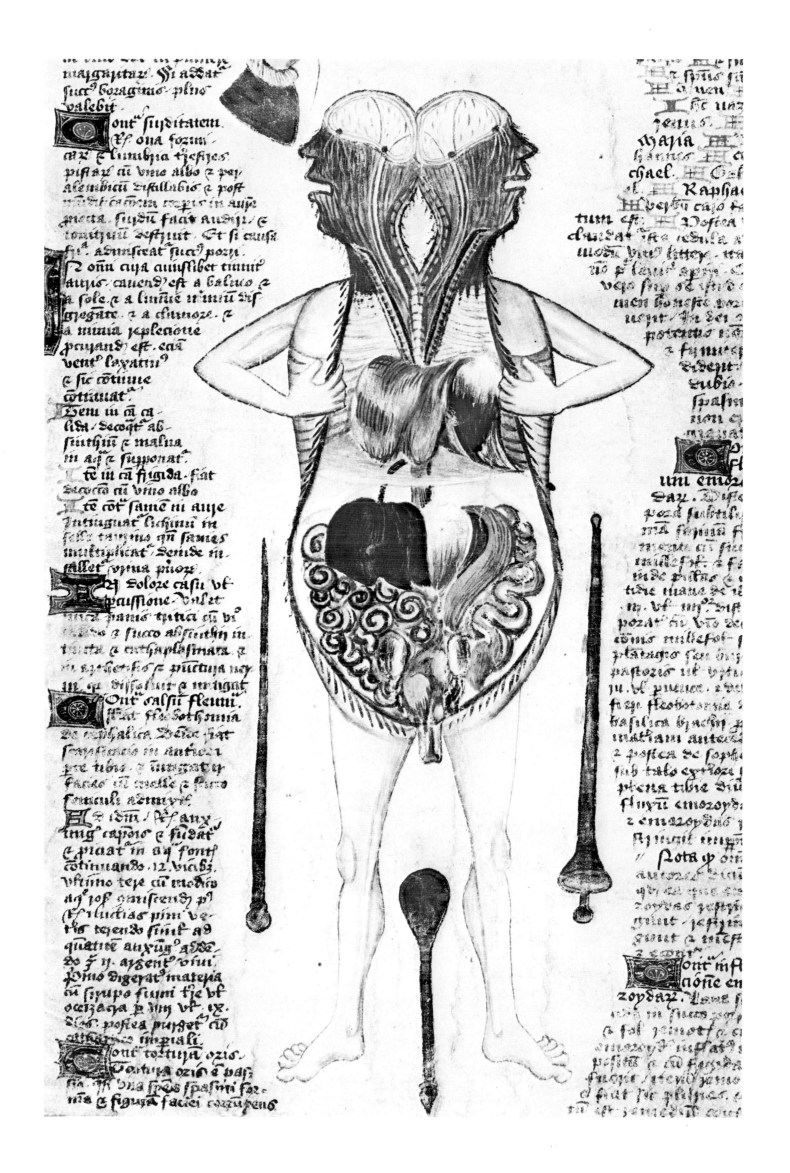

least for the entire period of fecundity, and their children are in fact weaned at a very early age.

In Hungary during the fifteenth century couples of the well-off class lived together on an average fifteen years and had close on four children. At the beginning of the ninth century the peasants of the Abbey of Saint-Germain near Paris had 2 ½ to 3 children living, probably at an age when they were able to help their parents, in addition to infants.

However, a high birth-rate did not necessarily entail very large families for it was more or less balanced by the high mortality rate due to general nutritional and hygienic conditions and to peculiar circumstances that led occasionally to the appearance and spread of terrible diseases.

Epidemics were far from rare in the Middle Ages. The most dreadful was plague, which was brought from the Levant. There were two forms: bubonic and pneumonic. The first was characterized by hardening and suppuration of the ganglions and caused death in 60 to 80 per cent of cases; the second was 100 per cent fatal in its primary form. Both are transmitted to man by the flea of the black rat and from man to man by direct contagion.

The first epidemic of bubonic plague appeared in 540 and continued in the Mediterranean countries until 750 with outbreaks at intervals of nine to twelve years. The second, in which bubonic and pneumonic forms were combined, began in 1347, recurred in 1374–75 and continued until the beginning of the following century. It reappeared at intervals until the eighteenth and then disappeared just as mysteriously as it had in the eighth. Perhaps it was driven out by cholera or pseudo-tuberculosis, a mild disease that has only recently been studied and gives absolute immunity. Its disappearance may also have been due to the decline of the black rat before the onslaught of the fierce grey variety.

Smallpox very likely reached the West about 750 and created enormous havoc. The Crusaders brought it back with them several times. Dysentery spread through the whole of Gaul in 580–82, and influenza was far more virulent than it is today.

Thus an important percentage of the population was killed off at intervals by epidemics due to famine following a bad harvest or to chance occurrences such as the arrival of a shipload of black rats. And, of course, the victims were mostly the weakest members.

But the diseases which made the strongest impact on daily life in the Middle Ages were endemic; the relative microbes had become permanent parasites of humans, 'sparing' their carriers or killing them only very slowly. Typical of those infections was leprosy, a word that in those days covered many other skin diseases such as psoriasis. Sufferers were isolated completely from the rest of humanity and left to rot away by slow degrees. Unless, of course, they happened to be members of the nobility. Baldwin, the leper king of Jerusalem, lived in the midst of his court.

In the twelfth and thirteenth centuries between 1 and 5 per cent of the population of the Western World were smitten with leprosy. The disease finally disappeared in a mysterious fashion; it may have been driven out by tuberculosis, for it has been recently proved that the tubercle bacilli oust those that cause leprosy. Before accepting this theory, however, one must first make sure that the 'phthisis' or 'languor' mentioned in the literature, which seems to have been extremely widespread and lethal, was identical with tuberculosis and particularly prevalent in the regions where leprosy declined. Other maladies, such as tubercular scrofula, called the king's evil because the king of France consecrated at Reims was able to cure it, gradually disappeared too. Charles X, in the nineteenth century, was rarely called upon to practise his miraculous gift. Also worthy of mention are diseases caused by malnutrition: Saint Lawrence's Fire (eczema) and Saint Anthony's Fire (erysipelas); so are those due to hypernutrition in some classes—dropsy, obesity and gout, to which Louis VI of France, William the Conqueror and Henry II Plantagenet were martyrs. The remedies prescribed by physicians, such as the Spanish fly poultices applied on the buboes of plague,

Dentists were not merely tooth-drawers; some possessed a large assortment of instruments.

The apothecaries knew a number of remedies: powders from the East or herbs crushed in a mortar and applied on the spot (right).

seem to have been of little or no avail against specific diseases. That those medicasters were far from popular is reflected in an abundant folklore, of which Molière was one of the supreme interpreters after the Guiot Bible. They had, however, a quantity of reasonably good recipes for mild ailments—cupping, blood-letting, firing, sweat baths, diets, highly spiced syrups, and various decoctions for evacuating the stomach or purging the bile. They were also able to cope with accidents to healthy individuals. They reduced fractures, as proved by a great many skeletons; attended to battle wounds, removing daggers or arrowheads and bathing with oil or wine; practised cauterization with red hot irons, and even performed trepanations with some success.

Diagnosis was based on urine analysis and the patient's outward appearance, and treatment included moral as well as physical assistance. But, except for a few good prescriptions handed down from the school of Hippocrates, recipes were mostly a mass of counter-indications, superstitions and

quackery. Further, real physicians were very rare among the huge rural populations, where healers, sorcerers and wonderworkers had it all their own way. Only people of extremely robust constitution could hope to recover from serious illnesses. Natural selection and the survival of the fittest were fundamental facts of life in the Middle Ages.

It must be said, however, that the towns and monasteries had, as a rule, hospices, hospitals, infirmaries, and even an occasional leperhouse or lazaretto. Built and maintained by the active charity of the Church and the faithful, they were served by monks or nuns. As a rule there were four departments: a lying-in ward for women, a section for the sick, one for the dying and one for convalescents. Two or three patients were bedded together, except for parturients and the moribund. But hygiene was quite strictly imposed; baths were frequent, the sheets clean and the food reasonably wholesome. This is proved by the many hospital account books that have come down to us, for example those of the Innocents at Florence and the Hôtel-Dieu at Soissons. Because of the free assistance they offered poor unfortunates, suffering rather from general debility than from serious maladies, those establishments were able to save a great many sick people but not, however, during epidemics.

But in spite of doctors and hospitals the death-rate was always very high, particularly at birth and during infancy and adolescence. There is a quantity of documentary evidence of this. First and foremost for royalty. Blanche of Castille lost 4 of her 12 children at birth and 3 others before they were 13 years old; only 6 of Marguerite of Provence's 11 children lived to the age of 20. And the death-rate was probably far higher among the classes where hygiene and nutrition were more deficient, medical science was unknown, and pregnant women and nursing mothers did heavy work.

Research on conditions in Hungary has established that infant mortality remained more or less constant from the tenth century to the fifteenth. Between 40 and 46 per cent of the skeletons that have been unearthed belonged to children under 14 years of age, and it is far from certain that all infants who died before being christened were buried in the parish churchyard. For the West as a whole it has been suggested that one third of all babies born viable died before reaching the age of 5. Life expectancy at birth was 21 years among the Hungarian aristocracy in the fifteenth century and not more than 28.7 years among the peasants over the entire period.

A man was considered old at 35. When Good King Dagobert died at 36 nobody found it out of the way. Not one of the Capetian kings of France reached the age of 60. Charlemagne and Rudolph of Habsburg were viewed with astonishment because they lived to be just over 70. It must be said, however, that octogenarians and nonagenarians were not unknown. In Tuscany at the beginning of the fifteenth century there were many people over 75, though that region was at a very low point of population pressure at the time. They must have been exceptionally hardy to cope with all life's hazards.

The fact that a short lifespan was the rule had most important consequences. The West was populated by young people; between 45 and 55 per cent of the population were under 20 years of age. They began their working life when still extremely young—between 5 and 7—and shouldered responsibilities at 13 or 15. A Germanic man came of age at 15 and could become king, squire, journeyman, master craftsman or head of a rural farm unit, as well as marry and build a family. But he seldom lived to see his grandchildren, who were at a great disadvantage compared with more recent generations by the absence of grandparents in the home.

On the other hand, death was taken for granted as an everyday occurrence. It was often very swift: a child took to its bed and was dead in a couple of hours; a giant like the 'Grand Ferré' got overheated, drank deep and lay down, never to rise again. And how many women were carried off by puerperal fever! The future here on earth meant little or nothing; all that counted was eternity. Death held no terror except when it was very painful or abnormally frequent, as during the great epidemics. It was only towards the end of the Middle Ages, after the Black Death and its consequences, that people began to regret the death of the body and long to live.

The population of the West underwent a very great change during the ten centuries which make up the Middle Ages. It was during the declining years of the Roman Empire, a typical phase of demographic deflation, that Gaul was invaded by Germanic tribes. They were not very numerous—at most 5-10 per cent of the romanized population—but vigorous and dynamic. In the sixth century the Mediterranean countries were still further weakened by a terrible pestilence. Instead, the germanized regions in Northern Gaul and England, as well as those east of the Rhine and north of the Danube, experienced a period of great prosperity. Land clearance was speeded up in the seventh and eighth centuries and the regions between the Rhine and the Elbe were settled. One of the consequences was the rise of the Carolingian Empire.

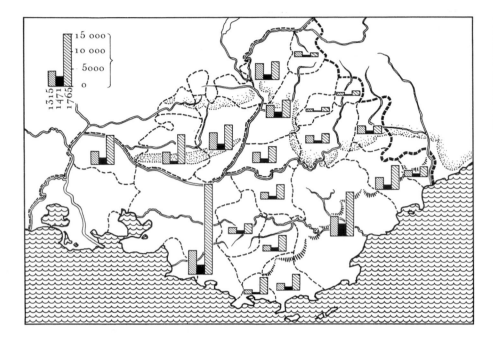

It is hard to measure the population decline in the West towards the end of the Middle Ages. Provence, where a copious source material has been preserved, is the one region for which we can form some idea of the overall development. In many places the population was reduced by half or even two thirds in 150 years: ruthless natural selection eliminated the weakest. The figures refer to the number of households.

The wars and massacres for which Normans, Saracens, and particularly the Hungarians were responsible may have slowed down the population explosion but did not bring it to an end. Indeed, the Christian West was strengthened by the incorporation of hundreds of thousands of young able-bodied men—the figure of 400,000 has been put forward for the Hungarians alone. Many of them, like the Danes of Normandy and the Danelaw and, later, the evangelized Slavs of Poland, were perfectly assimilated and helped to protect the population when the Mongol migration stopped in Hungary and Silesia.

At all events, progress is very clear to see from the eleventh century on. Whether or not we accept the very approximate figures advanced by K. Benett, the trend they reflect matches the vast areas cleared, the huge thrust of colonization east of the Elbe, south of the Pyrenees and even across the sea—in the Peloponnese and the Holy Land—and the great development of the towns. It has been calculated that the population of the West increased from 48 million in 1100 to 50 million in 1150, 61 million in 1200 and 73 million in 1300. The indices of

growth established by Slicher van Bath are 109.5 from 1000 to 1050; 104.3 from 1050 to 1100; 104.2 from 1100 to 1150; 122 from 1150 to 1200; 113.1 from 1200 to 1250 and 105.8 from 1250 to 1300. According to J. Russell, the population of England rose from 800,000 in the eighth century to 1.5 million at the end of the eleventh and 3.5 million at the beginning of the fourteenth. France, within its medieval frontiers which remained more or less stable after 843, is said to have grown from 5 million in the mid-ninth century to 14 or 15 million at the beginning of the fourteenth. A town like Metz saw its population multiply sevenfold, from 5,000 to 35,000 people, between the ninth century and the thirteenth. Others that started from nil, like Venice founded at Rialto as late as 810, and Florence which sprang up at the foot of the ancient Fiesole, could boast some 100,000 inhabitants at the beginning of the fourteenth century. At that point the population explosion slowed down but did not quite stop.

The overcrowded West suffered from chronic malnutrition. Even slight fluctuations in climate caused famines that killed off the poor and so debilitated the masses that their weakened organisms were unable to resist the first onslaught of an entirely new bacillus. The Black Death of 1348 spread like lightning, helped by a new carrier—the black rat; it is believed to have carried away one-third of the population overall and perhaps 40 per cent in England. Periodic recrudescences prevented a new start being made for a century and a half, except in Spain and parts of Germany and Italy. It is no exaggeration to say that during the Middle Ages the West developed in the interval between the two plagues.

These material conditions, and a hostile nature bravely confronted by a humanity whose strength and numbers steadily increased but whose victory was always in doubt, made a deep mark on man's attitude towards his environment.

A very young population has reactions that our gerontocratic civilization is unable to comprehend. Hardened warriors burst into tears: they were only 18 or 20 years old, some even less. Their enthusiasm was on a par with their credulity; despair suddenly followed temerity and violence gave way to resignation; one is amazed at their vanity and naivety. Their feelings ranged from one extreme to the other: love and hate were equally strong. Gambling and games of skill filled an important place in their lives. On the other hand, one must admire the maturity of little girls of 12, mothers of large families at 17, and 14 year old kings.

A population whose weaker members were ruthlessly eliminated by the natural conditions of existence where the strong had a better chance of survival than the wise, a population led by the strongest, most vigorous and most violent tended to revere strength and courage, view life as a struggle and be ready to fight at the drop of a glove. One sees this chiefly in the knightly class and the peasantry, less among the clerics and intellectuals. But the sword was for long mightier, and more necessary, than the pen. This is reflected in various customs: dubbing a knight by striking him on the shoulder with a sword; breaking a straw or throwing down a glove to signify a quarrel or a challenge; shaking hands on concluding a bargain at the country fair; the Christian crossing himself and joining his palms before his God, and the vassal before his liege.

An ill-nourished and under-nourished world, inadequately shielded against a rebellious nature, was tempted to dream of a Cloud Cuckoo Land where there was always plenty to eat, nature was enslaved once and for all and magic was the rule; particularly as in everyday life shortages were frequent and to be able to count on the mere necessaries was already an unattainable ideal. The rich and powerful were distinguished from the rest by super-nutrition; larger, more solidly built houses; gaudier, richer dress; splendid jewelry; and a munificence that was both spendthrift and vainly ostentatious. The overfed needed constant exercise, frequent blood-letting—wounds could have the same effect—they had tremendous vitality, amazing strength, a violent disposition and a 'sanguine' temperament. The underfed, debilitated by fasting and privations, forced at times to still their hunger with noxious weeds, were easier to delude and ready victims of terror and superstition.

A dreaded, hostile nature and a dark, untracked forest infested by wolves and robbers enhanced the feeling of insecurity. This made men all the more ready to seek security in association, unite in communities and accept any order that might be a guarantee of peace. But the close-knit unit formed by the village and its manor surrounded by woods or marshes was jealous of its independance and entertained only very slack relations with its neighbours.

Nonetheless, the excess produced by the population explosion and the survivors of local famines and general epidemics were forced to migrate to other localities where manpower was in demand. And the perpetual comings and goings on the roads, in the towns and at the courts of lords and kings blended and welded the Western World into a unit that was conditioned by the same climate, shared the same faith and the same basic view of a nature which, though tyrannical, was believed to have been created around man and for him.

MENTALITY
AND
SOCIAL LIFE

Nature in the Middle Ages differed from that of our times not so much intrinsically as in its action on man, who was far more strongly influenced and moulded by it. In spite of this it was never considered as a whole or studied systematically, except very roughly and from a peculiar angle—for instance, by peasants endeavouring to discover the conditions needed to obtain a slightly better harvest or astronomers observing the course of some natural phenomenon.

Man felt that he and nature were linked by unbreakable bonds, so he gave it a place in his overall vision of the universe, of which God was lord and creator and man the centre.

Documents which have come down to us prove how accurately details were often observed. The whole and all its parts had their place and meaning within that overall vision. Nature was the tangible mask, reflection or symbol of another reality, which was explained by religion and described by the Ancients. Their works, attributed with a fundamental importance, were screened, anthologized and transcribed by the Fathers of the Church and the great ecclesiastical authors of the Middle Ages on the basis of partial translations and interpretations by Syrians, Jews and Arabs. Preachers, confessors, catechists, even the most ignorant clerics repeated elementary or crudely simplified explanations of those works, which were thus made available to the faithful, namely to all the peoples of the West; they were also rendered in vividly coloured images on the walls of churches and cathedrals for the benefit of the illiterate.

The result was that a mentality which had the greatest difficulty in freeing itself from a visible nature at once overbearing and essentially misunderstood, fell under the sway of a religion that had an explanation for everything and was built in part on the science of the Ancients, considered perfect and immutable, to which nothing new could possibly be added.

The Western World was inhabited exclusively by Christians and every facet of man's daily life—morals

Christ, the Great Architect, measuring the universe. The concept of Christ as a man lavishing care on the earth was central to the Middle Ages.

A clepsydra probably used at the court of St Louis in Paris c. 1250.

Silver-mounted German sand glass dated 1483.

and his attitude to sin, family life and his relations with his fellows—was directly interpreted, influenced and even provoked by religion. In this respect western society was merely a reflection of the Divine Providence, which had assigned to every man his place.

But when it comes to details we find two distinct influences: on the one hand the substantial heritage received from earlier civilizations, which Christianity incorporated and utilized; on the other, the behaviours, traditions, customs, cognitions and superstitions that can be traced back to a Germanic, Gallo-Roman or Celtic past and were assimilated or handed down by the Middle Ages.

This explains why it is so extremely difficult to explain to people who live in the last quarter of the twentieth century the mentality that prevailed in a Pre-Cartesian era, basically Christian but imbued with classical or barbarian reminiscences, when nothing was methodically put in doubt. Attention was focused in a different direction, and many axioms that we consider false were accepted without question.

THE SENSE OF TIME

Time, and the changes its passage entails, is one of the fundamental problems that first penetrated man's consciousness and has always offered philosophers and theologians food for thought. There is no place in a study of everyday life to dwell on the shrewd conceptions of Thomas Aquinas or Albertus Magnus. But it is worth recalling that the overwhelming majority of people in the West continued to experience time in the very same way as their forbears had done in Graeco-Roman antiquity and their descendants would do in many rural regions of Europe until the mid-twentieth century.

The rhythmic passage of time was established by the sun—in the short term by the alternation of day and night; in the long term by the cyclic recurrence of the seasons of the year. This perfect and immutable rhythm, this fragment of eternity, was the work of God and therefore fell within the purview of his Church. Liturgical festivities marked the great astronomical events of the year. Prayers stressed the

Above: fourteenth century wall clock with alarm mechanism.

Sundials show hours that differ in length with the length of the day. More accurate instruments, such as the sand glass, the water clock or clepsydra and the mechanical clock (from the end of the thirteenth century), measure equal periods.

Night is falling, the moon appears in the sky, the night-watchman winds his horn to tell the hour, children hurry to reach home before dark and the gates are shut.

rhythm of day and night and throughout the West a network of churchbells informed the faithful of the major divisions of the day between two recitations of the Angelus. Only the clergy felt the need for even the most elementary notions of metrology; everyone was capable of establishing approximately the middle of the day, noontide, when the sun was at the highest point of its course. The hours were still counted in accordance with the Roman method: 12 hours of day and 12 of night. Noontide crowned the sixth hour of day (sixte), whereas the first (prime) corresponded to sunrise and the twelfth (vespers) marked the beginning of night. Tierce (the third hour) and nones (the ninth) were situated about the middle of the two halves of the day.

The third hour of night was marked by the office of compline; the sixth ended at midnight (matins); the ninth was celebrated by lauds. Need I say that these hours of day and night were only approximately equal? They differed from our hours of 60 minutes for the simple reason that only at the equinoxes did the days and nights have the same length, namely 12 hours each, adding up to exactly 24 of our hours.

At the winter solstice day lasted from 6 to 8 of our hours, depending on the latitude, or from 360 to 480 minutes; but it was still divided into 12 hours of between 30 and 40 of our minutes each. Conversely, at the summer solstice day lasted from 16 to 18 of our hours, so an hour comprised 80 or 90 minutes.

The hours grew longer or shorter from the equinox to the solstice; they were all of approximately equal length only on a single day in spring and autumn. This phenomenon is brought home to us very forcefully when we examine one of the many sundials we have inherited from the past, for instance the famous angel dial of Chartres Cathedral, which dates from the twelfth century. A gnomon perpendicular to the dial and lying generally in the axis of the earth casts its shadow on engraved lines that are determined by observation or reckoning. The median line corresponds to noon, when the sun passes through the local meridian; five lines to the left and six to the right, numbered as a rule from 1 to 12 indicate the other hours. The first tallies with sunrise or the end of the first hour, the last with sunset. These lines diverge and so reflect the varying length of the hours depending on the length of the day.

For the night and for days when the sun did not shine a different method was needed. Only very few people were capable of judging even very approximately what time it was from the position of the stars and the constellations of the zodiac, which change not only from one hour to the next but also from one night to the next. Candles that burned for three or four hours served the purpose—three sufficed to measure the whole night. Another instrument used was the hour-glass, in which sand passes in a thin thread at constant speed from one graduated container to another. The clepsydra or waterclock was based on the same principle but to ensure a constant flow the vase must have the shape of an inverted bell, which is very difficult to achieve empirically. The hours indicated by candle, sandglass or waterclock were identical but differed from those shown on a sundial, which varied from day to day. Yet the overwhelming majority of the population did not bother about that; they lived according to church time, which was marked by the liturgical offices and the great religious feasts. That was also the time observed by the powerful feudal lords, marked by quit rents and military service. Those in a dependent position were not really interested in punctuality; they were neither harried nor in haste. A great deal has been said about the extraordinary indifference to the passage of time shown by the rural masses; they felt no need to know their age, count the years, calculate the time of day, or observe an exact timetable.

The Middle Ages were drawing to a close when a great intellectual change first appeared in towns where trade and industry flourished. It was marked by the definitive adoption of hours all of the same length, indicated by mechanical clocks that took the place of the church bells. The advent of lay, rational, urban time that tallied with the motion of the stars was probably due to the influence of merchants who were conscious of its value and had to decide in advance on their journeys, balance their books, and calculate rates of exchange. Patricians and master craftsmen, anxious to avoid being taken in by their workers, must have followed in the merchants' wake, and it is not by chance that the first modern clocks were more often installed in the towers of civic buildings than in the steeples of churches and cathedrals.

However, several centuries passed before this new way of counting time was generally adopted, measured exactly and instinctively sensed by the rural masses and the urban population of the West. This is brought home to us if we take the trouble to note the terms people commonly employed to express the future, the past, and concepts linked with the passage of time. Even when town time had spread to the countryside, the sense of time evolved only very slowly in a world so absolutely dependent on the sun and the seasons.

At the beginning of the twentieth century the day of a European peasant still gave a very good idea of how time was employed by all classes of the population during the Middle Ages. He was awakened

Above: a fourteenth century lantern. Right: The Church organized the Christian year. The major dates on the calendar coincided with religious holidays usually celebrated with processions (see illustration), fairs, pilgrimages and benedictions.

by a peal of bells shortly before dawn so as to be ready to work at sunrise. After crossing himself and murmuring a prayer, he put on his clothes—shirt, breeches, hose and shoes—and only then washed; this was necessarily a very perfunctory process since it was performed when he was fully dressed. Very few people had to time to act on the advice contained in *The Secret of Secrets*: to take a little exercise, wash their hands and feet with cold water in summer, rub their teeth and gums with a leaf, anoint themselves with oil, and take an electuary made with rhubarb or aloes to purge the bile. On the other hand, a great many went to church every morning to pray or hear Mass and, if the distance was too great, never failed to prolong their daily devotions in proportion. Breakfast was not eaten until after prayers; Holy Communion, which could only be partaken of when fasting, was a very frequent practice. Consequently, work began at prime or thereabouts, that is, towards six o'clock. We shall see that people's occupations varied, as was natural, with the social stratum to which they belonged. Peasants went out to the fields; women busied themselves about the house, washed their children or gossiped with the neighbours.

For the nobility and clergy the timetable was no less strict because of the duties inherent in their condition. About tierce a second meal or at least a solid snack was eaten to fill the void left by digestion of breakfast; some townsmen took themselves to the tavern where they gulped down a drink to revive their strength. Dinner was at noon (sixte), followed by a break that varied in length within wide limits. Peasants and craftsmen very soon went back to work; the nobles took time off to watch a show, enjoy a nap, gamble or go hunting; clerics rested or spent some time in meditation. Monks, during Lent, had to wait till nones, about three o'clock in the afternoon, to eat their dinner and were so famished that they managed to have nones moved forward to about midday; that is how midday came to be called noon in modern English, and afternoon the remainder of the day. When night fell and vespers were sung all professional activity was brought to a close.

Peasants and their animals had to return home when it got dark; craftsmen, who were obliged to do their work where all could see and hear—besides having no adequate means of illumination—put up their shutters. A resin torch, an oil lamp or a tallow candle was lighted here and there, but most people made do with the light cast by the flame in the hearth. Only the rich could afford fragrant wax candles, which cost a lot of money. Lack of lighting facilities cut short the evenings, and people did not dawdle over their supper. By compline (about 9 o'clock) the fire was covered in virtually all homes, leaving only a handful of harmless embers for the next morning, and the whole family was more or less comfortably in bed. Even in well-to-do circles one bed accommodated several people. Nobles, clerics and peasants were alike in not wearing a night-shirt: everybody slept naked between sheets or blankets. Monks and nuns, who had to rise every three hours to recite their offices, kept all, or at least part, of their clothes on and were entitled to a pallet each.

The Church not only called attention to the hours of the day; it organized the entire year in the Christian West. The winter solstice was marked by the great festivities of the Nativity (25 December), the Circumcision (1 January), the Epiphany (6 January), the Adoration of the Magi and the Baptism of Christ. During the previous period, Advent, there were three fast-days a week: Monday, Wednesday and Friday. The weeks that preceded Lent were marked by other festivities that varied with the social stratum but were particularly typical in the rural environment where we shall come across them again: Candlemas on 2 February, celebrated with pancakes and the blessing of the candles; Shrovetide just before Ash Wednesday, when the faithful crossed their foreheads with hallowed ashes to symbolize the fate reserved for the body. Then began forty days of abstinence from meat, except on Sundays and at Mid-Lent, in preparation for Holy Week. The Annunciation was celebrated on 25 March; Palm Sunday commemorated Our Lord's entry into Jerusalem. On Holy Thursday, those who could do

The astrolabe was used to measure the height of the stars above the horizon. Probably invented in Greece, it reached the West through the intermediary of the Arabs. It was the ancestor of the sextant. Above left: miniature showing how the astrolabe was employed. Above right: design of an astrolabe from a treatise on geometry. Right: a magnificent thirteenth century astrolabe, thought to be Spanish.

so received twelve poor men at their table, and on Good Friday the bells were silenced for three days. This was followed by Easter, the great festival that marked the end of Lent and celebrated Christ's Resurrection with the distribution of the eggs and the rite of spring. Then there were the Rogation Days, the Ascension and Whitsun (fifty days after Easter, commemorating the descent of the Holy Ghost to the Apostles). Corpus Christi was introduced in the thirteenth century. It coincided with the season when the crops were blessed, pilgrimages took place, tournaments were organised, campaigns started and the great fairs were held. It was also the time of love. Midsummer Day, 24 June, heralded in the summer, the season of heavy work in the fields, which lasted until Michaelmas, 29 September, and was broken only by a few feasts, of which the Assumption, 15 August, in honour of Our Lady, was the most important. After that came the commemoration of All Saints on 1 November and preparations for Christmas.

Since time was ordered by the Church, the new dating systems introduced gradually in the West to establish a few fixed points in its ceaseless course were naturally based on the major events of Christian history. The ancient systems based on the foundation of Rome in 753 BC or the first Olympiad in 776, with dates expressed in function of the governing Consuls or the years of the Emperor's reign were abandoned, and from the sixth century, following in the footsteps of Dionysius Exiguus, the clergy took as a starting point the Incarnation of Christ. By the ninth century the new chronology, whose historic importance is known to all, was employed in most western lands. Instead of 1 January or 1 March, as in ancient Rome, the first day of the year was 25 December (Christmas) and 25 March (Lady Day) or Easter, the greatest of all Christian holidays. The trouble was that Easter is a movable feast; it falls on the first Sunday after the vernal equinox and the fourteenth day of the paschal moon and therefore ranges from 22 March to 25 April. Consequently, a legal year that went from Easter to Easter could have from eleven to thirteen months. A number of days at the end of March or the beginning of April separated by a twelvemonth might belong to the same calendar year and therefore create confusion. For example, since Easter fell on 31 March in 1252 and on 20 April in 1253, the year 1252 had 365 plus 20 days and all the days between 31 March and 20 April 1253 were dated 1252 in legal documents as were those from 31 March to 20 April 1252.

It is probably due to pressure from the merchants that the beginning of the year was finally established at the Circumcision, reverting to the ancient Roman usage for the civil year. But it is worth stressing that in the West different systems continued to be used side by side for a very long time without apparently troubling the inhabitants, who were closely linked in mentality and by the constant practice of a religion which organized time after the same fashion. The Venetians began the year on 1 March, the Florentines and English (under the Norman kings) on 25 March, the Papacy on 25 December, the French from the twelfth century at Easter; the Spaniards reckoned the commencement of the Christian era 38 years before the birth of Christ. Seemingly, therefore, the method of dating was not considered of fundamental importance and it is tempting to see in this lack of precision a continuing indifference to the passage of time.

The days of the week took their name from the Roman or Germanic gods to whom they were dedicated. Those names have remained virtually unchanged, except for the day of the sun (Sunday, Sonntag), which in Latin became *dies dominica* (dimanche, domenica, domingo). The months kept their Latin names, which reflected the ancient Roman usage; since their religious year began on 1 March, September, October, November and December were really the seventh, eighth, ninth and tenth months. Instead, the days of the month were no longer related, as in Rome, to the Calends (1st), Nones (5th or 7th) and Ides (13th or 15th), but were designated either by numbers (from 1 to 31), as we do now, or very often by the name of the saint celebrated on each.

The rigorous precision insisted on today was unknown in the Middle Ages. Though balances were used, the measurement of solids and liquids was very uncertain; it made a great difference whether a measure was level or heaped.

24 June was called St John's Day or Midsummer Day rather than 'the twenty-fourth of June' and only very seldom, except in the early Middle Ages, 'the eighth day before Calends of July'. The year was mentioned only in official documents, chronicles and historical works. The common run of the illiterate, when relating events of the past, undoubtedly specified the date only by reference to a season of the year or a religious festival. The number of years that had elapsed interested neither the story-teller nor his audience. And in a world where death struck fast and frequently, there was little sense in attempting to foresee or anticipate the distant future on earth.

In the Middle Ages the vast majority of people in the West did not define their position in time as we do today. They lived in the present—a rather vague present that covered a few months or years. Time was organized by the Church, but with no great precision or certainty, within the faltering framework of the hours, days and seasons.

THE NOTION OF SPACE

Space too was sensed, understood and measured differently in the Middle Ages from the manner it is today. The complicated, imprecise systems of weights and measures then in use have no exact modern equivalents. Each little country, each micro-region, even a single village had units of its own for measuring capacity, weight, length and area; though mostly derived from Roman measures, they varied in type and size not only from one country to another but within a matter of miles. Even the revival of international trade did not lead to the introduction of a rational, generally accepted system. There were, in fact, a few local simplifications, notably in the Languedoc, but as a rule merchants made do with volumes of conversion tables so weighty that nowadays we would not dream of using anything of the sort. Here, by way of example, is a brief extract from a Florentine Merchants' Manual compiled in the first half on the fourteenth century:

'100 fine Venice pounds equal 96 Genoa pounds;

1 silver mark, Venice weight, equals 9 ounces 3 deniers Genoa weight;

1 mina, Genoa weight, equals 1 ¼ bushels;

100 gross Venice pounds equal 147 pounds 1 ounce 20 ¼ carats
in Genoa at 144 carats an ounce, or 1 ounce 3 deniers 9 grains or
24 deniers an ounce or 24 grains a denier weight;

10 rods in Genoa equal 35 ells in Venice;

100 fine Venice pounds equal 92 to 93 pounds in Pisa;

18 ells of cloth, Venice measure, equal 17 ells in Pisa;

1 Venice pound of silver, equal to 1 ½ Venice mark, equals 13 ounces in Pisa.'

On the other hand, thousands of standard measures that were rendered useless by the introduction of the metric system have been preserved. Even within the limits of the territories where they were accepted they were copied and employed quite

Charlemagne attempted, with no great success, to introduce a roughly uniform system of weights and measures throughout his empire. 'Charlemagne's Pile' (above) was the name given to a series of standard weights established at a far later date. Made up of bronze bowls that fitted one into the other, it was only recognized within a very narrowly limited territory.

Precision balances were introduced at the end of the Middle Ages for rare or precious commodities. The difficulty was to agree on the unit of weight, which varied from one region to another. The balance on the left came from Prussia.

imprecisely. As a general rule the measurement of space was anything but accurate. There was much talk of hogsheads of wine, sacks of wheat and bales of wool, but the weight and capacity of each hogshead, sack or bale varied within extremely wide limits. What is more, a measure of capacity could, for instance, be used 'full' or 'heaped'. And the same unit corresponded to quite different quantities depending on the substance for which it served and the way it was handled, without apparently troubling the user in the slightest. In Paris, for instance, a hogshead of oats was equal to 240 bushels or 572 gallons, whereas a hogshead of wheat was equal to 144 bushels or 343 gallons. In the same town a hogshead of wine 'on the dregs' was very different

from a hogshead of 'filtered' wine, and had nothing in common with the hogsheads previously mentioned: a hogshead of wine was barely one tenth of a hogshead of oats.

By and large, figures were little known and poorly used. This is true not only of the overwhelming majority of country people. It is very doubtful whether a lord of the manor, even when he was a member of the clergy, possessed the mental equipment needed to map out a campaign, count his vassals, check his dependants and collect the requisite weapons and supplies. But he had an excellent visual memory for the men who had put their hands in his, he could plan a raid, empirically and with a certain approximation, and muster his men. But very seldom

The books kept by Francesco di Marco Datini, of Prato, in the fifteenth century are among the first to display a reliable accounting system. This balance sheet (below) dated 1 January 1410 was established for the firm's subsidiary at Avignon. The text is in Tuscan vernacular and the sums are written in Arabic figures, which were introduced in the tenth century.

The notion of numerical accuracy was quite alien to Medieval Man. Chroniclers tell stories of numberless armies, when they really amounted at most to a few thousand men.

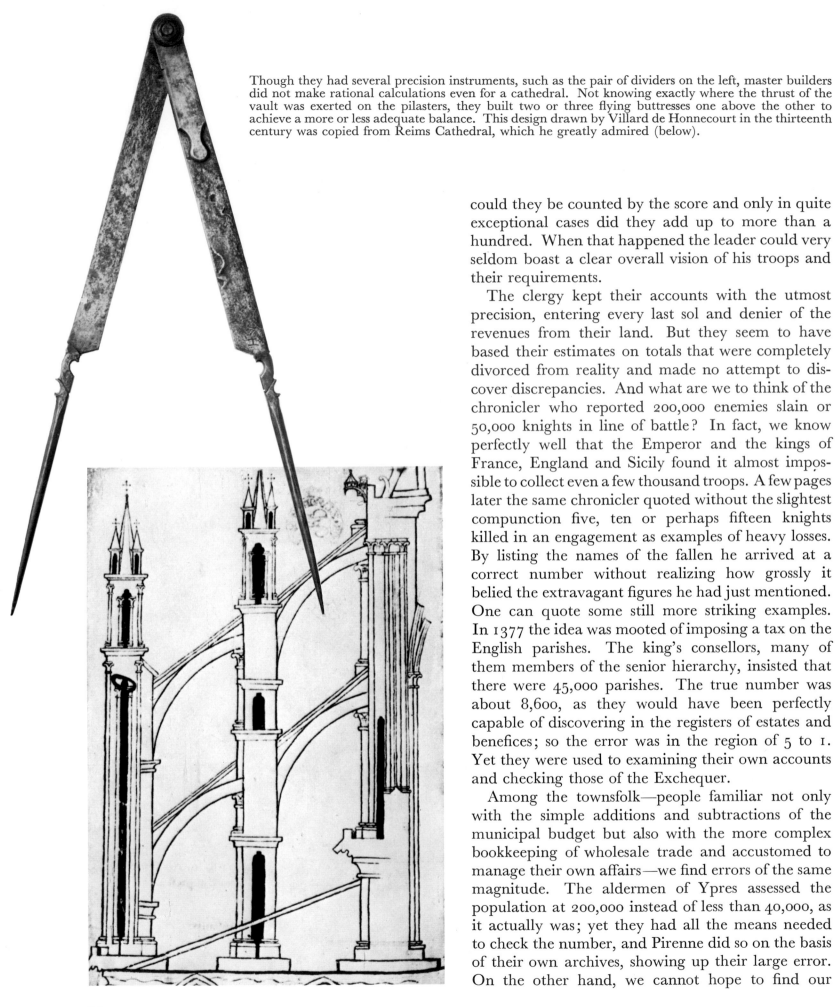

Though they had several precision instruments, such as the pair of dividers on the left, master builders did not make rational calculations even for a cathedral. Not knowing exactly where the thrust of the vault was exerted on the pilasters, they built two or three flying buttresses one above the other to achieve a more or less adequate balance. This design drawn by Villard de Honnecourt in the thirteenth century was copied from Reims Cathedral, which he greatly admired (below).

could they be counted by the score and only in quite exceptional cases did they add up to more than a hundred. When that happened the leader could very seldom boast a clear overall vision of his troops and their requirements.

The clergy kept their accounts with the utmost precision, entering every last sol and denier of the revenues from their land. But they seem to have based their estimates on totals that were completely divorced from reality and made no attempt to discover discrepancies. And what are we to think of the chronicler who reported 200,000 enemies slain or 50,000 knights in line of battle? In fact, we know perfectly well that the Emperor and the kings of France, England and Sicily found it almost impossible to collect even a few thousand troops. A few pages later the same chronicler quoted without the slightest compunction five, ten or perhaps fifteen knights killed in an engagement as examples of heavy losses. By listing the names of the fallen he arrived at a correct number without realizing how grossly it belied the extravagant figures he had just mentioned. One can quote some still more striking examples. In 1377 the idea was mooted of imposing a tax on the English parishes. The king's consellors, many of them members of the senior hierarchy, insisted that there were 45,000 parishes. The true number was about 8,600, as they would have been perfectly capable of discovering in the registers of estates and benefices; so the error was in the region of 5 to 1. Yet they were used to examining their own accounts and checking those of the Exchequer.

Among the townsfolk—people familiar not only with the simple additions and subtractions of the municipal budget but also with the more complex bookkeeping of wholesale trade and accustomed to manage their own affairs—we find errors of the same magnitude. The aldermen of Ypres assessed the population at 200,000 instead of less than 40,000, as it actually was; yet they had all the means needed to check the number, and Pirenne did so on the basis of their own archives, showing up their large error. On the other hand, we cannot hope to find our way through the labyrinth of medieval bookkeeping. Even in the accounts kept by merchants in the fourteenth and fifteenth centuries, who were the first to master figures, a careful check of the balance sheets and the profit and loss accounts reveals omissions and inaccuracies masked by the formal precision of the mathematical operations. The situation is obviously still worse when it comes to notaries and the clerks employed by lay and ecclesiastical lords. One ought to be able to draw up a balance sheet on the basis of the accounts that have come down to us, divided into receipts and expenditures; but, to start with, the receipts are in an incredible mess. Very often sums entered under that head were immediately used to pay a debt or a purchase, which is consequently listed among the receipts instead of the expenditures. as it should be. Inaccuracies also crop up in the summaries and even in the books themselves. At the start these were kept with every care, only to end up in a more or less illegible scribble, with notes in the margins and at the foot of the pages, entries that though cancelled were carried over to the final totals, and so on and so forth. One might be tempted to believe that the clerks and their lords were brainless bunglers, who forgot what they were trying to do while they were still at it, hastily finished the job as best they could, or simply gave it up before the end was reached.

When we consider the grandest monuments erected during the Middle Ages, the tens of thousands of churches and castles that are still standing today, we are amazed at the lack of unity and accuracy in their execution and the unfinished state in which so many of them were left. True, we are full of admiration for those achievements and realize that their very magnitude was an obstacle to their completion. And we shall never tire of revisiting the finest of them and wondering at their extraordinary perfection. It is also possible that buildings more geometrically exact or more completely finished would have less charm and rouse less powerful emotions. Nor does it detract from their value to recall how little knowledge of mathematics and physics the master builders possessed, how few really efficient machines they could count on, and how entirely lacking they were in precision instruments. In their dual functions as architect and foreman, they often employed methods which were empirical and inexact. How many vaults and spires, for instance at Beauvais, collapsed or were left unfinished! And not only for lack of money. Those that are still existant very often owe their preservation to meticulous maintenance and ceaseless restoration work through the centuries. Some were 'completed' well or ill during the nineteenth or the twentieth centuries; others are still unfinished. We may bear in mind the catastrophes that might have happened at Bayeux, Evreux, Chartres and Amiens in the fourteenth or fifteenth century But let us not forget Cologne, Ulm and Milan.

When we go into details we are struck by the many cases of faulty execution—chapels symmetrically positioned that differ in size; rose windows that are slightly off centre—and of faulty conception: flying buttresses designed to back up the pilasters that support a vault are often erected between the points where the thrust is applied; to offset the effects of this error there are sometimes two or three buttresses in place of one. The thirteenth-century French architect Villard de Honnecourt offers a striking example, and at Reims of all places!

However, in his day there was already a noticeable improvement in the handling of figures and a greater search for accuracy, at least by philosophers and mathematicians like Roger Bacon and some merchants. But as far as the great mass of the population was concerned the indifference to time and space was simply incredible; so was their inability to master figures and reason rigorously, precisely and what we would call logically. A writer could combine in a single page, without the slightest compunction, a personal observation, an exact number or a precise detail with a contrary statement lifted wholesale from an ancient author or a religious manual; though it utterly contradicted what he knew from experience, he accepted it without question as the absolute truth.

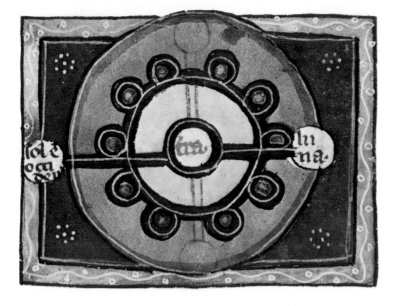

Many representations of the universe were restricted to the earth, with the moon—and the sun—revolving round it.

This map of the heavens dates from the twelfth century. Each of the seven planets then known (Mercury, Venus, Earth, Mars, Jupiter, Saturn and the moon) describes a circle in the sky, governs the days of the week and has a 'house' in one, or sometimes two, of the twelve signs of the Zodiac. These latter govern the months and are already shown in the shape given them today.

THE VISION OF THE UNIVERSE

This lack of rigour in grasping figures and following a train of thought was only partly due to a lack of technical and scientific knowledge. The notions received from the Ancients were more than sufficient for following a path that to our modern eyes would seem far more progressive. Yet for almost a thousand years, scholars, philosophers, scientists, clerics, laymen with a smattering of letters, and the entire population of the Western World accepted without any real question a conception of nature and the universe that had been evolved towards the end of the classical period following in the footsteps of Aristotle, a philosopher who had lived eight centuries earlier and whose theories had been more or less revised and corrected by Christianity. This is true even of such great and original thinkers as the Frenchman Gerbert of Aurillac, the Italian Thomas Aquinas, the Englishman Roger Bacon, the Catalan Ramon Lull and the German Albertus Magnus.

During that lengthy period all the details of that philosophy were recopied again and again without the slightest attempt at subjecting them to a critical examination or bringing them up to date. And it is no exaggeration to say with C. Langlois that it was not the scholars who were capable of achieving an advance, but 'the common herd, who held the same beliefs and convictions for a thousand years.'

It was a self-evident fact that God created the universe. That axiom could be interpreted in different ways matching different levels of reflection. He may have thought it up from all eternity; He may have lifted out of the primeval void the matter with which he fashioned it in the six days of the Bible story; He may have laid down the laws that govern the course of events. These laws could be suspended by the Creator at any time; by so doing he worked a miracle. It was a fact, for instance, that an inexplicable eclipse of the sun took place on the day of the Crucifixion, converting the great astronomer Dionysius the Areopagite.

There were four major elements—earth, water, air and fire—enclosed as in an egg-shell by the domed

The famous *Tapiz de la Creación* in the treasury of Gerona Cathedral illustrates the first chapter of Genesis. In the centre, Christ as the creative World and also as 'The Lord of Creation'. With His right hand He blesses the universe; in His left He holds the Book of Revelation. Two circular inscriptions from the Bible frame scenes arranged round the figure of Christ. Above His head, the Holy Ghost between light (on the right) and darkness (on the left). Lower down, arranged symmetrically, the two phases of the separation of land and water. In the lower semicircle, Adam reigns over the animals (right) and Eve is brought forth from his side as he lies asleep among the flowers (left). Below, the animals that live in the sky, the earth and the waters. The circle of the Creation is inscribed in a rectangle that represents the heavenly Jerusalem, announced by four angels at the four corners of the tapestry, who blow their trumpets to signify the end of the world.

sky. The circle was the most perfect of all shapes; this was amply demonstrated by the vaulted arches of houses and bridges, the circular section of vats, barrels, wheels and the like; by the fact that less space is wasted in circular containers, and that the circle, like God, has neither beginning nor end. The egg was a favourite image used by writers who wanted to make difficult concepts generally accessible. Timaeus explained to Placidus that the shell represented the firmament, the white skin the earth, the albumen water, and the yoke fire. Beyond the firmament was a heaven where angels and the blessed dwelt, then the circle from which the rebellious angels had been cast out, and lastly, the splendid heaven where God had His throne. The visible sky was made up of several layers of a very pure, bright, rarified air that revolved ceaselessly, producing delightful music that could be heard in paradise. The stars shining in the far distance were related to the sky as knots are to the tree; many of them were of huge size and all exerted a direct influence on the earth. Ptolemy says in his Almagest that they numbered 1,022; he counted them all and grouped them in 47 constellations. The twelve most important constellations constituted the signs of the Zodiac: Aries, Taurus, Gemini, Cancer, Leo, Virgo, Libra, Scorpio, Sagittarius, Capricorn, Aquarius and Pisces, within which lay the path of the seven planets; the sun resided for one month in each. Thus the signs directly governed the seasons and the months. The planets influenced the days of the week which were named after them; they were closer to the earth than stars, and the closer they were, the smaller were the circles they described. Saturn took thirty years to travel through its orbit; then came Jupiter, Mars, the sun—the true centre of the universe, from which all heat came—Venus, Mercury and, lastly, the moon, which was the closest to the earth and reflected the sun's light like a well polished mirror. The *Sphaera Mundi* contains a great deal of information about the heavenly bodies; unfortunately the figures differ from one manuscript to another and even from one passage to another in the same manuscript. For example, the distance between the earth and the starry stratum was said to be equal to 10,055 times the earth's diameter, whereas there were 585 diameters from the earth to the sun. The latter was $166 \frac{3}{20}$ times larger than the earth, which in turn was $39 \frac{1}{4}$ times larger than the moon; from the earth to the moon the distance varied from 12 to $34 \frac{1}{2}$ diameters.

The sky was the privileged seat of the two lightest elements, fire and air. Fire was an extremely dry, bright air which sometimes appeared in the shape of lightning, produced by a clash between winds and falling to earth as a thunderbolt. The air might be more or less dense depending on the proximity of heavy elements. One of its functions was to support birds, which swam in the air as fish did in the water; it could bend a rod held aloft in all directions; air in movement was called wind.

Water was mostly represented by the sea, which owed its bitter taste to the mountains of salt it dissolved. The rivers flowed into it; they also sprang from it through the veins of the earth, which filtered and removed its bitter taste. If they passed through sulphurous caverns those waters burst forth hot and salty, as at Aix in Gascony (Dax) and Aix-la-Chapelle. Rivers were responsible for earthquakes.

Earth was the basic element. It was the centre of the universe, round which the sky, the stars and the planets revolved; it was also a geographic reality, surrounded by the circular ocean and sheltering and sustaining man and his environment. The earth was often believed to be round and scholars held that it measured 20,428 miles in circumference and 6,500 miles in diameter. These figures were calculated by Eratosthenes and, at some 1,650 yards to a mile, were not too far out. That some people saw the earth as a flat disc was of no great importance because that is how it had to be represented on the two-dimensional plans which were studied then.

What chiefly interested the common people was their immediate environment: the mineral, the vegetable and, still more, the animal kingdom. Taking their cue from the ancient authors, treatises

on stones discourse on their immutable qualities. Many of them were precious aids or remedies to be contemplated, touched, worn on the person or swallowed in beverages. Here, for example, is what Philippe de Thaon had to say about magnetite, the lodestone which attracted iron and had the same colour. It was found in the water of the River Jordan and in India, and served to confirm a woman's fidelity. For that purpose it was only necessary to place it on the sleeping woman's head: if she was chaste she turned over on her stomach; if not, she turned on her back. Magnetite cured dropsy, but a man who drank it three times in a row became impotent. It was useful for robbers because when placed on burning coals its odour gave the impression that the whole place was on the point of collapsing; all the inhabitants ran out of their houses, leaving them at the robbers' tender mercies. The seventy-eight stones generally named and described comprised few common minerals; rare or fabulous stones aroused greater interest. Special studies were devoted to the twelve gems of the rational (Exodus XXVIII, v. 17–20—Authorised King James Version), agate, alabaster, beryl, coral, cornelian, crystal, emerald, jade, jasper, lapis lazuli, onyx and sapphire.

The vegetable kingdom was not studied any more systematically. Authors mention aloe, nutmeg, myrrh, incense, pepper, camphor, sandalwood and other precious or aromatic plants that were credited with medicinal properties. But pictures of them were extremely rare and people pronounced their names without having a clear idea of what they were really like. Common plants were so familiar to the country-people that they were hardly given a thought unless they had a symbolic significance.

The animal kingdom instead made a strong impact on the mind of Medieval Man. Nobles hunted big game and bred dogs, horses and falcons; peasants bred domestic animals and fought the beasts of prey that threatened them. Philosophers studied both and clerics used them in their sermons. The most important animals, both real and imaginary, are described in the bestiaries and pictured on the walls and windows of cathedrals and other public buildings. Few insects are mentioned, except for the bee, which was viewed as a worthy bird, and the prudent ant, which had its place among the 'beasts' or mammals.

Fish seems to have been the generic name for all the creatures that lived in the water and for those without legs that lived on land. In the Middle Ages they were believed to be innumerable, though that encyclopaedic scholar Isidore of Seville—following in Pliny's footsteps—counted 144 species. Here are a few of the most important: the whale, made famous by Jonah, wallowed on the surface of the water its back covered with sand, weeds and bushes and when mariners landed there and started to light a fire, it suddenly dived and drowned them all. The porpoise rummaged the sea-bed; the eel and the lamprey were closely related to the snake; the Nile crocodile was 20 feet long and wept as it devoured its human prey; the crab attacked oysters by blocking their hinged shell with a pebble; the dolphin showed its strange love for men by saving them from storms; the hippopotamus was a sort of horse with the tusks of a boar and the hooves of an ox. There were also syrens, basilisks, huge dragons that could fell an elephant with a stroke of their tail, salamanders that lived in fire, and adders, of which the females killed the males during copulation and were killed by their offspring at birth.

But it is birds and land mammals that are given most space in the bestiaries. The phoenix, griffin and roc perpetuated ancient fables; the eagle, the vulture and other birds of prey are correctly described. The ostrich could digest iron and buried its eggs in the sand, where they hatched of themselves in the heat of the sun. Cranes, crows, doves, halcyons, herons, hoopoes, ibises, parrots, partridges, peacocks, pelicans, storks and swans are described in detail. So is the cock, a brave fighter and the handsomest bird of all, with crown and spurs.

The 'beasts' are far too numerous to be named here. First comes the lion, whose name in Greek means king; he was feared by all the others and the only things he feared were white cocks, scorpions,

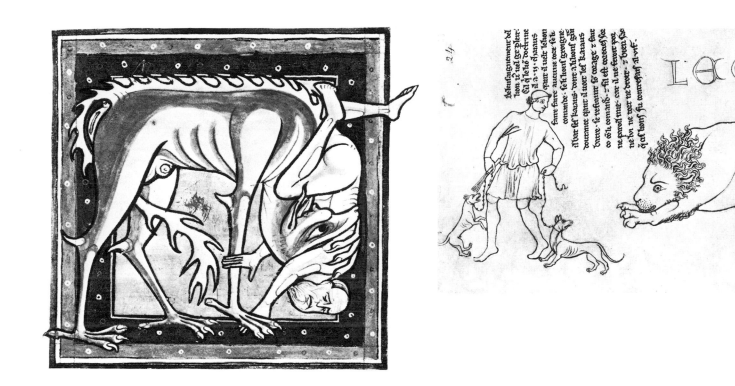

The Romanesque repertories contain a wealth of fabulous beasts. Some, like that above, were terrifying products of the illuminators' imagination and are completely alien to us. According to Dante, the griffin (below), half eagle, half lion, represents Christ's dual nature. In his sketchbook Villard de Honnecourt copied a lion after nature. This was a rare occurrence and proves that he succeeded in freeing himself from the many symbolistic legends centred round the noble beast. (Above, right.)

Left: This map from an English fourteenth century Psalter shows Christ blessing the earth. Our planet is represented as a flat disc framed by the winds, the clouds and the phases of the moon. Beneath the figure of Christ and the full moon is the Garden of Eden from which flow the rivers Ganges, Euphrates, Tigris, Gihon and Phison (Nile). In the centre, Jerusalem. To the right, between the moon and Jerusalem, a dark area represents the Red Sea. Another dark area, beneath Jerusalem, represents the Mediterranean. Lower still, we can decipher a few well-known names: Roma, Gallia. The North is at the bottom of the map.

Right: The so-called world map of Christopher Columbus drawn between 1488 and 1492 gives a very complete idea of the world before the discovery of America.

fire and squeaking wheels. He was a generous, understanding friend to man, slept with his eyes open, and erased his tracks with his tail. The weasel was made pregnant through its ear and gave birth through its mouth. The huge, chaste, clever elephant was handicapped by having no knees and so could not rise after a fall. We have seen that the wolf, lynx, stag, roe and red deer and bear were familiar to all.

Domestic animals are described accurately and with great realism. The ox, square and heavy, with large ears, a broad forehead, wide nostrils, gullet drooping to the knees and long, hairy tail. Sheep and ewes, simple-minded, gentle, timid, supplied milk, meat, wool and hide. The camel, with one hump or two, lived to be a hundred, could go without water for three days and was exhausted by the sexual act. The various breeds of dogs and horses are precisely listed and their qualities insisted on: chargers for battle, palfreys for riding, pack-horses for carrying loads.

The same taste for disordered analysis and description is displayed in geographical treatises—very often a good dose of credulity too. The inhabited portion of the earth was divided into three great regions: Asia to the east comprised the Garden of Eden defended by fierce beasts and a wall of fire whose gate had remained shut since the Fall. The fountain that watered Eden produced four rivers —the Nile that flowed through Ethiopia and Egypt, the Ganges that irrigated India, the Tigris, and the Euphrates. Asia was as large as all the other inhabited lands taken together and comprised India with its twenty-four countries, Persia, Chaldea, the kingdoms of the Magi, Armenia, the land of the Amazons, and that of Gog and Magog near the Caspian Mountain. Closer to us was Asia Minor, which was well known from the descriptions of travellers to Byzantium and pilgrims to the Holy Land.

Africa was the smallest of the regions. It started at Gades and the Pillars of Hercules—Cadiz and the Straits of Gibraltar—and stretched eastwards to Egypt; the blackamoors lived there. Carthage stood before the two Syrtes, which were shunned by ships because the sea was so rough. Further south were the Troglodytes, the Garamantes and the Ethiopians.

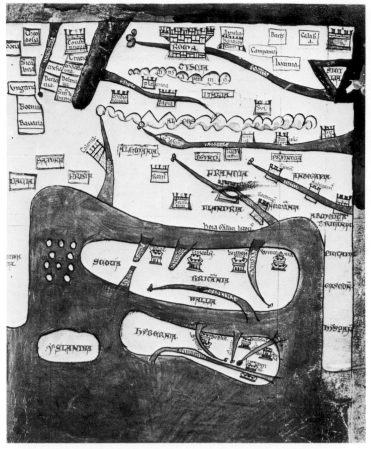

Map making developed greatly during the Middle Ages. The first maps were purely symbolical but gradually became more accurate and complete. Above: a map of Western Europe designed about 1200. North is on the left, South on the right.

Below: the plan of Saint-Jean-d'Acre on a thirteenth century map. With its help a traveller would have had no difficulty to find his way, for instance, from the port to the Hospital of St John, recognizable by the crosses of Lorraine that crown it.

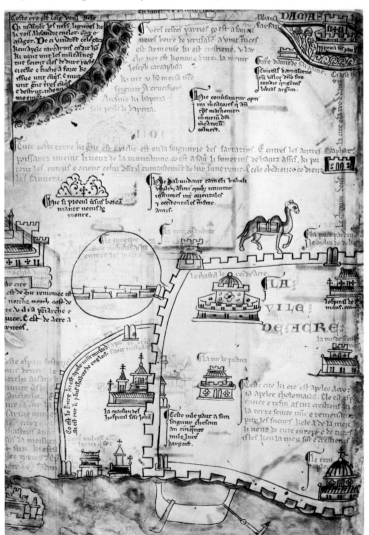

According to *L'Image du Monde*, a work that was widely read and copied, Spain, Italy, Sicily, Syria, Palestine and almost the whole of the Mediterranean Sea belonged to Africa.

These distant continents were described and discussed by a host of authors, who filled them with fabulous, outsized creatures lifted from the most credulous and ignorant Latin compilers like Solinus and the Greek Herodotus—the 'father of lies'. Europe, instead, seems to have aroused little interest in the people who lived there. True, Constantinople was often spoken of with amazement and envy. The same applies to Rome, but a legendary Rome that had little resemblance to reality. The western core of the continent—France, Germany, England and Italy—is hardly mentioned by popular writers because they considered it too well known. It was completely ignored by the masses, who, if they looked beyond their narrow local horizon, saw only the fabulous or biblical lands described by story-tellers or represented on the doorways of the churches at Vézelay, Aulnay and the like. The dialogue of Placidus and Timaeus makes a feeble attempt to classify the nations by temperament. Germans, Flemings and Englishmen are phlegmatic; Lombards, Portuguese, Spaniards, Catalans, French and Picards are sanguine, gay and quick, always ready to make love and good at it; Burgundians, Provençals, Gascons and Auvergnats are quick, dry and inefficient; Bretons, Scots, Welsh and Irish are melancholy. Other nations that formed part of the Western World, such as the Slavs, Scandinavians and Hungarians, were not described by ancient authors for the simple reason that they had never heard of them.

Yet those nations were known in the Middle Ages. First, to the Roman clergy, who visited them or received subsidies, pilgrimages and requests for advice or help from them. But also to many German and French nobles, who had gone on expeditions with them even before the great pilgrimages organized in common and the Crusades. The overland routes to Constantinople and Jerusalem passed

The young Venetian merchant Marco Polo sailed from Venice in 1271. He travelled through Armenia and reached China via Persia, the Pamir Plateau and the Gobi Desert. At Pekin he was patronized by Kublai Khan, who sent him on missions to Cochin China, Tibet and India. Back in Venice sixteen years later, he published his *Travels*, in which he related his adventures. It became very popular after 1307 and gives a quantity of very precise details of myths and legends, such as the deformed monsters that inhabit the land of Mekrit on the east bank of Lake Baikal (above), the dragons of Karajang (below left) and the dog-men of the Andaman Islands in the Gulf of Bengal (below right).

through Hungary, just as those to St James of Campostella passed through France and North-west Spain. Studies on the Slav and Scandinavian countries and their inhabitants have been preserved: for the latter, see the Venerable Bede's history written in the eighth century, the life of the missionary Anskar in the ninth and Adam of Bremen's splendid descriptions in the eleventh, besides the memories and traditions handed down in the Danelaw and Normandy from the tenth and eleventh centuries. But those nations' pagan past was forgotten and their recent absorption into the western community made them quite uninteresting. The French romances of chivalry tell very briefly of Ogier 'the Dane'—he was really from the Ardennes—and Sone de Nansai made a long stay in Norway but had little to say about that country.

The West discovered central Asia, the Mongolian steppes, India and the Far East, the African coast and the Sahara in the twelfth and thirteenth centuries. But the information brought back from those regions by missionaries, merchants and explorers was either not assimilated by popularizers or was blended with the ancient myths and legends. In the maps that began to appear at that time the precisely drawn contour lines enclose features and place names based on sources over a thousand years old.

In the last analysis all nature, as Scripture says, revolved around man—the microcosm—and depended on him. In the words of the Florentine philosopher Brunetto Latini, 'all things in heaven and under it are made for man, but man is made for himself'.

To describe man as the Middle Ages saw him would be both irksome and pointless. Suffice it to say that, like the macrocosm, he was composed of four elements: blood, warm and moist, corresponding to air; phlegm or lymph, moist and cold, corresponding to water; choler, or bile, warm and dry like fire; melancholy, dry and cold like earth. Health and sickness, life and death were the result of variations in the relations between these elements.

The body had four principal members: the heart, from which the arteries sprang; the brain, seat of the soul, from which issued the nerves that made the body move; the liver, where the veins had their origin; the genitals, for the perpetuation of the species. The soul was the source of life; it was created by God and would never die; its faculty of discerning between good and evil was called reason and distinguished man from the beasts.

This vision of the universe, sketched in broad outline, may seem purely descriptive and analytical. Nothing could be further from the truth. The universe, as Gregory the Great said, 'comprises all things', and man was its centre. Therefore every part of it and everything that happened in it influenced the microcosm and had a meaning that had to be grasped. They were symbols of another reality and could easily be viewed in a biblical and evangelical perspective, based on an ancient culture and made available to every human being.

SIGNS AND SYMBOLS

These aspects of the universe may seem absurd to us because we do not know their symbolic significance. But at the time they were not only understood by all and sundry but were the only ones imaginable. If we dwell briefly on the meanings of the objects and phenomena that we have so far considered only in their outward appearance, we are struck by the close interdependence of microcosm and macrocosm—what Dom Stercks called 'the cosmological experience that permits an existential revelation of man to himself'. This was a typical trait of the medieval mentality. Numberless writings, such as Guillaume de Digulleville's *Pilgrimages* were based on a dense mass of symbols, which the author commented on with great pleasure. And the finest products of lay art, such as Jan van Eyck's Arnolfini marriage picture, were more highly valued for their symbolic content than for the painter's amazing technical mastery or his splendid rendering of real life.

Man's relationship to the Creation is suggested in this miniature from St Hildegard of Bingen's *Liber divinorum operum*. In the centre is the earth, then man created to be the lord of the earth; beyond man, the immensity of the universe; still further away, Christ dominates the whole. He is the centre and axis of the earth, of man and of the universe, beyond and above all Creation.

Numbers were a mine of meanings, notably those from one to twelve. Saint Augustine said they were the thoughts of God and therefore had an eternal truth. One needs no comment. Two represented duality—body and spirit, light and darkness, right and left, man and woman, wet and dry. Three stood for the Holy Trinity, God in three persons, and also for the human trinity: body, soul and spirit. Four (two times two, or three plus one) represented the perfection of the Trinity upset by the addition of a unit; it symbolized the material universe, the four rivers of Eden or the four Virtues, the four cardinal points, the four seasons, man's four members, the four letters of the name Adam, and so on. The multiplication of four by three of the material world by sacred time, gave twelve (also equal to six times two or eight plus four) which symbolized time past, the twelve Apostles, the twelve signs of the Zodiac, the twelve months of the year, the twelve tribes of Israel. Five, the number of man, was also the number of the universe; it symbolized the will. Seven was the sacred number: the seven-branched candlestick, the seven planets, the seven days of the week, the seven wonders of the world, the seven colours of heraldry, the seven seals, and the seven deadly sins. Eight (four times two) was the symbol of the Resurrection.

The basic geometrical figures were closely linked with these numbers, and their meaning was no less profound. At Aix the centre of the Palatine Chapel is an octagon, the emperor's throne was set on the seventh step of a three-tier system. Four of these figures composed the universe. First, the circle —perfect, homogeneous, with neither beginning nor end—represented heaven and symbolized time because the stars and planets travelled through it unceasingly along an immutable path. The circle led to the idea of the wheel, the cycle, and therefore of evolution and endless recurrence; to the spiral, which symbolized cyclic continuity combined with constant progress, like the vortex of the creation; and lastly, to the swastika, a combination of four common-centred crosses in rotation.

The centre of the circle and therefore of all space, round which all things were organized and from out of which all things were created, was the perfect image of unity—the indivisible, inchoate, immeasurable creative principle. It was the pure, transcendant, absolute Being. The square and the cross, impressive figurations of the number four and the material world, also have a centre and can be perfectly inscribed in a circle. Indeed, the square was viewed as a sort of circle with four corners; resting firmly on its four points and oriented in a certain way, it could represent immobility, stability and the division of space into four parts.

If the centre of this square—its omphalos or navel—was added to its four points, one obtained the symbolism of the number five; the universe in which heaven, earth, space, time and eternity were united.

But the true unifying element was the cross—the mediator and go-between—because it joins diamet-

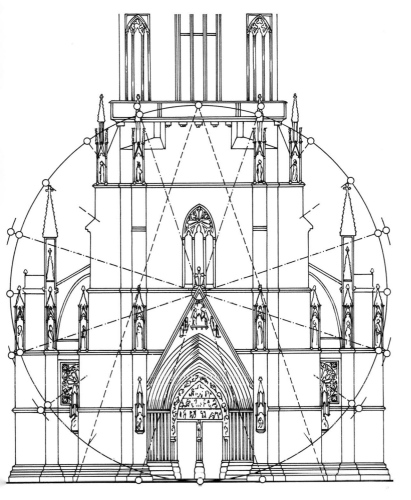

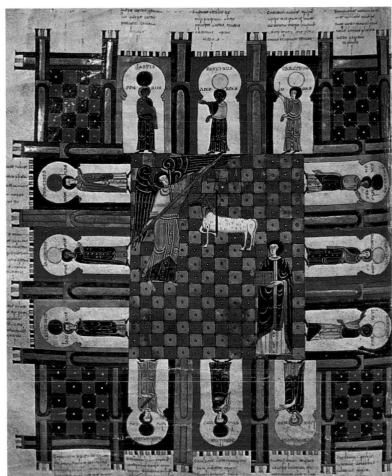

The proportions of the great religious buildings were frequently determined by symbolical constructions. The chief lines of the cathedral at Freiburg-in-Breisgau form a Maltese cross inscribed in a circle divided into twenty parts.

Many concrete applications of medieval symbolism are entirely alien to our modern mentality. Below, left: The garden of the cloister beside the cathedral of Notre-Dame du Puy is an example of this. The rectangle that frames the garden represents the created, planned world; the cross formed by the paving stones recalls the four rivers of Eden and the four branches of Christ's cross; the fountain, whose water reflects the sky, symbolizes the spring of living water and the mirror of the heavenly garden. Above, right: the heavenly Jerusalem is represented by a chessboard with twelve times twelve squares. The figure twelve is obtained by multiplying four by three, the symbolical multiplication of the temporal world (four) by the sacred world (three). The figure twelve also stands for the twelve tribes of Israel, the twelve apostles, the twelve signs of the Zodiac, the twelve fiery suns at the end of time, and the twelve gates of the heavenly Jerusalem. The angel is depicted on the chessboard to signify that he is 'to measure the city and the gates thereof and the wall thereof' with his reed of gold (Revelation XXI, 15).

The representation of one God in three Persons poses a problem that can never be adequately solved. When St Hildegard of Bingen (c. 1165) wanted to evoke the Trinity, she resorted to the symbol of the circle as the image of infinity. Christ, God and Man in one, is shown in human form.

rically opposed points within a square inscribed in a circle; and the centres of the square and the circle coincide with each other and with the centre of the cross.

Medieval symbology rested largely on these numbers and these geometrical figures. The earthly paradise was commonly represented as a circle with, in the middle, a square that stood for the famous fountain. The heavenly Jerusalem was a square with twelve doors topped by circles and arranged in four groups of three.

Passing from the plane to three-dimensional space we find that the sphere and the cube, the basic elements of Romanesque architecture, assumed the symbolic meanings of the circle and the square.

There were seven basic colours, each of which stood for one of the seven planets. But they also had more general symbolic meanings that were common knowledge. Black—sable in heraldry—associated with Saturn, was linked with the idea of sorrow and of a ruthless, steadfast will. Red—gules—stood for Mars and was the emblem of both charity and victory. White—argent—represented the moon and symbolized purity, honesty and sincerity. Yellow—or—identified with the sun, evoked intelligence and judgment. Green—vert—was the colour of Venus and of hope. Blue—azur—evoked Jupiter and the sky and violet—pourpre—Mercury. This elemental symbology made its influence felt chiefly in the twelfth and thirteenth centuries with the spread of heraldry, whose strict and unchanging rules were already clearly established at that time.

Signs and symbols were not always confused, and one can see how enriching the distribution was for medieval thinking when one considers, for example, how the path of the heavenly bodies was interpreted.

Modern astrology in its most elementary and best known form, namely individual and general horoscopes, explains a great many things that we are apt to consider with the utmost scepticism but in the Middle Ages were accepted as the very foundations of reality. People believed that even the smallest star exerted an influence on mankind. As a matter

The Iron Crown of Lombardy, used at the coronation ceremonies of the Holy Roman Empire, and now kept in the Cathedral at Monza, Italy.

The crown of the Holy Roman Empire was fashioned for Otto the Great between 953 and 962. The arch was remade and the cross added between 1027 and 1039. Like the high priest of the Old Law, the Emperor wore under his crown a mitre with two horns, one on either side of the arch. Here too the symbolism of forms, figures, gems and colours is very instructive. The crown comprises eight plaques; its octagonal contour evokes the union of the two squares of the earthly Rome and the heavenly Jerusalem, whose golden walls and gates are studded with pearls and precious stones. These latter add up to 12 × 12 = 144 (the number of the Apocalypse). Each of the plaques at front and back has these rows of large gems—green emeralds, blue sapphires—which represent more directly the twelve tribes of Israel, like those on the pectoral of the high priest of the Old Law, and the twelve apostles. The other plaques represent the kings of the Old Testament: King David inspired, King Solomon the Wise; the others are thought to represent the prophet Isaiah who had had the vision of the Pancreator flanked by two seraphim and who told the sick king Hezekiah that he would live 15 years longer to serve his people. This is an allusion to Otto who, in 957, was just as ill as Hezekiah when Isaiah informed him of what God had in store for him. Thus the wearer of the crown reconciled the Old and New Testaments. He was the instrument of Christ as evangelizer, judge and pacifier; and the Holy Roman Empire which he upheld was one of the links in the chain that bound the Jerusalem of David and Solomon to the heavenly Jerusalem.

According to the notion current in the Middle Ages, man and the universe are bound by mysterious ties. Thus the twelve signs of the Zodiac correspond to the different parts of the body (right). It was also believed that astrologers could foretell and explain, almost scientifically, certain aspects of human behaviour by suitably observing the sun and the planets (left).

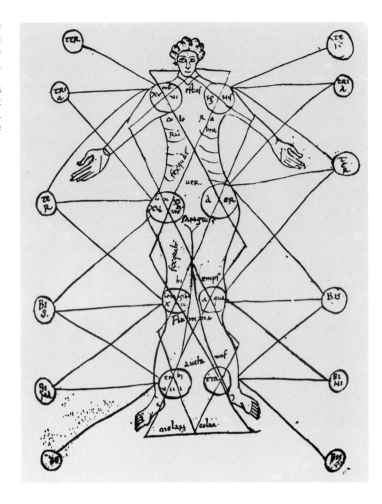

of fact, our ignorance of the effects of cosmic and other rays makes it difficult for us to refute that assertion entirely. The larger the star and the closer it was to the earth, the stronger was its action. The planets, as Sidrac says, 'govern by the will of God the land, the waters, the winds, human beings, animals, birds, fish and all things that exist'.

An individual's destiny depended largely on the planet that was in the ascendant on the day of his birth and the sign of the Zodiac in which it was situated. Venus was the planet 'of love and of the instruments of crime and joy. He who is born under that planet will have a vain and feeble heart. He will be loved in childhood and well fed. He will grow up to be proud, importune and cowardly. He will gladly perform disloyal acts and will love many instruments. He will be covetous and mean.' Saturn reigned over thin, careless, dark, dry, slow, beardless men of feeble will; Jupiter over good-tempered, gracious, amorous, bearded men, who run no risk of going bald; Mars over irascible,

quarrelsome, violent, brainless, proud, bald men. To the planet's influence was added that of the sign. For example, 'if Gemini is in opposition to Venus' when a man is born, 'he will be poor for a time'; if Cancer, 'he will be neither rich nor poor and will live long'; if Virgo, 'he will be a poor minstrel and die young'; if Leo, 'he will be rich and respected and live long.' The signs of the Zodiac were grouped in threes: the Ram, Leo and Sagittarius were hot and dry like fire; Taurus, Virgo and Capricorn cold and dry like earth; Libra, Gemini and Aquarius hot and moist like air; Cancer, Scorpio and Pisces wet and cold like water.

These influences were accentuated or mitigated by those of the planets. For example, the moon was cold and humid. Each planet had its 'house' in a certain sign: the sun in Leo, the moon in Cancer, Saturn in Capricorn and Aquarius, and so on. If their virtues were of the same order they could be reinforced in conjunction, paralyzed in opposition, and attenuated in sixte and carte. The days of the

Left: The so-called sword of St George was the typical weapon of the knight. The hilt forms a cross above the monogram of Jesus. The blade is bright, or as pure as a true knight should be. The butterfly issuing from its cocoon on the pommel symbolizes the Resurrection. Above right: The pelican feeding its young with its blood, on this late fifteenth century plate, is a symbol of Christ the Saviour.

Below right: According to legend, the unicorn was a shy and untameable creature. Only a virgin, by caressing it, could capture one, and while the beast was held in her arms, the hunters could kill it. William of Normandy thought that the death of the unicorn stood for Christ's sacrifice, killed by the Jews (the hunters) in the arms of humanity.

THE PORTRAIT OF GIOVANNI ARNOLFINI AND HIS WIFE
by Jan van Eyck

This magnificent picture by Van Eyck, though seemingly so simple, is full of symbolism. Did the painter intend it as a portrait of himself and his wife Margaret in 1434? The inscription *Johannes de Eyck fuit hic* could actually be translated as 'This man was Jan van Eyck.' But in all likelihood it is the double portrait of Giovanni Arnolfini, a great Lucchese merchant settled at Bruges, and his wife Giovanna Cenami, a Parisian whose family also came from Lucca. Very probably the couple who commissioned and paid for the picture prescribed most of the details and certainly the general idea, leaving the composition and execution to the artist. All the details of the painting, from the nails in the floorboards and the dog's silky coat to the pattens and the man's undisguised ugliness, are imbued with a meticulous, precise realism. They also throw into relief the luxury of the couple's bedchamber and clothing: the young woman's two-stranded necklace, the lap-dog, the glazed windows, the carved furniture, the magnificent chandelier, the convex looking-glass—a great rarity—decorated with ten miniatures depicting scenes from the Passion. Only Venice could have produced an article of that sort, just as only Lucca or a few other Italian towns could have woven the sumptuous violet velvet of the man's coat, the clipped black velvet of his hat, the delicate blue silk of the woman's undergarment. The lace may have been made at Bruges or Malines and the heavy madder-red coverlet in Flanders. But the luxurious furs (dark sable and rich, snow-white fur) must have come from Prussia or Russia, like the wax of the candle. Oranges, carpet and red leather slippers call to mind a Southern or Islamic land (perhaps Spain). The whole setting evokes the occupations of a great merchant who imported rare products from so far away and the wealth he had accumulated. The style and materials of the clothes reveal the influence of an aristocratic *milieu*, and precisely that of the court of Burgundy, which set the fashion for the whole Western World at that time. Like a born nobleman, this merchant, who was also counsellor and money-lender to the duke, wears a hat in the shape of an inverted truncated cone and a velvet and sable surcoat; the latter was slipped over the head because garments open in front, after the manner of the Turkish caftan, were not introduced to Europe via Venice until the end of the fifteenth century. The hose and the doublet with gold-embroidered cuffs set off the sombre hues of the man's costume. His young bride, instead, is dressed in white, bright green and sky blue. Observe the luxurious length of her fur-lined robe, whose full, slit sleeves are adorned with deckle-edged scallops. Her very fine cambric head-dress rests on hair done up in 'buns' and enclosed in a gold net. The silk undergarment emphasizes the curves of her youthful figure, visible even under the heavy outer robe thanks to the girdle that marks the waist, sculpts the bosom and especially the stomach (which has caused some critics to believe that the young bride was pregnant).

The picture shows the young woman on an equal footing with the man. In that merchant society she was not only a wife and future mother, but also her husband's invaluable helpmeet; she brought him her fortune and her family influence, and assisted him in the management of his business. If widowed prematurely, she would take it in hand herself with her children, to whom she gave an excellent education. The realism of both composition and detail was intentional. It is in keeping with the merchant's rational, precise mentality and the artist's seeing

eye. But if the painting reflects the mentality of a new society, it is also a touching symbol imbued with the spirit of the Middle Ages: the gesture of the husband's hand and the candle burning in broad daylight on the sunny side of the room are clues to its recondite significance.

What it represents, in fact, is the wedding of the Arnolfini couple. Reflected in the looking glass are the two witnesses, who stand facing the bride and groom. One is in all probability the painter himself. That would explain the inscription, 'John van Eyck was here in 1434,' and make the work a marriage certificate of a novel sort but no less valid than a notary's deed. The three successive rites prescribed by the Emperor Gratian's decree, which dispensed with the presence of a priest, are here performed simultaneously. The groom raises his right hand under God's eye (the nuptial candle in the six-branch chandelier); the ring is slipped on the fourth finger of the bride's left hand; their hands are joined. There seems to be a sort of sacred enclosure centred round the bright note of those two joined hands. And in this perspective the details attain their full symbolical significance.

The bride and groom are fully dressed for setting out on the great journey they will undertake together. Their mien is grave, serious, thoughtful—notably the husband's for he realizes his responsibility. Their eyes are fixed on the same path and the same goal. Their movements are so slow as to be almost imperceptible, consistent with the notions of certainty, fidelity and stability. The groom draws the young bride very gently towards him and forwards along their joint route; she seems to consent and gathers up the folds of her gown to walk more easily. The very short shadows apparently denote the midday hour, the moment when the sun stands still at the zenith. The blossoming tree outside the window evokes springtime, youth and the joy of togetherness.

But the couple have discarded their shoes to tread the holy ground of the nuptial chamber; the bride stands by the bed, which she will lie on first. The oranges, fruits of paradise, conjure up the idea of the Fall (carnal intercourse), which only Christ's Passion (depicted around the looking glass) could redeem. The little dog, like those on noblewomen's tombs, symbolizes fidelity; the lions carved on the settee stand for strength and courage. The union in one small room of the vegetable, mineral and animal kingdoms also recalls the unity of the cosmos centred round the man and woman from whose union new men are born. The allusion is stressed not only by the bride's prominent stomach but also by the sculpture of St Margaret vanquishing the dragon above her head. The symbolism of the composition is developed in that of the colours. The groom's black and reddish garb stands for will power and authority; the bride wears green for hope and love, blue for fidelity, white for purity. Thus two human beings, dissimilar—he sombre and ugly, she radiant and beautiful—but complementary, are joined together by their clasped hands as equals under the eye of God.

This painting is an end-product because based on the religion and symbolism of the Middle Ages, when, as Abbot Suger said, the purpose of art was to lead men through the visible world to the invisible certainties. But it is also the first attempt in the West to produce an impression of sacredness in a purely human context depicted with meticulous realism, without resorting to a religious subject but rendering an intimate scene pervaded by the presence of God.

week had a special relationship to the seven planets; the influence of each returned every seven hours and each day took its name from the planet under which it commenced. For instance, Venus reigned over Friday—named after Frigga, the goddess of love—at 1 hour, 8 hours, 15 hours and 22 hours.

In keeping with these beliefs, every astronomic phenomenon was interpreted as a sign that had to be regarded with the greatest respect because it was addressed to man and exerted a direct influence on him. The passage of a comet, the appearance of a luminous path in the sky, an aurora borealis, or an eclipse announced an event of major importance, often a dreadful calamity like a deluge, a cloud of locusts or a rain of ashes. The so-called *Astronomer's Chronicle* compiled during the Carolingian period described the eclipse of 5 May 840, and goes on to say: 'Although this prodigy was in the natural order, it was consummated by the sad event that followed: in fact, it foretold that the supreme light which shone for all on a candlestick in the house of God, namely the emperor of most pious memory, would very soon be withdrawn from humanity and that his departure would leave the world in darkness and despair.'

Lapidaries and bestiaries are full of symbolical information. To touch or wear a stone, to see an animal, to wear its fur, to depict it or speak of it had a meaning or gave a warning. Take for instance the twelve gems of the rational: red jaspar signified love; green jasper faith; white jasper gentleness. Sapphire promised heaven; chalcedony closeness to God; emerald Christian hope; sardonyx chastity or humility; sard the sufferings of the just; chrysolite the heavenly life; beryl purification; topaz the crown of a holy life; chrysoprase the reward of virtue; hyacinth the grace of God; amethyst Christ's martyrdom. By a sort of transmutation, stones that represented the heaviest element, earth, assumed in their transparence and brilliance the qualities of the lightest and purest element, fire.

In the vegetable kingdom, the rose represented the Virgin; the apple sin; the mandragora lust and the devil. The grape stood for Christ, whose blood was drained by a mystic wine-press.

Animals were particularly rich in symbolic significance. For example, the turtle dove, simple, chaste and inconsolable in widowhood, was the emblem of the 'Holy Church of which God is the spouse'. The eagle, which lost interest in its young if they could not bear to look at the sun, taught parents to disown their children if they refused to serve God. The lion was king of the world, son of the Virgin Mary, who on the day of judgment would have no pity on the Jews. He was four-square in front and slim behind, a blend of the divine and human natures. His splendid tail meant that we are subject to God's justice. When he pawed the ground in fury he reminded us that we are the ground that the lion Jesus pawed on and that God afflicts us for our own good and chastises those He loves. The hunted lion erased his tracks with his tail, a symbol of the Incarnation, for God became man secretly in order to outwit the devil, who discovered His ruse too late. The lion slept with open eyes because God's death was only apparent; he trembled when he saw a man for the first time because God made man and humiliated Himself by doing so. The lioness gave birth to a dead cub (the Virgin giving birth to Jesus), which was restored to life the third day by the male's roar (the power of God). Thus Christianity took over the least important facts established by the ancient scholars, giving them a revised form and a new interpretation.

Every animal evoked some aspect of man. *Reynard the Fox* gives most of them in simplified form. There we find King Noble the lion, Tibert the cat, Bruin the strong but clumsy bear. Heraldry set great store on these interpretations; humble animals and those that stood for vulgar or base vices were not represented on coats of arms.

There was nothing that could not be given a symbolic or allegorical interpretation. A bird on a square (the dove on Noah's ark or the phoenix on its pyre) symbolized eternity. The knight's arms comprised a shining sword because a knight was pure; it two edges signified civil and canon law; its point served to kill the enemies of the Church; Christ's name engraved on the blade meant that Jesus must always be in the knight's mind; the big, round pommel was like the world that honoured a knight, and so on and so forth. Even the horse's four hooves recalled the four great virtues: justice, prudence, temperance and fortitude. The same was true of the priest's robes. The amice reminded him that he must not slander or lie; the alb that his hands must be clean; the girdle that he must avoid lust; the maniple that he was the reaper of souls—it was the remnant of a towel with which reapers of old wiped off their sweat. Some of these symbols may have been imagined by inventive authors and therefore not accessible to the masses. But most of them were commented on and explained in simple words by the clergy, and even the illiterate could decipher quite easily the image of the world on the walls of the cathedrals.

In this connection, it is worth recalling the words of the bishops at the Synod of Arras in 1025 as reported by C. Terrasse, E. Mâle and J. Huizinga: 'What simple illiterate souls cannot learn from the scriptures they are taught in church; they know from the pictures.' This is reflected in the words the French poet François Villon put into the mouth of his poor old mother towards the end of the fifteenth century:

> *Femme je suis, povrette et ancienne,*
> *Ne rien ne sçait, oncques lettres ne lus.*
> *Au moustier vois, dont suis paroissienne*
> *Paradis painct, où sont harpes et luts,*
> *Et ung enfer ou damnés sont bouillus.*
> *L'ung me fait peut, l'autre joie et liese...*

> A poor old woman am I,
> I know nothing and cannot read.
> In the Church where I go
> I see a Paradise painted
> In which are harps and lutes,
> And a Hell, in which the damned are boiled.
> One gives fear, the other joy and gladness.

ATTITUDES AND BEHAVIOUR

A religion that so precisely defined and conditioned man's vision of the universe had necessarily a no less far-reaching impact on his behaviour. For that reason a serious study of life in the Middle Ages should start with a brief exposition of Christian dogma and ethic.

Sin was ever-present. Hell was near because death was on the prowl. All a man could do was ask the priest to call down God's mercy on him, or else go to Confession regularly, receive the Sacrament frequently, and resolve more or less firmly to resist temptation. Practising Christians, whose life is based on their faith, can understand the immense moral compulsion that fear of damnation must have exerted on those tens of millions of uncouth creatures, whose violent, elemental urges put them almost constantly at odds with the Ten Commandments.

The medieval Christian's first preoccupation was to gain salvation. He knew that his soul would be weighed by the archangel Michael while the disgusting horned devil stood by, attempting to weigh down the balance and demanding his due.

97

The Church taught by word and picture the ways a man could save his soul and enter paradise. To do so he had to admonish sinners to live more worthily (1), comfort the sick (2), feed the hungry (3), visit prisoners (4), harbour the homeless (5), bury the dead (6) and clothe the naked (7). If he did all this throughout his lifetime, he could hope that his soul would be carried off to heaven when his last hour came (8). These scenes were taken from a manuscript, but they were also painted and sculptured on to the walls of cathedrals, where they form a sort of popular catechism.

That compulsion differed, of course, from one individual to another. Many people lived in sin, but there is ample proof that many too endeavoured to avoid sinning and when they did so fully realized it and accepted their responsibility.

The medieval Christian's religious instruction comprised the frequent repetition of, commentary on, and therefore to some extent assimilation of the ten Commandments, the twelve Articles of Faith, the gifts of the Holy Ghost and the seven Cardinal Virtues. More important still were the warnings against the seven deadly sins—the seven heads of the Beast of the Apocalypse: pride, covetousness, lust, anger, gluttony, envy, and sloth. Seven branches spring from each of these sins: pride, for example, produced disloyalty, spite, conceit, ambition, vanity, hypocrisy and shame. These produced offshoots in their turn: disloyalty, for example, led to ingratitude, rage and apostasy. There is no place here to expatiate on the Christian's fight, as a soldier of God, against sin; on the temptations he succumbed to most frequently, or on his constant practice of the theological virtues—active charity, love of his neighbour, and the others. Their fundamental importance must, however, be stressed for they were the very essence of his daily life.

Proof of this is offered by some elementary themes—salvation, the Apocalypse, the devil, the supernatural—which people pondered on at least superficially and reacted to.

Death itself was not a shock for frequency made it familiar. Children died almost daily. At intervals, as we have seen, whole families were carried off by war, famine or an epidemic. The body too was of little consequence. In the *Besant de Dieu* we see King Louis VIII of France 'become carrion in a few hours'. In any case, happines was not to be found on earth, where sickness, poverty, reproaches and insults were the common lot, and all that could be expected if life was long enough was a horrible old age. 'The head falls, the teeth rot, the breath stinks and so does the whole body.' Death impressed the masses only when it was extremely painful or spectacular, like

that of sufferers from Saint Anthony's Fire, who were poisoned by the ergot fungus of rye and died amid dreadful convulsions. Was it the unusual aspect of that sort of death or its diabolical connotation that made the greater impression?

On the other hand, death was not final, for the immortality of the soul was a dogma accepted almost without discussion. The problem was to know who would be admitted to eternal life on leaving this earth, where all is imperfection, inequality and sin.

The Church asserted that the virtuous would go to heaven and that the chances of that were equal for all; better still, they were greater for those who had suffered and struggled. This was confirmed by the literal interpretation of Christ's words, 'The last shall be first' and 'Blessed are the poor in spirit', and His parables like that of the Pharisee and the publican. This basic principle, which was largely responsible for preserving social order in the West, seems to have been universally accepted. But though it fed the anxiety of the rich and powerful it was not much comfort for the poor. Other explanations of the Scriptures fostered new fears. The Church taught that God was omniscient and knew the names of the elect from all eternity. If this was true it was logical to believe in predestination. A great many people were convinced that whatever a man did, good or bad, would be of no avail. This fear is echoed in widely read adaptations of Boetius and the *Roman de la Rose*. Complicated arguments were employed to safeguard free will. The most convincing, at least for the dull-minded, compared God to a hidden observer who sees people travelling along a road; some turn right, others left. Though He leaves them perfectly free, God knows where they are going. However, it does not take a profound thinker to have difficulty in reconciling such attributes of the Godhead as omniscience and omnipotence, justice and goodness, and at the same time find a place for free will if they are accepted. And how can the average sinner be sure he is on the right road? Different answers to these questions led to different attitudes.

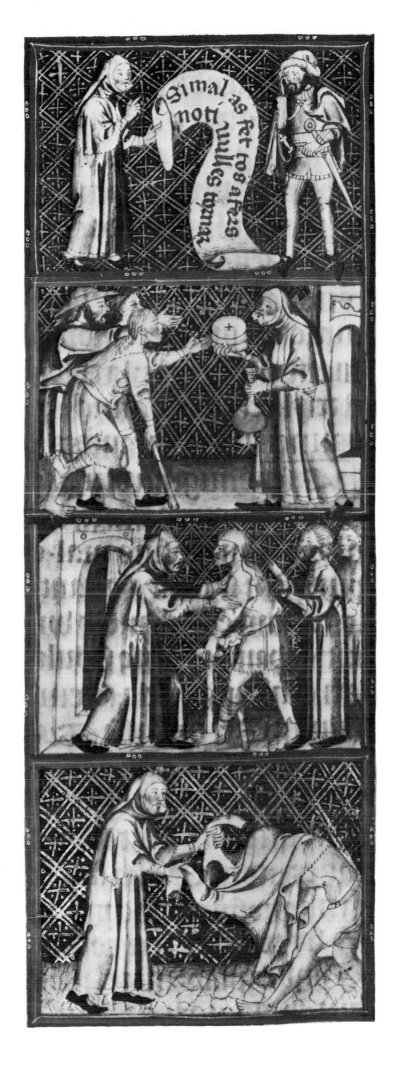

Laxity, it seemed for some, was logical enough. If you can do nothing to change a fate sealed from all eternity, why not defy the censorious and enjoy the best you can obtain here on earth? In the sixth century those who felt in that way found allies in wrong-headed men 'whose perverse intelligence refused to believe what is written or accept what is proved, scorning as fictions things they have seen and even making fun of them'. In the twelfth century some cried: 'Who cares about death? Let us take what good things come to us every day. Afterwards, come what may!' Death would end the fight, and after that nothing was left of either body or soul. Others said that a good God could not have created hell or brought into the world a man doomed to trouble, toil and misfortune. At that time poor, riotous clerks called Goliards roamed the roads singing the praises of wine, woman and song, critizing a social order founded on money, parodying the Gospel of Saint (silver) Mark. Others voiced their dissatisfaction by professing or practising heresies. Many in the South of France at the end of the century were converted to Catharism, whose practices were less strict and whose dogma was simpler and more edifying. Others did not go so far as that but continued to sin without remorse or contrition, went to Confession, paid large sums in the shape of alms to pious Christians who did penance in their stead and who interceded with the saints for their sinful benefactors' pardon. It seems, however, that the majority did their best to live as Christians and went through life a prey to terror and anguish. We can find in the literature stories from the Merovingian period about crowds who saw the sword of God's wrath unsheathed and were terror-stricken at the idea that the end of the world was at hand, to be followed by the terrible Apocalypse prophesied by Saint John and the Last Judgment. We know with what fear the millennium was awaited by a 'humanity still prostrated before a terrible, magical and vengeful God who dominates and crushes it' (G. Duby). The West may have been gradually advancing 'from a religion of ritual and liturgy to an active Christianity', but progress was extremely slow. Portrayals of the Last Judgment by a just and terrible God on the tympana of the Romanesque churches had not yet been superseded by the beautiful, suave images of the Good Shepherd that adorned those in the Gothic style. The end of the Middle Ages was marked by the Flagellants and Savonarola.

Worldly goods could not ward off the fear of hell. Many Christians abandoned the world for a hermit's life; others renounced the wealth acquired at the cost of endless toil and greed. The urge felt by tens or hundreds of thousands of men to make pilgrimages to the local relics of saints or to sanctuaries of international fame like Rome, Constantinople or Saint James of Compostella, and later to join the Crusades was the symptom of a great unrest, but also of a great hope. In fact, most pilgrims and Crusaders were convinced that the superhuman journey would gain them remission of their sins and admittance to the heavenly Jerusalem they had so often heard described. Meanwhile, though his day to day conduct hardly changed, hope of heaven slowly replaced fear of hell in the sinner's heart.

The devil was omnipresent, well known and well feared too. The Prince of Darkness employed every possible trick to do evil. He was depicted horribly ugly, with wings and claws, surrounded by his court of stinking demons. But he was known to be cunning personified, and in order to tempt man could assume any shape—handsome youth or wily serpent—use specious arguments, clothe his hatred in honourable words, win the confidence of fools, or trip up a saint. His one and only aim was to fill hell and torment sinners there for all eternity. Having to stand up to so strong an enemy made a Christian's life a constant struggle. He needed the help of the angels and frequent miracles to save him and build up his confidence. So wonders were part and parcel of his daily life; as were the superstition and credulity that went with them. Though Christianized or even a thoroughgoing Christian, he could not free himself from a certain dualism. Miracles, which suspended

The poor place all their hopes in the world to come. Why should they not be treated there like poor Lazarus, who was welcomed at the gate of heaven by an angel of God? In vain the miser saves his money in a big purse. There is no escaping the devil who pursues him on the central portal of Chartres Cathedral: he cannot take his money with him into hell.

the normal sequence of events, were the work of God obtained by the intercession of the angels and saints, their relics or a vast range of holy persons hermits, ascetics, wandering clerks, impassioned preachers. The *Golden Legend*, written at the end of the thirteenth century by Jacopo da Voragine, who later became Archbishop of Genoa, is a series of anecdotes that had been known and repeated for a very long time but never before collected. Chronicles and romances of chivalry are imbued with the same atmosphere and animated by the same pure, benevolent forces that make themselves felt daily and are finally victorious over evil and secure eternal life.

On the other hand, belief in the existence of the devil and his escorting demons gave practitioners of sorcery and magic an immense prestige. Christians

were repeatedly taken in by magicians and false prophets who worked what looked like miracles, and there is no need to go back to Saint Gregory of Tours (538–94) for proof of the existence of famous charlatans: there were enough of them all through the Middle Ages. At that time anything out of the ordinary, anything that was incomprehensible, wonderful or terrifying was considered supernatural and therefore attributed to the devil unless obviously due to divine intervention. This belief was not confined to peasants; the works that mention it were written chiefly by clerics and nobles and based on their own experience.

The *Great Chronicles of France*, written in the fourteenth century, tell the story of a black cat 'brought forth by sorcery', in which prelates were implicated.

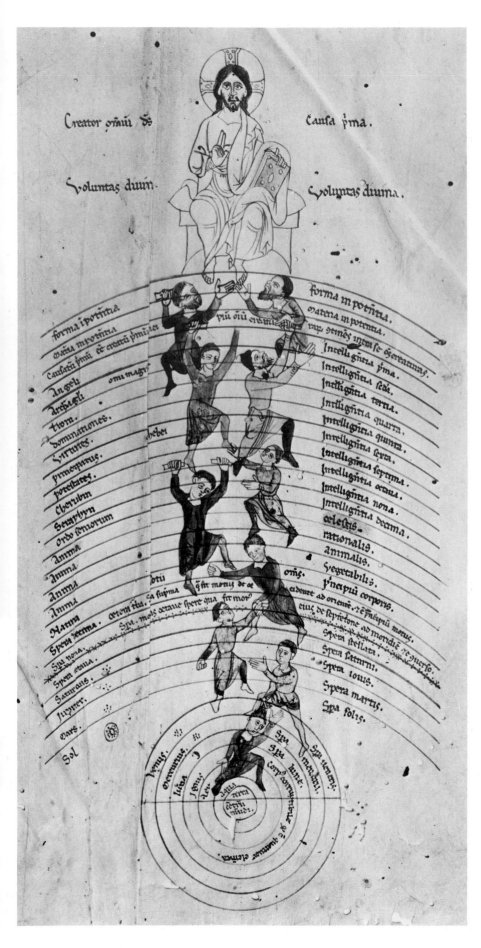

The various stages of the road that leads to God are represented here (left) as an ascent. The mystic surmounts a number of circles, first planetary—the orbits of the moon, Mercury, Venus, the sun, Mars, Jupiter, Saturn—then heavenly (the choirs of the angels) to reach the feet of the 'Creator of all things'.

The Golden Legend proves that Christianity was impregnated with the lives of the saints and their miracles. Right: St Francis of Assisi—we can recognize him by the halo and stigmata—preaches to the birds. His love for God's creatures confirmed his love for their Creator.

And Bernard Guy's *Inquisitor's Handbook* lays down how sorcerers, fortune-tellers and the like were to be put to the question. This seems to prove that even the judges believed in their powers. The text states that sorcerers used images of wax or lead, gathered herbs on their knees turned towards the east, made people swallow hairs and fingernails, worked spells and incantations with fruits, plants and ropes to cure the sick, fecundate the barren, foretell the future and discover secrets.

Those tools of Satan were extraordinarily numerous and easy to recognize. People who were lame, blind, cross-eyed, deaf, dumb, hunch-backed, or deformed in any other way conjured up the idea of vice and the devil's wiles in the minds of normal people. All the more so those who suffered attacks of madness and were often believed to be 'possessed'. Mental disease was common owing to undernourishment, fasting, vitamin deficiency and the use of hallucinogenic herbs. The epidemics of lycanthropy studied in the Germanic territories were closely linked with famines. Cases of hysteria and broomriding multiplied in a society burdened by sexual and other taboos. In minds moulded by ecclesiastical ideology, morbid neuroses aggravated by the fear of hell, usually took a religious turn. Religious mysticism led people to see the devil everywhere, and their attitude to a neurotic convinced him that he was possessed and endowed with magic powers by the forces of evil. If he was not cured by an exorcist who whipped him or asperged him with holy water, he ended up by selling his soul to the devil and became a sorcerer. Put to the torture by the rack, the boot, or red-hot irons, he confessed to having had intercourse with male (incubi) or female (suc-

cubi) demons, monstrous copulations that were quite incredible and crimes that he could not possibly have committed. In the end he might even do something of the sort in a moment of delirium, either alone or with other sufferers, conducting orgies, profaning the Host, practising vampirism, killing children, and giving all manner of perverse lewdness a free rein.

If the inquisitors forced him to admit his responsibility, recognized his powers, and discovered by torture his insensible point (anaesthetized by excessive pain) which was believed to be the 'devil's mark', what could be expected of narrow-minded, credulous, greedy nobles, ignorant, deprived priests or simple peasants? All they wanted was to defend themselves against spells and philtres, make use of propitiatory formulas, wear charms and amulets or, better still, buy a particle of those occult powers or a knowledge of what the future had in store. Unable to master nature on the material plane, they dreamt of doing so by magic means. And of course, as a result their credulity strengthened the sorceror's own belief in his powers and gave him a still more important place in western society.

Another factor may well have been a latent hostility to a Church ruled by the rich and powerful and to the Christian society of which it was the soul. The act of dedication to the devil may have been a way to break up and dominate that society. It was in any case a way to rediscover the pagan rites of the Celts, Teutons and other Indo-Europeans and the ancestral gods that the Church identified as demons. Well-known examples were the extraordinary obstinacy with which the Lutetians in 983, the Slavs between the Oder and the Elbe, and the Prussian peoples from the tenth to the thirteenth century, fought to keep their 'false' gods, refusing to be converted and accept the domination of the Christianized Poles and Germans. But very much the same thing had happened in Germany and Gaul; the Church had succeeded in Christianizing many ancient superstitions, replacing the cult of the gods with devotion to the saints, spreading the use of

The line that separated Christian miracle from pagan magic was not always well defined. This rock-crystal ball mounted in silver is a 'magic ball' dating from the Merovingian period.

The devil was an ever-present danger. His attacks could be repulsed by exorcism and the Virgin Mary's efficacious protection. But once he had persuaded the unfortunate clerk Theophilus to conclude a satanic pact, only Our Lady could save him from hell.

holy medals and the habit of continually making the sign of the Cross. But memories of the Gallo-Roman, Celtic or Germanic past were never cancelled. During the Merovingian period people still worshipped Diana, Venus, Jove and Mercury, who had ousted the indigenous Gallic gods, as well as springs, trees and upright stones—even when topped by a cross. Many traditional rustic ceremonies can be traced back to ancient rites in honour of the sun or earth, over which Christianity threw a transparent veil. Those indestructible pagan myths were mirrored in tales told at the fireside, some of which were handed down to our grandparents, and in the romances of chivalry that were so popular with knights and ladies and have been preserved in book form. Examples that come to mind are Merlin and Viviana in the Druidic forest of Brocéliande; Aymon's four sons and their horse Bayard; the solar or initiatory symbolism of Gawain and Perceval; Rabelais' *Gargantua*, who some scholars have seen as personifying the Celtic trinity; and fairytales like 'Sleeping Beauty' or 'Snow-White and the Seven Dwarfs'.

The Middle Ages received and passed on a host of ancient myths and legends. They were more or less thoroughly filtered by the Church, which was forced to adopt some as they were and loaded others with new meanings and interpretations. In this way the Church may have allowed many old superstitions to take root and introduced new ones; but it was also responsible for a moral coercion and a longing for perfection which in the long run left a permanent mark on the mentality of Western Man.

THE CHRISTIAN FAMILY

The family was the cornerstone of Germanic society. But it was a special type of family—a basic, complex social group, a sort of collective personality. Though it had the same Indo-European origin, the Germanic family was very different from the Roman family. In the latter the *pater familias* governed only

his direct descendants, whom he provided for and represented. In the former all the males capable of bearing arms had their say, even when their common ancestor presided over the assembly. The Roman family recognized the private property of its members and was governed by public law. The Germanic family cultivated a virtually untransferable collective domain and was a law unto itself. During the rapid fusion that took place in the first centuries of the Middle Ages the Germanic family gained the upper hand. It was the only valid social organization that offered a refuge to the individual, who would have been crushed entirely without the active assistance of his kinsmen. This family feeling was an essential trait of the western aristocracy for centuries; we shall discuss its causes and effects later.

The medieval urge for union and mutual aid led to associations of different kinds among the working classes—confraternities, guilds, communes and rural communities. But in the twelfth century, and still more in the thirteenth, the large family group seems to have everywhere experienced a decline. This was due to obvious demographic factors that led to the parcelling out of the heritage; at the same time improved farming methods and the acquisition of new lands favoured more concentrated and productive units requiring fewer hands and less space. But there were also religious and political reasons linked with the growing influence of Christianity and the strengthening of the central authority. Violence was progressively held in check by the truce of God or the efforts of the sovereign, and there was less need for the protection offered by the family group. When the custom of making a will became more general, the fragmentation of the inheritance was speeded up under the influence of Roman law, the notaries in the Mediterranean countries, and the Church; the latter was the prime beneficiary of bequests and the interested custodian of deeds over which only the ecclesiastical courts had jurisdiction. Another factor was the growing importance of the close family unit made up of the married couple and their minors or unmarried children. In Tuscany at

The marriage of this English lord and his lady may have been rather an agreement between clans than a free choice by the spouses, but the sacrament they administered to each other, the family they founded, and their mutual affection are as if combined in, and confirmed for, their posterity by the gesture that joins their effigies sculptured on the Greene Tomb at Lowick.

the beginning of the fifteenth century 77 per cent of the households, accounting for 56 per cent of the population, comprised fewer than 5 persons. The family of 6 or more survived longer in the rural districts than in the towns, which where the new, dynamic element of the Western World.

That the small family unit took so long to assert itself may seem strange in view of the fact that the sacrament of matrimony was central to the Christian doctrine. In the first centuries of the Middle Ages the only immediate family that slaves, small tenant-farmers, foreigners, exiles and those married outside the clan or fief ever had, was usually the one they founded themselves with the priest's blessing; but they were often adopted by their spouse's family and in most cases they and the majority of their children

stayed in the same place, on the same estate and in the service of the same clan from that time onwards.

At the top of the social ladder marriage was always viewed as a bargain to be concluded between family or allied groups. What is more, for centuries the dispositions of canon law were flouted; notorious concubinage and multiple marriages were common until the time of Charlemagne. And the Church took such a broad view of the canonical cases of nullity—consanguinity up to the seventh degree, spiritual kinship, impotence, moral compulsion, to name but a few—that the separation of couples was tolerated and many homes that had been spared by death were broken up. Abandoned husbands, repudiated wives and many widowers returned to the bosom of the family in which they were born,

The document on the left is the marriage contract of Isabelle, daughter of Enguerrand de Marigny, and Guillaume de Tancarville in 1309. A contract of this type prevented the husband from appropriating the wife's dowry, over which she kept all her rights, and established a settlement as a source of revenue to provide, if necessary, for the needs of his widow. Women were better protected under the influence of Germanic law than under Roman law.

Traditional wedding gifts included small, valuable pieces of furniture which the groom offered the bride on the morning after the consummation of the marriage. A typical one was this partly gilded silver casket notable for its elegant decoration: a crowned lion—emblem of strength and courage—and a unicorn—emblem of purity and virginity—frame the newly wed couple.

where they found their unmarried siblings and other relations who took care of their children.

But the Christian marriage has two major characteristics that made it far more solid than the German and Roman bonds and stressed the cohesion and stability of the close family founded upon it. First, it is a sacrament; and the Church took good care that it was not administered at certain times —shortly before Christmas, Easter and Pentecost— nor before a certain age: 14 years for boys, 12 for girls; nor against the will of the parties. The wedding was preceded by the betrothal—a solemn promise in the presence of a priest, followed by the exchange of rings and kisses. The wedding ring was first worn on the middle finger of the right hand, later increasingly on the ring finger of the left hand, which was believed to be connected directly with the heart by a nerve (perhaps a vein). After the period of the bans—40 days—the spouses administered the sacrament to themselves by exchanging their consent; but a priest was present under the church porch to give them assistance, bless their union, lead them into the sanctuary and say Mass for them. The ceremony was accompanied by a quantity of folkloristic detail, both Christian and pagan: the bride's white dress and flowing hair; the procession to the church; the grain thrown on the bride and groom; the flowers strewn in their path; the banquet, toasts and gifts. Very often the groom carried the bride over the threshold of his house, where her closest friends undressed her and put her in his bed. A marriage validly contracted and consummated could not be dissolved. The spouses had to live together, be faithful to each other, and bring up their children; the husband was the head of the family. Such thirteenth-century works as *La Lumière aux Lais* (Light for Laymen) voiced the view that marriage was a routine, a means to prevent vice and beget children, the last and least of the sacraments. But they could not deny its basic social importance.

Marriage was also a contract which the Church enforced through the ecclesiastical courts. Many of

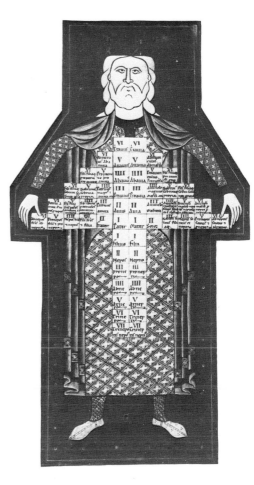

Time in the guise of a crowned king, displays a table showing the various degrees of kinship in accordance with Gratian's decree. Marriages between close relatives were forbidden and generally considered null and void, even if consummated by free mutual consent. The pope was the sole judge of their validity.

The wedding was often preceded by a solemn betrothal in the presence of a priest, who blessed the ring that the affianced husband slipped on to the finger of his future spouse. The wedding, which took place 40 days after the betrothal, involved merely their mutual consent.

This picture is a telling reflection of the medieval mentality. It represents all possible degrees of kinship and affinity between man and wife. The church held a very strict view of this and would not allow persons to marry between whom there was only the seventh degree of consanguinity. This, of course, was in a necessary effort to prevent interbreeding, which in the days of limited movement from village to village was a real risk, and could result in the 'village idiot.'

its clauses were aimed expressly at protecting the wife, who had formerly occupied an extremely lowly position, particularly in Rome.

At the betrothal ceremony the groom had to pay a deposit; if he wanted to recover his liberty, it cost him four times as much to make amends. The husband settled one-third or even one-half of his estate on his wife to ensure her livelihood in case he died. He also had to pay a 'morning gift' (*Morgengabe*) as a thank-offering or to compensate her for the loss of her virginity. Roman law recognized the wife's dowry, usually an advance on her inheritance, which she recovered when the marriage was dissolved. No doubt, the husband's marital authority gave him the right to manage the couple's property, including both settlement and dowry; but without his wife's consent he could not dispose of acquests (property acquired jointly during the marriage) or even of any property he or she inherited (which till the twelfth century was supervised by the whole family).

A married woman's legal limitations did not stem from a fundamental inferiority; in fact, if the husband became incapable of managing his estate, his wife took up the task. When trade developed, her right to do business was recognized subject to the husband's authorization.

All in all, the woman's status in medieval society improved greatly with the passage of time, particularly between 1100 and 1300. True, the Church never let her take part in the liturgy or perform public functions: Woman was made from one of Adam's ribs and was responsible for his fall, so she had to obey her husband, keep his home, bear his children, and see to their education. Thomas Aquinas, in the thirteenth century, said woman was 'indispensable for the preservation of the species, for food and drink... She was created to assist man but only in procreation because for all other tasks another man would be far more efficient.'

But she was readily recognized as man's equal on the spiritual plane. Noblewomen crowded to Fontevrault and Saint Waudru at Mons, and the great female saints were universally revered. The importance of the cult of the Virgin Mary is demonstrated by the many chapels and churches dedicated to Our Lady and the enormous spread of representations of the Virgin Mother of God. On the legal plane, a woman could make a will and, from the thirteenth century, be called as a witness.

Various works, one of them the famous *Four Ages of Man* written by Philip of Novara about 1265, speak of women without a trace of condescension. The important place occupied in history by queens, nuns and shepherdesses—Saint Geneviève, Brunhilda, Hildegard of Bingen, Eleanor of Aquitaine, Joan of Arc and Catherine of Siena—is well known. Moralists demanded rather less of women than of men. They should not be bold, wanton in word or deed, flighty, covetous, beggarly or spendthrift. For a woman, giving away money except for charity was a fault because before marriage she did not have to make presents and afterwards she should leave that to her husband; in order not to ruin him if he was generous, or to shame him if he was stingy, or to give others the idea that she was just as free with her body as with her money. A woman had a great advantage over a man: if she was a virgin before marriage and a chaste spouse after—here the influence of a Church temporarily in the service of males is clear to see—all her faults counted for nothing. A man, instead, had to be 'generous, courteous, fearless and prudent'. A woman had to learn first of all to have 'a goodly and simple demeanour'. A poor girl could become a rich lady by deserving to make a good match, whereas a girl of high rank could remain unmarried or marry beneath her if she had a bad name. There was little use in learning to read or write unless she wanted to be a nun, for books put wrong ideas into a girl's head and knowing how to write was an invincible temptation to enter into correspondance with men who sent her love letters. It might be well to play an instrument, sing and dance. All girls should learn to sew and spin, for if they were poor they had to do those tasks themselves and if

Tasks were clearly defined and apportioned within the family circle. The men fought or worked out of doors; the women took care of the house, cooked the food and educated the children. Here young girls learn to embroider and do tapestry work under their mother's supervision. This detail of the altarpiece of the Virgin and St George at Barcelona is simply a stylized reproduction of a common fifteenth century family scene.

Left: while the husband wields the hoe, his wife spins as she suckles her last born; another child, stark naked, plays under its mother's eye.

Below: The woman of the house saw to the feeding of her family, giving each his share not forgetting beggars and the poor.

they were rich they would be able to direct and appreciate them. Broadly speaking, they should know how to run a home, in other words do all the chores. The *Ménagier de Paris* in the fourteenth century tells us all that was required of women and all the things newly weds did not know.

Very young girls were warned against lewd old men and against boys 'for it often happens that boys and wenches love each other when small and, when they are able to, get together as other people think nature wants them to'.

It was the usual thing for parents to try and marry off their daughters at 14 years of age. Very abundant popular literature shows us how a married woman was viewed by her husband and other men. It would seem that, at least during the twelfth and thirteenth centuries, many more husbands were upbraided, beaten, opposed and cuckolded by loud-mouthed, hectoring, domineering wives who wore the breeches than the other way about. Obviously those stories must be taken with a grain of salt for some of them are very like caricatures: the flighty wife who greased herself with sheep's gall or dog's fat, cast spells, administered poisons, told lies and was unfaithful; the wife who tortured her husband

by making him repeat the same thing ten times over, deafening him with her cackle, contradicting all he said, giving him beer in place of wine or yeasty gruel in place of bread, waking him when he wanted to sleep, scolding him when he was silent, interrupting him when he opened his mouth. Women were turbulent, quarrelsome, hypocritical—they met their lovers in church—disobedient, envious, superstitious, cruel, lustful, hard to please and never satisfied. They insisted on their conjugal rights and if a husband was too tired to comply tore out his hair or slapped his face; when instead the husband felt like it, the wife refused. We should not pay too much attention to *The Complaints of Mahieu* or the satires on procuresses or women who drank, but all those works show up the extremely important part women played throughout society during the Middle Ages.

It would be wrong to believe that only women of the lower classes who fed their husbands and brought up their children were recognized for what they were worth. Noblewomen were just as busy, and some of them married commoners or bondmen (or even fell in love with clerics). They performed very important functions in managing the fiefs for which they had to do, and receive, homage; running their

The 'joys of married life' inspired a great many satires. Some husbands were free with blows (above left) but there were also wives who reversed the situation to their own advantage and the discomfiture of their lord and master (above right). Left: This water tank calls to mind the misadventure of the Greek philosopher Aristotle, the great master of medieval thought. He charged Alexander with forgetting his glory for the love of a woman. She revenged herself by seducing the philosopher and compelling him to get down on hands and knees and let her mount his back. A nice image of the 'superiority' of woman and a typical example of the excesses to which love can lead and how it can worst even a philosopher.

families, and replacing husbands and brothers who went on, or died at, the Crusades; in the development of Catharism and in the days of the troubadours. God had a preference for women for, as Robert of Blois said, 'he created woman in paradise, willed to be born of a woman and appeared first to women after the Resurrection'. The 'courtesy' that first developed among the nobility of Southern France reflects this view of womanhood: not only active and capable but also esteemed and praised, equally far removed from the termagant and from the enslaved wife of previous centuries. It must also be said that her devoted knight, whose love she finally rewarded, was not her husband, and that adultery, though contrary to the Christian doctrine, was considered quite normal. Even King Arthur's beautiful queen, Guinevere, eventually slept with Lancelot. At that time too the laws became less severe towards the adulterous woman. During the Merovingian epoch her sin had entailed repudiation, an exemplary punishment, sometimes even death. Later, canon law stipulated almost identical punishments for men and women who committed adultery.

The improvement in a woman's lot in the twelfth and thirteenth centuries was not due solely to the Church. Indeed the Church had changed its views very little since the dawn of Christianity and, in many cases, would not dream of freeing a woman from her duty to her husband. But, as it seems impossible that an evolution which had been very slow for a thousand years was suddenly speeded up by mere chance, the leading medievalists—first among them R. Fossier—now advance an interesting theory. Between 1100 and 1300 there may have been a relative shortage of women; this they attribute to a biological cycle that alters the proportions of the sexes at birth during certain periods or, more probably to a higher death-rate among women in childbirth, as a result of which men were more favoured than women by improved conditions.

A statistical study based on a multitude of documents shows that in the twelfth century for every 110 men there were only 90 women and in the thirteenth the relative figures were still 105 and 95. In Tuscany, at Florence and Arezzo, a census taken at the beginning of the fifteenth century showed 110, 118 and even 138 men per 100 women. Woman's prestige and monetary value were enhanced by her relative rarity. The proportions were inverted not long after, at least in Germany. At Nuremberg in 1449 there were 121 women for every 100 men and at Basle in 1454, 124.7 to 100. So man achieved the position he has managed to keep, against all attacks, to the present day.

This question is closely bound up with the basic problems of daily life raised by man's relationship to woman. For instance, was love viewed, felt and made as it is today?

Even a rapid glance through the literature reveals substantial differences. Not so much in preliminary behaviour. Love at first sight was very frequent, from Chilperic and Arnegonde to Tristan and Iseult. Jehan stopped speechless in his tracks when he first caught sight of Blonde. Stories of man's first approaches to the adored one, the strength and purity of platonic or spiritual love, of faint-hearted lovers too shy to speak and maidens taking pity on love-sick youths are nothing new. But there are details we find quite extraordinary. For instance, Jehan and Blonde embraced furiously every night for two years, 'kissing and playing all the games of love but one'. When they finally married after several years' separation, we find that Blonde at least was still a virgin: 'In a little hour they were masters at the game they had never known. Love and nature taught them.' That game was played only after receiving the priest's blessing. The Church, which thundered against fornication, seems to have exerted a very strong influence on sexual life in the West during the Middle Ages. We have already seen that the fear of sin was very real and lust, at least outside wedlock, was the most deadly sin of all. Did that fear prevent men and women from following their most natural bent? Did the exaltation of the Virgin Mary, who together with confessors and widows formed the élite of primitive

The back of this looking glass is adorned with three love scenes. On the left, a youth bends his knee before his beloved, probably swearing to be faithful to her. On the right, he draws her towards him to kiss her. In the middle, a noble lady hands her lover a sword as a pledge of love and honour; this makes him her champion and entitles him to wear her colours.

Right: an extraordinary sculpture of St Louis and Marguerite of Provence dating from about 1290. It shows them as a happy married couple. In fact, the Saint dearly loved his wife, who bore him eleven children and followed him to the Holy Land. Here he wears a Crusader's garb, holding a model of the Holy Sepulchre in his right hand and the shield with three fleurs-de-lis with his left.

Sometimes the noble lady scares the chaste youth to whom she offers herself; below, Joseph runs away from the wife of Potiphar.

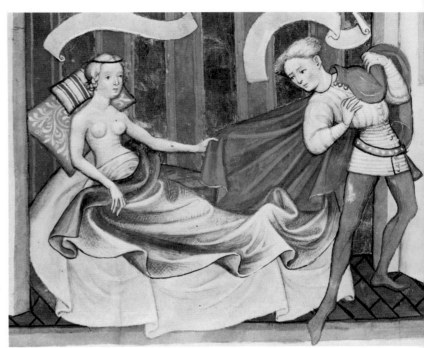

Christian society, encourage continence and celibacy? Recent studies in France and the United States based on medieval Penitentials and textbooks for confession, which concerned all classes of society, help us to answer these questions. Without going into details of the different forms of bodily love, it is worth recalling that sins against nature —sodomy, intercourse with animals, homosexuality between men and, to a lesser degree, between women—were often punished more severely than crimes such as the abduction of young girls and the raping of nuns. Those crimes were certainly committed, since they were provided for and the rate of punishment fixed. But they cannot be explained by sexual inhibitions due to religious vetoes. In fact, simple fornication was punished far less severely: reckoned in days of penitence the ratio was about 180 to 1, at any rate for men. Masturbation too was forbidden and punished. Prostitution, instead, was more or less tolerated as a means to relieve the prurience of adolescents, prevent attacks on virgins, and avoid adultery or make it less frequent. It was organized chiefly in the towns. We

Above right: a representation of Venus in *Le Livre des Echecs amoureux* (The Book of Love's Mishaps). Pictures of attractive naked women were rare before the fifteenth century.

If we are to believe literary documents, lying on the same bed (above) did not necessarily imply fornication. One is amazed at the details they go into. If a female partner was still a virgin after years of intimacy, what is meant by 'enjoying the thousand games of love' or 'kissing each other again and again'?

But scenes of steam baths, towards the end of the Middle Ages, with men and women bathing together stark naked (below right) denote customs very different from our own.

Below left: Even monks were not free from concupiscence; when one was caught in the act he was set in the pillory with his accomplice and exposed to the insults of the populace.

know from police regulations that there were prostitutes for both rich and poor in Paris; Venice too had a solid reputation in this respect. They could be recognized by the colour of their dress. But in most rural districts their position is far more difficult to define. In any case their paying partners were guilty of sin. Relatively few were those who went a step further and took part in orgies or the collective sexual frenzy which, as we have seen, was sometimes a feature of sorcery.

Most of those who did not choose continence or chastity married. Love-making was explicitly permitted only between husband and wife and then subject to certain conditions that may not always have been observed: excessive pleasure was frowned upon and only the natural position was allowed. Above all, there must always be the possibility of procreation; this was so strongly insisted upon that intercourse with a pregnant wife was disapproved. This last obligation raised a very serious problem. As we shall see, young people had a hard time in western society even among the nobility; in particular, men were seldom able to marry within ten years of puberty because marriage meant children and therefore the means to rear them. For women conditions varied enormously with the time and place. Noble English girls were usually married at 24 in the reign of Edward I, but the average age dropped to 20 under the Tudors. At Florence, and in Tuscany generally, at the beginning of the fifteenth century over three-quarters of the girls in both town and country married before they reached 19 and 34 per cent were under 16. On an average a husband was 14 years older than his wife. If we do not count nuns, 90 per cent of women were wives or widows before they were 22. Instead, only 75 per cent of the men were married by 42 and at least 10 per cent remained single.

In any case late marriage for men seems to have been the rule. So what were the millions of adolescents and young adults to do before they could found a family? Did they avoid fornication in obedience to the behests of the Church and wait for marriage before making love? Though this does not seem reasonable, it may well have often been the case. Except in some great families, especially towards the end of the Middle Ages, the lot of the illegitimate child of an unmarried mother was far worse than under Germanic law. Being treated as pariahs, bastards were easy to pinpoint. A certain number belonged to noble or powerful families; normal fiscal laws reveal others, and so does the '*Echoites de Bâtards*' inherited by the lord of the manor, for instance in Burgundy. But as far as one can judge from the available information, they do not seem to have been very numerous in proportion to legitimate children. On the other hand abortion, which often involved the intervention of witches or the performance of magic rites, was considered on a par with infanticide and cruelly punished. Apparently, therefore, conception outside wedlock, at least by unmarried women, was quite rare. The inference is that such illegal relationships were either infrequent, which seems unlikely, or involved contraceptive practices that were onanistic in the broad sense and against nature because they led to avoidance of the natural position. The Penitentials condemn and punish sins of that kind, particularly when committed by married couples united, like Jehan and Blonde, 'by love and nature'. They are less clear on other situations perhaps because, fornication outside wedlock being in itself a sin, unnatural or incomplete copulation to avoid begetting a child whose birth would reveal the crime, may have been considered as a last resource. And what about the Nicholite clerics whose wives and children were less and less tolerated? Did they aggravate the enormity of their sin by the scandal of begetting children through using the natural position? And what about the thousand games of love played by Jehan and Blonde? Or, as related in the little book by Jehan de Saintré, the affair of the Dame des Belles Cousines with the knight who had the key to her bedroom? Or the lady who pleaded not guilty because, though a gentleman did sleep in her bed, they did not indulge in ugly thoughts or actions?

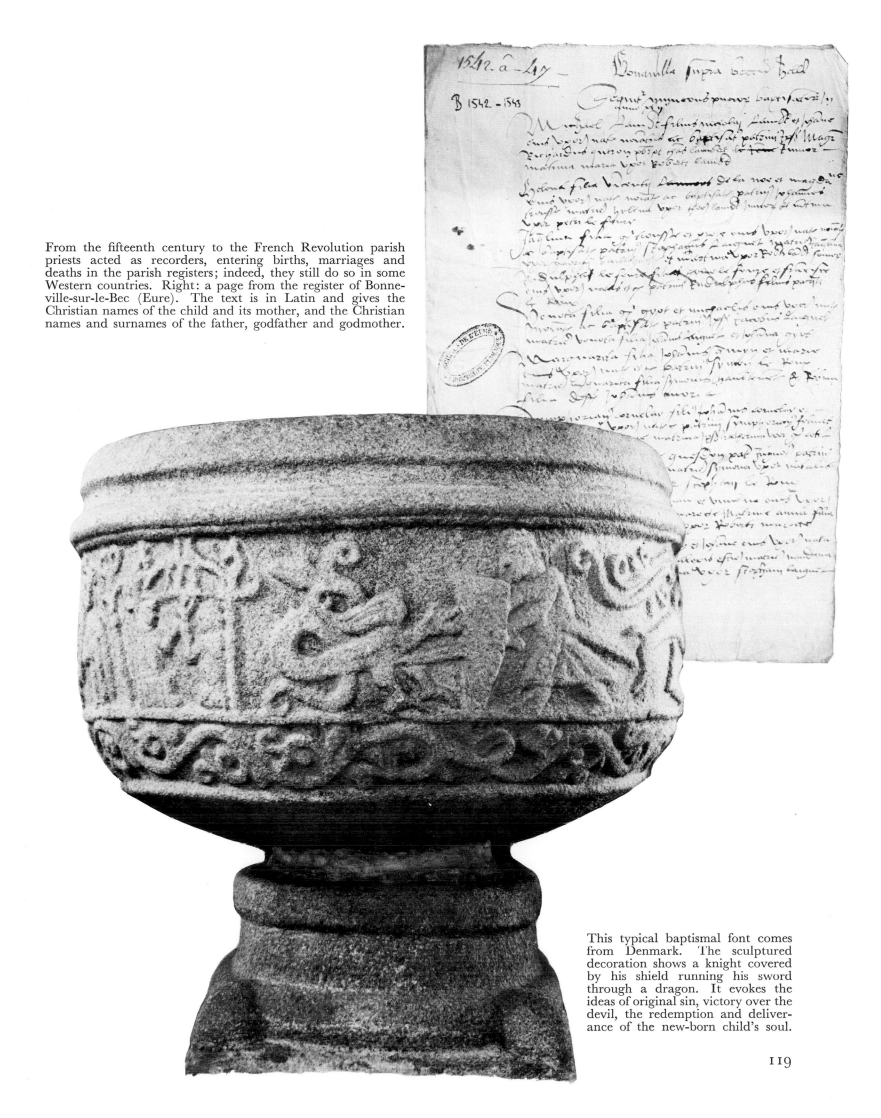

From the fifteenth century to the French Revolution parish priests acted as recorders, entering births, marriages and deaths in the parish registers; indeed, they still do so in some Western countries. Right: a page from the register of Bonne-ville-sur-le-Bec (Eure). The text is in Latin and gives the Christian names of the child and its mother, and the Christian names and surnames of the father, godfather and godmother.

This typical baptismal font comes from Denmark. The sculptured decoration shows a knight covered by his shield running his sword through a dragon. It evokes the ideas of original sin, victory over the devil, the redemption and deliverance of the new-born child's soul.

119

Babies were christened a few days after birth because of the dreadfully high infant mortality. Baptism by sprinkling, usual nowadays, was not introduced till the end of the Middle Ages. Previously, the new Christian was immersed in the font in the presence of the priest—here a bishop, as we can see from his crozier and mitre—the father and the godparents; these last were often very numerous.

Under these conditions legal marriage must have been strengthened by prenuptial experience of incomplete, passing, uncertain love affairs; in comparison the conjugal love tolerated by the Church must have seemed more satisfying, more lasting and calculated to give more complete satisfaction to both spouses.

Courtly romances, particularly those written north of the Loire, speak of the marriage that crowns the passion of two lovers as a commonplace event. In his *Cligés* and *Erec et Enide* Chrétien de Troyes sings the praises of conjugal love with no idea of immediate procreation.

With all the more reason in most literary works marriage is viewed as the normal recompense of mutual inclination; even Mahieu confessed that he married for love. Moralists and satirists draw a comparison between the women they condemn and the many more who love, serve, advise and help their husband and are his brightest jewel. 'A good wife is a very grand thing', says the *Livre des Manières*. Historians, painters and sculptors, have handed down innumerable examples of loyal, mutually trusting couples whose love was crowned by marriage, but also of many whose love was born of marriage. The latter are particularly numerous in the highest class, which was best known to the sources, though the large number of illegitimate children in that class proves that free love was no exception, as with Philip the Fair and Jeanne of Navarre, the Emperor Maximilian and Mary of Burgundy, Charles V and Isabella of Portugal.

Could one say of them that which the author of *Sone de Nansai* wrote as a conclusion to his story? Sone was an emperor, his first three sons were kings and the fourth became pope. His wife, Odée of Norway, loved her children and yet 'she loved the emperor her lord and husband more than she would have loved twenty children. The love she felt at the start took root in her heart, grew, blossomed and increased every day.' This is a phenomenon that has always existed. But why deny that the amazing rigourism of the Church and its immense influence on western society were to some extent responsible for the strengthening of the marriage bond, the improvement in woman's status and the difference between love in and out of wedlock?

Christian marriage had a logical consequence, mirrored in Thomas Aquinas's famous words: 'A home is not perfect if it is not swarming with children.' Procreation was meant to be the first objective of the indissoluble couple, and in principle their children, like Jesus, were kings. We have already seen that there were, in fact, a great many children. More, perhaps, in families that lived at the limit of subsistence and where the mother was fertile for a very long time despite intervals of temporary amenorrhoea. There is also proof that children were desired. Mahieu scoffed at the many

In aristocratic circles, marriage was less a personal than a family matter: two children were often affianced when still very young. The engagement was consecrated by the Church and became a consummated marriage when the betrothed reached the marriageable age, about 15 years old (right).

Only women attended births and helped to deliver the child. Except in the case of royal confinements, all men, even physicians, were kept away. The infant was bathed in a pan and tightly bound in swaddling clothes.

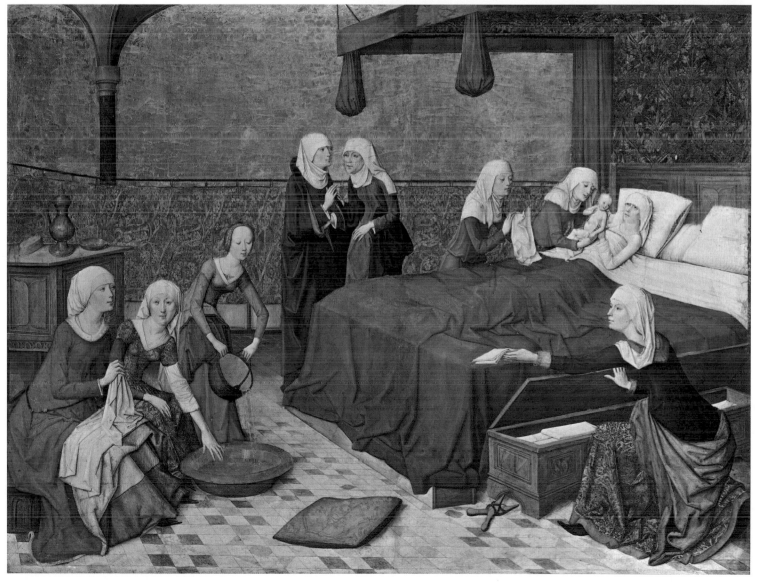

people who married in order to have children to hand down their name. The *Livre des Manières* has a moving phrase: 'It is good to have children', and the naive reservations it makes are extremely interesting because they prove that people stole, borrowed, neglected to pay tithes, and worked themselves to death for their children, 'whose caresses drive them crazy'. Sidrac warns men not to love their children too much because many love them more than they love themselves. And Philip of Novara shows us that God favours the little ones that love and recognize the mother who gives them her milk, and are objects of love and pity for the father who rears them. Under these conditions the birth of a child and the first weeks of its life as a rule brought great joy.

All too often the infant was not viable and soon died. Many were born deformed and, considered a sign of God's wrath, ran the risk of being suppressed —a practice that was current under the Merovingians and continued in Norway up to the twelfth century—or else left at night at the church door like illegitimate babies. The Penitentials say that an undesired infant was sometimes overlain by its mother in the bed where it slept by her side.

But the normal procedure—and, it is to be hoped, the most frequent—was for the women who delivered the mother to wash the new baby with all due care, swathe it in swaddling clothes, and place it in a small portable cradle where it was frequently rocked. No time was lost in having it christened to make sure of its going to heaven in case it died untimely. Special periods were originally set aside for that purpose, namely Easter, Christmas and Saint John the Baptist's Day, but the Church gradually agreed to perform the rite at other times; so it often took place within three days of birth. Christening was a solemn ceremony even in poor families. Relatives and friends crowded around the godparents who helped to immerse the white-robed infant in the font—baptism by aspersion, customary nowadays, was only introduced at the end of the Middle Ages. The priest gave the child its Christian names and recommended it to its guardian angel and patron saints. After the ceremony the adults presented their gifts and sat down to a banquet; the mother was left to take care of the child.

Philosophers and art historians have long remarked on the apparent indifference to children during the Middle Ages. In fact, the innumerable representations of the Infant Jesus are hasty, inexpressive and purely symbolic. Until the appearance of the Renaissance 'putti', angels were depicted as little winged adults. Very few artists or writers observed and depicted children as they really were. Excellent parents said that they expected much 'good fruit' from their children when they grew up; they very likely viewed childhood as a passing unpleasantness. Philip of Novara says bluntly: 'Small children are so dirty and tedious in infancy and so naughty and fanciful when a little older that one would not bring them up at all were it not for the love God gave us for them.' He obviously became fond of his own children more and more as they grew up. The dreadful infant mortality rate should also be borne in mind. Perhaps one-third of all children died during their first five years and many fertile couples lost all their numerous offspring before the age of puberty. The *Livre des Manières* mentions the case of the Countess of Hereford, and ample confirmation is provided by the exploration of cemeteries and a study of the genealogies of royal families and rich merchants: for example, the Capetians and the merchant Etienne Benoist of Limoges. Small children were, as R. Fossier says, 'under suspended sentence of death.' Consequently, it was only after they had passed the critical age that their parents took an interest in them and prepared them for their place in society.

Before that their presence was merely tolerated. They were allowed to play with knuckle-bones, tops, dolls and cards, do fight sham battles as Bertrand du Guesclin did with the young scamps of his own age. Punishment started very early for 'the sapling had to be bent while it was still slim and tender'; later it would break. Children were to be scolded, then beaten even if they cried, for they were violent and tended to do a lot of nasty things like stealing and using bad language. They were first taught the two Commandments: Love God and love thy neighbour; then they learned a trade. The two best careers were the Church and knighthood. There were, in principle, no limits to a cleric's advancement: he could become a prelate, a saint, or even the pope. But it was necessary to start very young. In the early Middle Ages babies were entrusted to the monks, who knew exactly how to bring them up; Suger, in the twelfth century, began his education at 5 or 6. Future knights started training between 7 and 10. In Florence at the beginning of the fifteenth century little girls of 8 were placed with an employer and 'forgotten'. Boys apprenticed at the same age often continued to live at home; and they went back there on marrying. Both boys and girls were treated as adults when they were 13 years old. If they were financially independent they could marry.

Broadly speaking, Christian society offered children some degree of protection. Abortion, infanticide, and contraceptive practices in wedlock were mortal sins and punished as such. Continence was recommended during the menstrual period to avoid begetting deformed children; during pregnancy to avoid damaging the embryo; and during breast-feeding because it was believed that the mother's milk was formed by the menstrual blood, which would be put into circulation by a new embryo and cause the death of the nursling.

On the other hand, children were viewed rather as small adults. They were dressed exactly like grown-ups and were admired for the qualities that brought them close to adults. Examples of this are Jesus in the Temple, the presentation of the Virgin, and the discretion and thoughtfulness displayed by the saints in childhood. Children were objects of interest for the sake of what they would produce in the future—and that future was very near. Otherwise they do not seem to have been adequately watched over or respected. No known books on

Above: thirteen century toys from which our dolls and lead soldiers derived. Below: hide-and-seek, blind-man's-buff and many other children's games have changed very little since the Middle Ages. Among the nobility, playing at tourney stimulated the future knights' fighting spirit.

A school scene—the teacher, brandishing a cane, expels a pupil.

child care date from before the fifteenth century, whereas there are many on horse breeding. It was not uncommon for employers to rape the little girls in their charge; their tender age does not seem to have been an aggravating circumstance and the criminals very often received a pardon. Parents burdened with numerous offspring, many of them not wanted, sometimes showed culpable negligence bordering on indifference. It is hard to say whether children were neglected because death struck so brutally or vice versa.

The vocabulary, at least in French, is very imprecise as far as infancy is concerned. The word 'infant' was generally used to describe an adolescent, a 'youth' was one who had not reached the age of majority which was fixed at 13 or 15 years by laws derived from the Germanic tradition. We shall find these youths when we come to study the different social and professional classes; their lot varied greatly, but they all seem to have shared certain general characteristics. Life being so short, pro-

ductive activities began at a far earlier age than they do nowadays, and ended earlier too. From the twelfth century, as the number of youths increased with the improved living conditions, so did that of their elders. And it was the latter who possessed the women, the wealth and the honours, though they did not always have strength and ability. This delayed the promotion of the young men and provided a focal point for their dissatisfaction. There were many examples of young nobles forming gangs and of young clerics joining forces against their seniors. The calamities that happened in the fourteenth century put these young men in the majority. This explains the enthusiastic or violent reactions of those generations as well as their instinctive mistrust of their elders. Treatises written during the previous period by old men in their seventies or eighties show us how severely they were judged. Young men, they said, saw nothing, understood nothing and feared nothing; they took no care of sickness or death; they despised the old, whom they beat, wounded or killed; they rebelled against their lords and wrangled with their priests; they were so lewd that they had to be married off as soon as possible. Mahieu adds, in his jeremiad, that they could not wait for their parents to die: those who were poor in order to be rid of them; those who were rich in order to step into their shoes. Violent conflicts arose in the bosom of the family: mothers were jealous of their daughters; fathers fought with their sons over their farms of fiefs; they even killed each other. Parricide was common. Maternal uncles helped nephews against their father and his clan. This is confirmed by history—from Fredegond to the Plantagenets and Frederick II—and semi-fiction—the *Chanson de Roland* and *Huon of Bordeaux*. It was also a symptom of an important development: the growing affirmation of the individual.

This struck a decisive blow at the family authority inherited from the early Middle Ages, which was already threatened by the recognition of the married couple's independence and the new legal, social and moral status of woman.

LEGAL STRUCTURES

Canon law, identical from Scotland to Cyprus and from Portugal to Palestine, was the major unifying factor of the Western World. Elaborated slowly by the Church through the centuries, it had found its definite form by the twelfth. It welded the West into a single family, separated from the Orthodox branch of Christendom since 1054, and was closed to the Jews and resolutely hostile to Islam.

Though the influence of canon law on everyday life was pervasive, it was not always apparent. The cases over which the ecclesiastical courts had jurisdiction were extremely important, as we shall see later, but the problems posed by normal human relationships lay rather within the sphere of public and private law. It is interesting to note that very often their practical solutions were quite different from those we find at the present day.

Modern legal concepts owe far more to Roman than to Germanic law. As a result, we would feel more at home in the city states of Classical Antiquity than in Western Europe during the Middle Ages. But it would be a mistake to believe that the homely notions which governed the barbarian societies completely ousted the majestic legal structure erected by the Romans. For one thing, the Church as a body was founded on Roman law and the Germanic emperors adopted a great many of its provisions. Secondly, part of the West kept to the Roman system of written laws, while areas like Venice and Southern Italy were long influenced or dominated by Byzantium. Lastly, there was a remarkable revival of the study of Roman law in the eleventh and twelfth centuries, notably after 1088 at Bologna, where the Italian jurist Irnerius taught, and after 1160 at Montpellier in connection with courses given by Placentinus.

Under the influence of the Germans, the period of the invasions, however, led to the introduction of a number of concepts, at once elementary and fundamental, that resulted in a profound modification of the spirit of the law.

For example, the notion of the state as something entrusted to the emperor by the people for the common weal disappeared. The barbarian warriors had no idea of social discipline; at most they formed a personal bond with a freely chosen chieftain to whom they delegated discretionary powers. Little by little the chieftain became a king, elected from among the male members of an illustrious, consecrated line—Balthes, Amals or Merovingians— endowed with magic powers. Conquered territories belonged to the victorious king, who disposed of them at his pleasure, donating some lands and dividing the rest among his sons. By and large he kept the peace, administered justice and laid down laws in accordance with a broad interpretation of tribal law and had the right to command, constrain and punish. The Church gradually succeeded in imposing the idea that the king—later the emperor— received his authority from God; this was confirmed by the consecration of Pippin and the Carolingians. But that legal authority was soon limited by economic factors which worked against centralization. Charlemagne's endeavours were doomed to failure and his attempt to strengthen the centralized state by insisting that personal bonds had a general validity merely speeded up a process that was already under way resulting in the break-up of his empire.

We shall see that the feudal system involved a hierarchy of powers, or at least a series of individuals invested with different degrees of authority—military, administrative, judicial—who were linked by purely personal ties entailing duties that were very light but rigidly defined.

With few exceptions, such as England and Sicily, the nations of the West until the twelfth century recognized only local potentates and had no idea whatever of the state.

The situation was very similar where the notion of landed property was concerned. Complete, freely disposible ownership in the Roman and modern sense of the term gradually disappeared until it survived in the Western World only in the shape of such fossils as the allodium. In the feudal society there existed above all a series of rights possessed by different persons and superposed on the same fief, which formed almost the only basis of 'property'. A rough example may help to make the process easier to grasp: The king had neither money nor other means of rewarding a man who served him faithfully and was bound to him by a personal tie; so he granted him a fief or benefice, an estate that would enable him to fulfill his military duties. The estate was distributed among a number of peasants, who worked it and made it productive. The king and his vassal were the owners in chief of the estate which they were entitled, each at his own level, to dispose of in part. The peasants had the use of the land, which they too could dispose of by sale or other means. It should be noted that the Germans were more familiar with collective than with individual ownership; this had an impact on the existence of communal lands and the rights of the family over the property of an individual.

The concept of law had also to be defined anew. In Roman times the law was chiefly territorial, as it is today. In the early Middle Ages, instead, it was chiefly personal. The first step in a legal process was to ask the parties: '*Sub qua lege vivis?*' (Under what law do you live?) Each Germanic tribe —Burgundians, Visigoths, Salian and Ripuarian Franks (if the laws preserved under this last name are authentic)—had its own law, which differed from that of its neighbours. The difference was more marked in private and criminal law; public and administrative law was somewhat better regulated. Thus a suit between a Burgundian and a Salian Frank raised problems that were almost insoluble. But the territorial character of the law, which reappeared in the feudal period, entailed no less vexatious complications; in fact, every lord acting as judge applied the law of his fief and every fief had a different law. Actually, the word 'law' is not proper in this context, for it evokes the idea of provisions that are written, codified, harmonized and generally accepted. The West had for centuries an extremely fragmented economy and was organ-

ized vertically from the ground up. As a result the juridical situation was the outcome of local usage that developed through the initiative of individuals or groups. This situation, based on ethnic influences and ancient customs, was preserved over a long period peaceably, and without contract, by group consent. Thus usage constituted a form of law but, being unwritten and handed down only by tradition, it lacked certainty and rigour and gave undue importance to questions of detail; it seldom rose to the level of general principles. In some respects it was very typical of the medieval mentality discussed above. With all its defects, however, this customary law was highly respected and each local community was passionately attached to its customs. In the part of France where this system prevailed—broadly speaking, north of the Loire—customary law was not codified until a very late date. Various collections were privately compiled—in Normandy from the thirteenth century—but it was not until the end of the fifteenth century that the king ordered an integral transcription.

These customs and the 'laws' that derived from them were based on notions that were equally alien to the Roman spirit and to our own. The basic concept of justice, court procedure and hierarchy, appeals, and the settlement of the minor disputes that enlivened daily life in towns and villages, raised problems that were interpreted and solved with originality and often with primitive common sense.

For example, the members of the courts were not professional judges but the freemen of the district, hundred or county, advised by people with legal knowledge—elders, notables, assessors or sheriffs— and presided over by a representative of the king. The latter might be the count or one of his deputies, the hundredman or provost, who after consultations pronounced the sentence and saw that it was carried out. From the ninth century the number of freemen diminished and they were restricted to the lower courts—like that of the hundreds—and even there their services were often dispensed with. The lord or count usurped the administration of public

The wheel of fortune was a very common symbol during the Middle Ages. Its lesson seems to be that even kings and emperors could not escape the hazards of the human condition. Today's king can be tomorrow's beggar; this was a subtle but momentous innovation in the orderly society.

The 'justices of the peace', who were close to the people, received complaints and conducted the first inquiries. If the manorial court procrastinated or showed excessive partiality, organizations like the German Femgericht in the fifteenth century administered justice in its place.

justice at one or two levels: a lower court for minor offences and a higher court for capital crimes. But the principle of judgement by their peers did not disappear entirely for commoners. Many traces remained in the North of France; in the Empire some regions—for example Frisia—were left in the hands of free commoners, and everywhere the distinction between public law *(Landrecht)* and feudal law *(Lehnrecht)* and the relative courts was scrupulously respected. In England the hundreds were permanent institutions and the place of freemen on juries was laid down once again in 1194.

But it was the knightly society that was chiefly responsible for the preservation of the ancient Germanic principle of non-professional courts composed of the accused's peers. The criminal law on which those courts were based was altered beyond recognition by the great invasions. The Roman conception survived only in connection with such

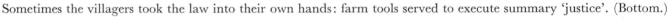
Sometimes the villagers took the law into their own hands: farm tools served to execute summary 'justice'. (Bottom.)

serious offences as forgery, desertion and treason, which were held to damage the king and therefore society as a whole. But assault and battery, and even murder, were private affairs that involved solely the victim and his family, which latter formed the basic cell of Germanic society.

What is more, even the most heinous crime went unpunished if the culprit was in a position to purchase immunity. All he had to do was pay compensation at a rate strictly fixed in relation to the victim's rank and the gravity of the injury inflicted. In principle one third of the sum *(fredum)* went to the king. In cases of murder the members of the victim's family shared the *Wergeld*, the blood money, according to the degree of kinship. If payment was defaulted, the injured family exerted its right to private revenge—the *faida*. The murder of a German cost twice as much as that of a Gallo-Roman, but not because one man was held to be worth less than the other. The price of the crime was the same, say 100 sols, but in the first case the culprit had to pay another 100 sols to indemnify the family; since the Roman family did not exert the *faida* it had no right to the relative compensation. Adding the king's part, we find 150 sols for a Roman—100 for the crime plus 50 for the *fredum*— and 300 sols for a German—100 for the crime, 100 for the family and 100 for the *fredum*.

Court procedure was no less primitive. For a very long time the accused was held to be guilty, so it was for the defendant to furnish proof of innocence. There was no investigation and no witnesses were called. The defendant either cleared himself by purgatorial oath or produced to the court a number of co-jurors that varied with the gravity of the crime he was supposed to have committed. The more relatives that came to swear in his favour, the better his chances of acquittal. For it was held that a crowd of honourably-known individuals would not support a criminal, and therefore the very fact of their taking an oath proved his innocence.

If the defendant was unable to muster an adequate number of guarantors, or if he was not a freeman,

The trial by ordeal most frequently undertaken, and the most binding, was the trial by combat—the winner demonstrated the judgement of God.

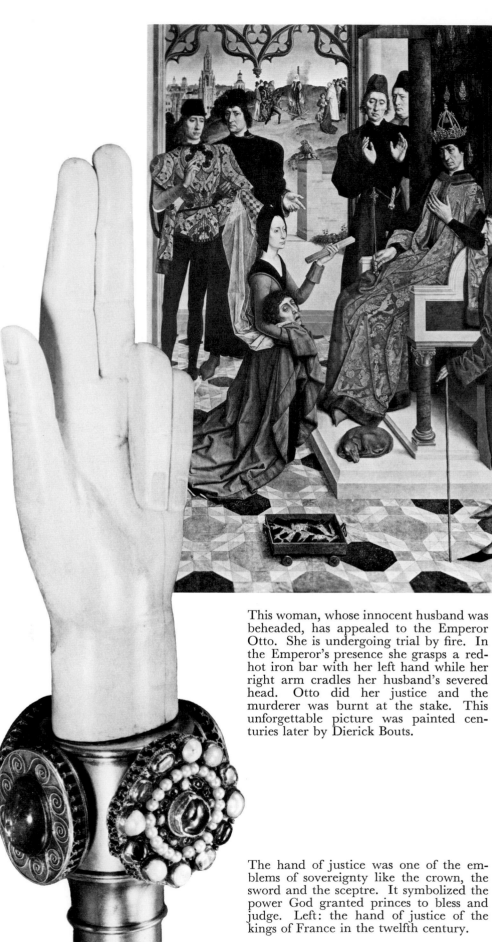

The administration of public justice was greatly influenced in the West by the ecclesiastical lords and still more by the kings, who were anxious to concentrate all authority in their own hands. The law courts held sessions, passed sentences and kept records (above). The guilty were taken to prison (below).

This woman, whose innocent husband was beheaded, has appealed to the Emperor Otto. She is undergoing trial by fire. In the Emperor's presence she grasps a red-hot iron bar with her left hand while her right arm cradles her husband's severed head. Otto did her justice and the murderer was burnt at the stake. This unforgettable picture was painted centuries later by Dierick Bouts.

The hand of justice was one of the emblems of sovereignty like the crown, the sword and the sceptre. It symbolized the power God granted princes to bless and judge. Left: the hand of justice of the kings of France in the twelfth century.

he could resort to trial by ordeal, as did the imperial seneschal in *Guillaume de Dôle*. This might involve thrusting a hand into boiling water or grasping a red-hot iron—the injury had to heal within a certain time; being bound and thrown into water—an innocent man would sink like a stone because water, being pure and blessed, rejected the guilty; or other tests of a similar kind. Sometimes the ordeal was bilateral, and the accused challenged his accuser to a legal duel. In every case proof was supplied by God, who made the innocent party triumph. Actually, it is difficult to be blind to the importance of strength, craft and wealth—for the purchase of a champion—on these occasions. But the procedure by rational proof and witnesses, produced by the plaintiff in feudal times, could not oust the trial of strength, for the ordeal was tantamount to that in the knightly society.

Private vengeance was not superseded, far from it. If a man declared guilty refused, with the support of his family, to pay the penalty or was unable to do so, the result was war between the two clans.

This custom was opposed with more or less success by the Church, through the truce of God, and by the sovereign, through arrest and the 'quarantaine du roi' (the king's forty-day truce). Saint Louis of France was one of those who banned private wars. But they still existed in the reign of Louis XIV and have survived to our own day at least in the shape of the duel.

It sometimes happened in feudal times that the court itself, in the person of the lord who presided or one of its members, was accused of 'distortion of justice' and therefore challenged to combat before the higher lord. Since each party fought with its own weapons, it will be readily understood that a serf, who was entitled only to an iron-shod staff and a buckler, hesitated to resort to that procedure except against an ecclesiastical lord whose champion bore the same weapons.

But by and large it was natural for the losing party to view a sentence as unjust and try to upset it. On the other hand, a decision was only considered definitive after it had been accepted by the two parties and their families.

In Roman law appeal procedure was recognized and organized to perfection from a lower court to the provincial governor, the prefect of the praetorium or even the emperor in person. The Merovingian kings and after them the Carolingian emperors seem to have acknowledged the principle, if they did not always apply it. But the lower court judges were apparently responsible for their decisions. An assessor whose sentence was modified had to pay a fine; a plaintiff whose suit was dismissed received a beating or had to pay heavy compensation. So the possibility of challenging a wrongful judgment existed side by side with the Roman tradition that denied a judge's culpability.

The fragmentation of the Carolingian empire and consequently of the courts limited appeals to the level of the count or the high justiciar. In France it was not until the thirteenth century, under Philip Augustus and Saint Louis, that the king ceased to arbitrate disputes himself and instead set up a hierarchy of appeals culminating in his court of Parliament. Till then for the lower orders virtually every sentence was definitive, while for powerful people it was perpetually questioned by trials of strength in the shape of duels and private wars.

The few examples we have briefly considered suffice to prove that, as far as their legal structures were concerned, our ancestors had very different concepts and customs from those of our own day. The notion of the state was replaced by personal ties and relationships; political power was concentrated and close at hand but its geographical limits were narrow; a distinction was drawn between ownership and possession; customary law, uncertain and a slave to detail, competed with and often replaced written law, which was for a time personal before again becoming territorial; the administration of justice was incompetent, based on pecuniary compensation, accepting as proof to a late date an oath, ordeal or duel, and hardly subject to revision except by force when the strongest won.

Even when he could count on God's assistance, a prince was always a man and could not escape the cares and anxieties of his state. Henry I of England (1068–1135) must have had his share for we see him here dreaming of his subjects' reproaches and, perhaps, of their revolt. Bottom: Those who pray, bishops and abbots with mitres and croziers, submit their grievances. Middle: Those who fight, warriors fully armed, seem to threaten him. Top: Those who work, peasants with spade, scythe and pitchfork, present a parchment with their claims. Henry Beauclerk's was certainly not an isolated case.

WESTERN SOCIETY

The Christian society, some factors of which were discussed above, was perfectly integrated in a vision of the universe based on the Divine Providence. This makes it very difficult to define it in terms of the present day.

Take the word 'freedom'. What sense could it have in a society in which legal freedom did not necessarily go hand in hand with economic or political freedom, and where these different freedoms were quite relative? The pope himself was 'the servant of the servants of God' and all Christians, though allowed a certain free will, were bound to obey divine laws of extraordinary severity.

Fraternity existed only in theory. All men were brothers as a matter of course, but even in the great western family, so many of the so-called brethren were enemies or inferiors, and therefore not to be associated with, that most of them were virtually ignored in everyday life.

What do we find when we examine the notions of equality and unity?

All Christians, men and women alike, were equal before the sacraments, before death and before the throne of God. All Christians could enter God's service—even women by becoming nuns—and be entrusted with the highest responsibilities. Suger, Abbot of Saint-Denis and regent of France, was of humble birth; so were Hildebrand and Gerbert, who became famous as Popes Gregory VII and Sylvester II. But what strikes us most is the unity of western society, all the more remarkable because its basic cells—castellany, seignory and parish—were often extremely individualistic. The West, despite differences of race, language, law, socio-professional and economic level, was the great Christian family. To employ an expression popular in the Middle Ages, based on Saint Paul's First Epistle to the Corinthians and the parable of the talents in the Gospel of Saint Matthew, it formed one body and all its members were jointly responsible for, and contributed equally to, its life.

Obviously each member had its own duty to perform, as in the days of the Late Empire, the Republic and Menenius Agrippa. Honorius of Autun (Augustodunensis) in the twelfth century said that the prelates were the head of that body, the doctors its eyes, the masters its mouth; fighters were its hands; spouses its belly; peasants the feet that support it. God in his mercy assigned the task of each and guaranteed the harmonious operation of the whole.

Here we have, clearly defined, a notion elaborated between the end of the eighth century and the beginning of the ninth. Every man has his place provided for him by God and must perform the duties entrusted to him in agreement with the canonical authority.

Apparently this basic notion was firmly anchored in men's minds, for any attack on the order willed by God, any attempt to change place, was viewed as a crime deserving of the gravest temporal sanctions, quite apart from being a sin.

Let us now see how each man was assigned his place in the medieval society and the criteria on which it was based. In principle, if we consider only the religious criterion, there were two sorts of functions providing the foundations for two orders: *clerus et populus*, the clergy, dedicated to the service of God, and the laity. Or, considering the many laymen who aspired to saintliness, the order of monks, the order of clerks and the order of laymen. This Carolingian concept was dictated by the churchmen, formulated by their pupil and protector the Emperor Charlemagne's son and successor, Louis the Pious, and reiterated by the popes.

But the Late Empire adopted other legal and social criteria, which some prelates continued to apply as late as the tenth century; they divided society into a great many 'categories'. Other criteria were strength, power and wealth.

The great achievement of the tenth and eleventh centuries was to unify the religious and economic criteria, rediscovering and sanctioning the classic distinction of Indo-European society, perhaps indeed

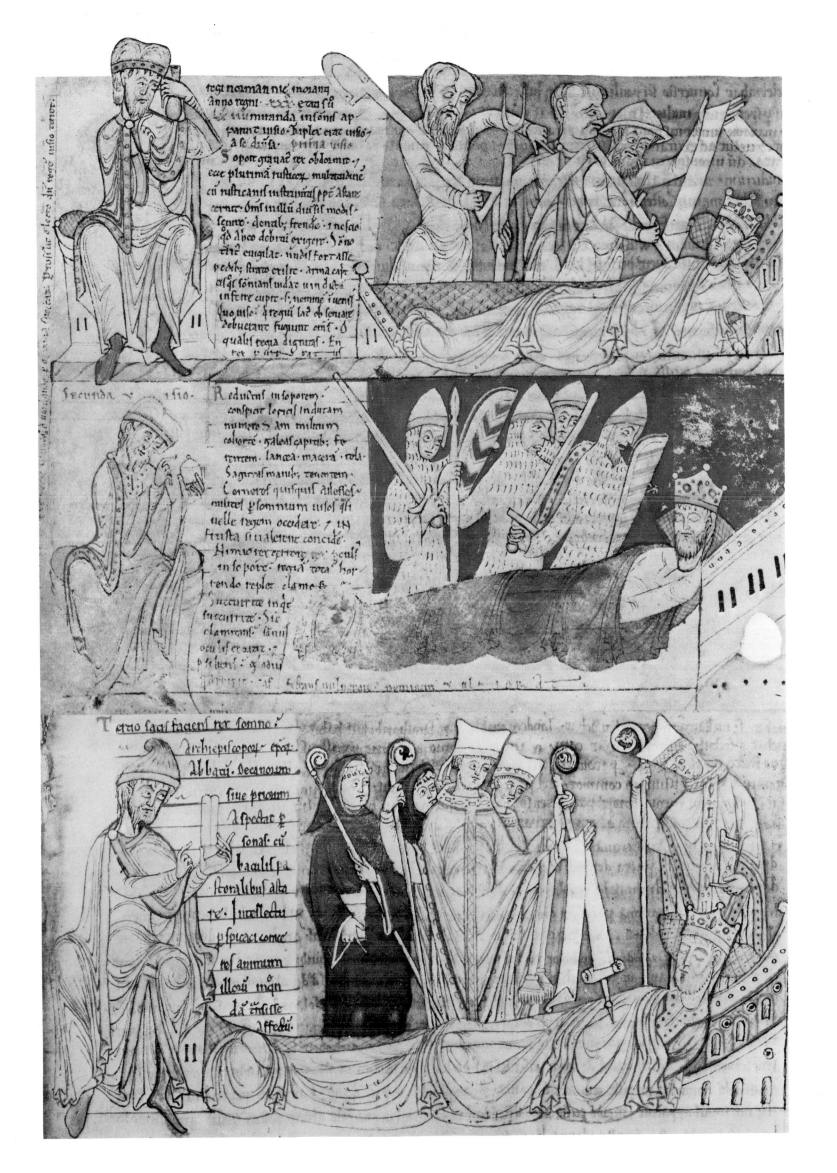

regi noeman ni̅c̅ morant̅
anno regni · xxx · et an̅ s̅
li̅ mirranda infon̅s ap
paruit uisio. triplex erat uisio
a se diu̅sa. prima uisio
Soport grauat̅ rex obdormit̅ ·
ecce plurima rusticoꝝ multitudine
cu̅ rusticanis ustrumu̅s ṗṗe lectu̅
cernit̅. Om̅s in illu̅ diu̅si modis
seuiu̅t · denti̅b; frendt̅ · ⁊ nescio
qd̅ a̅ eo debit̅ exigere. S ono̅
cu̅ euigilat · u̅de s̅ fortasse
pedib; strato crist̅e · arma cap̅
et se s̅onianc̅ uidt̅ u⁊n die
inferre cupt̅ · s̅ nemine i̅uent̅
quo uiso · a̅ regni lat̅ eb seruare
debuerant fugiunt om̅s · O
qualis regia dignitas · En
rex ꝑuip̅ ꝯ ua̅ · us

secunda ⁘ uisio.
Reductus in soporem ·
conspicat̅ legreis induta̅
numero 5 am militu̅ꝝ
cohorte · galeas capiti̅b; · for
tentem · lancea · macera · uela
Sagittas manu̅s · tenente̅m ·
Cornerol quisquis aileslles
milit̅ ꝑ somnium uisos iam
uelle regem occidere · ⁊ in
frusta si ualerent concide.
Hi mio rex terrore ꝑ̅ ꝑculs
in sopore · regia̅ tota̅ hor
rendo replet clamore ·
Succurrite in qe̅
succurrite · Sic
clamtanc̅ famu̅
ocu̅lis ꝑexurit · ⁊
ꝑ tachenc̅ · ⁊ q̅ adui
q̅ ꝯmuenti · asl chanf uulgron̅ · uemuam̅ ⁘ al · t an · ?

Tetuo sacis facens rex somno ·
Archiepiscopoꝝ · epoꝝ·
Abbati̅ · Decanorum
siue prioru̅
Aspectat ꝑ
sonas · cu̅
baculis pa
storalibus aita
re · mtellectu
ꝑspicaci comee
res animu̅
illoꝝ m̅ꝗn
da̅ ꝯsisse
Affectu̅

of every primitive society at a certain phase of its development. In England Albertus Magnus spoke of men of prayer *(jebed)*, men of horses *(fyrd)* and men of work *(weorc)*. About 1020 Adalberon of Laon explained to the king of France that 'the house of God, which was believed to be one, is divided into three parts: the first pray, the second fight, the third work'. Those who worked he called 'serfs' though some were legally freemen; he used the term to designate those who tilled the soil—which was the only source of wealth—and made it produce. They were subject to 'masters' whom they fed and by whom they were defended and protected.

Adalberon's definition is also interesting because it shows that the lay society was clearly hierarchized: the peasants were under the men of war. The latter submitted in turn to the churchmen, who were absolutely indispensable as intermediaries between man and God; they alone were able to ransom the souls of their fierce protectors by prayers, relics and the intervention of the saints and angels. In France this tripartite organization was maintained until the revolution of 1789. It matched the social situation at the time when the knightly class was established; the clergy tended to become a caste and economic activity was centred on the land. Being sanctioned by the Godhead—itself a Trinity—it created a permanent framework that it was sacrilege to alter; but if this was undoubtedly a guarantee of social peace, it excluded all possibility of evolution. The system soon found itself in contrast with the economic situation. In the twelfth century, and still more in the thirteenth, there arose an extremely dynamic class of people who, though neither peasants, nor warriors nor clerics, were excellent Christians, namely the merchants. Were they to remain in the order of the workers? Some theologians said yes; others held that a new socio-professional division was needed, but subject to sanction. The number of categories, 'conditions' and, a little later, 'estates' increased considerably but they were still classified, implicitly or explicitly, in two groups: a spiritual group ranging from monks and nuns to the

pope, and from students to priests, and a temporal group ranging from women to the emperor, and from peasants to the prince. That is how Guillaume de Digulleville's pilgrim interpreted the statue of Nebuchadnezzar's dream as representing the lay world—from its gold head, which represented the king, to the soles of its feet, half iron and half clay, which represented the workers and peasants (already united!).

This reflects a vision of a dualistic, hierarchized society in which only the clerical group and the summit of the lay group, namely the nobility, were more or less clearly defined. But new conditions which tended to bring together the dynamic world of town and road with the static world of the countryside resulted in certain changes even among the clergy. The monks and part of the lower clergy remained in the country; the new religious orders founded by Saint Francis and Saint Dominic took to the road or joined the secular clergy and the prelates in the towns. Even among the nobles —divided into rural, urban and court—the slow but inevitable acceptance of wealth as a criterion and the new money-making mentality helped to accentuate these distinctions in the fourteenth and fifteenth centuries. Thus, among the laity, great merchants, men of war, monopolizers, favourites of princes improved their position in the *de facto* hierarchy to the disadvantage of the gentry and the new serfs. At the same time the *de jure* hierarchy —headed by the nobles among the laity—became more flexible through the insertion of a more or less well-off 'middle class' between the nobles and the serfs (peasants), while among the clergy the lower orders formed a separate class whose material and moral standards could bear comparison with those of the most underprivileged laymen.

Lastly, it is worth noting that the Christian society excluded or segregated a great many individuals: heretics, who were the most dangerous because they endangered its unity; Jews who, because impossible to assimilate and not easily tolerated, were hunted, pestered, often expelled and

There was no room for non-Christians in the monolithic society of the Middle Ages. The Jews, after being tolerated for a long time, were viewed with dislike from the eleventh century and later persecuted. Above: An order issued by St Louis and bearing the seals of his barons attempted to stop the only activity they were still allowed—lending money at interest (usury). That occupation was strongly disapproved of, if we are to judge by this scene (right), in which a Franciscan friar, in dark habit, and a Dominican, in black and white, refuse to accept alms from two usurers.

occasionally massacred; the crippled and the sick, particularly lepers; exiles, vagrants and foreigners in general, whom hard times often turned into brigands, were viewed with suspicion. Not to mention the poor, who had no permanent means of subsistence and for that very reason were a threat to the social order. They might be tempted to steal or rebel; besides which, if God punished them in that way it meant that they were lazy, worthless sinners. In early times it was a work of mercy to succour the poor; in the fourteenth and fifteenth centuries they were distrusted and driven out. A careful study of daily life in the West during the Middle Ages must not be restricted to the socio-professional categories into which the Christian society was traditionally divided; it must also take into account the way of life of those pariahs and insist on the fact that though in theory it formed a rigid framework that framework displayed a quantity of cracks.

Above all else, we must never lose sight of two essential considerations if we are to understand a situation that cannot help but surprise us *a priori*. First, Western Man in general, no matter what his material or spiritual level, had notions of space and time that were totally different from ours; he viewed the universe from the standpoint of Antiquity, corrected and filtered by Christian symbolism; he lived in the fear of sin and damnation surrounded by a nature at once miraculous and diabolic; he conceded to the clan, the couple, woman, love, children and young people a place that we find extraordinary; and his ideas about ownership, law, justice and the state were not quite the same as ours. Secondly, society formed part of the divine order and was divided into functional or socio-professional categories such that normal daily behaviour within a given category was very constant, though totally different from that within the neighbouring categories. Even if they shared the same vision of the universe, lived in the same place and enjoyed the same revenue, a peasant, a rural noble, a village priest and a townsman who had purchased a local estate had totally different ways of life. The divine order ratified, crowned and tended to perpetuate what economic, social and functional causes would have rendered variable, unstable, and diverse.

136

I WORK FOR ALL: The Life of the Peasantry

The Western World, as we have already seen, may be viewed by and large as a vast forest gradually encroached upon through the centuries by tilled fields. Numerically, at least, the rural population had an overwhelming importance: it accounted for 90 or even 95 per cent of the total. Even at the end of the Middle Ages, in a country as intensely urbanized as Italy, at most 40 per cent of the inhabitants lived in the towns.

If we leave aside the thin layer of landed proprietors, both lay and ecclesiastic, and a certain number of secular and regular clergy who lived in the country, we find that at least 90 per cent of the people in the West were peasants. Although the percentage diminished since then, the peasantry formed the majority of the population right up to the nineteenth century and, in some countries, does so still. This is an extremely important point and contrasts both with the Graeco-Roman world, where the peasants formed the majority of the population and gradually crystallized around the urban nucleus of the city state, and the Islamic world, which was a steppe dotted with towns that exerted a direct influence on the rural population.

Centuries of heavy toil in the fields; a life conditioned by the rhythm of the sun, seasons and climate; close permanent contact with the soil, the mountains and the vegetation gave the Western World its basic character just as these factors had influenced the Indo-European or neolithic populations before they were urbanized by the Romans.

And it was not merely the physical characteristics of those populations that were influenced by the daily experience of their way of life. A great many traditional ways of speech and thought have their roots in that rural past, on which the evolution of the Western World was based and conditioned.

The Latin verb *laborare* (to work) produced the French verb *labourer*, which means to till the soil. And in fact, the peasant, whose entire life is devoted to tilling the soil, is the worker par excellence. E. Faral has shown him in the act of 'turning the soil, carting marl, harrowing, sowing, moving, tend-

In the Middle Ages land was the chief wealth, but without ample manpower its yield was poor. The peasants had no knowledge of artificial fertilizers; their tools, spade, rake, scythe, and sickle, and farming methods never improved. Consequently, all available labour was mobilized and the whole family helped to bring in the harvest. In the picture on the opposite page the married women wear a head-dress while the spinsters are bare-headed.

Most farm implements were made of wood. Even plough-shares had only a metal tip; it developed later into a coulter (right) for ripping the ground and protecting the share. After the eleventh century scythes (left) and pruning-knives were made of iron.

ing livestock, clipping sheep, doing other tasks', and described him after thirteenth-century French literary sources as 'a strapping fellow, a brute as black as coal, with a head of shaggy hair, eyes far apart like animal's, whose flat nose with nostrils spreading to his ears overhangs a thick-lipped red mouth full of yellow teeth'.

It is hardly believable that all the peasants in the West were created after the same model in tens of regions through ten centuries. However, it is possible to view their daily life as governed by a number of conditions that were the same for all and sprang from their basic function, which was to till the soil.

THE LIVING CONDITIONS

The work of the peasantry depended on the means at their disposal for acting on their natural environment. Climatic conditions and the rhythm of the seasons required domestic plants and animals more or less suited to the latitude and the normal vegetative cycle; the soil had to be employed in relation to its fertility or an effort made to improve that fertility. But the most important problems were those linked with ploughing, sowing and reaping and therefore with agricultural technology and methods of cultivation. Archaeological diggings have not provided any information about the tools employed by the peasants before the middle or the end of the Middle Ages. We learn why from texts and pictures: until then most implements were made of wood and therefore disappeared in the course of the centuries.

On a royal domain in the rich Lille district during the Carolingian period there were two scythes, two sickles, and a few iron-shod spades; the ploughs had a wooden share with only the tip in iron, since this metal was reserved for weapons. Between the ninth century and the thirteenth the increasing numbers of smiths in the rural districts, linked with the spread of heavier, sturdier and more efficient implements, was a development of major importance; for the

After the farm-workers, the wood-workers (joiners and carpenters) formed the majority of the rural population. Cartwrights and blacksmiths followed hard on their heels; they worked with tongs, hammers and anvils. This miniature, dating from the eleventh century, shows that saws and anvils had the same shapes that we know today.

peasant society, first of all, in which the rich farrier occupied a leading position, but still more on account of the technical advance he stood for. To realize this we have only to picture in our mind the unshod ox or horse pulling a wooden plough, while the peasant prunes his trees with a wooden blade, turns his soil with a wooden spade, crushes his wheat between two hand-operated grindstones, and his wife prepares his meals, without the help of a knife, in pots, most of which cannot bear the fire.

Heavy iron ploughs—or at least those whose major components (share, mould-board and coulter) were made of iron—brought about a veritable revolution. Being expensive, they were owned by few people or belonged to the community; this strengthened the

community spirit. Being heavy, it took a team of oxen or, increasingly, horses to pull them; this posed problems of yoking, of breeding large animals, and of manpower: a driver was needed for the team and a ploughman at the handles. Being strong and sturdy, these ploughs could till deep, heavy soil and therefore cultivate fertile land that had previously lain fallow, besides working ground full of roots without repeated breakage. By cutting a dissymmetrical furrow and turning over the clods, the soil was ventilated, helping it to fix the nitrogen of the atmosphere and so recover its fertility more quickly. They may even have contributed to changing the shape of the fields. The heavy, cumbersome yoked team was difficult to turn, so it was an advantage to

cut the furrow as long as possible; the ploughs were best suited to strip fields and helped to promote that shape—even if they were not responsible for the initial change in shape. Those heavy ploughs, many of them equipped with a mobile wheeled limber, were employed chiefly in France north of the Loire and on the clayey soil of England, Germany and the German-Polish plain. The Mediterranian countries, where the land had been under cultivation for centuries, kept to the lighter swing-plough drawn by an ox or an ass, which cut a straight, shallow furrow.

The introduction and spread of other costly but efficient implements also helped to ease the peasant's lot. For example, an improved press combining torsion and pressure, operated by a capstan or a central screw, enabled a larger quantity of olives or grapes to be pressed faster and more completely, thus leaving more hands free for other tasks.

The use of the motive power supplied by water and, later, by wind opened up still vaster prospects. At the end of the eleventh century so small a country as England had 5,624 mills situated in 3,000 localities. France could boast at least ten times as many, and two centuries later hundreds of thousands of flour and oil mills were installed throughout the country on the banks of streams and on dams; these latter formed lakes that modified both the landscape and the water system. Wind power was used in Castille from the tenth century, but was hardly known in the rest of Europe before the twelfth.

Those mills had a great impact on life in the rural districts. On the one hand, they freed a large por-tion of the manpower that had previously been needed to move the primitive grindstones inherited from a bygone age. On the other, a building of that sort, built sometimes of timber but increasingly of stone and often fortified, complete with dam and power-plant, the main parts of which were made of or strengthened with iron, required an important investment that only a landed proprietor could provide. To recover his outlay he had to impose on the peasants who brought him their grain such heavy taxes that they were tempted to make do with their old grindstones, which cost them nothing.

This led to conflicts, for the landlord obliged his tenants to use his mill and confiscated their hand-mills. The case is known of a monastery that paved its cloisters with the grindstones wrested from the peasants. The grasping miller enriched by the wheat extorted in payment and his pretty, flighty wife, free to enjoy herself while her husband supervised his millstones and the peasant waited for his flour, were well-known characters of the rustic scene.

The efficiency of the traditional motive power provided by draught animals was also greatly improved by the introduction of new techniques. For instance, the heavy plough posed the problem of the team and a demand developed for stronger, faster and more vigorous beasts. Oxen were shod and horses, formerly used more for war than for transport, were increasingly employed. Horse breeding was restricted by custom and by their frailty, which made them expensive. But the spread of oat production—in Picardy, for example, after the mid-

For centuries the heavy plough was drawn by oxen. On the opposite page they are harnessed in tandem pairs, with the yoke still wavering between neck and horns. The introduction of the mobile limber and the collar harness for horses was a great improvement. Horses work faster than oxen, consequently the ploughman's task was lightened and the yield increased (right).

Water mills were more powerful and more widespread than windmills, besides being independent of the fickle winds. Solidly built downstream on a mill leat, they ground huge quantities of grain into flour. The miller was also able to catch fish with nets set in the race.

In the tenth or eleventh century millers learned to use wind power to grind corn. The windmill reached the West from Islam and is still in use a thousand years later in countries like England and Holland that have steady winds.

Oil and wine presses were improved and, more important, their power was greatly increased. Some could be operated by two men (above). Others, like this thirteenth century monster (below) preserved in the Château de la Marquetterie (Champagne), needed ten; it weighs 12 tons and a pressing took 24 hours to crush all the grapes it contained.

twelfth century—undoubtedly helped to promote their use. On the other hand the ox, slower but stronger and less delicate, disappeared in some regions where agriculture was very advanced. However, as late as the eighteenth century it had not been completely ousted by the horse in the Paris district and still less in the southern countries.

Quite apart from the type of draught animal employed, the method of applying its force was improved. Peasants no longer harnessed an ox at the withers but set the yoke on its frontlet or, better still, on its horns; this enabled it to apply its strength to greater effect. Horses during Graeco-Roman Antiquity and the early Middle Ages had been attached nearly always by the neck so that they were half strangled at the very first pull; now a collar was invented that rested on the breast and ribs.

Lastly, to enable the plough to be pulled by a larger number of animals—eight oxen were often used in England at the end of the eleventh century —they had to be harnessed in tandem and not in a row. The Ancients had mostly harnessed their beasts abreast, as in the quadriga where the two wing horses pulled aslant with the result that their force was largerly wasted.

Thus the western peasant possessed effective utensils and appliances. Farming methods were also improved so that output increased considerably in both quantity and quality.

Land needs repose if it is to recover its fertility, and the custom of fallow was universal in the West until the introduction of the potato and forage crops. To curtail that period and make it more effective, farmers endeavoured to assist nature. In some privileged localities it was possible to obtain a harvest every year by spreading manure or burying leaves; some soils could also be improved by mixing with marl or chalky earth or correcting their acidity by the addition of heath-mould. The fallow land was carefully watched over, sometimes even worked. Flocks put to pasture on it enriched it with their droppings. One or more preparatory tillages ventilated the soil and buried the weeds.

Besides which, probably as early as the Carolingian period, the land was no longer left fallow every other year but only one year in three. This was possible because the systematic cultivation of spring wheat, oats and barley gradually provided an adequate crop rotation. A peasant's land was divided into three parts; in the first after the November tillage he sowed winter wheat, buck wheat, and spelt; in the second in March he sowed spring wheat; the third was left fallow. The following year the first part was fallow, the second under winter wheat, the third under spring wheat, and so on.

This method of rotation showed its true worth when applied on a large estate or the entire territory of a village. In that case all the arable land was divided into three soles, each peasant having a plot in each. Every year the plots in the same sole were left fallow or sown with the same type of wheat (winter or spring). This system had some great advantages, one being that two-thirds of the territory was always under cultivation instead of half. There was less waste of energy; the community's livestock could graze on the fallow land without fencing; the sown soles promoted the community spirit of the villagers. Furthermore, a hard winter or a poor crop could be compensated by a good spring that gave a big harvest of oats or barley. The sole system spread chiefly in the twelfth and thirteenth centuries, coinciding with the great encroachment of tilled fields on the forest following large-scale clearance work.

For all these reasons yields increased. During the Carolingian period a crop equal to three or four times the seed was a rare occurence. Some calculations—based, it is to be hoped, on bad years—would seem to prove that the seed was barely recovered or at most with a very small surplus. In the twelfth and thirteenth centuries, instead, a crop equal to five, six or even eight times the seed seems to have been the rule.

Some cereals, such as barley, give a better yield than oats and the like. This explains why oats, though preferred by horses and used for porridge by

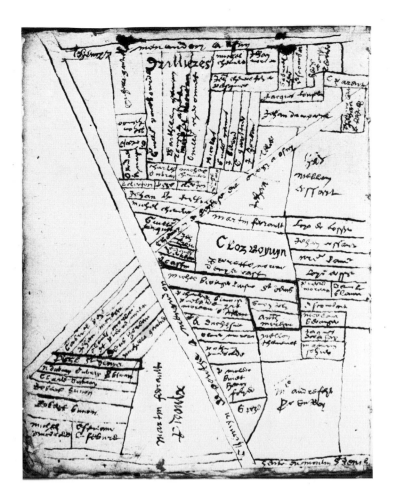

At the end of the Middle Ages fields and orchards were accurately measured. That the rudiments of land surveying were known is proved by a treatise written by Arnaud de Villeneuve in the fifteenth century. But few detailed cadastral surveys have come down to us; this one for the hamlet of Cergy (above) dates from 1528. In recent years the shortage of documents has been made up for by aerial photography, which shows how estates have been parcelled out. In this slanting view of Farlow (Shropshire) the quick-set hedges mark the limits of the patches successively cleared.

143

man, never ousted barley, which was indispensable for beer and coarse bread. Other crops were introduced, notably pulses, like peas, beans and lentils, and cabbage, which are rich in protein and they served to boost the caloric value of the workers' diet, besides making it more balanced. The introduction of hemp, flax and woad supplied raw materials for the textile industry and encouraged some lucky speculations, while providing diversification which softened the impact of bad times.

There were also grape vines—grown wherever it was possible until international trade was able to ensure the supply of wine to countries where the grape did not ripen easily—and olive trees in the Mediterranean area. The various kinds of fruit trees had all been known since ancient times except the apricot, which was imported during the period of the Crusades. In spite of this, medieval peasants did not have at their disposal the vast range of products available to their descendants in the eighteenth century. The sugar cane was already cultivated in Spain and Sicily, but did not reach the Venetian islands in the Mediterranean, such as Crete and Cyprus, until the end of the Middle Ages. As for potatoes, tomatoes, tobacco, maize and new sorts of beans, they were only introduced very gradually in modern times; this is also true of the sugar beet.

The livestock bred by the medieval peasantry was not different in kind from what we find nowadays, but the relative proportions of the various species has changed beyond recognition. Poultry comprised of a great many breeds of barnyard fowl as well as swans and peacocks; only the turkey was unknown. Big animals were scarce; there were few horses until the thirteenth century, except on large estates, and few oxen, except for those needed for farm work. There were some cows here and there to ensure reproduction, but except in regions like Norway and Denmark their milk was little used, and then more for cheese than butter. Those large animals required fodder that was rare and expensive: oats for the horses; hay and grass for the cattle. Winter stabling was often a serious problem because there was little

This peasant is pruning his vines with a bill-hook. The tool, which also has a sharp edge for cutting dead wood, continued unchanged in use until pruning-shears were introduced late in the nineteenth century.

The chick-pea was already known in Antiquity and its cultivation (opposite page) was very widespread. It supplied the peasantry with proteins that helped to balance their diet.

Sheep and shepherds were to be seen everywhere (opposite page). Sheep were a major source of income for poor and rich alike. Cattle, instead, were not so common because they need a great deal of fodder and there was not enough hay to feed them during the winter. Milk was preserved as cheese, more seldom as butter (above).

There were well-stocked aviaries where swan and peacock lived side by side with common fowls (left).

natural grassland to supply hay, so many animals were butchered before winter set in. November was the 'bloody' month.

Sheep were far more common and more highly appreciated, particularly from the twelfth century when they brought prosperity to the English countryside and the Spanish mountain districts. Almost every part of a sheep could be utilized: the milk for cheese; the skin for leather or fleece in the full-grown animals, for fur in the young ones; the meat was salted and preserved; even the horns and gut could be made into musical instruments. And sheep could always find pasture in the glades of the community forest or the fallow fields that they enriched with their droppings.

The pig was another fundamental factor of the peasant economy as early as the period of the bar-

barian invasions, when it shared with fowls and their eggs the task of providing almost all the food of domestic animal origin. Sixteen articles of the Salic Law are devoted to the pig. In the days of the Carolingian emperors peasants filled their modest abodes at the beginning of winter with hams, flitches of bacon, black puddings and rillettes, which helped to balance their diet till Lent. Pigs were easy to keep; the half-wild black beasts with long, stiff bristles and tusks like those on a boar's snout lived in the communal forest, feeding on beech-nuts, acorns and chestnuts under the remote supervision of a swineherd.

A peasant household also held quite a few dogs of breeds that are far less well known than those raised by the nobles. Cats were rare though they had been imported from Egypt in Roman times;

they were to be found chiefly in a few wealthy families, where they had to compete with tame weasels and stoats trained to hunt rats that were less fierce than the brown species of our own day.

VILLAGE AND HOME LIFE

The peasantry sometimes dwelt in isolated houses, but as a rule they lived in villages situated more or less in the centre of the farmland.

That land was constantly extended during the Middle Ages. During the Merovingian period the vast western forest had been broken only by a few small clearings. In the seventh century they began to expand around small hamlets. From the eleventh, when the great population explosion began, each peasant nibbled surreptitiously at the march and woodland round about his holding. This has left its trace in old surveys, in the names of localities and still more in the landscape produced by those operations. A peasant did not pay the old taxes on the land acquired in this way, but he had to pay tithes to the Church and when his lord realized what had happened he dunned him for a share ranging from one-sixth to one-fourteenth of the produce. At times the wasteland situated between two developed territories was occupied by a small number of persons who

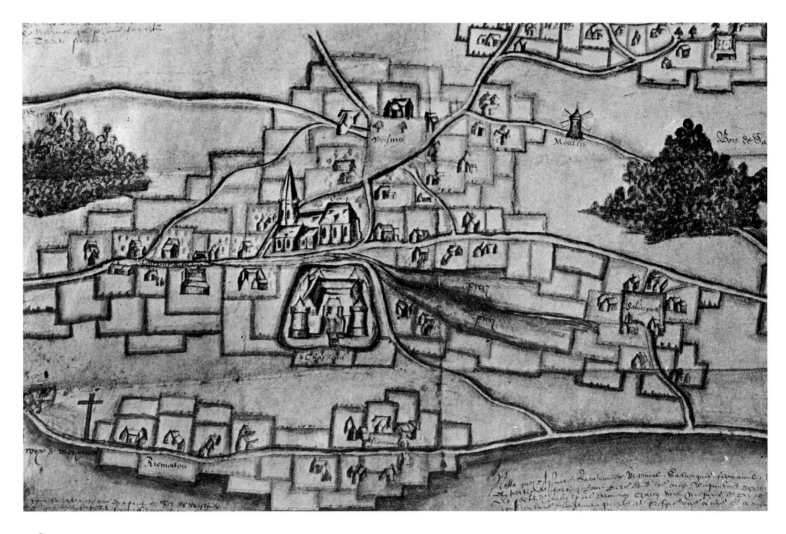

Above: Rysum in Lower Saxony gives a good idea of what a medieval village looked like. Built to an approximately circular plan, it has a very sensible system of roads and streets. The streets branch out from the centre like the spokes of a wheel, ending at the outer ring road that encircles the village. In the centre, towards which all streets converge, stands the house of God.

Opposite page: village life was centred round three poles—the church, the castle and the home. The church was the house of God, sovereign Lord and Judge, and the dead members of the community were interred in its shadow. The castle in the middle, the mill (upper right) and the gibbet (lower left) reminded the villagers that the lord of the manor had the right to order, restrain and punish. Besides the common land, small enclosed plots around the houses marked the limits of strictly family activities. This plan shows the village of Wismes (Pas-de-Calais).

Left: An aerial photograph of the hamlet of Middleton (Yorkshire) stresses its peculiar layout. The houses with their front gardens line the street on both sides; the plots of ground behind them are also perpendicular to it.

The materials used for building village houses varied from one region to another and also with their owners' means. Above: The house in which the reformer Ulrich Zwingli was born at Wildhaus (Switzerland) was built entirely of timber. Others had a timber framework filled in with pisé, like this one at Ightham Mote in Kent (left). At Bignor in Sussex there is a half-timbered house with small brick areas resting on a dry-stone base and thatched roof (opposite). Stone walls and tiled roofs, as in this farm at Stratford-on-Avon (below), were rarer.

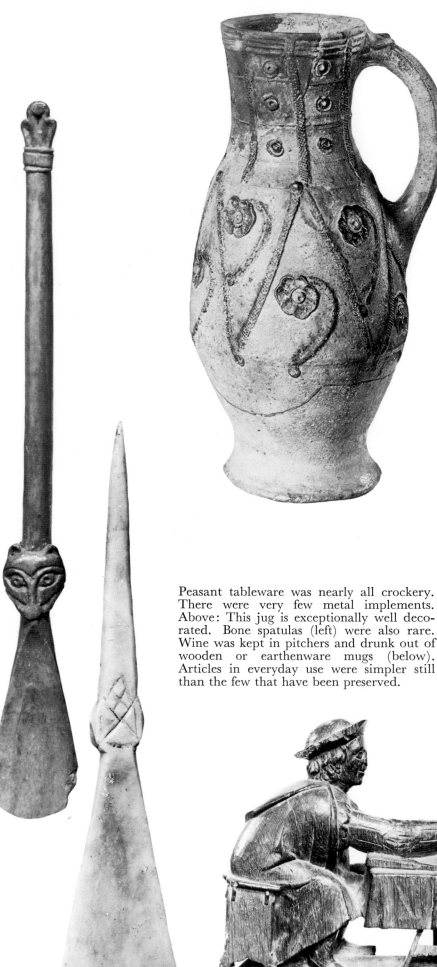

settled separately on the new land. Many farms of this type, of a certain area and all of a piece, were enclosed and gave rise to the typical wooded landscape we see today.

It also happened that whole villages were established under the management of a lay or ecclesiastical lord or a group of lords. The reasons for this may have been economic, military or political, but the result was always the same. Peasants called in from all over the country or supplied by the over-populated villages in the vicinity formed a new settlement with its own land. Each of these new arrivals was given a house and garden with a few fields for which he had to pay a share of the produce; his animals could feed in the nearby forest in return for payment of grazing dues. Justice dues, for which there was a fixed scale of prices, were payable to the lords who had settled him and ensured his protection.

This process was very widespread and can be observed in various countries: in France, at Lorris in the Gâtinais and the eighty villages that copied it; in the old countries of the West, at Beaumont in Argonne and its 500 French and Imperial daughters; in Spain reconquered from the Muslims; and in East Germany colonized on its Slav marches. It continued at least from the eleventh to the thirteenth century,

Peasant tableware was nearly all crockery. There were very few metal implements. Above: This jug is exceptionally well decorated. Bone spatulas (left) were also rare. Wine was kept in pitchers and drunk out of wooden or earthenware mugs (below). Articles in everyday use were simpler still than the few that have been preserved.

won scores of millions of acres for agriculture, and founded tens of thousands of new villages. A number of them were abandoned when the boom period came to an end in the fourteenth century, but the unpromising situation of the peasantry at the end of the Middle Ages should not make us forget the previous dynamic expansion.

Most settled areas in the West, both ancient and modern, had the same general arrangement. Three concentric zones extended from the forest to the village: at the edge of the wood, pastures, meadows, cleared ground and wasteland grazed by the communal flocks; closer in, land sown with cereals, under rotation, with vineyards and orchards on south-facing slopes; lastly, the village itself surrounded by crofts and garden plots that were kept tilled, hoed, ventilated, and fertilized with domestic waste. These plots, the result of years and years of care, helped to fix the position of the village. In some cases archaeologists in search of traces of a village that has disappeared have had the soil carefully analyzed: a high content in phosphorus anhydride and potassium salts marks the site of those crofts and therefore indicates the proximity of the one-time settlement.

If the village was planned in advance when clearance work was organized, it had a regular layout:

Comfort and wealth are very relative notions. The man toasting his toes before the fire might well be the lucky owner of the cauldron and three-legged pot on the right. Replace the chimney-piece with an open hearth of beaten earth and substitute earthen for the metal utensils, and you will realize the difference between a rich townsman and a peasant.

Very few fine pieces of furniture have been preserved. They are mostly cupboards (left) and chests (below) that belonged to well-off families. The peasants usually used low bins for keeping their few possessions. Many have locks and keys. Sometimes the cupboard consisted merely of a wall recess with or without a door.

154

Autumn was sowing time. The sower cast the grain on the ploughed field, taking it from a box (above) or bag.

This fifteenth century miniature depicts very precisely a ladder cart with rimmed wheels; the two horses are harnessed in a very flexible manner still employed today.

chequer-board (as in Provence), herring-bone, or linear (as in the Normandy villages and those settled by German colonists). Sometimes the houses were built haphazardly round about an open space dominated by the church; sometimes they were crowded behind ramparts. But they were never very numerous—a few dozen at the outside—and most were of the same simple type.

We have the good fortune to know about some villages that were recently excavated. They have put us in a position to synthesize the sparse elements provided previously by unreliable pictorial representations (miniatures executed for the nobility), the interpretation of texts (inventories and descriptions of buildings), and a few reverently preserved relics of doubtful authenticity ('Joan of Arc's house' at Domrémy).

To compare them with the dwellings of French peasants is no easy matter because documentation on the latter is widely scattered and of various origin. They differed greatly from one region to another, so that a synthesis is far more difficult to make. Cottages built chiefly of timber have disappeared completely except for the very lowest courses, as at Montaigut in the Albigensian territory, which are very hard to interpret. Elsewhere, as at Dracy, Saint-Jean-le-Froid and Condorcet, peasants lived in houses built mostly of dry stone; they were quite roomy, but heavy rather than solid, and uncomfortable. Construction methods have remained unvaried from the Middle Ages, if not earlier, to the present day; the stones were quarried locally or at least regionally and placed one on the other with clay as the only binder and since they often rested on the live rock, elaborate foundations were unnecessary. Pits dug in the ground or cut in the rock nearby served to store provisions and water was supplied by a spring or well that sometimes belonged

to the community. The floor was beaten earth. The walls—still standing to a height of about seven feet at Dracy—have only one opening, the doorway, set as a rule awkwardly in a corner. Were there windows, inevitably very small and set high up in the walls, at least in this part of Burgundy, as shown in some pictures? Or should we imagine a windowless ground floor comprising a wine cellar and areas for stowing ploughs and other gear, and an upper storey for living quarters? It seems unlikely that such rustic walls of very doubtful verticality could support so great a height, particularly as the roof was made of extremely heavy stone slabs that have been found on the site. Their weight is more than enough to account for the thickness of the walls that still exist as well as for the lack of openings. In Picardy far lighter structures—a brick base topped by a dry-stone wall that supported beams and wattles embedded in a mixture of mud and straw—have only tiny windows under the thatched roof.

On the other hand, there was no such thing as a typical peasant house. Each region had a design that suited local conditions and was often continued until the early twentieth century. How great was their diversity is clear to see in the countryside at the present day: walls of mud, timber and stone; roofs of tiles, thatch, slates and slabs of stone; with one

storey or several; with the stabling and storage separate or under the same roof. It is not even certain that all the houses had the traditional large all-purpose room where the inmates lived, worked, cooked, ate and slept around the hearth, which dispensed heat, light... and smoke.

Nor have we a precise idea of their contents, except what can be gleaned from the peasant furniture of the seventeenth and eighteenth centuries now preserved in various museums, for instance at Brou for the Bresse district, or from descriptions provided by pictures, wills and other documents.

Actually, the items dating from the fourteenth and fifteenth centuries exhibited, for instance, in the Musée des Arts décoratifs in Paris, belonged to a wealthy minority, and bins, chests and beds seem to have been the only pieces of furniture in general use at least in the poorer homes.

Beds were often very wide, as evidenced by the story of the Ogre's seven daughters in 'Tom Thumb'. Only the uprights were of wood, and the sleepers lay on straw or a mattress with or without sheets. A cloth blanket or a coverlet made of fur (mouse-deer or sheepskin) was often used to keep out the cold because night-shirts were unknown and everyone slept naked. Sometimes curtains were drawn around the bed to form an alcove.

In this autumnal scene, taken from the fifteenth century prayerbook known as *Les Très Riches Heures du Duc de Berry*, every detail is in keeping with a natural order that recurs invariably each year. One peasant sows the grain, a second breaks up the clods and covers the seed with a harrow, while a scarecrow appears to shoot arrows at the greedy magpies that swoop down on the field. But perhaps the reality was not quite so idyllic as this splendid calendar page would have us believe.

Scythes just like those employed today spread with the use of iron in rural districts (right). They were sharpened with a whetstone (opposite page). The scythe is perfectly suited for grass but not for corn because, being so sharp and heavy, it mows too fast.

Opposite page: in late spring the wheat is tall and dotted with cockles and cornflowers. Some peasants take advantage of the brief respite before the harvest to walk in the fields, pick flowers or enjoy the prospect of a good crop. Others prefer making love.

Sugar was employed exclusively by apothecaries. Other people used honey, supplied as a rule by wild bees.

What a kind husband! He takes his wife to the fields in a wheelbarrow. This one is peculiar in having three wheels for running on good paths; on rough tracks and in the fields the big front wheel served as it does today.

Tables often rested on trestles and sometimes were covered with a cloth. The table was set for a meal and afterwards removed and people sat on benches, for chairs were a luxury. The excavations at Dracy have brought to light an incredible number of keys of admirable workmanship, many of them in the same room. Seemingly the bins had locks and even lowly peasants had several of them, as the literature tells us. They were used for holding some foodstuffs, bread, salt and clothes. Inventories dating from after the thirteenth century lead one to infer that as a rule people had few clothes and that their material was of poor quality. There was no such thing as peasant costume and, as I have already said, the universal custom was to wear several articles of clothing one over the other. The only difference in dress between a peasant and a nobleman was the material: until the fourteenth century the fashion was the same. All wore a long outer garment which had to be hitched up for work in the fields, linen hose, strap shoes, a shirt of linen or hemp, a doublet, a gown or a coat and over all a woollen cloak complete with hood. Regional differences began to appear at the end of the fourteenth century in the head-dress and the general design. A man could be recognized as a stranger because he did not wear the local costume.

Many peasants, male and female, owned a more valuable article of clothing that was kept for special occasions and perhaps handed down from father to son and from mother to daughter. It was usually an outer garment, possibly of good-quality cloth and lined with fur. In the poorest families it was sometimes pledged to secure a loan or was the first thing impounded by a creditor—a sure sign of its relative value.

The major finds unearthed by archaelogists in the remains of peasant dwellings are kitchen utensils: a few andirons, fire-dogs, spits and articles in pewter or other metal; a certain number of bronze pots and kettles; and a vast quantity of shards that attest the use of pot-bellied jugs and other earthen vessels for drinking, cooking, serving and preserving. Many have elegant lines, are varnished, coloured or decorated, and made of fine clay whose texture varies with the type. This pottery bears witness to the existence of an industry and trade of some importance. Bearing in mind that a number of coins and metal ornaments have also been found in the ruins of the simple houses in the little village of Dracy, mixed with this fine earthenware, fibres of carbonized cloth and a great many keys, one cannot help thinking that even poor peasants were moderately well off.

Food and drink has already been mentioned in chapter one. It may be worth recalling, however, what an important part cereals played in the peasants' diet, compared with the few proteins supplied by fresh-water fish, small game (rabbits and birds), leguminous plants like lentils or peas, and domestic animals—poultry (eggs), swine and cattle.

A pig yielded 175 to 200 pounds of more or less fat meat; an ox 330 to 440. We have seen that a family of five or six that made do with one pig and a few capons a year ate as much meat as that of a Provençal peasant in the nineteenth century and incomparably more than a similar family in Africa or the Far East. At Saint-Jean-le-Froid in the fourteenth century, sheep were common throughout the district and their wool was processed in every home—as the many spindle whorls discovered show. Yet 41 per cent of the butcher's meat was supplied by oxen—judging from the bony matter that has been found there—compared with 34 per cent of pig, and 18 per cent of sheep and goat.

A great deal of beer and wine was drunk in the country, especially as the local brews and vintages could not be transported and sold at a distance because of the keeping problem. In alcoholic content and method of preparation these local wines differed greatly from the wines of Malmsey, Beaune and Saint-Pourçain and the Hamburg beer which gave rise to an important trade.

A peasant daily life was spent in an atmosphere of thrift and austerity, conditioned by the rhythm of the sun and the seasons. The working day lasted from sunrise to sunset and was, therefore, much shorter in winter, when the fields required less care. For the same reason it was only in winter that country-people stayed up after supper, but they never kept late hours unless the men had to cut hemp for the womenfolk to spin. In fact, that would have meant keeping up the fire to provide heat and light; and bed, where straw and blankets offered better protection against the cold, was a strong temptation. Collective night watches lasting until dawn were frowned upon the Church on the pretext that they encouraged licence.

Many illustrations of the life of the peasantry through the months have come down to us in the calendar miniatures contained, for example, in the Carolingian *Recueil* of astronomy and reckoning in Vienna and the *Très Riches Heures du Duc de Berry*; in sculptured medallions (at Amiens, Saint-Denis and Chartres); frescoes (at Laval); and stained-glass windows (such as the Zodiac window at Chartres). One can get a very good idea of the essential peasant activities through the year by examining one of the foregoing and reading Verson's *Chant des Vilains*.

At Amiens, for example, the medallions are arranged in four groups of three, recalling the four seasons. December was the month when the pig was slaughtered. Virtually all known calendars show a scene of this kind. Here the peasant bends down to cut the throat of the pig, which he grips between his knees; by his side another butchered animal slung head down drips blood which is collected in a basin for making black pudding. January is symbolized by two-faced Janus seated at a well-stocked table and served by the two man-servants who perhaps represent the old year and the new. This illustration of the festivities connected with the beginning of the year is frequently replaced or set off by the picture—here attributed to February—of a hooded figure who sits poking the fire in an attempt to warm his naked feet and hands. Obviously winter was the dead season during which the peasants settled the affairs of the previous year but did not yet prepare for the one just starting.

Archery is a good way to pass the time on a Sunday. It also provides the lord of the manor with excellent marksmen for defending his lands and castle.

Right: the balls are only roughly spherical and probably filled with bran, but the game—it seems an ancestor of modern baseball—is no less exciting for that.

Opposite page: September brings the autumn and ripens the fruit in the orchard. Men's dress was practical for climbing trees but there were dauntless women who did not let their long gowns deter them from doing the same. Part of the fruit was dried for that was the only way to preserve it.

Work was interrupted by holidays and other festive occasions. In Spain the first bullfights took place towards the end of the Middle Ages. On the left the beast, goaded by many banderillas, is excited by the cape of the torero, who has taken refuge among the spectators; on the right it charges a man who has ventured into the ring. Local colour is stressed by the costumes and the Moorish arches.

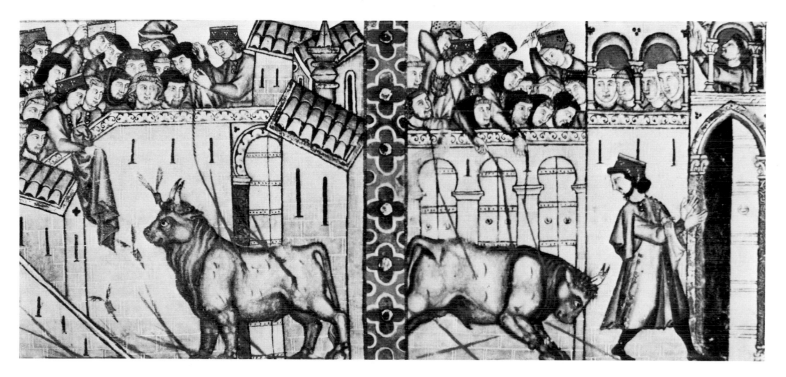

This two-handled cup in glazed earthenware has its place in the Norman folklore. After the wedding, when the bride and groom were bedded their friends and relatives went on carousing; but about midnight they broke into the bridal chamber and invited the spouses with lewd jests to quaff a cup filled with a reinvigorating potion called bride's broth.

Country people are fond of having a good time. These French peasants sing and dance to a music that is mostly quite beyond our ken for, like all genuine folk music, it was passed on orally from one generation to the next and the few transcriptions that have come down to us are far from complete.

At blind-man's-buff children and adults alike enjoy the blunders and clumsiness of the blindfold player. There is a tradition in France that the game got its name from a knight called Colin who, having lost his sight in a battle, laid about him blindly with a mallet. His courage was perpetuated in the game of *colin-maillard*, the French for blind-man's-buff.

March witnessed the digging of the ground with big clods overturned and broken up, particularly around the vine plants. The calendars evidently copied ancient models that had originated in the Mediterranean lands where wine growing was all-important; but the spread of Christianity introduced the vine throughout Western Europe, even as far north as England.

April, falcon on wrist, conjures up the start of the hunting season and other noble occupations, which are sometimes shown in March. When this is so, April recalls tree and vine pruning, the use of milk for making butter or cheese, and the first time animals born during the winter are let out of doors. It is always the season for paying the first rents after Christmas to the lord about to leave on a campaign.

May is represented by an old man seated in a blossoming orchard; this recalls the mildness of the season and the last days of leisure before heavy work starts in the fields. In some calendars the pastimes of the nobles are pictured in May.

June, wearing a cap, brandishes a long-handled scythe with an almost straight blade in a flower-dotted meadow; sometimes he is shown clipping sheep or tilling the fallow.

July reaps the corn with a small sickle leaving long stubble for later grazing; he wears a hat for protection against the sun, and the sheaves pile up behind him.

August beats the grain with a flail on the threshing floor; sometimes he is shown as a winnower scattering the chaff in the wind, while the grain falls under its own weight into a tub.

September witnesses the fruit harvest: here probably apples knocked down with a pole; sometimes bunches of grapes picked on the vine plant or trellis are depicted, though as a rule October, represented with back basket, cask and grapes trodden under foot, is the month traditionally dedicated to wine.

November is the time for tillage and for sowing winter wheat: the sower takes the seed from a wallet and flings it with a sweeping gesture over the newly turned clods.

Fortunately the peasant's year was not all hard labour: the workdays were interspersed with a certain number of holidays. We have already seen that the great feasts of the Christian year coincided with the major astronomic dates that had a direct impact on the countryman's activities—Christmas with the winter solstice, Easter with the spring equinox, St John's Day with the summer solstice, and so on.

The festivities centred round Christmas, which marked the end of one year and the beginning of the next, derived from a solar rite that can be traced back to long before the dawn of Christianity. That was the time when pigs were slaughtered and the last grain stored in the sheaf was threshed in preparation for the copious supper that followed midnight Mass. The celebrations were accompanied by games and shows that have gradually been condemned to oblivion: games of chance; feats of skill like archery —which was often promoted by the lord or king because it was good training for military service; songs and dances in which men dressed as women— like the peasant of Melun who, probably to ape the devil, 'donned a woman's fur lined cloak with the fur outside and covered his face with a woman's coif'. Sometimes there were games in which people represented characters in plays, but they were more usually performed by townspeople.

Innocents' Day was 28 December; 1 January was All Fools' Day. Between the two, New Year's Eve (31 December) was a great occasion for merry-making. Actually the year number changed as a rule on Christmas Day, Lady Day (25 March) or Easter Sunday; but 1 January was considered the first day of the new year in spite of that. On that day in France children and young men went from door to door singing a traditional song: 'L'au guy l'an neuf', and received gifts from the householders.

Twelfth Night, the vigil of the Epiphany, the feast of the Three Magi when the cake with the bean was eaten, ended the festive Christmas period.

After Candlemas, 2 February, with its candle-light procession and pancake dinner, came Quadragesima, the first Sunday in Lent, a time when there were 'bonfires round which the good people are accustomed to gather and dance, and the youths and the children to jump over the fires when they get smaller', or when the young peasants carried straw torches through the fields.

Shrove Tuesday, the day of the mummers, was the occasion not only for banquets and drinking bouts but also for famous matches of a game the French called '*soule*'; it was the ancestor of football but far rougher.

Those winter pastimes—together with the long weeks of fasting which coincided with the slack season when provisions were running out but people had less appetite because they worked less—were brought to a close by the Easter cycle celebrated with the famous eggs, rediscovered with pleasure after the long fast, the hallowed bread, the green boughs of Palm Sunday, and all the other marks of celebration.

May was the month of the first blossoms on trees and hedgerows. On the eve of May Day the village youths went out to the forest to cut branches, which they placed before the doors and windows of the houses where there were marriageable girls: strangers were not asked to join in the fun.

At Whitsun peasants began to be less afraid that frost might nip their tender crops and work in the fields increased. Priests who did not get up in time to say their prayers and sluggards who preferred to stay abed were roused by dousing with cold water amid peals of laughter. In the evening the young people danced on the flower-studded meadows.

St John's Day, the beginning of summer and the longest day of the year, was celebrated with bonfires. A green bower was erected before nightfall to shelter sleeping fairies or as a shrine for the Virgin Mary's statue.

Harvest Home, celebrated by dancing on the new threshing floor—very useful for flattening it—and the civil ceremonies that coincided with the feast of the Assumption (15 August) were a blend of rustic, pagan and sexual customs placed, oddly enough,

under the patronage of Our Lady and sometimes even held in church. The vintage festival, Michaelmas (29 September) and St Remigius' Day (1 October) marked the end of the harvest period, when rents were paid and leases fell due. All Saints and All Souls ushered in the season when nature sleeps. Religious ceremonies included ringing the bells for the repose of the departed, while cruel pagan customs involved the wholesale massacre of various animals, such as goslings and pigs. After that the approach of Christmas and the preparations for that great event put in the shade the various saints' days in the rural calendar.

Outside the public holidays, various occasions offered peasants an opportunity to gather, make merry or speed the passage of bad times. They were mostly family events hallowed by the Church, such as christenings held shortly before the churching of the mother, who was liable to a fine if she was not solemnly purified by the parish priest. The ceremony was followed by a feast to which friends and relatives were invited, while the young mother's father and husband gave her a few creature comforts, such as cushions, an easy-chair, a cloak or the like. One of the texts on this subject that have come down to us tells of a peasant 'who had the intention of killing a pig and some kids he wanted to dress for the feast at the churching of one of his daughters who had given birth to a child and was to go to Mass the next day'.

Betrothals and weddings were important events in the life of the village. If the groom was not a local man he usually paid a round of drinks for the young men whom he robbed of a possible wife; sometimes the bride, who was guilty too, offered them bread. After the customary banquet and carousing the young men often went to spy on the couple during their wedding night and sometimes organized a mock serenade. The publication of the banns, hailed by a song from the local youths, was paid for by the bride's father with bread, meat and wine. The right of '*culage*', '*congnage*' or '*couillage*'—French terms that are self-explanatory but untranslatable—claimed originally by the lord and later, increasingly, by the young men of the village, was paid more usually in money than in kind. A wealth of folklore grew up around weddings throughout the Western World.

Another tradition that has continued to the present day demanded that a family offered a banquet to all those who attended a funeral. Even the humblest peasants insisted on observing the custom and distributing food to the poor who then gathered.

Given the inordinately high birth, death and marriage rates already noted, even in a village that counted only a few score souls family occasions were numerous enough to justify a gathering of this type every month.

SOCIAL RELATIONSHIPS

We have seen that the peasant society displayed a number of general characteristics, linked mostly with the economic and material conditions, which resulted mainly in a simple life in home and village, centred on work in the fields. It would be a mistake, however, to view that society as a monolithic entity and speak of the daily life of the typical peasant as if there was only a single category. There were, instead, very considerable differences due to such factors as time and place as well as to the status or wealth of certain social groups.

For instance, some peasants were slaves, while others were serfs. And among those who may be considered freemen, some were well off or even rich and economically independent—the yeomen—while others had practically no land and were forced to hire themselves out as day-labourers. Many, though not really impoverished, were utterly dependant on their lord, their landowner or their creditors. All had, or could have, a house and a family, and all scraped a living from work on the farm; but daily life was not the same for all.

Right up to the Carolingian period there is clear documentary evidence of the existence of rural slaves in the ancient sense of the term: namely individuals who were personally subject to their

There was hardly a region that did not invent some brutal sport. Cock fighting was popular in Flanders and the North of France. Judging from this miniature, the birds do not seem to have fought to the death for their spurs are not armed with sharp metal blades. That refinement of cruelty was invented later and led to the banning of the sport in quite recent times.

Dice was the most popular gambling game. Many were the cheats who cogged the dice or played other tricks; many too were the kings and princes who endeavoured—never with complete success—to ban a game that was cause of quarrels.

Men and women make hay under the steward's watchful eye, while woodmen fell trees. The movements of woodcutters and mowers are keenly observed and denote methods that remained unvaried for centuries.

owners, had no property or chattels, and were herded together near the place where their master or his agent resided. Some lived in separate cabins with their womenfolk and children, who also belonged to the same master.

As a rule those slaves were settled on holdings, which means that they had the use of a small farm, for which they paid rent—sometimes at a very oppressive rate—to the master, who owned both the land and their persons. This type of tenancy was often very ancient, since the stock of slaves was not easy to renew. In fact, from the Late Empire period to that of Charlemagne, there were few wars to provide the victors with large numbers of captured enemies as slaves. And gradually the Church prohibited the enslavement of Christianized peoples. The slave trade was in the doldrums and consequently a slave became a highly prized commodity. Besides which, it was no easy matter to propagate slavery by natural reproduction for breeding was an extremely costly business: a young slave could hardly do any work before he was 8 years old and the death rate, particularly during the first three years, was very high.

It should also be said that slaves worked very inefficiently in small gangs and therefore the large estates were under-exploited. Consequently, it was an advantage to divide the surplus land of a domain into holdings and settle slaves on them. Under this system the slaves supported themselves, could beget families—thus supplying their owner with young slaves at no cost—and till the land more effectively to their advantage and his. Lastly, since each holding was small, the slave settled on it had some time left for working on the land farmed directly by the master, which was called the 'reserve' or home farm. When needed for tilling or harvesting he helped his mates who lived on the reserve, whereas in the dead season he kept himself and so cost his master nothing.

These tenant slaves, who were very numerous during the Carolingian period, had a certain economic and personal independence. As a rule they were baptized Christians and were allowed to marry instead of living in concubinage as was the ancient custom. The master could not kill them nor beat them too hard. So their lot was somewhat improved.

But both those who had holdings and those who worked on the master's domain were hereditary slaves. They could be bought and sold; they had no legal personality, and their master, who was responsible for their actions, was also their judge. Needless to say, they could not take an oath because the penalty for perjury was to have one hand cut off, and that would have damaged the master to whom their whole body belonged. They could not become priests, nor marry outside the domain without their master's consent, nor do military service, nor appear in court.

From the ninth century the number of those peasant slaves gradually diminished and by the

Peasants were obliged to do a certain amount of work for their lord under the eye of a supervisor. The jobs included road maintenance (right) and repairs to bridges, the castle and its outhouses and farm buildings.

On large estates, like those belonging to the crown or the monasteries, the steward had the task of summoning the workers and distributing the jobs. These men have brought their implements—bill-hooks for pruning vines or fruit trees, spades for digging, scythes and sickles for mowing.

Within the villages, the steward allocates the work according to each man's strength and skill. The organization is faultless. The sheaves are tipped on to the threshing floor and beaten with flails; the grain is winnowed, put into sacks and stored in the granary. The straw will be used to bed down cattle.

eleventh they were hardly distinguishable from serfs. Their gradual disappearance was due basically to the new structure of seignory and the impossibility of renewing the stock of slaves. Until the end of the seventh century the trade had been supplied by the tribes conquered by the Visigoths; until the eighth by the Slavs seized by raiding Lombards; until the beginning of the ninth by the enslaved captives of the Franks; until the beginning of the tenth by those sold by the Normans, and until the middle of the tenth by the Hungarians. But by the end of that century the situation in western Europe had been stabilized and the Christianization of Poland, Bohemia and the Scandinavian countries had begun. On the other hand the few slaves offered on the market— the word 'slave' derived from 'Slav', the national appellation of the Slavonic peoples—were sold to Byzantium or the Islamic countries where slavery was still usual and slaves brought high prices.

As a result, by the thirteenth century peasant slaves were found only in the Scandinavian countries and East Germany, along the trade routes followed by slave gangs on the way to Russia, Byzantium and Islam, and in the countries that bordered the Mediterranean to the West. In Spain and Portugal raids organized by the Christian conquerors supplied great numbers of Muslim slaves in addition to Negroes imported by traders and Christian Sardinians kidnapped by unscrupulous fellow-believers or by pirates. In Provence, Italy, Sicily, the Venetian islands and the Latin states of the Levant most slaves worked in the towns, the males serving as craftsmen's aides, the females as domestic servants. But in Sicily, Liguria and Crete many worked on the land; this may have been due to the drop in population, but more probably to the difficulty of using draught animals on the steep slopes or to the necessity of cultivating new crops or making the most of small plots.

This led to the presence in the country round about Genoa, Barcelona, Palermo and Candia of a certain number of Greeks, Bulgarians, Russians and Tartars, whom their masters lost no time in having

Four fifteenth-century statues on the Town Hall at Überlingen represent peasants carrying different tributes. From left to right: money, vegetables, grain and meat.

baptized. The conquest of Madiera, the Azores, the Canary Islands, the Antilles and the American continent by Western Europeans accustomed to employing slave labour on the land explains how an organized slave trade could continue well into the nineteenth century and make a profound impact on the settlement of both North and South America.

Living conditions varied greatly even among the rural slaves. During the Merovingian and Carolingian periods most of them were herded together in the immediate vicinity of the owner's house and worked under the supervision of an overseer, while their womenfolk spun and wove in the women's quarters. There were also settled slaves who lived on their own for two or three days a week cultivating their small holdings and occupying cabins where they brought up their families. In the Mediterranean countries at the end of the Middle Ages slaves cost so much money that their owners employed them singly, took care not to wear them out prematurely by overworking them, and ended up by considering them more or less as farm-hands.

Incidentally, all slaves could save up money to purchase their freedom; those funds were seldom impounded by the master.

At the end of the Middle Ages old slaves were virtually always emancipated when they could no longer do enough work to pay for their keep. From the Merovingian period many slaves were set free by their owners' will. Very likely the small number of half-free men found in the country districts of France during the Carolingian period were identical with these freedmen, whose way of life and economic situation differed little from those of real slaves.

The same might be said of the serfs—the term derived from 'servus', the Latin word for slave—who were so typical a feature of the countryside in the Middle Ages. But, apart from the linguistic connection and the very strong feeling at the time that they formed the most depressed social category, serfs were entirely different from slaves.

Serfs were only partly descended from the ancient slaves. In fact, in Carolingian times the vast majority of the rural population consisted of tenant farmers who had the legal status of freemen. They did not own the small holdings on which they were settled and for which they paid rent and performed services. They could not leave the estate, nor dispose of their holdings, nor marry without the landowner's consent. But in principle those 'coloni' could not be evicted and enjoyed certain rights. Though economically dependant on the landowner, they were considered freemen by the state. Under Charlemagne they were liable for military service or for a tax in lieu payable in cash or kind; they could take oaths and were responsible before public courts. It should be noted, however, that though under Germanic law all freemen belonged to the district court, they took less and less part in its proceedings. In many cases they applied not to the count's court, which was gradually monopolized by the big landowners, but to the lower court of the hundred presided over by the sheriff or headman of the hundred, who was subordinate to the count.

To draw a map of serfdom at the beginning of the twelfth century involves reducing all forms of servitude to one common denominator—a very difficult matter. It would seem more sensible to define its territorial distribution after Robert Fossier (opposite). From the thirteenth century serfdom survived only in England, the Languedoc, the Pyrenees, the Empire and France, from Poitou to Austria. Everywhere else the majority of peasants were free.

Some historians have suggested that those peasants should be termed half-free. There were, in fact, freemen settled on freeholds (allodia) independently of the domanial system. Unfortunately, it is very difficult to study them because their lands are only mentioned in documents when they were donated, bequeathed or sold to a lay or ecclesiastical lord; in other words, when they were incorporated in a domain. During the tenth and eleventh centuries many of those freemen became dependant on a powerful neighbour to whom they surrendered their land and their freedom in exchange for adequate protection. Some placed themselves at the service of a saint and of the clergy who represented him on earth; others exchanged a stable for a servile tenure involving heavy duties. The very generalized trend of these duties from personal to territorial, for complex but clearly defined reasons, explains how a great many men who were free, half-free or freed were reduced to the economic level of settled slaves. They were subject to field service though they still paid the taxes that their forbears had freely accepted as voluntary dependants. Once they had lost the right to bear arms and, later, to appear before the public courts, usurped by the descendents of the count or their landlord, they ceased to be viewed as freemen and could neither testify nor dispose of their holdings. It should also be said that occasionally free peasants were forcibly enslaved: in the thirteenth century in Southern France by Simon de Montfort's barons because suspected of the Catharist heresy; in Spain by the lords of the Reconquista because rebellious Muslims; in England in the twelfth century when Anglo-Saxons were deprived of their rights by the Normans and came to be viewed as serfs.

The diverse origin of these serfs explains their uneven geographical distribution. R. Fossier recently established a map showing the approximate percentage of serfs in the various regions. It gives between 0 and 10 per cent in Normandy, Picardy, Saxony, Lombardy, Old Castile and most of the Scandinavian countries where the slaves did not become serfs; between 12 and 25 per cent in Pied-

mont, Aquitaine, Ile-de-France, the Rhone valley, Tuscany, Flanders and Burgundy; and 50 per cent or more in the Lower Loire, Poitou, Berry, Champagne, Upper Lorraine, Franconia, Bavaria and Bohemia.

Another problem is to define the notion of serfdom, in view of the fact that there were different degrees of dependance and that the available texts are often conflicting. Judging from R. Fossier's summary, it would seem that medieval scholars nowadays stress three major aspects. The first is moral and, in keeping with the ancient view of slavery, involved public flogging, shackling of escaped serfs, restrictions on marriage, prohibition to enter religious orders, etcetera. The second is personal and involved payment of a poll tax, and very heavy, lifelong, daily work in the service of the master who in some cases owned the serf's very body.

Where dues linked with land tenure were concerned, these seem to have differed very slightly, if at all, from those paid by free tenants—field service, quit-rent, a fixed or proportional fraction of the produce, and the like. It was only in the matter of inheritance that the serfs were at a disadvantage. Not that the lord seized everything at their death as in the case of mortmain, for that would have discouraged the will to save or to work more than the absolute minimum; but a part of the heritage (half the land, or the best goods or animal) went to the lord. In cases of escheat, when there was no direct heir, the lord was sometimes entitled to resume possession of the entire holding.

Marxist historians have endeavoured to transcend all the differences of detail between one group of dependant peasants and another, and considered serfs those workers 'who do not enjoy complete personal freedom: there is no personal slavery but the peasant is bound to his master *(Homo proprius)* and later to his domain *(adscriptus glebe)*. Thus the status of free peasant tended towards a status of bondage under which every peasant, though disposing of implements and the usufruct of a farm, is bound to an owner in chief, the lord, by all sorts of personal obligations and dues.'

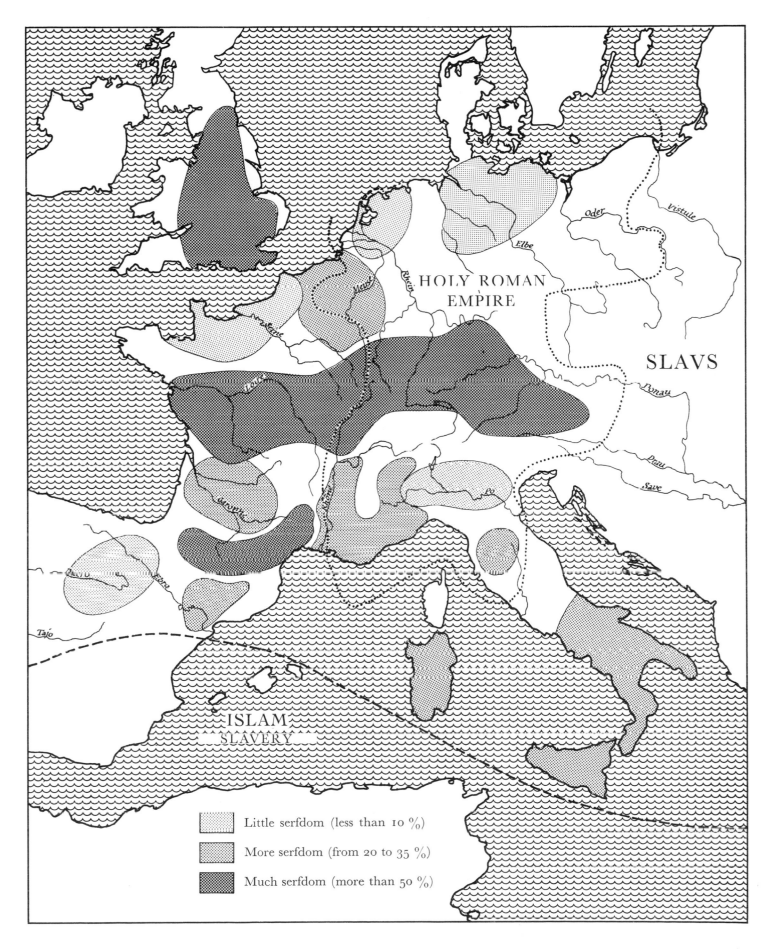

SLAVS

HOLY ROMAN
EMPIRE

ISLAM
SLAVERY

Oder
Vistule
Elbe
Rhein
Meuse
Donau
Drau
Save
Po
Tajo
Ebro

Little serfdom (less than 10 %)

More serfdom (from 20 to 35 %)

Much serfdom (more than 50 %)

From this angle, part of the peasants whom their contemporaries viewed as freemen were serfs; and at certain periods they may well have made up the majority of the population of Western Europe.

Be that as it may, serfdom, which first appeared in the ninth and tenth centuries and had become established by the eleventh, diminished and in some regions even disappeared in the thirteenth. Fugitive serfs won their freedom in the towns where they settled; serfs summoned to clear the land on a neighbouring domain stayed on as free strangers; many others, having put aside a little money saved from the sale of their scanty surplus, wanted to remove the degrading blot of servitude. They bought their freedom from their lord, either singly or collectively, at a very high price, while at the same time field service was reduced to a minimum because of the greater supply of manpower and the smaller area of the reserve. But the economic situation of those freed serfs was not always to be envied. Many of them had incurred a debt in order to gain their freedom and put their land in pawn. The most unfortunate had to work as hired labourers to make a living and became dependant on their creditors.

When bad times set in at the end of the thirteenth century and the beginning of the fourteenth, many former serfs seem to have fallen into a state of impoverishment and mendicity. Most of them either entered the service of a rich master or became serfs again. They joined up with ruined peasants who were too poor to stand on their own feet or pay the poll tax. In East Germany, where the peasants who had voluntarily settled the virgin lands were freemen, the lords—they were called Junkers—began to exert a rigid control in the fifteenth century. In Russia serfdom appeared very late, when the country started to be westernized, and continued until the end of the nineteenth century. Thus right up to the French Revolution there existed in the West a class of underlings who were often bound to the land and were just as heavily burdened as their predecessors.

On the other hand, the differences in the living standards of the peasantry were stressed by the rise of a thin, yet solid stratum of well-off, even rich, yeomen farmers. True, before the time of Charlemagne there had been, alongside the great landowners, some small freeholders who were liable for military service but were mostly engaged in husbandry. But that class had been reduced in number during the eighth and ninth centuries for two major reasons: first, because some freemen became vassals and entered the knightly class; and secondly, because others became dependants or serfs. The survivors joined forces with the freedmen and independent coloni to form the very numerous medium peasant class—of which we know little more than that it was subject to the lords who owned the land and the castles that protected it, or were vested with the right to administer justice. The richest or most favoured of the peasant class succeeded in finding a place among the gentry, being knighted or the like.

But the thirteenth century also saw the rise, in the village communities in which the peasants were concentrated, of a well-off minority who owned not only livestock, ploughs and other means of production, but also the most extensive and fertile farms. Some of those yeomen farmers were descended from the gentry who had not been able to maintain their rank and had set to farming the remnants of their estates themselves. Most of them were peasants who had made good either as a lord's domestic serfs, or on a less fragmented or more fertile holding, or because they were stronger or luckier than their fellows. They had achieved a dominant position in the community and joined together a number of plots by lending money with the land as surety or buying up escheated plots or allodial tenures whose price had dropped when the pressure of population diminished or because the impoverished owners had gone away.

In extreme cases those well-off peasants farmed some seigniorial rights and so gained entry to the nobility without enjoying the king's favour or holding high office.

Those yeomen farmers had a far easier life than the other peasants, the serfs or the rural slaves. We must bear this in mind even if the natural and technical

Payments in kind were delivered at the castle, where they were counted and checked. When the quantities were fixed, measures like this one in the Castle of Dinan (Nord) were used.

The ecclesiastical lord collected a variety of dues: rents in cash and in kind from his lands, fees payable to him as a lord and those payable to the Church. Revenues in cash were counted and booked (right); payments in kind were carefully checked (above).

problems that beset the rural society allow us to take a global view of it; it still had its slight influence.

On the other hand it would be wrong to overstress these differences. In fact, from the Merovingian period, the settled slaves and coloni of the big estates were linked by strong economic ties. This was all the more true of the free smallholders in whom the Frankish tradition of pasturage, common usage, sheriff's or hundred's courts, group departures for the army, strengthened the community spirit. This had sprung, in the Romanized parts of Europe, from collective liability for the Constantinian tax and had been fostered by common economic interdependence due to the rotation of crops, the overlapping of plots, and the passage of flocks entailing the fencing of sown fields. The village community crystallized around its church in the same way as the domanial community grew up in the shadow of the manor. The importance of these units in Frisia, Sweden and England up to the end of the eleventh century is well known, but they also continued to exist in Western Europe during the Carolingian and post-Carolingian periods.

There were other cohesive factors too. First, in the old communities subject at least to the military authority of the lord with the economic and fiscal consequences that involved; those communities sometimes merged with ancient domanial units and, in particular, formed more solid defensive ties among themselves aimed less at the lord than at new arrivals or dissident members who wanted to evade their control. Secondly, in the new communities; most of these were established under the authority of a lord for a prolonged joint effort—colonization or clearance work—which often involved collective activities such as crop rotation, maintenance of dams or watching over commons; other communities sprang up around a church or under the protection of a patron saint. They were founded on well-defined customs or privileges applied under the supervision of a headman and had a partly independent court as well as one or two deliberative assemblies, membership of which was first limited to freemen and later made accessible to all male villagers. The assemblies were a typical feature of those communities. Their frequent meetings enabled the peasants to become better acquainted and settle disputes of minor importance. They strengthened ties of all kinds and offered the possibility of compounding or redeeming the talliage and extending immunities. When the lord defaulted they sometimes took his place in maintaining order and organizing defensive operations.

The lord was another cohesive factor, particularly if he held the right to command, constrain and punish. That right was originally public and was usurped at the dissolution of the Carolingian empire by officials to whom it had been delegated, notably the counts. The administration of justice was split

The exasperated peasants sometimes revolted, but they seldom succeeded in keeping their freedom for any length of time. Above: the peasant leader Peter Amstalden in 1478 administers justice in the Swiss village of Schupfheim.

Top right: the poorest peasants possessed only their hands and a few very simple implements. They had the greatest difficulty in paying their taxes, and their creditors pressed them hard for any debts they incurred.

Opposite page: The pillory erected in front of the bailiff's house at Braine-le-Château was a reminder of the duty to be prudent and obey the lord. This must have been quite a common sight in towns and villages throughout the land.

Very often the clergy acted as counsellors, intermediaries and moderators by turns. Above: In 1478 the discontented of Niklashausen (Baden) gathered to listen to advice from the parish priest Pfeiffer.

To quell revolts the lords or the municipal authorities sent in soldiers who, in the heat of battle, exceeded their orders and gave their taste for violence a free rein. Not a soul was spared. The doors were broken open with a battering ram and the houses pillaged and often set on fire either carelessly or on purpose. The miniature on the left shows a band of soldiers storming and sacking a village in Swabia.

The banner of the peasants of Entlebuch dates from the fourteenth century. It bears a tree whose seven branches represent the seven communes of the valley. But it has a deeper symbolic meaning: the tree represents life, the three roots the Trinity, the seven branches the days of the Creation, and the four leaves on each branch grow towards the four points of the compass.

When pushed to extremes, the peasants sometimes formed bands to take vengeance for the extortions they were forced to endure. They preferred to attack when they were certain of victory. A solitary knight did not have a chance: he was slaughtered with hatchets and daggers. After committing their crime, the 'redressers of wrongs' disappeared; they could count on the population keeping silent (below).

On Sundays and feast days the common people gathered round their parish priest to sanctify the Lord's Day. In the castle lords and servants assembled in the chapel to listen to the chaplain. The nobles sat on benches, the servants on the floor, but the sermon was the same for both. The voice from the pulpit dwelt on the truths and commandments intended equally for the weak and the powerful, the poor and the rich.

up into three grades, high, low and middle. As a result a powerful lord, who was also high justiciar, took advantage of his situation to force all the peasants of the neighbouring parishes, whether freeholders, dependants of small landowners, or those settled on his own lands, to pay heavy dues in exchange for his alleged keeping of the peace. These 'customs' or 'imposts' became established in the eleventh century. The most well-known are the economic monopolies which the French call 'banalités': the lord, perhaps as a very big landowner but probably as heir to the public authority, built a mill, a wine press or a bakehouse, or kept a stud bull or boar; they were made available at a price to the peasants, who were obliged to make use of those facilities. The lord was also empowered to forbid his peasants to compete with him when he disposed of the dregs of his wine casks; he could exact talliage when he needed money, billet his servants on the tenants and requisition provisions. As a rule he owned a castle—the lord of the manor was the king-pin of the fighting class—and took that as a pretext for additional extortions: the peasants had to keep the castle in repair and the roads that led to it, feed the garrison and their horses, and pay for the right to take refuge within its walls. They were also liable to be called up as militia infantry, watchmen or fortress guards; to be exempted they had to pay.

All this offered the villagers a great many occasions to meet and discuss matters, and so fostered solidarity in the face of their common obligations. The small landowners who were not rich enough to have a castle, and therefore became vassals of those who had one, also gave their tenants, both serfs and freemen, occasion to join forces and work together; many of them were part of the village community, on which they exerted a strong influence.

Sometimes the lords provided a focal point for the discontent of the rural communities of the whole region. When that happened the peasants united against the nobles to impose a truce of God in agreement with the clergy, as in the Angoumois at the beginning of the eleventh century; or acted to stop the pillage and armed robbery by brigandish nobles, as in Northern France. All through the thirteenth century they took concerted action to abolish anachronistic services and oppressive taxes. But the real terroristic revolts against the nobles, known as the Jacqueries, took place in the fourteenth and fifteenth centuries, a critical period marked by the decline of the Church and the nobility and the concentration of power in the hands of the king. The causes were many, but there is reason to believe that in Flanders before 1328, the Ile-de-France in 1358, Aragon and Catalonia in 1350 and 1388, Languedoc, Normandy and England from 1381 to 1383, it was the well-off peasants who took the lead in a struggle aimed chiefly at safeguarding their privileges. They were quite naturally joined by the humble, sweated peasants and a few poor wretches, but that did not give their action a less clearly selfish character.

The movement was really revolutionary only where a new ideology opposed to the traditional order sought to replace the classic Christian doctrine. This was the case of the Lollards, the followers of John Wycliffe, in England (1408–20) and the Czech Taborites and Adamites, who sprang from the Hussite heresy and preached an elementary communism; they opposed the nobles not only because of

class hatred but were also inspired by anti-German nationalism. The vast revolt of the *Bund ob dem See*, which spread to Swabia, in South-West Germany, and the regions around Lake Constance and Saint-Gall at the end of the fourteenth century and the beginning of the fifteenth, succeeded at one point in controlling sixty towns and strongholds, razing thirty castles and temporarily subduing a great many lords; but it ended in a miserable compromise. It was not until the peasant war of 1525 that the struggle against the nobles was pushed to extremes.

During the whole course of the Middle Ages the explosions of peasant fury were very limited in both place and time. They were not a feature of everyday life, unfolding in the shadow of the castle or around the parish church. Indeed, the church and its priest rather than the castle and its lord were the major factors in the peasants' life and forged the ties that made them a community. It was to the church that they went to attend Mass, listen to a sermon, hear the news, and even meet to organize the struggle against the lord. There they joined to worship their patron saint, receive the sacraments, have their children christened and bury their parents. They kept the building in repair and sometimes even fortified it as a refuge in case of need; they paid tithes at the church door, held fairs and markets on the square before it, and welcomed pilgrims and strangers there. It was in the church that the poor were given food. The church bell marked the hours of the day and rang the Angelus to call home belated workers from the fields.

There is no denying that the peasants led a hard life, particularly the poorest of them; but it must have been some comfort, if cold, to feel a member of a community, with the very real advantages that involved. The castle was seldom, the church never, the focal point of the hate of those who lived in their shadow or under their law. More often than not they were seen as guarantees of a law and order for which they were responsible and which may have been strict but in the long run was advantageous and therefore accepted.

I FIGHT FOR ALL: the Warrior

If we are to believe the mediocre dialogue of Placidus and Timaeus written by a French clerk in the reign of Philip the Fair (1285–1314), the origin of the knightly class should be sought in ancient Greece. There the boldest, most solidly built males were entrusted with the task of defending the community. But those 'knights' followed in the footsteps of their Hebrew colleague Nimrod who, after building a first stronghold, attacked all the people who happened to come within reach and held them to ransom. The sums they paid were the first taxes. Thus might triumphed over right. 'For, in the natural way, all things of every sort that come from the earth are common to all men. But, by reason of force and greed disordered and wrongly used, lands and provinces have been and are today variously appropriated and divided into empires, kingdoms, duchies, counties, baronies; and the common people outrageously taxed, plundered and ruined.'

These ideas, probably current in the fourteenth century, dated from the thirteenth. They were not original and merely mirrored the mentality of certain social groups at what was a critical time for the fighting class. It is far from certain that they matched a real situation and that the problems they posed were central to the feudal society. The strongest members of that society, having gradually formed a hierarchized class, may well have forced the workers to accept their protection under threat and at the cost of heavy taxes and extortions.

THE RISE AND GROWTH OF THE KNIGHTLY CLASS

A classic scheme that covered the entire Western World and was valid for close on a thousand years (from the eighth century to the eighteenth) shows us a 'vassal' doing 'homage', namely taking an oath of fealty and promising to give military service, to a 'lord'; the latter, in return, undertook to protect him and granted him a source of revenue, termed a 'fief', which was usually a piece of land.

This monumental Gothic sculpture belongs to Bamberg Cathedral. The rider is believed to be St Stephen, King of Hungary (969–1038). He gives the impression of being a noble lord rather than a fighting man.

The pledge of fealty and devotion on the one hand and of protection on the other, given and received by two free men who were as a rule warriors, and the personal bonds that tied them, derived probably from the Indo-European society if they were not indeed indispensable features of every primitive society. Comradeship existed among the ancient Gauls and Germans; in Rome the bond between patron and client was very strong; so were those, in the days of the Late Empire, between big landowners and smallholders, between the emperor and his barbarian guard, between a chieftain and his henchmen.

The arrival of the Germans and the spread of Germanic customs destroyed the Roman concept of the state. The victorious warriors and the wealthy aristocracy had a dominating influence on the mass of the vanquished workers and slaves, and the lot of the poor freemen was very hard in those troublous times. This stressed the existence of two fundamental needs—subsistence and protection.

The freemen who had no means of their own did their best to find a leader or patron who would protect and feed them, while the leaders were on the lookout for fighting men to guard them and boost their power. The result was a contract or mutual bond between two people who were equal before the law—the 'senior' who was older and had a purely moral superiority, and the 'junior' who was younger and became his disciple. One promised to protect and keep the other, who implored his protection, promising him obedience and military aid, and surrendered his independence for life without losing his freedom.

The first Carolingians, while still mayors of the palace, gathered around them a great many of those protégés, who helped them to seize the throne. Once they had become kings or emperors, they demanded from some of their fighting men, in addition to the oath of fealty taken by all the freemen of the Empire, a personal bond that was far more exacting. Those faithful supporters, called *vassi dominici* (royal vassals), were granted public offices and became the permanent leaders of the army. Thanks to their strong position they had vassals of their own, whom they led to the army or the king's court of law.

The monarch encouraged the freemen to enter the service of the magnates and the latter to become his vassals; he hoped in that way to strengthen the reborn state by a network of subordination of which he would hold all the threads. Actually, vassalage was far more exacting than mere fealty to the king, who came to be separated from the rear vassals by the mediate lord. The latter's power grew for various reasons. In the eyes of the local population he was alone in the fight against successive waves of invaders —Normans, Saracens and Hungarians; the quarrels between contenders for the Carolingian succession made his homage a salable commodity, on a par with simple fealty, and ruined the monarchs who tried to buy it in turn; a great lord to whom part of the royal powers had been delegated and who had many vassals of his own enjoyed a *de facto* independence limited in law solely by the obligations he freely accepted towards the king. It must be pointed out, however, that as early as 895 vassals began to choose more than one lord. In the thirteenth century some had twenty lords, one no fewer than forty-three. And the ties of vassalage spread through various steps. By the tenth century only the lowest rank of vassals, who really needed protection, were still closely dependant on the mediate lord who shielded and supported them.

There is a famous document which gives a good idea of a vassal's obligations and shows how relatively unimportant they were. It is a letter from Bishop Fulbert of Chartres to Duke William of Aquitaine, written about 1020, and the prescriptions it contains applied to vassals of low standing. Needless to say, they must take the lord's interests to heart. They must also advise him, sit on his court, help him to administer justice, notably in judging their peers, and show their solidarity with him at all times. They must further give him military and pecuniary aid. Military aid was a very heavy burden because, when

The Norman kings of England and Sicily created direct vassals who owed them personal service and so formed the largest feudal armies in the West. Here a knight receives his sword from the sovereign in person after swearing fealty to him.

After the Conquest of England, William the Conqueror in 1087 had a survey made of all the resources of the country. The results were recorded in the Domesday Book. The work got its name from the precision and justice with which the inquiry was made; there was none other like it in the Middle Ages.

the infantry fell into disrepute in the eighth century, it demanded a charger, a strong sword, a lance and very well made defensive armour (helmet, breastplate and shield) and involved constant training and a service that theoretically was limited neither in space nor in time. Pecuniary aid was not greatly developed before coins became common; it was restricted to half-a-dozen exceptional occasions—the knighting of the lord's eldest son, the marriage of his eldest daughter, the payment of a ransom, the departure for a crusade, and a double obligation towards a new emperor. In fact, the trend was towards a strict limitation of the various types of aid, which multiple vassalage, royal intervention and the introduction of the wage system rendered less effective and useful. In principle the vassal's obligations were balanced by those of the lord, who protected him almost as if he was a member of the family, gave him presents, food and clothing, and granted him a

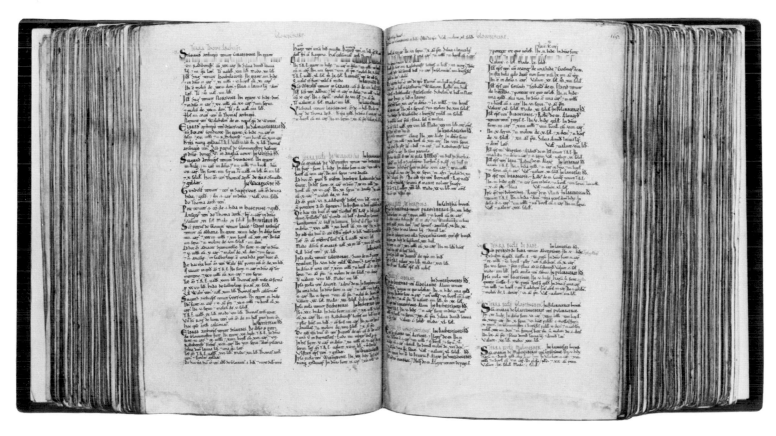

The sovereign power can be recognised by its attributes. The Emperor Otto III (above left), crowned and seated on his throne, holding the staff and globe which prove his spiritual and temporal authority. Above right: the coronation glove of the kings of Sicily. Below: the coronation robe of Charlemagne with golden eagles on a purple ground. Opposite: the globe surmounted by a cross.

184

Charlemagne, after the manner of a thirteenth-century king, grants a fief to one of his barons in the presence of a bishop. He hands him first a banner, then an unsheathed sword (top row). The knight will owe homage and assistance to his sovereign, whom he salutes here (bottom row) on taking leave. Armorial bearings served first to identify individuals, later families; they spread through the West.

On receiving his fief a knight built himself a castle aided by his men—if he had the means to do so—and became a lord of the manor (above).

source of revenue to enable him to do his service. This mutual relationship between lord and vassal and their legal, if not hierarchical, equality was emphasized by a ceremony which became definitely established between the end of the eight century and the tenth. The future vassal, on his knees, placed his joined hands between those of his lord, who raised him to his feet—in France and Italy from the end of the tenth century he kissed him too; it also became customary in the early eleventh century for the vassal to take an oath resting his right hand on a sacred object. This symbol of homage and fealty was followed by the investiture: the lord presented the vassal with a sceptre, a banner, a wand and a sod, as an emblem of the material counterpart of his vassalage, namely the grant of a benefice or, from the tenth century, of a fief.

From the early Middle Ages a fighting man who entered the service of a lord had to possess the means to acquire and maintain his arms and war-horse, besides feeding himself and his family. The lord could keep him at his side, lodging him in his house and paying all his expenses, but it was no easy matter

to collect large quantities of stores and lodge and feed a vast number of dependants; this led him to pay them a wage or rather, since money was very scarce, to grant them a source of revenue called a benefice. But even the richest lords could not continue to give land in full ownership to their followers. In the long run it ruined the Merovingian kings in spite of the conquests, confiscations and heritages that more than once restored their patrimony. On the other hand, it was hardly right for a man who left a lord's service to keep the benefice which could be viewed as the counterpart of that service. Lastly, Roman law recognized a type of tenure called *precarium*, which was adopted in a greatly modified form by the Franks; under the Merovingians it was used to enable lands to be granted in usufruct to a beneficiary either for a term of years or for life without the owner losing his vested rights.

The first Carolingian emperors stressed the military nature of the services performed by the vassals to whom they granted benefices of that type, namely lands in temporary tenure; when the service ended the usufruct ended too and the benefice reverted to

The present-day layout of Castle Bolton in Yorkshire bears witness to the relations between the lord and his tenants in ancient times. The castle stands in the centre of the estate; the villagers' houses line the road that leads to it. Each house faces the road and backs on to the fields. The life of the community was circumscribed by the manor.

the lord, who granted it to a new vassal in exchange for the same service. High officials, like counts and bishops, who took an oath of fealty to the king received a special endowment termed an honour, also in the shape of a piece of land, for the purpose of performing their duties. In this case too when the duties ceased the honour reverted to the sovereign. Thus a king's vassal could accumulate, in addition to his own allodial lands, a benefice as a counterpart to his status as a vassal and an honour if he was a count. He must have found it difficult to distinguish between those three different types of property. So it was natural that when the bonds that tied him to the sovereign were relaxed, the honour and the benefice, confused with the allodia, risked being considered as hereditary.

The hereditary benefice, usually in the shape of land, was exactly the same as a fief. The Capitulary of Quierzy in 877 explicitly sanctioned the hereditary principle and to some extent treated honours and benefices on a par. In Italy the constitution of 1037 gave formal sanction to the hereditary transmission of fiefs by the emperor's rear vassals. It must be said that very often to avoid that would have been no easy matter. In fact, where was a new vassal to be found outside the family of the previous one? Furthermore it would also be practically impossible to dislodge the family from the fief it occupied. And when a small landowner in search of protection surrendered his allodium to a lord who handed it back to him as a fief, how could his legitimate heir be deprived of a holding that had been in the family from time immemorial? On the other hand, a vassal already in possession of a fief for which he had done homage to a lord was obliged to do homage to another lord if he wanted to keep a fief that he happened to inherit. Thus heredity was one of the causes of the plurality of homages, on a par with the lord's desire to receive surcties and the vassal's cagerness to be granted several fiefs. Thus the fief, which was the concrete object of the contract between the lord and the vassal, became also the primary one, and the service became secondary.

The king was the supreme judge of both the weak and the powerful. St Louis punished Enguerrand de Coucy for hanging three noble youths found armed with bows and arrows in his woods.

To begin with a man who became a vassal received a benefice. In the ninth and tenth centuries some who wanted to receive a benefice or had inherited one were willing to do homage and swear fealty in order to obtain legal possession. From the eleventh century the overwhelming majority became vassals only to obtain or keep a fief.

Thus the fief developed into a hereditary benefice whose holder did homage, swore fealty and performed military or other service for the lord who remained its owner in chief. The fief retained most of the features of the benefice. When granted in usufruct it had to be adequately kept up; it could not be diminished or disposed of (by sale, donation or transfer to the Church) without the lord's approval, which could only be obtained by paying a fee equal, for instance, to one-fifth of the selling price, redemption, donation or due. On a vassal's death his fief fell vacant; the lord, as owner in chief, authorized the heir to 'take it up' on payment of an oppressive fee termed 'relief'; and the vassal was bound by what was called the right to shelter to receive his lord on his estate. Conflicts between heredity and the performance of military service by the holder of a fief no doubt arose when the heir was a minor, an unmarried woman, or there was more than one heir, but usage often tended to mitigate and check them. A fief as a source of revenue was not necessarily based on land; it might consist of certain rights, to collect tolls, court fees, etcetera, like those granted by the emperor to the Countess of Hainaut; ownership of groups of serfs; or a money income in countries and at times when coins were more common and great lords and monarchs had large revenues.

But as a general rule a fief was linked with the land and consisted of a domain with a certain number of peasants whose labour put the feudal vassal, in his capacity as rural lord, in a position to keep himself and carry out his duties. In fact, he collected quit-rent, tithes, or a share of the produce of newly cleared land. Dues like those for permission to marry outside the domain, and the privilege of day-work on the reserve when the latter was extensive and manpower scarce. Frequently a number of rural manors, some of which might be allodial, were centred round a castle whose lord, from the end of the eleventh century, exerted the right to command, constrain and punish.

As we have already seen, all the peasants of those manors were under various obligations; for instance, to respect the economic monopolies termed *banalités* in France, pay talliage, obey requisitions of all sorts, appear in court, and pay the fines inflicted by it.

In the early days the typical feature of the feudal system was that basic unit, a castellany with from ten to thirty rural parishes, sometimes more, in the

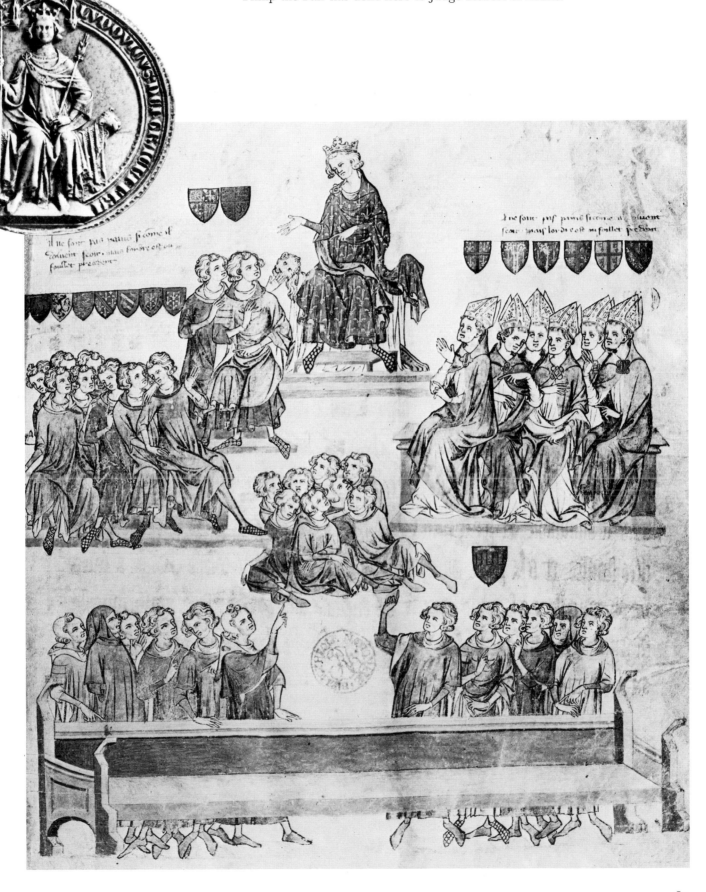

The 'great seal' was affixed to royal documents; this is Louis X the Hutin's.
The king could also summon his lay barons (below) to solemn sessions, as
Philip the Fair has done here to judge Robert of Artois.

A king's prime duty is to administer justice; he must therefore
be accessible to all comers. Here Alfonso X the Wise (1221–
1284) of Castile and Leon is judging his Christian and Muslim
subjects. Alfonso was famed for his absolute impartiality and
tolerant attitude towards his people. The king's canting arms,
the castle of Castile and the lion of Leon, are embroidered on
the fabric which covers the throne.

firmly established on their lands and bound by the
solid ties forged by insecurity and economic adversity.
They tended to form a caste that led the same life
and strengthened the bonds of kinship by marriages
between clans. A knight could not even imagine the
possibility of sinking to the level of a peasant. His
rank became hereditary, like the fief he received, and
the initiatory, magical rite of dubbing by which a
man entered that class of specialized fighters, though
theoretically open to all brave or rich men, became
increasingly the preserve of knights' sons.

Membership of the nobility did not, however,
depend exclusively on martial prowess. Other
typical traits were wealth based on land, authority
over the peasants and serfs, and linear descent from
a divine or heroic ancestor. But whatever their
origin, the nobles were the only people who ate
their fill, enjoyed total freedom, and had the time to
train and the means to fight on horseback. A forceful
picture of eleventh century society shows us the com-
moner as a peasant on foot carrying his hoe and,
towering above him, the armed lord on horseback.
By degrees the nobles developed a similar mentality
fostered by the same education, the sharing of the
same heroic, martial ideal, and the need to defend
themselves against the same dangers when the
population boom threatened their hereditary estates.
While accepting a hierarchy based on wealth, power
or authority, their clan spirit was strengthened on the
horizontal plane by collective warlike exercises in
unit or column formation. At the beginning of the
thirteenth century, however, a dual crisis developed
within the knightly class. In addition to the lack of
revenue, which had long tended to limit marriage,
preserve the right of primogeniture and keep a family
on its hereditary estates at all costs, there was now
the loss of the military monopoly it had long enjoyed
to the communal militia infantry, the mercenaries
whom the great lords often paid with the commuta-
tion taxes—called *écuage* in England—exacted from
their vassals, and to men of servile origin who were
trained in mounted service by their lord and master
from the eleventh or thirteenth centuries.

shadow of the castle. The man who had been
sufficiently strong, rich or powerful by birth to build
or usurp it was subject only to a distant lord—count,
prince or monarch—whose supervision was very
slack if it existed at all. He governed, judged and
punished the peasants. What is more, he was surrounded by armed horsemen who helped him to
keep law and order; some of the latter were domestic
henchmen who did homage and whom he fed or
settled in rural manors granted them as fiefs; others
were already settled vassals or small landed proprietors who were not powerful enough to have a
castle and had become his vassals by receiving from
him as fiefs the lands they had formerly held in
freehold. These small feudatories occupied a subordinate but honourable position. They were
grouped in close-knit clans and families, which were

Although supreme lord, the king was compelled to accept limits to his powers and grant his subjects freedoms and guarantees like those contained in the Magna Carta of England in 1215 (below).

As the premier nobleman, the king settled disputes over armorial bearings, as 'Good King René' is doing here.

The king was commander-in-chief of the army. Its core was formed by heavily armoured knights who were flanked by a steadily increasing number of foot soldiers, whose pikes could stop a cavalry charge.

while strengthening the
..lies, first among them the
..nse of the petty landowners.
..ed many details to this overall
.., where vassals of all levels, from
..or to territorial princes, had been
..dependent, the Capetian monarchy
its hold under Philip Augustus and
.. in the thirteenth century; later Louis XI
..e of Beaujeu succeeded in 'domesticating' a
..many nobles.

.. England the feudal system imported from
..ormandy by William the Conqueror became very
strict and highly centralized under the Plantagents;
and in spite of Magna Carta and the growing power
of Parliament, the Tudors had little reason to envy
their predecessors when faced by a nobility decimated by the Hundred Years War and the Wars of
the Roses.

In the Empire the Ottonians at the end of the
tenth century and the beginning of the eleventh
regained control of the great vassals and the lesser
lords, basing their power on ecclesiastical feudalism;
but after the House of Hohenstaufen, from mid-
twelfth to mid-thirteenth century, the German kings
succeeded only in consolidating or establishing a
strong territorial basis for their family *(Hausmacht)*,
while the gentry were domesticated or enregimented
by the princes of states that varied in size but were
all equal centralized and independent.

The princes enjoyed a very different status *(Für-
stenstand)* from the counts *(Grafen)*, lords *(Herren)* or
knights *(Ritter)*. This latter class was filled with
impoverished nobles and former officials of kings or
lords. Many of them were of servile origin but,
having for that reason won the confidence of the
master on whom they were totally dependant, they
had been entrusted with important functions and
had done military service on horseback. The admission of those knightly serfs to the German nobility at
the end of the Middle Ages was a phenomenon of
capital importance.

.s,
.ght
.Some
.ghts by
. England
.ing livestock
.asture; in East
. industrial scale.
.new activities—in
.ing. Some collected
.ncreased tolls and de-
.ts in kind. But the major-
.. and moved to the towns,
.h the peasants, or relied on
.richer or luckier than them-
.ered their services to princes or
.rs married their sons or daughters
.sants or burghers. Ruined families
.ldren to feed and bring up—they would
.n unable to do it suitably in any case—
.away and disappeared. They were constantly
.aced by new arrivals, who were ennobled by the
.ngs, by the exercise of the duties of aldermen or
judges, or simply by slow, tireless usurpation, living
the life of the nobles without being entitled to do so
by birth. In France and England the wars of the
fourteenth and fifteenth centuries speeded up the

Castles built of stone were preceded by simple timber structures erected on natural or artificial mounds. Here William the Conqueror's soldiers are setting fire to the mound of Dinant shortly before the Norman Conquest of England.

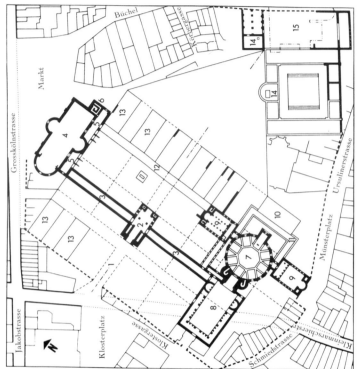

The first strongholds were built between the ninth century and the tenth. Charlemagne's palace at Aix-la-Chapelle was based on a Roman plan transformed in a very original fashion (see model above). At the top, the imperial edifice; on the right, the baths; on the left, the main gate and the court room; at the bottom, the Palatine Chapel. The plan of the palace (above left) shows the following points: 1. Main Avenue; 2. Monumental Gate; 3. Passageways; 4. Throne Room; 5. Arcaded Gallery; 6. Tower; 7. Palatine Chapel; 8. Atrium; 9. Annexes; 10. Court Room; 11. Portico; 12. Timber Connecting Gallery; 13. Buildings; 14. Imperial Baths; 15. Foundations of Roman Baths. The Werla Palace in Brunswick built by Otto I was totally different. It was built on a hill and fortified with moats and walls. Times had changed and safety came first (bottom).

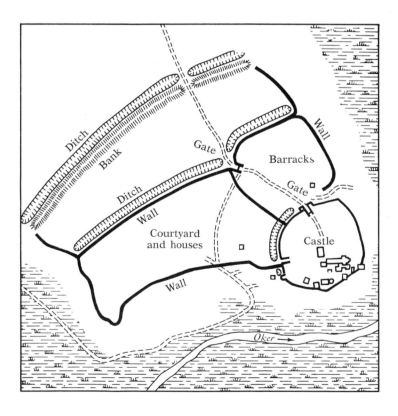

THE DAILY LIFE OF THE NOBILITY

No matter what their financial situation might be, the nobles differed from the rest of the population by their peculiar mentality and way of life. Also by their abode—castle, manor house or city mansion— their luxurious apparel, their abundant and costly fare, their mutual relationships, their life at court involving receptions, dances and games, their courtly sentiments, their strong family ties, and their unproductive, mostly violent occupations—hunting, military training, tourneys, wars, and the like.

It is virtually impossible to describe in any detail the habitat of the magnates before the time of Charlemagne. The rare contemporary texts which mention it are entirely lacking in precision. And very few excavations have uncovered more than Late Empire villas that were still lived in and more or less well kept up during the Merovingian period. Some had been fortified clumsily and in haste, but none

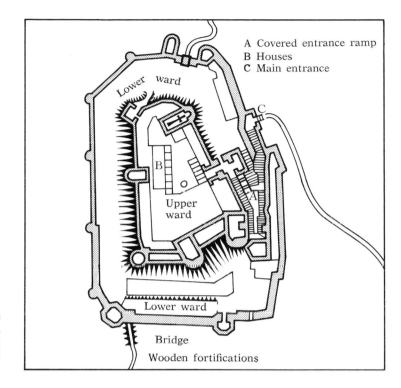

A Covered entrance ramp
B Houses
C Main entrance

Lower ward

Upper ward

Lower ward

Bridge

Wooden fortifications

The plan of the Krak des Chevaliers was inspired by the same safety principle but represents military architecture at its peak of perfection (right). The miniature above shows workmen building a castle; the major features are clear to see: moat full of water, single gate, drawbridge, ring wall and keep.

was redesigned from the ground up for defensive purposes; it is not even certain that they were surrounded by a fence or palisade.

In this respect the royal villas of the Carolingian period did not present any fundamental difference from those of an earlier date. They consisted of a main building surrounded by commons and huts for domestic slaves and peasant dependants. It must be said, in this connection, that for the period from Charlemagne to Otto the Great the excavations have laid bare only princely or ecclesiastical buildings. We have no way of knowing whether less exalted lords lived in houses of the same type.

Nevertheless, it is interesting to compare Charlemagne's palace at Aix-la-Chapelle, finished at the beginning of the ninth century, and the 'palace' of Werla built under Henry the Fowler and his son Otto in the early and middle years of the tenth century. The first found its inspiration in Rome; the second was already a stronghold.

For a long time it was believed that in the tenth and eleventh centuries Western Europe 'bristled' with castles to cope with invasions from without and anarchy within. As a matter of fact, neither the documents nor the vestiges that have been preserved justify that belief. On the contrary, very often the castles were not built until the twelfth century and each one incorporated ten, twenty, thirty or more parishes. So it would be more correct to say that they were thinly spread on the ground. True, some of the thousands of castles erected during that late period were subsequently rebuilt or replaced and have left no trace; besides which, aerial photography and other methods of archaeological investigation have revealed a vast number of mounds that date in fact from the tenth and eleventh centuries.

The overwhelming majority of those mounds mark the position of a stronghold where a lord made his permanent home. Diggings carried out in England, the Netherlands, Denmark, Germany, Bohemia,

The counts of Flanders built a monumental castle, the Gravensteen, at Ghent (above left) where they resided from the early thirteenth century. Its massive outer wall is encircled by a wide, winding waterway and the keep is 100 feet high. The Gravensteen may be viewed as a combined fortress and residence in urban surroundings. Beaumaris Castle in Wales (above) is one of the finest in Britain. It was built to a concentric plan, has a double enclosure and a massive keep astride the walls opposite the heavily fortified gatehouse. A great many castles of this type were built in the West from the thirteenth century on. Haut-Koenigsbourg (left) is set like an eyrie on a rocky crag that dominates the plain of Alsace between Strasbourg and Colmar; its keep dates from the thirteenth century. The Krak des Chevaliers in Syria (below), erected by the Knights of St John of Jerusalem, stands on a partly natural knoll. It has two enclosures; the most exposed side is protected by the living quarters and a massive fort. This is an excellent example of the rectangular plan adapted to a difficult site.

The bishop of Sion, who was also count of the Central Valais, had his residence in the fortified church of Valère (opposite page) built in the thirteenth century on a steep hill which dominates the town.

PARTS OF A CASTLE

1. Machicolation: corbelled stone gallery with loopholes for shooting downwards at a steep angle. (Saint-Servan)

2. Bretesse: isolated corbelled cell for defending a gate. (Aigues-Mortes)

3. Crenelations: rectangular gaps in parapet for shooting at the enemy. (Gisors)

4. Round Way: passageway on top of a ring wall protected on the outer side by a parapet. (Carcassonne)

5. Hoarding: corbelled timber gallery on the top of a wall. (Carcassonne)

6. Gate and Drawbridge: entrance to a stronghold and defensive feature with bridge over the moat in front of the gate. (Vitré)

7. Enclosure: defensive system comprising curtains (plain walls between towers), bailey (space between two walls) and moat. (Carcassonne)

Poland and, more recently, France, leave no doubt on this point. Lords of slight importance increased the height of a natural knoll or raised an entirely new one with earth brought in and piled up by the forced labour of the peasantry; on the summit they built a tower of timber—a material easy to come by at little cost, which did not require skilled workers— thus making a simple castle defended by a moat, a palisade and the steep sides of the mound. The adjoining courtyard, traces of commons and often of a chapel make it clear that this was a permanent residence. There is no denying the resemblance to the 'typical' feudal castle and one can readily believe that, whereas castles built of stone were relatively rare because extremely costly, mounds crowned by a timber tower were very numerous indeed.

As a matter of fact, there was no such thing as a typical feudal castle. They varied enormously with the time, the place, and the rank and fortune of the builder. At the end of the Middle Ages Le Jouvencel's hero amid a ravaged, deserted countryside gazed at 'places inhabited by poor noblemen, namely castles and strongholds that were not large buildings but paltry closes built along old lines... The chamber of the watch-tower was open to the sky and very windy, so that the warder was not well protected on all sides from the wind. In like manner the porter was very subject to heat and sun in summer and to cold and frost in winter...' Many manor houses inhabited by needy nobles were in the same state.

On the other hand, the density and distribution of those castles—and their shape too—varied not only with the period but also with the region—England, Northern France, the Rhineland, borderlands like the two Castiles whose name and coat-of-arms are so suggestive, Southern Italy, Wales, the Slav marches of East Germany, the Holy Land, and many others.

For all their diversity, those castles had at least two features in common: they were permanent residences and designed for rational defence. At first glance, the defensive function was seemingly the most important. Built on a hill, near a river or overlooking a marsh, the structure displayed—to

The mass and height of the huge castle of Vitré (Ille-et-Vilaine) overwhelms the houses that nestle at its foot. Built to a triangular plan on the west of the town, it is flanked by three chief towers at the corners: the keep or St Lawrence Tower (right), the Montafilant Tower (left) and the St Magdalene Tower (in the distance). It is integrated into the town's defence system to provide a last refuge for the lord and the townspeople.

those who observed it looking upwards from the outside—a first enclosure consisting of a palisade or dry-stone wall with or without a moat and a separate section called a barbican to protect the weak point formed by the gateway; a second enclosure several feet thick and up to 200 feet high, as at Angers, girded by a deep moat crossed on a drawbridge and preceded by rows of stakes driven into the ground between moat and wall making the lists; a number of square or round towers with loopholes for shooting arrows through flanked the great curtain wall, which was crowned by a round way shielded by battlements; the round way was also protected by hoardings, of timber at the end of the twelfth century and later of stone, with openings called machicolations for

dropping heavy rocks, molten pitch or boiling oil on the attackers. The double gate with inverted hinges was preceded by a portcullis and surmounted by a walled space from which assailants could be shot down; it was set in a stout bastion whose narrow entrance was often staggered. Inside the enclosure was a courtyard, usually dotted with storehouses, stables, kennels, kitchens, a chapel, a bakehouse, wells or a cistern, workshops for blacksmiths, wheelwrights and the like. At the highest point, often built against the curtain wall, stood a massive tower of considerable height—over 200 feet at Vincennes— and sometimes a group of strong, compact structures; this was the keep, the last line of defence. Fortified towns were built to the same pattern, surrounded by

Inside the castle walls the inmates enjoyed a certain comfort and even luxury. Left: this handsome knocker proves that not every room was open to all comers. Above: the dining hall in this picture is quite luxurious with its fine chimney-piece, glazed windows, carved press and costly tableware. Right: the Count of Foix's great hall was magnificently decorated, as befitted so puissant a lord.

circular walls and dominated by a citadel or castle with towers or a keep which served as a refuge.

But a castle was not built only for defence against a possible enemy or to dominate the countryside from its point of vantage. It was also meant to offer accommodation to the lord, his family, his retainers, and even his vassals and friends. It consisted in the main of a hall and one or more apartments.

The hall was generally found in the keep and, where possible, was very vast because it was there that the lord sat to administer justice, receive visitors and dependants, entertain guests, or simply to eat, converse and even sleep with his henchmen.

The furniture consisted mostly of benches covered with cloth or tapestry, folding chairs, stuffed cushions, chests and, occasionally, cupboards and presses cut in the thick walls. The floor was strewn with scented herbs, flowers and reeds to drive out the strong odour

given off more by the highly-spiced dishes than by the inmates; the latter in fact often found facilities for washing and bathing. Carpets were rare and the walls were sometimes covered with hangings or tapestries, lined with pelts, or plastered and painted. They were often decorated with trophies of the chase, heraldic devices, family trees recalling the lord's descent—with his arms and those of the kinsmen on whom he could count for assistance in time of trouble. A monumental fireplace, in front of which the table was laid on trestles, served to mellow the atmosphere and was the chief source of light during the long winter evenings—being more efficient than wax tapers or tallow candles set in sconces and chandeliers.

Adjoining the all-purpose hall, where some men even slept at night, there were smaller chambers whose use was more clearly defined—bedrooms in

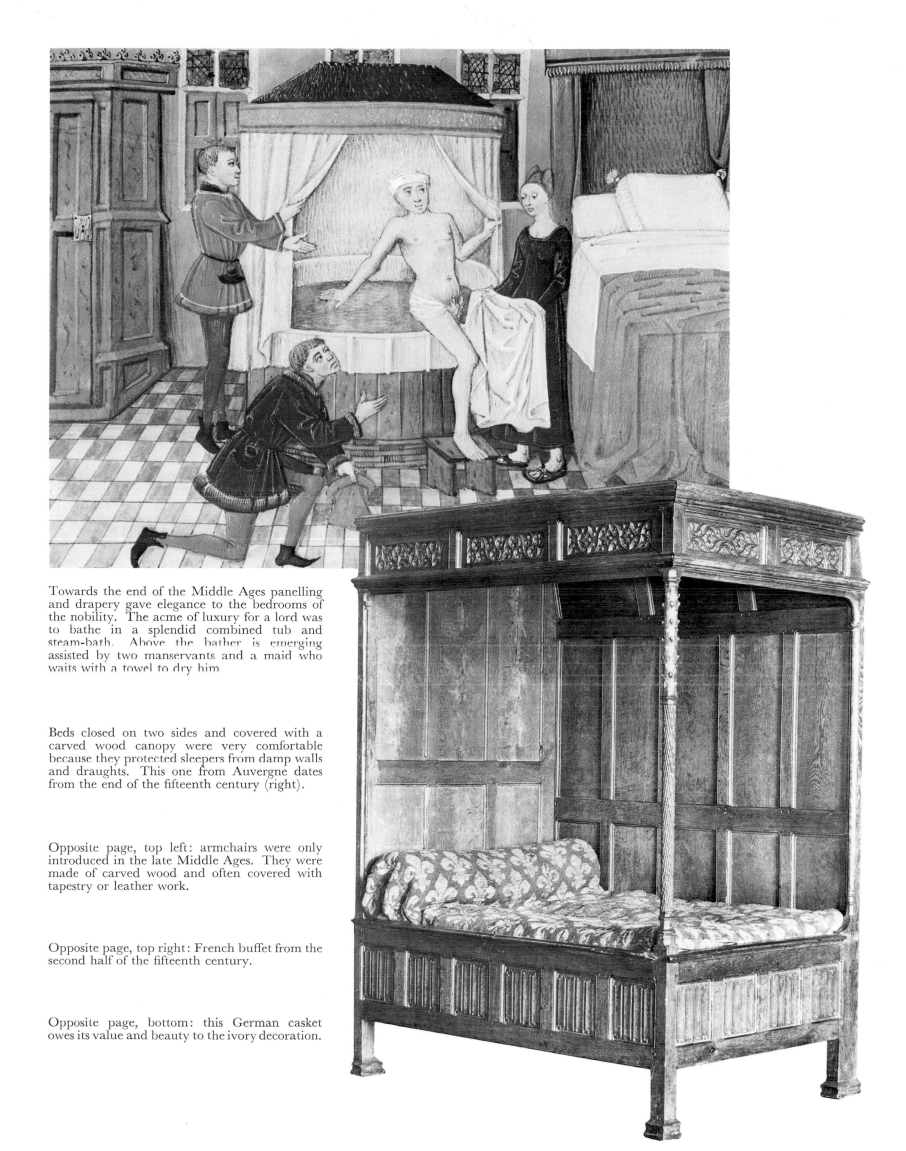

Towards the end of the Middle Ages panelling and drapery gave elegance to the bedrooms of the nobility. The acme of luxury for a lord was to bathe in a splendid combined tub and steam-bath. Above, the bather is emerging assisted by two manservants and a maid who waits with a towel to dry him

Beds closed on two sides and covered with a carved wood canopy were very comfortable because they protected sleepers from damp walls and draughts. This one from Auvergne dates from the end of the fifteenth century (right).

Opposite page, top left: armchairs were only introduced in the late Middle Ages. They were made of carved wood and often covered with tapestry or leather work.

Opposite page, top right: French buffet from the second half of the fifteenth century.

Opposite page, bottom: this German casket owes its value and beauty to the ivory decoration.

Top: kings and noble lords had a well-stocked wardrobe. It was the place where their clothes were looked after and stored in chests.

Outside the great wall or in a secluded courtyard there was often a garden encircled by a fence or trellis that served for growing rare flowers, aromatic herbs or fruit trees; a fountain provided music and coolness. An ideal place for friendly conversation (bottom).

the towers with neither window nor fireplace, containing a huge curtained bed with straw mattress, sheets, blankets or a coverlet that was often gorgeously decorated; guard-rooms; soldiers' quarters; latrines; and a chapel. On the ground floor were the kitchens and stables; in the basement, store-rooms for foodstuffs and equipment, with sometimes a dungeon or the mouth of an underground passage leading outside the walls. Beyond the walls was the orchard, where the lord might walk and the ladies meet their lovers. Some royal and princely castles, such as Pierrefonds and Haut Koenigsbourg, which have been restored with more scholarship than taste, were designed with a keener eye for comfort; in the villas that studded the Italian countryside in the fourteenth and fifteenth centuries this was pushed to the point where defence disappeared.

In any case, even a lesser lord was obliged to display a certain luxury in order to establish his prestige and moral authority and distinguish himself from the other social classes. This was also why he indulged in lavishness and waste, whether or not he could afford to do so.

He had, for instance, to keep open house and a full board, in addition to feeding a crowd of servants and retainers. There were always visitors or guests, besides vassals and rear vassals who came to do their service, attend court or give advice. They brought with them their own servants and sometimes their families, all of whom were delighted to leave the wretched manor house where they were so bored. The copious midday meal which lasted well into the afternoon, was preceded and followed by ablutions because people ate with their fingers. Young maids brought in the dishes—which were covered to keep the food warm—to the knights and ladies, who were often seated alternately, two of them sharing a bowl and a goblet. The table was adorned with a few handsome pieces of plate, such as water jugs and salt cellars, and covered with a plain cloth on which everyone wiped their hands. Sometimes jugglers, tumblers, bearwards, story-tellers, minstrels, harpists, lute-players and the like amused the company

between the courses and provided subjects of conversation; the guests themselves sang songs celebrating war, love and wine, or joined in the chorus.

After dinner there was dancing to the accompaniment of vocal or instrumental music; the dancers, either in pairs as today or in groups, 'carolled' for hours on end. Other people preferred to pass the time playing dice, backgammon, chess, cards or bowls. Chess was known as early as the ninth century but became popular at the time of the crusades. Cards were imported from India via Germany in the fourteenth century; the picture cards represented Ogier the Dane, Joan of Arc's brother-in-arms Lahire, Lancelot of the Lake, and Hector de Galard.

As a rule some of the ladies and the maids joined the lady of the house in a separate room to sew, embroider or spin, chatting and singing the while or telling stories or fairytales. Sometimes they inspected the kitchens, attended to the sick and wounded, or bathed the men who had returned exhausted from the jousts or the chase.

The arrival of a distinguished guest, or an exceptional event such as the knighting of a son, the marriage of a daughter, or the birth of a child, were pretexts for organizing splendid festivities, of which we know the details from chronicles and the enormous cost from contemporary account books.

High living and revelry were not the only characteristic traits of the nobility. Fine clothes and splendid jewelry were also class symbols. Up until the mid-fourteenth century the nobles were fond of rare and costly materials, heavy woollen cloth woven in Flanders—Brussels scarlet and Ghent striped—or finished in Florence by the artisans of the Calimala Guild, silks from Cyprus, Damascus or Lucca, fine linen from Reims, all enriched with the bright colours and infinite shades obtainable through the advances in the dyer's art—these were described by such poetic names as naive green, gay green, light woodland green. They also wore fine, costly furs which had become scarce in the West and which they endeavoured to keep for their own exclusive use: squirrel (minever), the alternation of whose grey back and white belly gave vair; ermine, whose milky whiteness was emphasized by the black tip of its tail; very young lamb, whose fleece was as fine as astrakan; dark-brown sable, the most expensive and precious of all, which in heraldry gave its name to the tincture of the deepest black.

After the middle of the fourteenth century dress became a distinctive mark of sex, class and nationality, and fashions changed rapidly. The nobility, while remaining loyal to certain 'noble' materials, such as vair and ermine, which trade now supplied at a low price, dictated or followed the fashion. One glance was enough to distinguish a penurious, ill-dressed nobleman who seldom left the country from one who was rich, well-connected and on the crest of the wave.

In addition to himself and his family, a lord had to dress his retainers too. The more clothes he had to supply, the more powerful and magnificent he was considered to be. We still have the bills for liveries dating from the fourteenth and fifteenth centuries incurred by a number of magnates of the Empire, the Count of Hainaut, the Duke of Brabant, the Count of Savoy; in France, the Countess of Artois, the Count of Flanders, the Duke of Burgundy; in Italy, the Duke of Mantua; besides those of sovereigns like the pope and the kings of France, Aragon, England and Sicily. About 1345 the pope alone dressed over 1,500 persons twice a year; the Countess of Artois and the Count of Savoy dressed close on 200 each. Minor nobles who took advantage of the livery of those princes had to dress their own vassals and retainers in their turn.

The court system explains how the same fashions, the same games, the same artistic, intellectual and musical trends, the same way of life and the same mentality spread through the whole western nobility. In France, for instance, the court of Philip the Fair and his sons was visited by other European sovereigns, such as the kings of Navarre, Sicily, Scotland, Majorca and Bohemia, accompanied by a train of lords. Each of those lords, like his French counterpart, was attended by a number of vassals and so the chain continued. There were frequent gatherings at each rung of the social ladder, and marriage between princely families of different countries and the ensuing festivities helped to weld the western nobility into one great family—though, as a matter of fact, many brothers were mortal enemies. It was exclusively in the bosom of that family that the curious phenomenon of 'amour courtois' and the ritual of chivalry developed and became so prominent a factor of daily life in the eleventh and twelfth centuries.

Marriage was often the outcome of an agreement between families. A lord could select a husband for a minor heiress and give advice on the marriage of a vassal of either sex. Love matches were probably fewer among nobles than among commoners, but that does not mean that the bond was less strong. The population boom did not spare the nobility and added to the number of young bachelors who were dissatisfied to see women, wealth and power concentrated in the hands of their elders. What is more, the crusades brought western fighting men into contact with civilizations where the harem was the rule and women were experts at pleasing the males. On returning to their native land, at the courts of their lords or the castles where they broke their journey, those knights became acquainted with women whose husbands were old, incapable or absent. Banquets, dances, hawking and the like offered many occasions for meetings. It may also be worth recalling the relative scarcity, for biological or local reasons, of women in castles thronged with men-at-arms; the complex influences of Catharism and Waldensianism in the Languedoc; the proximity of a Spain imbued with Islamic culture, where the Duke of Aquitaine may well have come in contact with Andalusian poetry when he went there to help in the *Reconquista*; besides the Celtic tradition of women who were half-fairies and ensnared and fettered the men of their choice.

Whatever the reason, it seems certain that from the twelfth century a new idea of love spread from the Languedoc to the nobility of all Western Europe

Meals in a great lord's house were ruled by etiquette. This was particularly true of the wedding banquet for Clarisse de Gascogne and Renaut de Montauban (above). The young bride dines alone with a maid of honour at either side. The lords sit at a different table and admire her graceful bearing. The service is supervised by a major-domo. Three musicians enliven the princely feast.

There was little in the way of individual tableware. Spoons were introduced first, followed by knives. Forks were relegated to the kitchen or wielded by the major-domo. Left: this very rare table knife was offered to Louis IX of France at his coronation. Another rare piece is the German or Flemish nutcracker below, which dates from the fifteenth century.

—a love at once chaste and ardent, which conflicted with religious taboos and was perfectly in keeping with the youth (15 or 16 years) of those who experienced it. There is no point in arguing about the issue of that sort of love: it probably ended in most cases with the lady yielding completely to the supplications of her suitor, perhaps after a long period of caresses and games of love that stopped just short of the 'ultimate solace'. The original feature of that sentiment was that the flesh did not take first place and the woman was viewed as a mistress, if not as a goddess or even the Virgin Mary; she stood on a high plane and demanded homage, loyalty, dedication and worship, initiatory ordeals, service at her court and the like. In this way the lady raised her knight to her own level through a love that made him braver and more steadfast. This idea of *amour courtois* celebrated by the troubadours, many of whom were of noble birth, spread very soon to the nobility of Aragon and Castile, the court of Monferrato in Sicily, England, and in particular Germany, where it blossomed out in the Minnesang at the end of the twelfth century with Walter von der Vogelweide (1170–1228). It was a refined, aristocratic concept that took up a great deal of time and therefore could not penetrate the workaday world; an extremely intellectual ideal, in which long denial was itself a joy. Oddly enough, that courtly, religious love, though pure and constant, seems to have ignored marriage entirely. True, the loved one was sometimes a damsel and the two lovers concluded by marrying. But far more often she was a lady of higher rank, married to a powerful but aging lord for whom she might feel affection and to whom her body unquestionably belonged: all she could grant her knight was her heart and her thoughts, and it was only much later that she surrendered her body too. All the courts of Western Europe were greatly

208

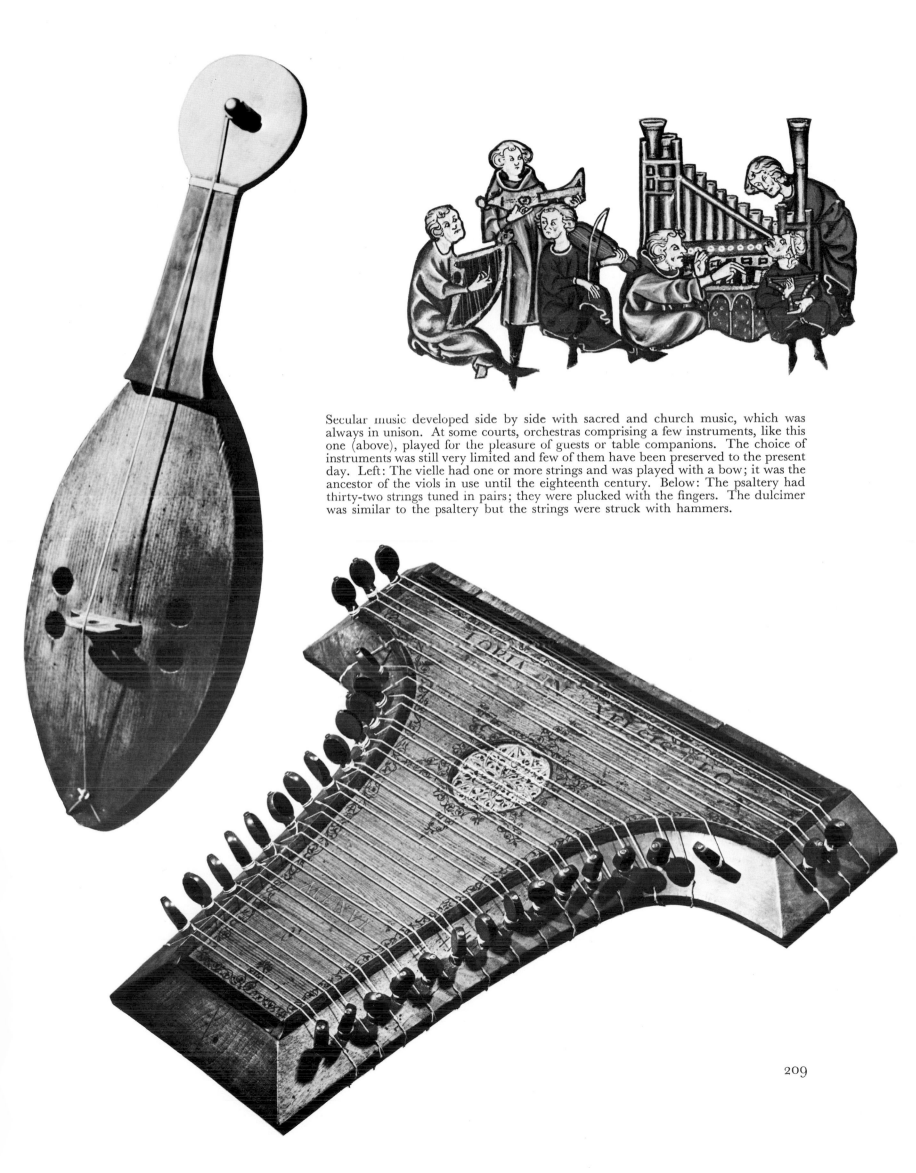

Secular music developed side by side with sacred and church music, which was always in unison. At some courts, orchestras comprising a few instruments, like this one (above), played for the pleasure of guests or table companions. The choice of instruments was still very limited and few of them have been preserved to the present day. Left: The vielle had one or more strings and was played with a bow; it was the ancestor of the viols in use until the eighteenth century. Below: The psaltery had thirty-two strings tuned in pairs; they were plucked with the fingers. The dulcimer was similar to the psaltery but the strings were struck with hammers.

209

Playing cards were introduced in the fourteenth and fifteenth centuries, probably from India via the German lands. French cards were designed at Charles VII's court. Above right: a knave of diamonds in the image of Hector de Galard.

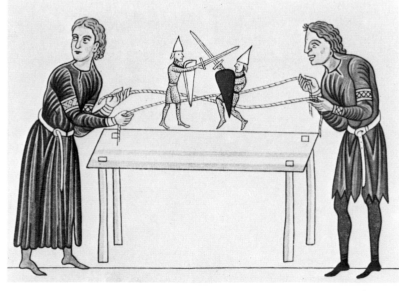

Puppets amused both children and adults because they often mirrored current events very wittily.

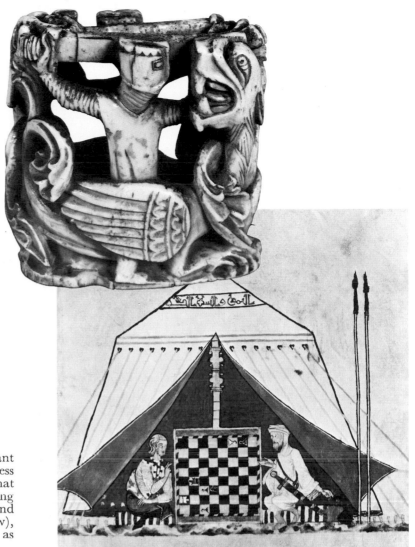

Another game popular with the nobles was chess. Imported from the Levant in the ninth century, its pieces were often works of art (top right). Chess offered knights situations similar to those they met with in war. For that reason, perhaps, it was played in castles and camps by Christians among themselves (above left) and by Christians and Muslims in the Holy Land and in Spain (right). Portable boards like the one in the Musée de Cluny (below), which dates from the fifteenth century, served too for other games, such as draughts, backgammon and morris.

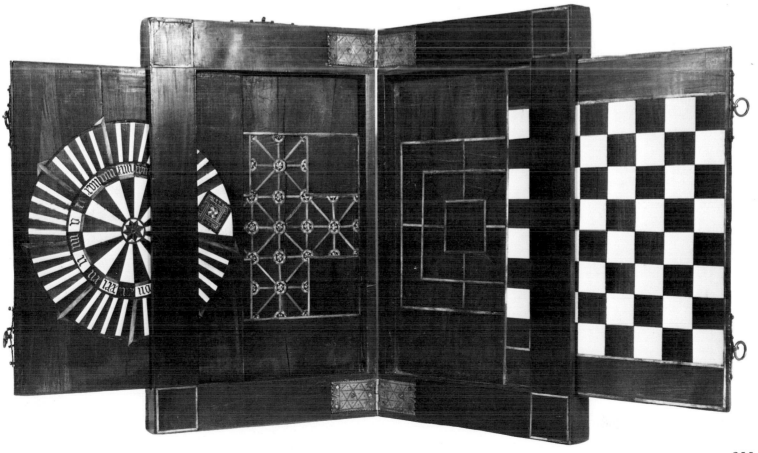

Over a very long period dress forms and materials changed very little and everyone wore the same type of clothes. But soon the lords could be distinguished by the quality, if not the style, of their garments; furs, silks, and gold and silver embroidery became more common. This tunic belonged to a twelfth century king of Sicily. Its simple lines recall those of the dalmatic but it was made of purplish turquoise silk with cuffs and hem handsomely embroidered with gold thread and pearls. In the fifteenth century this simplicity gave way to luxury.

influenced by courtesy till the end of the fifteenth century. There is no way of knowing whether all those who read or listened to the adventures of little Jehan de Saintré followed exactly the same way of life as their hero. But in any event, stories of that sort give an idea of the literary, musical and philosophical culture that thrived in those noble circles. The enormous popularity of tales of chivalry based chiefly on incredible feats of strength and courage is further proof of that influence.

The ideal of chivalry and its ritual, introduced and developed in the eleventh and twelfth centuries, were in principle basic facts of daily life. The consecration of the knight and the blessing of his 'newly-girt' sword are first referred to at the end of the tenth century. From that time ceremonies of that type are mentioned more and more frequently. Descriptions dating from the twelfth show us candidates for knighthood who, after serving a long apprenticeship first as pages and later as esquires, take a purificatory bath, dress all in white, and pass the night in prayer in the castle oratory or the nearest church. After Mass and the feast that followed it each candidate had his sword girded on by his sponsor, who then dealt him a swingeing blow on the cheek or the nape of the neck with his open hand; in some cases he touched him three times on the shoulder with the blade of his sword. This was the culminating point of the dubbing ceremony, for the round on horseback, the quintain and the ensuing festivities were optional. The blow may be considered on a par with the buffet given a child who has witnessed an important event to make sure that he will always cherish the memory of it. It may also have symbolized the transmission of the sponsor's martial valour to his protégé. More probably it was something like the American present-day custom of hazing (a form of initiation), which involves a novice in a number of tests before he is admitted to an exclusive group.

This is one more indication of how some customs of the ancient Germanic tribes were Christianized and hallowed by the Church. The blessing of the

The style of dress underwent a change in the mid-fourteenth century. Fine linen, silk and velvet were commonly used by the nobility and the well-off burghers. Fashions varied frequently after the example set by the courts of France and Burgundy (above). Women gave their breasts uplift with a muslin veil pinned at the back to form the equivalent of the modern brassière. Gowns were very long and widened towards the hem; they were embellished with braid, embroidery and fur. Sometimes the sleeves were so tight-fitting that they had to be stitched each time the garment was worn. Sumptuary laws enacted to check extravagance were seldom obeyed.

In every age clothes were adorned with jewelry, belt buckles, brooches, clasps, pins and the like. They were made of gold, silver and brass chased like the Merovingian belt buckle (top right); set with gems like this German clasp (bottom right), or coated with bright enamels.

sword was often followed by the new knight taking an oath that he would live in accordance with the law of the Church and to the honour of chivalry. The rules to be observed were set forth in a code whose interpretation was an inexhaustible source of new symbols. The most important were to defend widows, orphans and the weak; to serve good causes and pursue evil-doers; to help one's neighbour; to keep faith; not to kill a man who could not defend himself. But that slight tincture of Christianity did little to hide the fact that for a knight valour was the greatest virtue. Thus the Church not only perpetuated but also justified specialization in combat and the fighting spirit, and with it the domination of a certain social class. The commonalty that sustained the knight who defended it was like the horse that carried him: it needed whip and spur to drive it in the right direction.

Even if his means were not adequate for knighthood, a nobleman refused to work and his chief occupation was to train for war by engaging in sports.

The chase provided at once excellent training, an exciting pastime and a useful sport: it destroyed wild or dangerous animals and supplied meat to keep up the strength of those who sat at the lord's table. It demanded costly equipment and a large retinue. Its most refined and attractive form, which had the advantage that it was open to ladies, was falconry, which employed carefully trained high-flying birds like the falcon or low-flying birds like the goshawk to intercept rabbits, hares and other rodents and more especially herons, cranes, duck and other large birds. Dogs were trained to flush the game, run to the falcon's assistance on the ground, and kill the quarry without injuring it. Falconry was an extremely refined art. The Emperor Frederick II wrote a well-documented manual on it which was deservedly famous, and most lords and ladies had their portrait engraved, falcon on wrist, on the reverse of their seal.

Big dogs of selected breeds were used for hunting bear, deer, wild boar and hare. A pack of hounds was a typical feature of castle or manor house, complete with kennels and handlers. Gaston Phoebus of Foix, referred to earlier, who lived at the end of the fourteenth century, left unique descriptions in richly illustrated manuscripts; he tells us of the pleasure given by headlong gallops through woods, over fields and in the mountains, the fierce combat with bears, boars and wolves, the prestige a hunter enjoyed among the ladies and other gallant knights.

Fishing in lake and river was very often no less sporting; and both otter and salmon were the quarry of veritable hunts with harpoons, dogs and nets weighed with lead.

It must be said, however, that young noblemen did not pass all their time hunting. They took frequent riding lessons in the woods or over rough country, and made enormously long journeys on horseback merely for the pleasure of feeling a horse between their thighs, or perhaps to admire the beauty of the landscape or commune with nature.

Martial exercise of many kinds also served to brighten and fill the rather monotonous way of life in castle and manor house. Two men could train in a field or the castle lists, charging each other, breaking lances, each endeavouring to unhorse his opponent. They could also obtain good practice tilting at a quintain, which was a big dummy with shield and hauberk set, either fixed or mobile, on a post driven into the ground. The knight, riding at full gallop, had to overturn the dummy with a blow of his lance in the centre of its shield—he had only five tries, hence the name; if the blow was off centre, the dummy swung round the post and dealt the bungler a blow, strong enough to knock him off his horse, with a wooden pole attached to its arm.

Fencing with single stick, sword or lance was another popular sport among the young men. But the chief training for combat was provided by tourneys. We know all about those grand, colourful pageants indubitably of pagan origin that brought together the flower of chivalry. A fair held at the same time gave all the nobles present a chance to show their generosity. The spectators filled the stands and galleries raised above the space ringed

round by the lists or the closed field where the champions tilted either singly or in teams which represented a region or a nation. Heralds gave the signal for the jousts which, though the combatants wore thick armour, frequently caused injuries and sometimes death. The losers had to surrender their horses and harness as well as pay a ransom. The victors not only received handsome prizes—falcons, crowns and gilded fleeces—and gained enormous prestige among the ladies; they also earned a lot of money. So it is not surprising that many knights made it their profession to tour the lists. One of the most famous was a valiant English baron named William Marshall, who with a single comrade defeated 203 knights in the space of a few months; he hired 2 clerks to keep check of his earnings. The fights were sometimes very fierce. On one occasion Marshall's helmet was so battered that he had to resort to a blacksmith, who hammered it into shape on his anvil before he could take it off. Alongside those expert jousters a host of wealthy, pugnacious young men of royal or princely blood trained in the perilous game of war. As Roger of Hoveden said, 'a knight cannot distinguish himself in that if he has not trained for it in tourneys. He must have seen his blood flow, heard his teeth crack under fist blows, felt his opponent's weight bear down upon him as he lay on the ground and, after being twenty times unhorsed, have risen twenty times to fight.'

But the best training of all was war itself. The famous troubadour Bertran de Born sang of the joy he felt in springtime when setting out on a campaign. Le Jouvencel said 'war is a jolly thing', and Froissart spoke repeatedly of feats of arms and described with what regret old mercenaries recalled the good times when they made war. War, in fact, was the knight's first and foremost activity; it enabled him to achieve fulfilment, and to show his valour, his prowess, his

Dubbing a knight, for long a purely lay ceremony, took on a religious character under the influence of the Church. This is how it was carried out: after a night of vigil, the knight received the spurs, banner, shield (top left) and sword. This was sometimes followed by a blow with the flat of a sword—an act that could replace all other ceremonial on the battlefield (above right). He next took an oath on the Gospel (below) and received Holy Communion before fighting the Saracens or other enemies in defence of the faith or in the service of his lord or king.

In the Germanic lands the minnesingers, chief among them Wolfram von Eschenbach and Walter von der Vogelweide, celebrated courtly love. Lovers used little caskets like this delicately wrought in leather, ivory or precious metals to dispatch their love letters.

Left: courtly love was a product of the knightly society. A knight was bound to love a beautiful and virtuous lady before whom he bowed his knee in sign of veneration and obedience. For her sake he would do a thousand gallant deeds, for 'love was the spring from which all valour flowed.'

'O noble lady, I am and shall always be yours! A devoted slave at your behest. I am your servant and liegeman. I am yours for ever. You are my first love and will be my last.' These words by Bernard de Ventadour are well matched to the tapestry (opposite) entitled 'The Gift of His Heart.'

Hunting was a knight's favourite pastime and excellent training. Ladies too enjoyed hunting, particulary falconry (above) with sparrow hawks, goshawks and falcons. The birds are carried hooded on the fist protected with a leather glove. When the dogs have flushed the quarry, the hawks are unhooded and slipped; they fly at the quarry and strike it down. The dogs retrieve the game and the birds are recalled by their masters.

Big game hunting required a costly organization: servants, horses, hounds and mastiffs. The lord himself was armed with a spear and a hunting knife like this one, which belonged to Philip the Good (right). He also carried a horn for giving orders or signalling his position. The horn was sometimes of ivory, whence its name of oliphant (from elephant). Some were works of art (far right).

The chase consisted in locating the quarry, laying on the hounds to make it break cover, pursuing it, thwarting its wiles, hunting it down, and killing it with knife or spear. The miniature left is taken from the finest treatise on the chase, written by Gaston Phoebus Count of Foix and Viscount of Béarn.

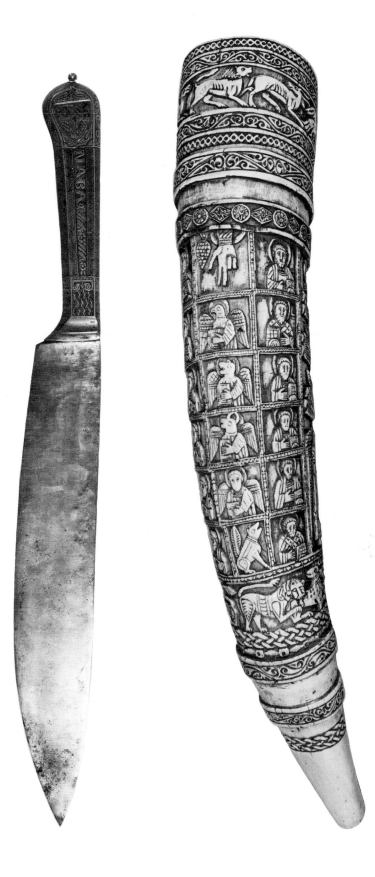

experience and his loyalty to his lord or his faith. Fighting under the same banner strengthened the bonds of kinship and comradeship. War also gave him a chance to leave his drab manor house, where limited means condemned him to a shabby way of life, and take advantage of his lord's liberality, the booty won, the ransom of captives, supplies requisitioned from the peasants, or quite simply brigandage on the roads and pillage in the farms. What is more, even a low-born fighting man knew that 'once he had a helmet on his head he was a noble'.

The wars so keenly desired by knights and esquires were waged for many different reasons. For private vengeance, first of all, a privilege of the nobility which enlisted kinsmen and vassals; but also as a means to humble rival lords, conquer towns, crush revolts, and acquire new territory. Towards the end of the Middle Ages wars between monarchs tended to be waged on the national scale—England against France, Germany against Bohemia, and so on. The Church did its best, with varying success, to keep the peace in the West by a system of truces of God in the eleventh century, by instituting chivalry and mobilizing it against the infidels in the South (the Moors in Spain), the North-east (the Balto-Prussians) and the Eastern Mediterranean (the Saracens in the Holy Land), or by arbitrating between belligerants. But it never succeeded in putting an end to acts of violence and occasionally was the first to start a war in order to further papal or theocratic ambitions.

But those frequent wars were limited in extent; they seldom lasted very long or involved a large territory. And the forces employed were never very numerous. The First Crusade mobilized 10,000 to 12,000 knights at the outside, making a total of 50,000 men; but that was a record. At Bouvines in 1214 the emperor Otto of Brunswick had 1,500 knights and 7,500 foot soldiers, many of whom belonged to the Count of Flanders and to Renaud of Boulogne. The army that Philip Augustus of France mustered against him was even less strong. The biggest force assembled during the Hundred Years War was Edward III's before Calais; it numbered

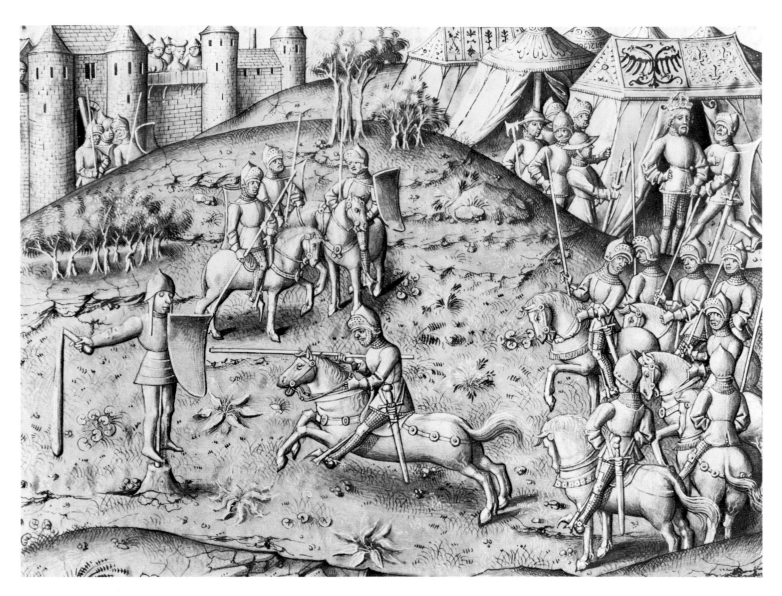

Training for war occupied a great deal of time. Above: a knight tilts at a quintain. He has five chances to knock down the swivelling dummy. If his lance thrust is off centre the dummy swings round and deals the unskilful tilter a heavy blow with its club.

The chief offensive weapons were the long lance, often broken at the first onset, and a broad sword of great strength and flexibility. Recent analyses of the alloys employed have proved how well the medieval smiths worked.

For protection against missiles and his adversary's sword, the knight wore a helmet and a long coat of mail that completed or replaced a suit of armour. His mount had a chamfron to protect its head and its body was covered by a caparison of jointed metal plates. A war horse or charger had to be extremely robust because he had to carry not only his rider but also the weight of both their protective armour, which could add up to over 130 pounds.

222

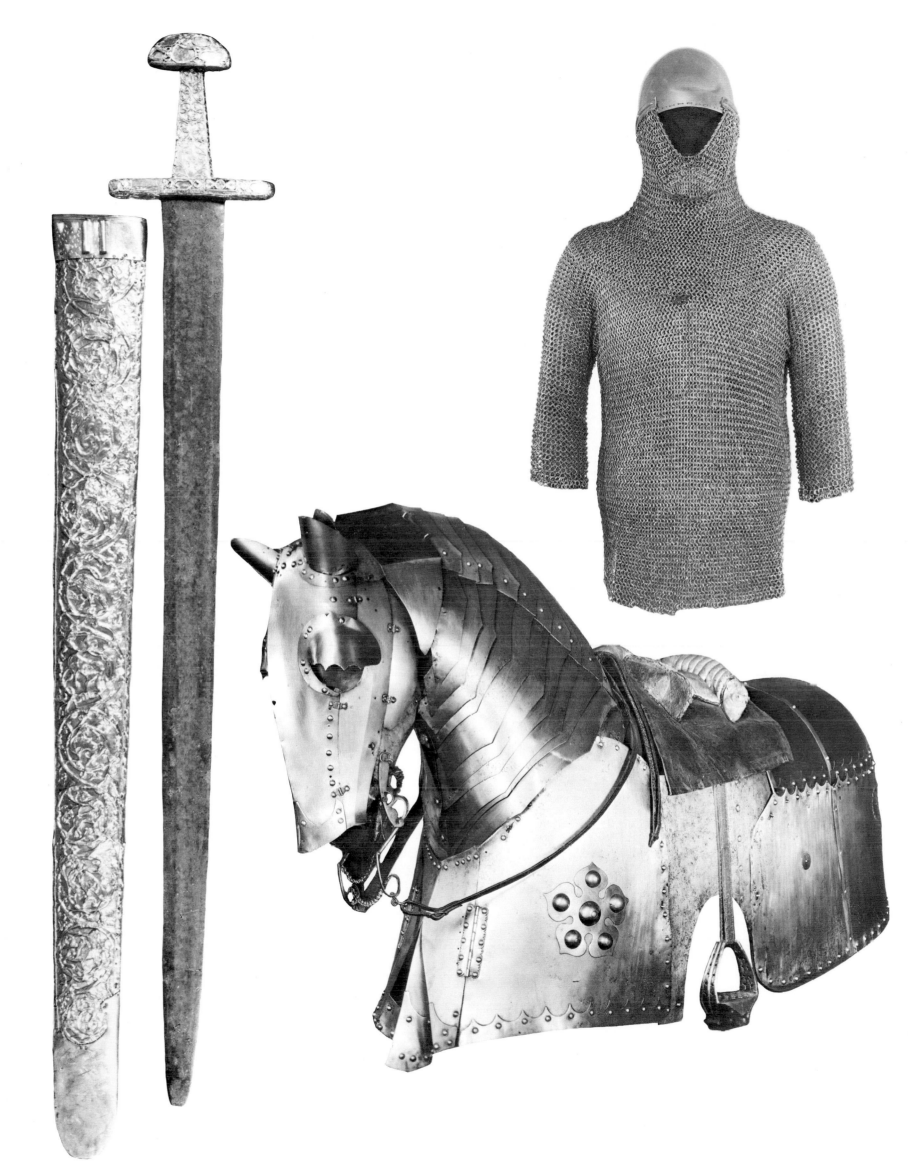

Tournaments were still more closely related to war than the chase. In order to avoid excesses they were regulated by very strict rules. First came the presentation of the champions and their banners (above), next the knight was dressed by his esquire (left) who stands by to assist his master (far left). When he was armed from head to toe, he chose the lady whose colours he would wear (opposite page).

This was followed by the parade (left) and once the preliminaries were over, the combatants charged each other, each endeavouring to unseat his opponent with his lance (bottom left).

After that the contest was resumed on foot or horseback with swords. The victor received the crown from his lady (opposite page). The vanquished, more or less severely wounded, forfeited his equipment, his steed, his freedom (which he had to buy back with a proper ransom) and sometimes his very life.

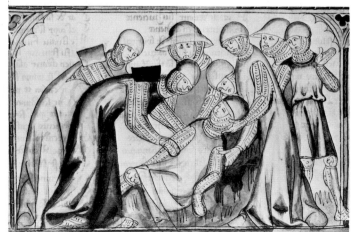

32,000 men but not all of them were English. John of Gaunt made his terrible raid in 1373 with only 4,000 fighting men. The king of France had the greatest difficulty in raising an army of 15,000 and in 1467 the Imperial Diet could muster only 20,000 against the Turks. On the other hand, a handful of defenders sufficed to make a castle or a fortified town almost impregnable. In 1436 Rouen had 2 mounted men-at-arms, 12 foot soldiers and 38 archers. Orleans resisted a siege of 7 months with fewer than 700 soldiers.

The knight, more and more heavily armed and mounted on a huge horse that was also protected to some extent, was the medieval equivalent of the tank. As a rule he was attended by an esquire and armour bearers, who were also mounted but more lightly armed. Towards the close of the period an army was counted by lances, which amounted to 1 knight plus 5 other men; so 1,500 lances equalled 9,000 fighting men. To those must be added foot soldiers, who were also able to ride if the need arose, and bowmen. Offensive weapons and defensive armour became steadily stronger and weightier; coat of mail, helm and buckler were gradually replaced by a heavy suit of armour with a breastplate weighing 55 pounds and a visored head-piece weighing 11. To break through all that iron needed an axe or a mace, which were carried in addition to a lance 10 to 13 feet long, a tempered sword and a dagger. A knight always risked being unhorsed with different kinds of hooks or short, broad-tipped pikes, and once on the ground he was incapable of rising. Foot soldiers wore a helmet weighing from 6 to 9 pounds called a sallet and a corselet of 20 pounds or more. The best way to disable a knight was to kill his charger or pierce his armour. The long-bow made of yew, about 5 feet long, which could shoot 6 or 7 arrows a minute at a range of 275 yards and was effective to over 160, did the first job very well. In the fifteenth century it found a rival in the heavy crossbow that weighed up to 18 pounds and could shoot only 2 bolts a minute but was a formidable weapon in the hands of an expert; its bolts, called

quarrels, were deadly up to 330 yards. Firearms, though known as early as the fourteenth century, were of no great importance until later and did not essentially modify either siege warfare or tactics in the field.

Pitched battles with flags flying were very rare indeed. Four of the most famous were Arsuf, in 1191, where Richard Cœur-de-Lion, surprised by Saladin when his army was in marching order, immediately joined battle and overwhelmed the Saracens; Bouvines in 1214, where Bishop Guérin of Beauvais made the French army face about and inflicted a decisive defeat on the coalition troops; and two of the great English victories during the Hundred Years War—Poitiers (1356) and Agincourt (1415). In general the more disciplined knights, who were willing to manoeuvre in formation and let their commander use his archers to the best advantage, were victorious as long as they fought against enemies equipped with the same weapons and obeying the same rules of the game; this was the case in wars between western noblemen. Encounters with the Flemish militia infantry (at Courtrai in 1302), the Turkish forces (Nicopolis in 1396), and the mobile fortresses of the Hussites, did not always end in the same way. In all those battles the vanquished suffered extremely heavy losses; if they were unwilling or unable to disengage, casualties ran as high as 50 or even 80 per cent. I might mention by way of example the French at Agincourt in 1415 and the English at Formigny in 1450. The rich lords were often spared because they were worth a good ransom; but for one king of France taken prisoner, how many great princes like Ottokar of Bohemia or Charles the Bold of Burgundy met an inglorious death at the end of a lost battle.

In the course of a campaign an army more often came up against a fortified place than against another army. That marked the beginning of a long siege which only guile, treachery, famine, sickness, or a political agreement could bring to a close. Sometimes, but not very frequently, a siege was carried on with great energy and the castle or

Knights were fond of fighting. The members of the same clan fought side by side in small groups. Siege warfare led to the revival of the art of building war machines such as the *ballista* (above). Here we see how difficult it was to take a fortress.

On the march heavy equipment-shields, helmets, coats of mail and suits of armour were loaded on carts in order to spare the warriors and their steeds. Some troops remained in arms to defend the convoy against a surprise attack.

In the fourteenth and fifteenth centuries battles were decided by cavalry charges. The mounted men were deployed, in order to make a frontal attack, behind a curtain of archers whose task it was to break the enemy counter charge.

The shape of helmets evolved continually. The so-called helmet of St Wenceslaus (above) is a conical casque with nasal (935). The one below is a basinet with movable vizor (early fifteenth century).

Left: In the fifteenth century the factions that arose during the political troubles caused by the Hundred Years War invented identification badges.

Left: This spendid painted wooden shield belonged to a lord of Rarogne in Switzerland about 1500.

Opposite page: For a knight war was a sport or game. Mounted on his charger and armed cap-à-pie, this one cuts a very fine figure. His armour sparkles in the sunlight; the plumes on his helmet and his steed's chamfron nod; his banner waves.

230

(exceptionally) the town was stormed. But that required enormous resources: saps and mines to wreck a section of the walls, battering rams and other machines protected by penthouses to breach them, turret bridges for bringing the attackers directly to the walls and a quantity of ladders for scaling them. It can readily be understood that a surprise attack at night on a poorly guarded fortress promised the best results.

Most wars were waged in the shape of raids. Forces far too small to take a town or castle scoured the countryside, pillaging, burning, spoiling, exacting ransom and leaving ruins in their wake; at most they engaged in skirmishes of slight importance with rival bands. It would be a mistake to overrate the damage done. Even John of Gaunt's great raid of 1373, though it covered 600 miles, from Calais to Bordeaux, did not lay waste more than 4,000 square miles. But armed bands led by minor nobles who very often had no connection with either side took advantage of those troublous times and multiplied the damage done by the mercenaries.

The burghers who governed the city-states of Italy and Germany had so little taste for fighting that they preferred to pay needy minor noblemen to do so in their stead. The great lords of the West, faced with the shortage, debility, indiscipline, or excessive cost of the nobles, also had recourse to bands of mercenaries engaged for a single campaign. But those troops, carefully nursed by their *condottieri*, who were loath to risk them in battle, and badly paid by their employers, disregarded the terms of their contract and became a scourge for townsmen and peasants alike. The establishment of regular armies made up of paid professional soldiers was the only way to keep fighting men under control. These armies first appeared at the end of the fifteenth century but were beyond reach of states that could not count on extremely high revenues. From then on the nobles had to cope with strong competition in a 'profession' they had monopolized for centuries; they became only one section of the 'fighters' and were not always the most highly regarded component.

Left: The sieges were long and hazardous; the artillery could not easily penetrate the thick sturdy walls. Crossing the ditch and scaling the walls were deadly operations, and it was more often by means of a trick, through starvation, or by treason, that the fortress was successfully overwhelmed.

Artillery first appeared in the fourteenth century. It became a formidable weapon in the fifteenth owing to its increased mobility and the importance it had gained in both siege and mobile warfare. The thunder of guns announced that the age of chivalry was near its end. Opposite page, above: This Austrian piece dates from the second half of the fourteenth century.

War became very hard for the knights when the enemy refused to respect the code of chivalry and the rules of the game. They had no defence against mercenaries or soldiers of fortune who overwhelmed them with a hail of rocks, as at the Battle of Brignais soon after the Peace of Brétigny in 1360 (above).

I PRAY FOR ALL:
the Seekers for Perfection

For centuries western society comprised only two orders, laity and clergy, and one of its most clearly defined sections was made up of those who prayed. When daily life was overshadowed by fear of sin and the obligation to say prayers, go to confession and receive communion, those who were allotted the function of intermediaries between God and man quite naturally occupied the highest rank and dignity. In addition, the vast numbers of clerics invested and inspired, directly or indirectly, by the pope of Rome exerted an enormous unifying influence on the mass of Christians who accepted his authority.

But all those clerics did not have the same function and rank of importance: far from it. They could perform their activities in the intellectual, the spiritual or even the material sphere, but at times those activities encountered obstacles or stirred up revolt. The clergy, admittance to which was gained merely by the ceremony of the tonsure, was only in appearance a homogeneous body. In actual fact it was highly diversified and contrasted; submerged in the mass of the laity, it too comprised poor and weak, good and bad, rich and powerful.

A first group of seekers for perfection was made up throughout the entire Middle Ages of both clerics and laymen, but the proportion of the former increased steadily as time went on. It was important in both numbers and influence and comprised all those who renounced the world for the service of God. Some lived a life of solitude—in fact, the word monk derives from *monos*, the Greek for 'alone'. The poor, chaste, humble hermits who populated the deserts and forests were well known to the peasants, who often brought them food, asked them for their advice, blessing and even miraculous intervention—thought this was disapproved of by the parish priest. Hermits were also well known to stray travellers, whom they sheltered and put on the right road; to hunters who chanced on their hovels; to forest and water wardens in search of wild honey or timber; to vagabonds, outlaws and the lovelorn who wanted to leave the world for a time.

The Church preached the true faith and instructed the believers —men and women, young and old, rich and poor, nobles, burghers and peasants. It was present everywhere: with monks and parish priests in the country; with chaplains in the castles; with the bishops and clerics in the towns, as at Tournai (left).

235

But most seekers for perfection were cenobites who formed a community, lived in a monastery, and followed a rule under the direction of an abbot or prior. Only a minority of them took vows and embraced the perfect life imposed by the rule; they were the professed monks, canons and the like. Some were priests (the fathers), but no religious order laid down that all professed members had to be ordained; for centuries they were viewed as laymen. The eleventh century saw the appearance of the first lay brothers, who took vows of conversion, stability and obedience, did menial work in the monastery and tilled the fields; they lived a life of silence, austerity, fasting and prayer, but were not necessarily clerks. The same is true of the 'novices' during their period of training and probation, and of the 'oblates' and 'donats'. The latter joined the monks in prayers, received board and lodging in return for surrendering all or part of their worldly goods to the monastery and, in some cases, were free to come and go as they pleased. Lastly, there were the many laymen, prebendaries, servants, bailiffs, craftsmen and others who lived in the shadow of the monastery, which they often made a very populous, active centre.

The head of the community was the abbot, who was chosen or elected by the fathers. He had enormous authority over the clerical and lay members of the community, besides managing the estate which was often very extensive; this gave him a most important position in feudal times as lord of numerous vassals and serfs. He was assisted in the performance of his duties by a staff of familiars, which comprised the prior—sometimes aided by a sub-prior—chamberlain, treasurer, physician, chaplain, cellarer and precentor. Some very important abbeys established subsidiaries on parts of their vast estates; they were all under the abbot's supreme authority, but he appointed a resident prior to attend to the daily business of each house, which in that case was called a priory. When several new or 'reformed' establishments were under the same rule, delegates of each met periodically under their common head to preserve the spirit of the founder, settle disputes, maintain their endowment and promote their 'order'. Those meetings were general chapters.

Thus the daily life of the monks was conditioned by two major factors—firstly, the rule they had adopted and its more or less strict application; secondly, the material situation of the monastery, namely the size of the community and the area of its lands. Let us consider a few examples taken from the great Benedictine family, the mendicant friars and the military orders.

There is no denying the importance of the disciples of Saint Augustine, Johannes Cassianus (†434) and Caesareus of Arles, still less of the Irish Saint Columban (540–615). But it was the rule of Saint Benedict of Nursia (480–547), revived by Saint Benedict Anianus (750–821) and the founders of Cluny (909) and Cîteaux (1098), that was the major influence in medieval monastism and its most perfect expression.

In 529 Benedict, together with a handful of followers, erected on the top of Monte Cassino two oratories and a monastery, for which the saint drew up a number of counsels and injunctions. He decided in favour of life in a community where each member watched over and assisted his fellows under the wing of the abbot; it was simpler, if less rich and edifying, than that of a hermit. The members of the order renounced their worldly goods and took a vow of stability, namely to remain in the same monastery until death; they also undertook to renounce the world and live in poverty, chastity and obedience to the abbot and the rule, which was the fundamental, constituent principle of the community. Thus poverty, humility, obedience and piety, not pushed to unreasonable extremes, were the typical features of the Benedictine way of life, in which time was happily filled by reading the Holy Books, manual work and sleep. The year was divided into three parts—from Easter to the end of September, covering broadly spring and summer; from 1 October to Ash Wednesday; and Lent; and the monks' timetable was closely linked with the course of the sun. They rose before dawn, recited matins (or vigils) and lauds, and attended to their various occupations until

The mendicant orders appeared in the early thirteenth century. They include the Carmelites (above), Augustinians (below right), Franciscans (below left), and Dominicans (bottom). They lived in the towns and preached absolute poverty.

the fourth hour; after that, from Easter to Michaelmas, they read until noon; in winter they recited the psalms and read the Bible or pious books until lauds or tierce, then worked till the ninth hour (in Lent the tenth). Dinner, at noon in summer and the ninth hour in winter, was followed by a period of rest or reading; in winter and, with all the more reason in Lent, dinner brought manual work to a close because it was eaten at the end of the day. In summer, after nones, which were slightly anticipated, work was resumed until vespers, followed by a second meal. After compline the whole community went to bed. On Sundays there was general reading except for those who had to say Mass or perform other services.

These injunctions were, it is clear to see, admirably suited to a rural community. Work included the cooking, done by each monk in turn, the making and repairing of clothes and implements; the tilling of the fields under the supervision of the cellarer. The food was adequate, though meat was banned entirely; in fact each meal—there were two from Easter to Michelmas—comprised two dishes plus fruit in season and each monk received some 10 ounces of bread and a pint of wine a day. The habit was simple but functional: footwear and stockings, two cowls and two light tunics for summer; the same in heavy material for winter.

The Benedictine way of life was modified during the seventh and eighth centuries by the extroversion of the monasteries which, in Germany and some other countries, were entrusted with the Christianization of the indigenous population and the spread of culture by organizing on their premises schools and workshops for copying manuscripts.

On the other hand, under the influence of the saintly bishop of Metz, Chrodegang, the priests of the most important churches, particularly the cathedrals, began to assemble in 'chapters' or 'colleges', eat in the same refectory, sleep in the same dormitory, and celebrate the Divine offices all together. The rule they adopted was inspired less by Saint Benedict than by Saint Augustine. It was necessarily more

The bishop was assisted by the members of the chapter, who formed a community in the shadow of the cathedral. In addition to the cloister, the capitular hall and other common rooms, as at Elne (Pyrénées-Orientales) below, they often had private apartments. At the end of the eleventh century the Cluniacs founded the Cistercian order and settled in locations with such evocative names as Clairvaux, Beaulieu and Vallbona. Part of the cloister at Vallbona is reproduced, bottom. However, not all monasteries were as isolated as that of the Benedictine Saint-Martin-du-Canigou (right).

flexible because those 'canons' had to attend to their various occupations; it also tolerated the wearing of less coarse materials, such as linen, the eating of meat and the possession of certain property. For these reasons it was preferred by a great many 'canonesses', who shied away from the hard life of the Benedictine nuns. Vows of chastity and obedience were compulsory and respected, but the virtual suppression of the vow of poverty was to have important consequences at a later date.

At the same time, side by side with this alleviation of the cenobite way of life, many monasteries reverted under the influence of Saint Benedict Anianus and the Emperor Louis the Pious (817) to the strict observation of the injunctions of Monte Cassino. Indeed, that rule was extended to all the monasteries in Western Europe except those that belonged to the order of canons. The reform, though applied in principle, tolerated a number of compromises. Abbeys which had expanded inordinately at the end of the eighth century endeavoured, without complete success, to revert to the separation of religious life and manual work from cultural life and relations with the outside world. The famous plan of Saint-Gall drawn up about 820 seems to have been the response to that urge.

Benedictine abbeys of this type were very numerous in the West during the Middle Ages and some of them still exist at the present day. But they were not alone. After 909 the Cluniac order spread far and wide; by the end of the eleventh century it had over 1,100 houses—some newly established, others reformed—totalling tens of thousands of monks. Cluny itself counted some 400 inmates. This vast number implied enormous buildings in addition to those for housing the servants and serfs. There were also rural priories dotted around the countryside, where a few monks resided during the season to supervise work in the fields. But the Cluniac way of life was not exactly that which Saint Benedict had laid down. Firstly, many of the monks were priests who had to say their daily Mass and spent so much time in liturgical offices, prayers and chanting that little was

In a treatise on the spiritual life, St Bernard, abbot of Clairvaux, took the theme of Jacob's ladder (left) to illustrate the various steps in the contemplative life (the ascending angels) and the graces it bestows (the descending angels).

The tonsure consisted in cutting a lock of hair on the crown of the head. It was performed by the bishop (top right) and transformed a layman into a clerk.

For the novice in a monastic order the first important step was taking the habit, which entailed the obligation to obey the rule and ... sent the devil packing (top left).

left for manual labour; intellectual work and the copying of ancient manuscripts were more highly prized. On the other hand, relations with the outside world became far closer. This was due in part to the size of the abbey's estates, which gave the monks great importance in the feudal society and demanded large-scale employment of servile labour to make up for their neglect of manual work. Another cause was the strict, almost feudal hierarchy that linked the subsidiary priories to the abbot of Cluny. But more important still in this connection was the monks' active charity, and their brotherly assistance to the poor and sick, their educational work among the laity, and the pastoral activities of those who were ordained priests or deacons. Besides which, the rule grew milder on the material plane. The common dormitory was replaced by separate cells; healthy, simple food was replaced by cooked dishes including fish of all sorts, eggs and dairy products replacing meat, which was still forbidden; wine was improved by the addition of spices or honey; and the black cowl was replaced by a fur-lined cloak.

The black monks, many of noble birth, had considerable influence on their vast lands worked by peasants or serfs and in the small towns and villages of the vicinity. Their church was crowded with the country people and attended even by the local lord; their sermons were given an attentive ear and their confessionals never lacked penitents. Their example was no less effective in improving the morals of clergy and laity alike than the power and persuasive action of the Church or the fear of hell and of a just and terrible God. The monastery was just as essential an element of life in rural districts of Western Europe as the parish church, whose incumbent was often appointed by the monks. On the other hand, the Cluniacs took little interest in the management of their worldly affairs; they lacked the competence to do so and, owing to their origin and their liturgical and intellectual preoccupations, viewed it as a matter of quite secondary importance. All idea of utility or profit was entirely alien to them and they made no effort to improve farming methods on their estates.

THE ABBEY OF SAINT GALL

Right: A model of the abbey gives a bird's-eye view of the whole as planned in the ninth century.

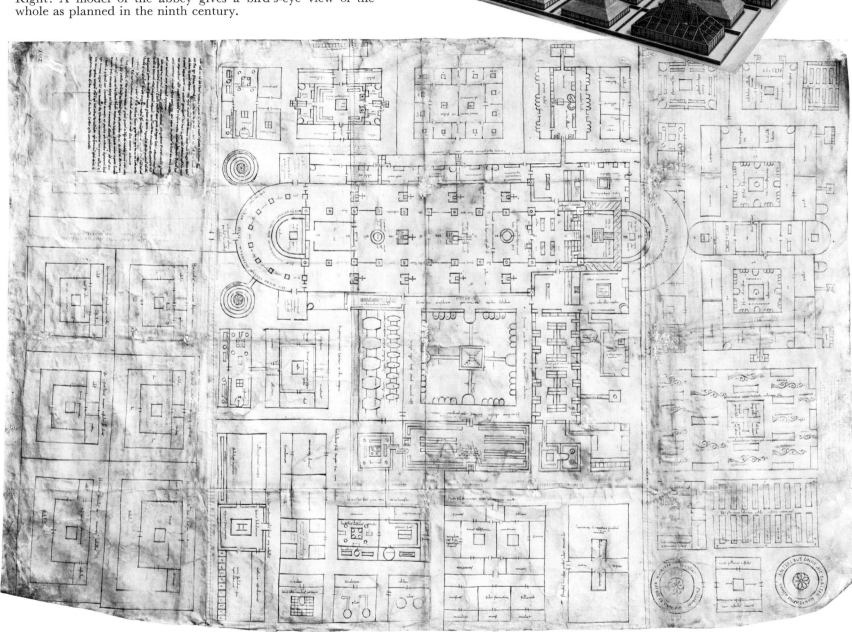

Above: plan of the Abbey of Saint Gall about 820. One can distinguish: to the North-west, the entrance, the vestibule, the guest-house and the school for the young noblemen of the vicinity; to the East and North-east, the noviciate and infirmary; in the centre, the cloister, library, dormitory and refectory; to the South and West, the commons and farm buildings.

The simplified plan on the right makes it easier to read the original (above). The major sectors are: 1. Church — 2. Sacristy — 3. Library and Study Hall — 4. Vestibule — 5. Parlour — 6. Dormitory — 7. Baths and Lavatories — 8. Refectory — 9. Wine Cellar — 10. Monks' Kitchen — 11. Bakery — 12. Guests' Kitchen — 13. Guest-house — 14. School — 15. Abbot's House — 16. Infirmaries — 17. Gardeners' Quarters — 18. Hen-house — 19. Barn — 20. Servants' Quarters — 21. Mill — 22. Almshouse — 23. Stables — 24. Imperial Apartments — 25. Cattle and Sheep — 26. Pigs — 27. Cloister — 28. Vegetable Garden — 29. Cemetery and Orchard.

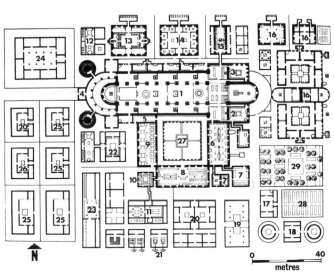

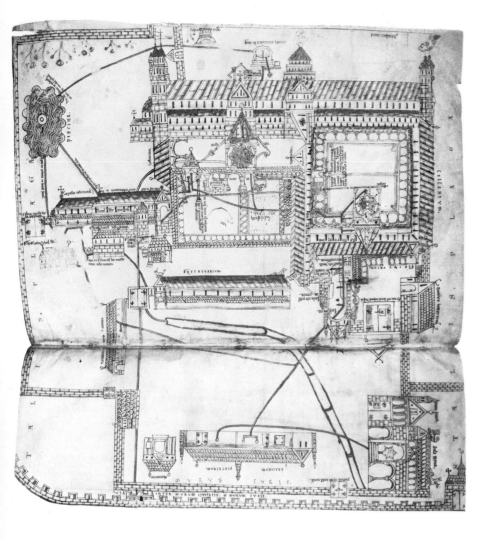

This ancient plan of the Benedictine Abbey of Canterbury shows the water supply system for the vast establishment. The water was pumped from a reservoir (upper left) into conduits that distributed it to the various buildings and in particular to the cisterns in the two cloisters below the church. This plan was drawn in 1160, ten years before the murder of Thomas Becket.

The erection of splendid churches of gigantic proportions—the only religious building in the West that outdid Cluny in this respect was Saint Peter's in Rome—and the time and money spent in organizing pilgrimages, hastening the *Reconquista*, and facilitating the departure of the crusades, inhibited investment and so hampered progress in agricultural techniques and betterment of the country people's standard of living. Lastly, when the Cluniacs played a part in improving the recruitement of the episcopate and took the pope's side against the emperor, they seemed to have betrayed the spirit of Saint Benedict. By the end of the eleventh century, though they may not have forfeited their esteem, they were apparently out of touch with the purest, most traditional aspirations of those who fought and those who worked.

The many monastic orders which arose at that time comprise the Carthusians (1084), whose members were hermits who lived in a community but took a vow of silence, the Order of Fontevrault (1100–01), which combined a monastery and a nunnery both under an abbess, and the Premonstratensians (1120), who spread chiefly in Germany. But the most important of all were the Cistercians (1098) and the military orders (1050–1168).

Although the black monks did not disappear from the western countryside, they were gradually superseded by the white monks who were first concentrated in wild and remote places. They rejected the slightest relaxation of Saint Benedict's rule, refused feudal dues, servile labour, ease and comfort. Their sole clothing was a tunic and cowl with an iron crucifix; their bed was a pallet in the common dormitory; their food was scanty; their church was bare and austere with no belfry, pictures, stained-glass windows or statuary. They insisted on reverting to manual labour with the help of lay brothers and to a spiritual life untrammelled by too splendid a liturgy; also to strict community life and complete decentralization. Under the vigorous leadership of Saint Bernard, by the end of the twelfth century the order numbered more than 500 houses. The Cistercians farmed their estates themselves and built a number of barns around their monasteries; they did a great deal of clearance work and, to make up for the shortage of manpower, greatly improved agricultural methods or went over to livestock breeding, which thrived very well on their damp soil; in England the wool produced by their sheep became an important export commodity. Cistercian monasteries were, as a rule, arranged so as to make the best use of water power. It was not very long before their well-run estates brought wealth to those seekers after absolute poverty. On the other hand, their contemplative way of life was upset by the various services demanded of them by the popes and bishops who had risen from their ranks; they were entrusted, for example, with organizing military orders in the Iberian Peninsula and the war against the heretics in the Languedoc.

In these fields they came into contact with orders which were specialized in such activities. The Cistercian order did not disappear—far from it. Indeed, from the end of the twelfth century to the end of the thirteenth the number of its houses rose from 525 to 694. But it lost the leading position it had monopolized for close on a hundred years. This was due in part to the growing preponderance of the

The Cistercians were zealous in the strict application of the Benedictine rule and so devoted a great deal of their time to manual labour with the assistance of lay brothers (above). The huge barns erected around their chief monasteries prove the importance of their agricultural activities. One of them still stands at Ter Doest near Lissewegen in Belgium; it dates from the thirteenth century.

Unlike the Cluniac churches, those of the Cistercian order were shorn of all purely ornamental decoration. The huge church of Pontigny Abbey (below), one of the 'daughters' of Cîteaux, is 354 feet long, 205 feet wide at the transept and 60 feet high. The most striking external feature is the absence of a steeple.

town over the countryside, which favoured the urban orders rather than the Benedictines, who kept in the main to the rural districts.

The first and most famous of the military orders was established in the mid-eleventh century in connection with an Amalfitan charitable foundation in Jerusalem, which at that time was occupied by the Egyptians. Their ideal, a nursing brotherhood, which they never relinquished, led the Hospitallers to escort and protect pilgrims on the road to the Holy Sepulchre and thus to become the first western order whose vocation for fighting was diametrically opposed to the Christian ideal of peace and charity. The Hospitallers were heavily armed knights recruited exclusively from the nobility, flanked by auxiliary brothers who acted very much like esquires; they lived in buildings that were half-monastery, half-barrack, trained in groups, engaged in frequent combats, observed a very strict discipline, and guarded strongly fortified castles. This way of life the Hospitallers shared with the Templars, the Teutonic Knights and the orders that had sprung up on the eastern and southern fringes of the West—the Brotherhood of the Sword in Livonia and the Knights of Saint James of the Sword and those of Tomar in the Iberian peninsula.

It should be said that the military orders had several centres in England, France and Germany, where they recruited members and concentrated the revenues of estates that were uncommonly well managed and constantly augmented by pious donations and legacies. The surplus of the receipts from the sale of wool by the Templars in England and of grain, furs, wax and amber by the Teutonic Knights in Germany were devoted to financing a permanent crusade against pagans and infidels. Incidentally, the Templars became specialized in banking activities and international clearing operations, which developed as a result of the great flow of money from West to East that was particularly intense during the period of the crusades.

As a matter of fact, the way of life of those soldier monks cannot be equated exactly with that of the nobility or clergy, still less with that of the bankers. Saint Bernard, a great admirer of the Templars, who played a part in their mercurial rise, said: 'Insolent remarks, worthless actions, immoderate laughter, complaints and grumbles, when noted, are always punished. They detest chess and dice; they abhor hunting; they do not find the usual pleasure in the ridiculous pursuit of birds... They shun and loathe mimes, magicians and jugglers, improper songs and satirical farces. They wear their hair short. One never sees them well-kempt, seldom washed, with shaggy beard, reeking of dust, soiled by their armour and the heat. They distrust all excess in food and dress, demanding only what is strictly necessary. They live all together without wives or children.'

The knights slept in cells opening off the same corridor; the brothers in dormitories. In spite of their active life and their two meals a day, they had to abstain from meat three times a week and kept two Lents—from Martinmass to Christmas and from Ash Wednesday to Easter. Rising at midnight for matins, they recited eighty-six prayers: thirteen to Our Lady, thirteen to the saint of the day, thirty for the living and thirty for the dead. At tierce and sext they said fourteen prayers, at vespers eighteen. Discipline was very strict: the slightest fault entailed beating with a stirrup-leather, while the punishment meted out for serious crimes such as larceny, heresy, lying, simony, sodomy or the disclosure of matters discussed by the chapter was far more severe, the worst being expulsion from the order. It has been asserted, without any real evidence, that the Templars cultivated esoteric—even heretical—doctrines. Apparently, they denied Christ three times by spitting on the Cross; but that may have been done in memory of Saint Peter or as a test of humility and total obedience. The legend that they were compelled to indulge in sodomy was already widespread in the fourteenth century. In fact, one reads in the romance of Fauvel:

They are ordered to spit upon [the Cross]
They kissed each other behind...
Which is very hideous to relate.

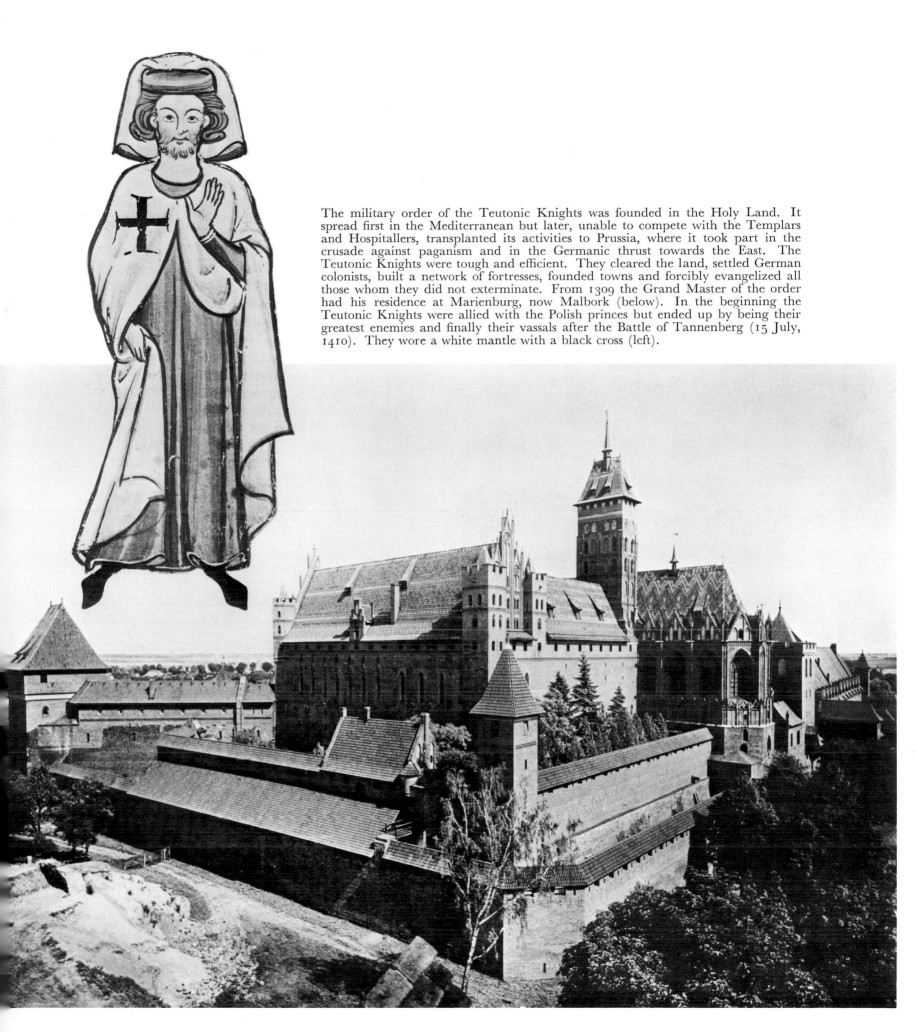

The military order of the Teutonic Knights was founded in the Holy Land. It spread first in the Mediterranean but later, unable to compete with the Templars and Hospitallers, transplanted its activities to Prussia, where it took part in the crusade against paganism and in the Germanic thrust towards the East. The Teutonic Knights were tough and efficient. They cleared the land, settled German colonists, built a network of fortresses, founded towns and forcibly evangelized all those whom they did not exterminate. From 1309 the Grand Master of the order had his residence at Marienburg, now Malbork (below). In the beginning the Teutonic Knights were allied with the Polish princes but ended up by being their greatest enemies and finally their vassals after the Battle of Tannenberg (15 July, 1410). They wore a white mantle with a black cross (left).

245

There may have been a time when it was the custom to bestow a kiss at the lower end of the spine as an initiatory ordeal. Or, quite simply, homosexuality may have developed within the order during the great crises it underwent in the thirteenth century. They were also accused of worshipping Baphomet—an idol that may or may not have been hermaphroditic—but that indictment rests on evidence at once tardy and far from well founded.

Be that as it may, the power, wealth and discipline of the Templars and the fact that they were stationed far away, on the threshold of the fabulous Orient, led to the acceptance of a great many legends and made them the object of a great many hates. Let me mention Wolfram von Eschenbach's words: 'The valiant knights have their residence in the castle of Monsalvat, where the Grail is kept; they are the Templars, who often ride far away in search of adventure; whatever the outcome of their battles, whether glory or humiliation, they accept it with a happy heart in expiation of their sins.' It must also be borne in mind that, like the other military orders, those guardians of the Grail went through a profound crisis in the thirteenth century, made all the more difficult by the loss of the Holy Land and the problem of finding a new place in a society where their financial activities stirred up envy and hate. The Iberian and Teutonic orders surmounted their crises far more brilliantly and the Hospitallers live on today as Knights of the Sovereign Military Order of Malta.

The critical period for the rural and knightly orders was marked by the contemporary rise of a considerable number of new orders that insisted on absolute poverty; their members roamed the roads or settled in the towns, which had come to be the nervous centres, hearts and arteries of the West. These 'mendicant' orders comprised the Carmelites, Augustinians, Sachets (who wore a sort of sack), Pies (dressed in black and white), and more especially the Minorites (Franciscans) and Preachers (Dominicans). They combined action and contemplation in a rule that was strict in matters of morals but more

The order of the Templars was founded in Jerusalem in 1119 under the title of 'Poor Knights of Christ and the Temple of Solomon' to protect pilgrims in Palestine. Later the knights acquired vast estates and amassed a huge fortune that made them the bankers of the merchants and pilgrims. The Templars earned a reputation for being fierce fighters (as suggested by the miniature above) and were feared and respected by their enemies. The meaning of their seal (top) is clear: the armed knight is dedicated to the service of the pilgrim whom he carries and protects. In the fourteenth century some kings were alarmed by the Templars' wealth and power. The pope suppressed the order in 1312 and all its property was transferred to the Hospitallers; in France Philip the Fair only handed it over after extracting as much money as he could.

flexible as regards stability and even hierarchy. These 'friars' gradually developed side by side with the 'monks'.

Saint Dominic (1170–1221) spent 10 years with the Cistercians preaching among the Albigensian heretics; this made him realize the necessity of offering new spiritual models to match the new problems of the human society, based on total return to poverty and evangelical predication. As a result, his first act was to set up at Prouille in the South of France the first nunnery for repentant and converted Cathar women (1207–1211). This was followed in 1215 by the establishment at Toulouse, in the very heart of the reconquered Albigensian country, of the first house of his order of Preaching Friars, based on the rule of Saint Augustine and the practices of Prémontré. When the founder died in 1221 the order was already divided into eight provinces: France, Germany, England, Spain, Hungary, Rome, Provence and Lombardy; the Holy Land, Greece, Poland and Dacia were added in 1228. Every year each convent appointed delegates to the general chapter, which elected the General.

Those who aspired to enter the order of Saint Dominic underwent a lengthy noviciate, during which they lived a cloistered life and made a serious study of theology. After taking their vows of obedience, poverty and chastity, they entered a monastery, where they continued their studies and were ordained as priests. From that moment, their life was spent in study, meditation, teaching, administration, pastoral work and preaching in town squares and the open countryside. They practised absolute poverty and demonstrated their penitence and self-denial by fasting and mortification. Their intellectual training made them uniquely persuasive preachers; dressed in the white gown of Prémontré overlaid by the black cloak of the Augustinian canons, they played a leading part in the universities. The two greatest scholars of the Middle Ages, Albertus Magnus and Thomas Aquinas, were Dominicans.

While the Preaching Friars dealt in dogma and aimed at their listeners' intelligence and reason, the disciples of Saint Francis of Assisi (1181–1226) sought to reach men's hearts with their words on practical moral issues. In their hooded robe of coarse brown drugget as worn by the poor of Umbria, with a length of rope knotted round their waist, they were the poorest of the poor. Renouncing the convent that offered material security and begging for their daily bread, they travelled as far afield as Egypt, Mongolia and China to preach the evangelical virtues of simplicity, humility, charity and love. Saint Clara of Favorino, an admirer of Saint Francis, founded the corresponding female order of the Poor Clares. By the end of the thirteenth century over 1,500 houses divided into 34 provinces followed the Franciscan rule, and the secular world was deeply penetrated by the friars' preaching and example. A great many lay men and women who were not prepared to renounce the world and marriage formed confraternities for the purpose of doing penance. This was the origin of the 'Third Order of Saint Francis', which at about the middle of the century counted close on 600,000 members in Italy alone— over 5 per cent of the total population! Others formed an association with the Dominicans.

Obviously, those mendicant orders, whose members lived a life of action amid the population of the towns or preached and heard confessions from all classes on the open roads, made an enormous impact. Any description of life in the Middle Ages must give the place they deserve to those friars and, in general, to all monks and other seekers for perfection. Few orders disappeared during that period and none ousted its predecessors; they all lived side by side for centuries. Wayfarers and pilgrims could count on finding board and lodging in the barns and priories of the Cistercians, the abbeys of the Benedictines, the foundations of the Cluniacs, the Premonstratensian nunneries and the commanderies of the Hospitallers, Templars and Teutonic Knights. On their way they joined Black Friars travelling from church to church to preach or to distant universities to teach or study, or Franciscans who, true to the spirit of their founder, had left their 'conventual' brethren to harangue and stir up the people within a hair's breadth of heresy and disobedience. In contrast to the secular clergy, who were more bound by tradition and hierarchy, the regular clergy were in constant transformation and renovation in keeping with the economic, social and spiritual conditions of the world around them; they formed the progressive wing of the Western Church.

THE CHURCH AND THE WORLD

The seekers for perfection were cut off from the world by the walls of their convents and from its multifarious conditions and ways of life by the strict observance of their rule; in other respects there was for centuries nothing to distinguish them from the general mass of the laity. On the contrary, the men who served God soon formed an order that was hierarchized on two counts: capability and authority.

All that was needed to become a clerk was the tonsure. The ceremony, repeated millions and millions of times, was performed in the presence of the bishop who, after intoning an introit or a Kyrie eleison, clipped the candidate's hair and beard as a visible sign of his—very partial—renouncement of the world in expectation of God's eternal kingdom. This was confirmed by the formula of dedication, recited in unison by the bishop and the new clerk. The latter, after receiving the tonsure, had to rise by stages through a series of orders before he attained the priesthood and the right to celebrate the Divine mysteries. Since there was a fixed interval between each order, he was 30 years of age—quite exceptionally 25—by the time he was allowed to practise the full powers of a priest. The orders were divided into major and minor. The minor orders were doorkeeper or sacristan who kept the key to the church, watched over the liturgical ornaments and was permitted to ring the bell; reader, who instructed the people by reading religious texts and could bless fruit and bread; exorcist, who had power over devils; and acolyte, who carried the cruets and candlestick. Then came the subdeacon, already under obligation of continence, who helped to celebrate the mysteries and was increasingly looked upon as having received

a major order. Above him was the deacon, who could preach, administer certain sacraments, such as baptism and even holy communion, who wore the stole and dalmatic. Lastly, the priest celebrated the mysteries and the Eucharistic sacrifice, gave blessings and administered most of the sacraments. The episcopacy was the highest grade of the priesthood but did not constitute a special order.

The strict hierarchy that ruled the clergy in the West was largely inherited from the administrative structure of the late Roman Empire, as they existed when the Christian religion was established in Rome. The basic nucleus was the ancient 'city'—a town with its surrounding country. When a number of those cities were grouped together to form a province, one of them became the capital or metropolis. The priest of the city was called 'episcopos', the Greek word for 'overseer', from which our word 'bishop' derived. He was to some extent answerable to the metropolitan, the priest in charge of the province, who at the time of Charlemagne was given the suggestive title of archbishop. But as Christianity spread and the country people—'pagani' in Latin, from which our word 'pagan' comes—were converted, the bishop ceased to be the only priest of the city. He was surrounded by a number of clerics who assisted and advised him; when the canonical rule was adopted in the ninth century, they formed the cathedral chapter. More important still, the parishes that grew up around the bishop's see and became the new nuclei of Western Christianity required the services of a great many clerics.

A parish often sprang up in a domain, centred in the village that had developed around the manor house, whose private chapel became the church;

This magnificent disc in gold, silver, enamel and precious stones was formerly fixed on a staff and served as a flabellum. The use of those ceremonial fans dates back to the first centuries of Christianity, when they were employed in Mediterranean lands to keep flies away from the Blessed Sacrament and the officiating prelates; in those early days they were made of parchment or feathers. Later flabella were also introduced in countries where their utility was not so obvious. They developed imperceptibly into precious objects, notably reliquaries like this, which dates from the thirteenth century. This flabellum, one of a pair, is in New York, its twin in Leningrad.

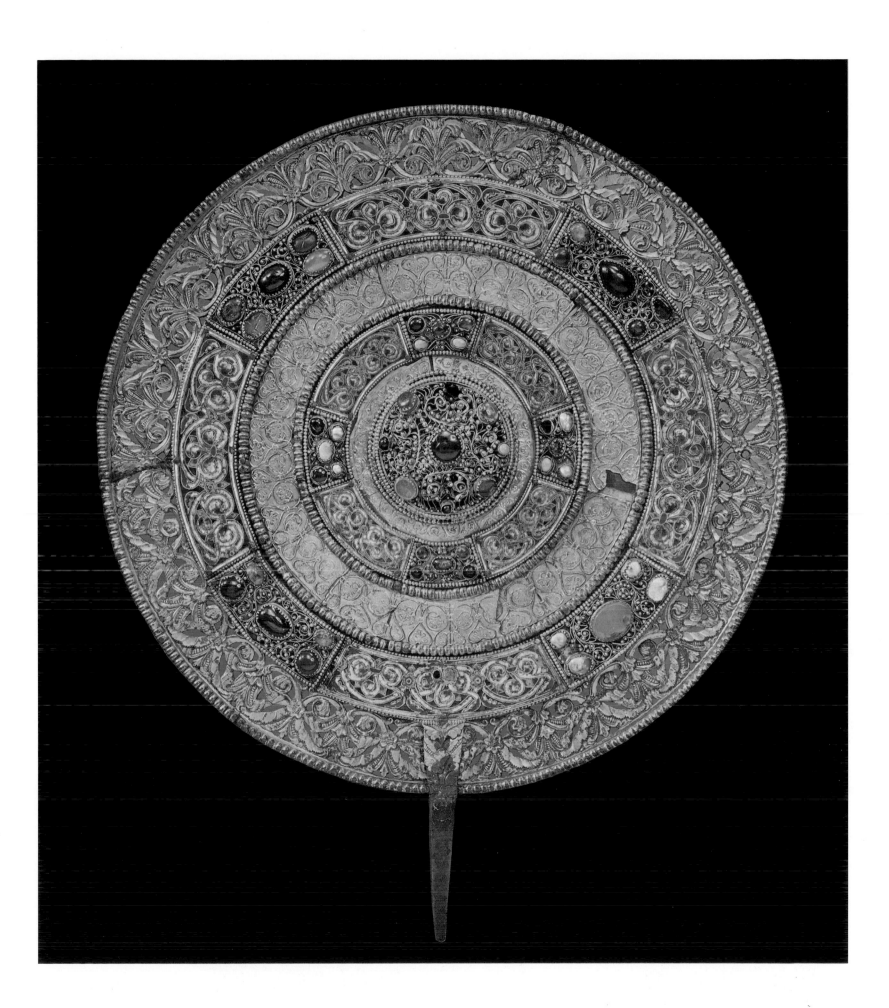

Churchmen set great store by the beauty and quality of liturgical objects: nothing was too fine for the Lord's service. Left: the abbot of Clairvaux's crozier, at once a commander's baton and a good shepherd's crook (twelfth century). Right: a liturgical comb in ivory; the carving in the middle represents the adoration of the Magi. Below right: the very ancient chalice of Ardagh (Ireland).

The mitre was the attribute of the bishop but was also worn by many abbots, termed 'mitred and croziered', who were directly answerable to the general of their order or to the pope. Mitres were often precious articles embroidered with gold and silver thread. The one on the right dates from the second half of the fourteenth century; the principal decorative motif represents the Annunciation.

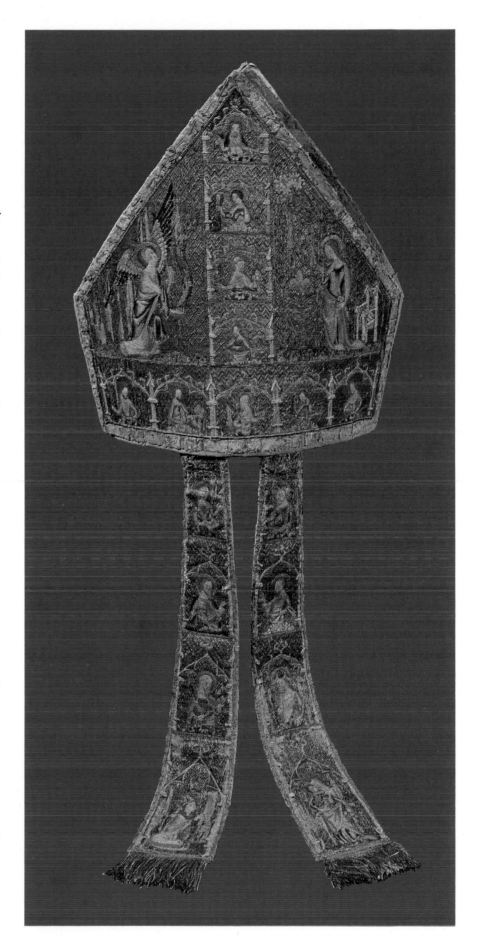

this gave it a strong economic cohesion. But spiritual cohesion was stronger still; its focal point was the vicar or rector who administered the sacraments, said the obligatory Sunday Mass, prayed, preached and spread the news. The church was the centre of gravity of the village; the churchyard *(campo santo)* was the place where the villagers gathered to make merry, pay the tithe or bury their dead. All this gave the parish priest great moral authority, but his economic situation was not always very satisfactory. As a rule he had at his disposal a piece of land which he often farmed himself; this put him in a position to understand perfectly the problems that beset his flock. He also received a quarter of the tithe, if it was not entirely payable to the feudal lord; the remaining three quarters went on the upkeep of the church, assistance to poor people and orphans and a contribution to the bishop. Another source of income consisted of the surplice fees, namely payments for marriages, burials and the like. He could also hope to receive pious donations and bequests. Therefore, under normal conditions, he had enough to live on and even to bring up the family with which far too many priests were saddled. His situation was worse if he was appointed by a monastery, a cathedral chapter or a lay patron; they paid him what they considered an 'adequate' share of the tithe but it was in fact far from sufficient. The destitution in which the humble rural clergy lived cannot be determined with any precision, but it certainly did not place them on a much higher level than their parishioners.

Sometimes, as the population increased and more land was cleared, a parish outgrew its possibilities and split up into a number of new ones. When this happened the parish priest became a 'rural dean' with a certain authority over the priests of the new parishes, which all together formed a deanery. A group of deaneries formed an archdeanery, and a group of archdeaneries formed a diocese. In the Romanized countries this latter unit very frequently corresponded to the ancient city and was spiritually subordinate to the bishop, who was the corner stone of the ecclesiastical hierarchy.

The clergy performed their educational tasks by word of mouth, both individually and collectively. Above: A cleric exhorts a youth. Left: The Sunday sermon was an effective method of imparting instruction and directives, blame and encouragement, to the people.

The bishop enjoyed an estate whose importance made him a great landowner and gave him a leading position in the feudal society. He was also vested with various powers, those of authority, jurisdiction, magisterium and administration over all the Christians in his diocese. Authority to consecrate churches, pronounce blessings, confer the sacraments of confirmation and holy orders. Jurisdiction gave him exclusive cognizance of matters concerning religion— blasphemy, marriage, wills—and all crimes committed by clerks, as well as the right to excommunicate. Magisterium duties included training clerics and instructing the laymen. Administration entailed his authorization of the erection of religious buildings and the dividing up of the parishes. He could count on very large revenues: in addition to his manors, fiefs, allodia, feudal dues and taxes on fairs, markets and so on, he received a quarter of the tithe and was the heir to any property left by a cleric. In his capacity as a temporal lord he lived surrounded by numerous lay staff, knights, noble ladies, and baliffs; as a ecclesiastic he was assisted in the performance of his duties by a great many clerks, coadjutors who replaced him if he fell ill, an archpriest for the cathedral services, a vicar-general, a chancellor who kept his seal and supervised a host of notaries, an official principal to whom he delegated— within well-defined limits—the right to pass judgment and grant pardons, and an archdeacon, a kind of petty prime minister who had his own little court, kept his own police and looked after the parishes.

However, the bishop was not all-powerful. On the one hand, he was hemmed in by the members of the cathedral chapter, rich canons who began by electing him and then gave him advice and housed him in the splendid cathedral which they had built and administered. Occasionally those canons enjoyed particularly large revenues, which made them richer than the bishop himself; in that case the dean or provost who was their leader raised his voice to make demands and complaints. On the other hand, some communities in the diocese also wanted to have their own way. For example, colleges of canons generously endowed by the princes or bishops who had founded them or enriched by pilgrimages and rights of all sorts which they had been left by will or had usurped; monastic houses, particularly those whose head was entitled to mitre and crozier and who had considerable wealth at their disposal. Some abbeys and priories were 'exempt', that is, totally removed

The church was the house of God, but also of the people. The pulpit was set in the centre of the edifice and was very conspicuous because the preacher had to be seen and heard by the whole congregation. In the church of Notre-Dame at Vitré the carved wood pulpit is a splendid example of the flamboyant Gothic style.

from the bishop's authority and answerable directly to the abbot-general or grand master of their order, who in turn was directly responsible to the pope.

Lastly, the bishop was always conscious of the proximity and impending authority of the metropolitan archbishop who, after confirming his election, had consecrated him and received his oath of obedience and was entitled to judge appeals from the decisions of the bishop's official principal. Higher up still—we may leave aside the 'national' primates (Canterbury, Lyons, Toledo and the others) who had only a vague precedence over their fellow-bishops—was the pope, the bishop of Rome, who was surrounded by the Sacred College, had his own territorial endowment in the shape of the Patrimony of Saint Peter, and enjoyed worldwide jurisdiction. It was during the Middle Ages that the pope became the autocratic sovereign who reigned at Avignon in the fourteenth century and in Rome from the fifteenth; he was the centre of a brilliant and numerous court supported rather by the revenues cleverly and meticulously collected throughout the West than by those provided by the papal state. Since Nicholas I in the mid-ninth century, he had been crowned; since Gregory VII at the end of the eleventh, he had been totally free of the emperor's tutelage; while Innocent III (1198-1216) made him the unquestioned head of all Christendom. The pope was the source of canon law; he demanded an oath of allegiance from the bishops, whom he appointed and could transfer from one see to another, and whose spiritual authority he controlled by removing many cases to his own court and sending legates to every part of the Western World. He alone had supreme power over the secular clergy and most of the monastic and mendicant orders. Last but not least, he had in his possession an enormous number of benefices and could therefore rely on a host of loyal and grateful clients among the ranks of the clergy.

The pope was flanked by the cardinals, true princes of the Church; each of them had his own civil or military household, whose members wore his livery, and a small court. After 1059 the cardinals

elected the pope and advised him in all matters, even the appointment of new cardinals. They frequently acted as legates, which gave them an opportunity to improve their knowledge of the West. Being few in number—generally a score or so—they were anxious to play an increasingly important part in the direction of the Church and could exert considerable influence on so-called 'transition' popes.

The solidarity and homogeneity of the clergy were strengthened by visits of legates to the metropolitans, of metropolitans in their provinces, of bishops in their dioceses, of archdeacons and deans in their respective territories. The same objective was achieved by assemblies held at different levels. The general council, the assembly of the entire Western Church, was convened very rarely because the pope

253

The organ is the musical instrument best suited to religious ceremonies. Its powerful voice and the range of its timbres makes the vast nave of a church its natural home. The organ in the church of Valère at Sion in Switzerland (right) is the oldest that can still be played. It is built after the fashion of the so-called 'Burgundian' organs (left) depicted in paintings of that period. The air is supplied by hand-operated bellows.

mistrusted it, but it became extremely important when schisms broke out in the fifteenth century. National, provincial and diocesan synods, whose meetings became increasingly frequent, provided opportunities for coming to grips at regular intervals with the major problems and at the same time strengthened the bonds between the prelates, the lower clergy, conventual monks and mendicant friars.

The integration of the clergy in the everyday life of the laity raised a number of problems at both the individual and the general level and helped to enhance the former's unique, privileged position if not its homogeneity. The vast lands owned by the Church, perhaps even as early as the Merovingian period and in any case during the Carolingian and post-Carolingian periods, accounted for between 30 and 40 per cent of the total area of Western Europe and enjoyed the privilege of immunity. This meant that they were exempt from taxation, the representatives of the king and count could not enter them, and justice and quartering dues were collected by the bishop or abbot at the head of the community.

It must be said that the Carolingian monarchs favoured the privileged ecclesiastical landlords because they saw their power as a local counterbalance to the counts, and required of them an oath of fealty in exchange for the 'honour', namely the estate with which they endowed them and whose immune character they stressed. When the Carolingian empire disintegrated, that bond of fealty was greatly relaxed and the ecclesiastical landlords became virtually independent. Many had a host of vassals, some of them counts, and usurped the powers of a count or even established territorial principalities. The evolution of those immunities is particularly striking in the Germanic Empire where, because of the favour of Otto the Great, they formed the nucleus of veritable states. The archbishops of Trier, Cologne and Mainz and the abbot of Fulda were the most famous of those powerful privileged prelates.

But ecclesiastical offices and functions had one basic feature which the others lacked: they were not hereditary. This resulted in a second difference be-tween the immunities and the fiefs which were constituted in the West during that period—the end of the ninth century and the beginning of the tenth. The incumbent was chosen by election.

There was seldom any problem at the lowest level, namely that of the parish priest. In fact, the parish church was often simply the lord's former private chapel and, since it had been built either by him or his ancestors, he viewed it as his property. Consequently, he kept the relative tithes, taxes and surplice-fees and appointed the incumbent, whom he selected from his own household, to make assurance doubly sure, and rewarded him with a tiny patch of ground. But at the level of the bishopric, if not already of the deanery, the normal procedure was for the clergy and the people to have a say in the election of their pastor. It all depended on the way in which that tradition of the primitive Church was interpreted. Popes Leo the Great and Stephen V (888) proclaimed that 'the election appertains to the priests; the people must be informed and not obeyed'. Actually, in this case the priests were not the lesser clergy, which was gradually set aside and replaced by the local clerics who had belonged to the late bishop's circle, namely the cathedral canons; these latter were the first to be informed of the vacancy and could therefore agree on the name of a candidate and force its acceptance. Sometimes the great abbots of the diocese insisted on the privilege of 'first say'; this means that they submitted a first name which then won the adherence of many who had an open mind.

The bishop-elect had to receive confirmation and undergo a public examination of his life and scholarship at a synod which, in theory at least, comprised most of the churchmen and in any case all the bishops of the ecclesiastical province and was chaired by the metropolitan archbishop. He was then consecrated by the metropolitan assisted by two of his bishops. The main features of the ceremony were the laying on of hands with the words 'Accipe Spiritum Sanctum' (Receive the Holy Spirit), the annointing of his hands and forehead with holy oil, and the delivery of the pastoral staff, symbol of his

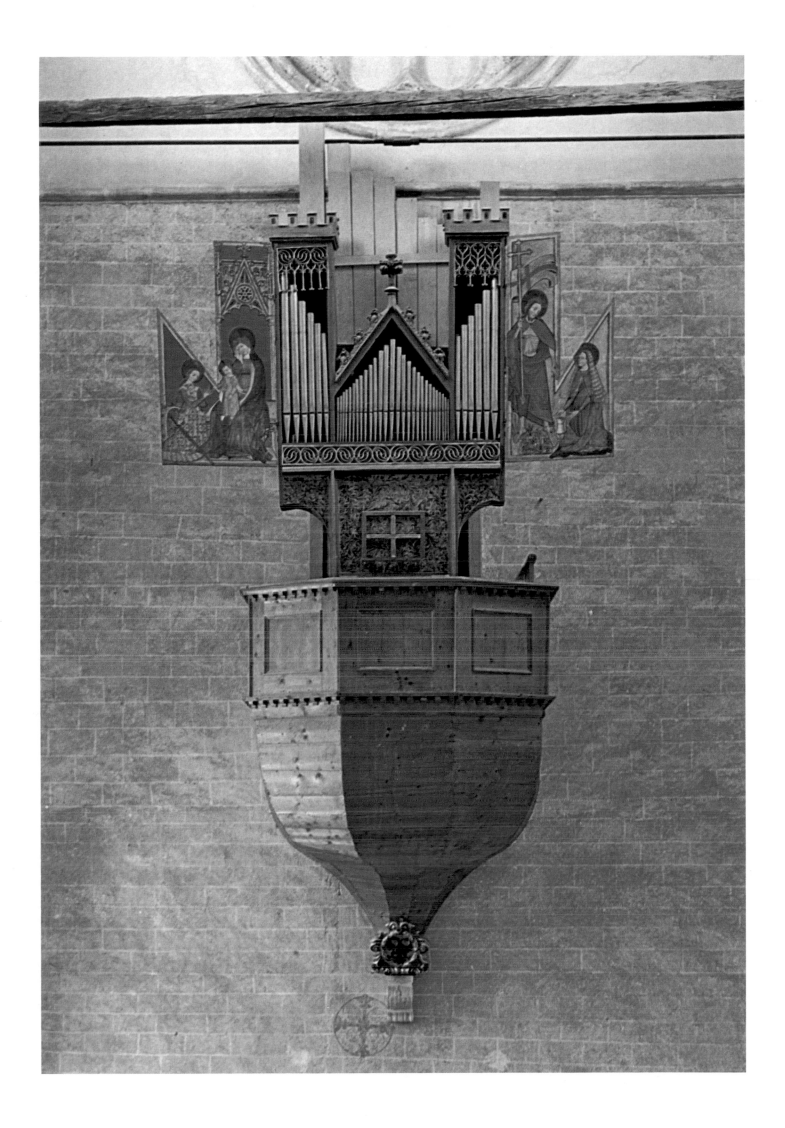

The Mass was the most important religious office. It was governed by a very precise ritual that varied with the prominence of the occasion and the celebrant. Above: The Mass of the Holy Relics involved a pomp and ceremony that made the divine rite a function at once splendid and impressive.

right to govern the diocese, with the words: 'Receive the staff, sign of sacred government, which lays upon thee the duty to fortify the weak, steady the irresolute, punish the wicked and lead the good in the way to eternal salvation.' The conferring of the ring recalled the bishop's mystic marriage with his church, from which he would not be separated until his death: only the pope could transfer a bishop from one see to another.

If the candidate failed in his canonical examination, the metropolitan and his suffragan bishops lost no time in consecrating another; this caused heated discussions, which often developed into open struggles. In principle the matter should have been submitted to the pope; in practice the decisive factor was the relative strength of the opposing forces, so the laity had the last word. Some laymen actually exerted a direct influence after the election—not the common people, who could do no more than confirm the elected candidate by acclamation, but the bishop's vassals, notably those who were not settled on estates in the country but lived in the city; being well armed, they were in a position to bring pressure to bear on the canons. The same is true of the local lords, particularly the count or viscount whose seat was in the immediate vicinity. But the weightiest intervention was that of the territorial prince who had usurped the royal privileges.

From the time of Charlemagne, if not earlier, the sovereign had acquired or recovered the right to grant an election or select a candidate. This right was more or less explicitly recognized by the popes, and in 921 John X declared that 'no bishop may be consecrated in his diocese without the royal consent'. Otto the Great appointed all his bishops, and at the end of the tenth century the king of France held nineteen bishoprics and four metropolitan sees (Reims, Sens, Tours and Bourges) which were his major sources of revenue. But many other princes usurped this royal right: the duke of Normandy appointed seven bishops; the count of Roussillon chose the bishop of Elne; the viscount of Bigorre that of Tarbes, and so on. This intervention by laymen in the affairs of the Church was deeply rooted in the feudal society. In fact, the temporalities of the bishops and abbots were endowments of land which enabled those prelates to perform their duties, and they were granted in exchange for an oath of fealty to the donor. As a rule, those honours and temporalities were considered as fiefs, the oath as an oath of vassalage, and therefore the essential ceremony was the investiture of the bishop (or abbot) elect with those lands before his consecration. It included placing his hands between the lord's, doing hommage and taking an oath 'as a man to his lord'; only after that the bishop elect received the symbol of his 'fief', not in the shape of a truss of straw, a lump of earth, or a banner, but the ring and crozier that were the emblems of his office. Hence, on this plane there was total confusion because the lord who invested the bishop elect was looked upon as owner in chief of those estates, which were only granted to the bishop for life. This enabled him to resume possession of the lands and depose the bishop, although this was contrary to canon law, dispose of them by bequest, sell them and give them in dowry. The bishop himself was viewed as a vassal who owed his lord aid and counsel. Lastly, since this lay investiture preceded the consecration which involved the bestowal of the ring and crozier, it thrust into second place, both literally and figuratively, the delivery of the crozier, that symbol of spiritual authority, by the metropolitan, and indeed the entire consecration ceremony. Taking the extreme view, it could be argued that it was the emperor who gave the pope the Patrimony of Saint Peter, appointed him and required him to swear an oath of fealty.

As a result of all this, the prelates were no less closely integrated than the rural clergy in the lay society. They lived in a palace or castle in the midst of their knights and vassals, made blood flow in hunt and battle, took pleasure in debauchery—in accordance with the Nicolaite doctrine—bought their election and sold sacred objects (simony). Prelates tended to be recruited exclusively from the knightly class: younger sons of noble families, friends one

The ecclesiastical hierarchy crystallized at a relatively early date and is clearly defined in this ninth century miniature. Below: the five minor orders—porter, reader, subdeacon, exorcist and acolyte. Above: the deacon, priest, and bishop, who is the guardian of the faith.

The pope is the bishop of Rome and the head of Western Christendom. He is surrounded by a college of cardinals distinguished by their peculiar hats.

Opposite page: not all clerics obeyed the Ten Commandments. They have been accused of four great failings—lechery (far right), drunkenness (right), and luxurious living (top right).

In solemn ceremonies and processions the Blessed Sacrament is carried and exposed to the people in a monstrance, designed first like a reliquary (left) and later like the sun. Whether plain or ornate, the monstrance is always made of precious metal: silver or silver-gilt.

The hosts for the Mass are made of a fluid mixture of flour and water baked in a mould like wafers. Below: a fourteenth century host mould with Christ and the twelve apostles.

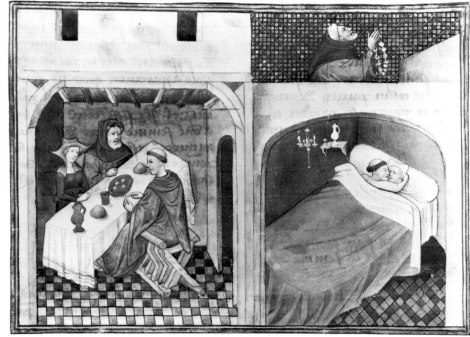

wanted to gratify, became bishops and abbots, daughters for whom no husband could be found were appointed canonesses. Indeed, it was a lucky chance when they were ordained and consecrated members of the clergy. Occasionally a layman became abbot, took up his abode in the monastery together with his family and his knights, annexing its revenues and leaving a mere pittance to the monks and the person who performed his spiritual functions. In any case, even when the layman elected to a bishopric sought consecration—and sometimes he was a man of great culture and unimpeachable morals—the fact remained that he became a churchman with neither vocation nor training and that his mentality and way of life were very similar to those of his brothers or cousins, lords of the nearby manors. In the eleventh century the Church, including a great many Benedictine and Cluniac monasteries, was profoundly infiltrated, penetrated and moulded, in body and spirit alike, by the outside world.

One can readily understand the importance of the so-called Gregorian reforms initiated by Popes

Gregory VII and Urban II and completed by Calixtus II in 1122. They went part of the way towards removing the great prelates from the feudal system by forbidding them to do homage to laymen, insisting on their being freely elected by the canons or directly appointed by the pope, and selecting many of them from among the monks and friars. By the mid-twelfth century scandalous prelates were far fewer in number, but unfortunately the lesser clergy were still entirely submerged in the rural community or closely bound up with the urban proletariat among which they lived.

Popular literature, satirical publications and the romances of chivalry had no pity for the secular clergy, the eminent prelates or the societies of nuns and canonesses. If we are to believe those works, their way of life was poles apart from the religious ideal. Their many vices included gluttony and drunkenness: the white monks were very fond of good-quality wine and among the black monks morals were very depraved; greed and deceit: priests of the lowest standing received payment for scores of

Masses that were never said; cardinals stole and robbed on a huge scale and took their booty across the Alps; clerics bought and sold, speculated on the price of grain, and even loaned money to the Jews; the white monks made a profit on everything, used churches for barns and churchyards for pigsties; and the simoniacal bishops, having incurred great expense to buy their see, had only one idea—to recover their outlay and make a fortune. Pride, sloth and hardness of heart were rife; there was little zeal in the performance of function or conformance to the monastic way of life. Nor should we forget lewdness, though it was less among the Benedictine monks and nuns than we have been led to believe.

The clergy enjoyed privileges, wealth and power that could not help exciting great envy among the knightly class as well as in the towns and villages. Satire, slander and calumny were the easiest forms of revenge. But a great many of these criticisms were openly discussed by preachers, pinpointed by episcopal directives, and proved true by numerous trials, records of which have been preserved in the pontifical archives and in the files of the sovereign princes. Heedless of their duties as priests, many clerks lived a life that was almost identical with that of the laity.

THE CHURCH, WARDEN OF THE WEST

Though seemingly so strongly influenced by the laity—to the point of being out of touch with many of the virtues expected of those who are dedicated to the service of God—the clergy actually enmeshed the whole western society in a strictly hierarchized system and a complicated series of obligatory rules and rites. They also supervised and guided initiatives, checked and controlled the acquisition of knowledge, preserved as far as possible the division of society in accordance with the order established by God, and bitterly withstood all those who disputed their monopoly of education and their vision of the world.

A study of ecclesiastical jurisdiction is a good way to obtain a picture of one side of this constant watch over society; it also pinpoints the difference in status between clergy and laity.

The Church had the sole right to judge many matters concerning all Christians and all matters concerning the clergy or those who were considered as clerks. Needless to say, the ecclesiastical courts were not identical with the lay courts that were maintained by the bishops, abbots and chapters who, in their quality as lords, had jurisdiction over their vassals and dependants. First of all, the Church exerted divine justice: it was a pitiless censor of all sins and, through the intermediary of the penitentiary, remitted those sins in consideration of a penance proportionate to their gravity; this penance must not be confused with the temporal punishment the sinner may have deserved. A crime for which a civil judge would have inflicted a term of imprisonment or a fine might be atoned for by a pilgrimage or a public penance. In extreme cases the bishop, the papal legate or the pope in person could pronounce excommunication against the culprit; this entailed his exclusion from the Church and therefore, in practice, from society because he was deprived of the sacraments, which were its corner stones, and of all contact with his fellow Christians.

On occasion excommunication of an individual or a collective was complicated by the addition of an interdict—an extremely grave spiritual punishment that debarred a town, a region or even an entire country from ecclesiastical functions and public worship. No Masses were said, no confessions heard, no weddings were celebrated; no communicants received the Eucharist and, when the measure was applied with the utmost rigour, no infants were christened and the dying were denied Extreme Unction. It put great numbers of innocent persons to the risk of eternal damnation simply because they were the subjects of a certain prince or inhabitants of a certain town. But for an interdict to be fully effective all the clergy had to obey it without exception and, more important still, the terrible sentence had to be reserved for the most exceptional cases. Otherwise people could come to terms with the interdict and the responsible sovereign could force some churchmen to disobey it or, as a last resort, obtain the election of an anti-pope who would set it aside. Fortunately, in most cases the culprit confessed his sin publicly or, more and more frequently, in private and redeemed his penance with alms, fasts, prayers or a pilgrimage, or earned through his merits in fighting the infidels or financing the erection of a church an indulgence, that is, the remission of part or all of the punishment incurred in this world and the next.

Human justice was resorted to for real matters *(ratione materiae)* or personal matters *(ratione personae)*. Real matters were those that concerned the sacraments, crimes against the faith and against sacred persons or places, wills, some oaths and pledges, ecclesiastical benefices and the estates of the Church. Personal matters comprised those concerning the clergy and other persons who were considered as clerks. It is easy to imagine that this removed an enormous number of cases from the civil courts since they could be submitted directly to the bishop of the official principal. Since marriage was a sacrament, all matrimonial questions lay within their jurisdiction, in particular the devolution of matrimonial property. The same is true of most cases of adultery and infanticide, as well as the vast majority of wills, notably those involving pious bequests. Crimes against the faith included simony, the traffic in sacred objects, magic, sorcery and, in particular, heresy. We shall see how the dreaded tribunal of the Inquisition was set up in the Languedoc in the thirteenth century to restore the Christian faith and the dominion of the Church in the lands where the Albigensian heresy had flourished. There were also the crimes committed in holy places and violations of the right of sanctuary.

In fact, any criminal could take refuge in an ecclesiastical building; by so doing he evaded all secular jurisdiction. The Church was strong enough not only to impose respect of that sanctuary, which had been too often violated under the Merovingians, but also to extend the right beyond the limit of thirty to sixty paces round about a church, thus including cemeteries and even entire villages on newly cleared land. The boundaries of those new villages were marked by crosses, many of which still stand. Needless to say, that fore-runner of modern immunity resulted in various abuses: ruffians pursued by the watch in the vicinity of a church had only to clutch a special ring supplied for that purpose to make sure of immunity; urban cemeteries were used as headquarters by bands of robbers, who took refuge there at nightfall; all sorts of people settled in the villages that enjoyed immunity.

Not all Church lands had the right of sanctuary. In the case of some fiefs held by the Church the lay lord who was their owner in chief was subject to the jurisdiction of the public court, so this latter had to decide on the position of the estate before the competent authority was established with certainty. The same is true of the tithes, some of which were attached to a fief. As for oaths, if calling God and the saints as witnesses ought normally to involve the jurisdiction of the ecclesiastical court, the fact that the bond between lord and vassal and the feudal system as a whole was based on an oath would have placed the immense majority of civil and criminal cases in the hands of the Church. On the other hand, a great many contracts were drawn up before the official principal by mutual consent of the parties, especially when trade developed and written proof became increasingly necessary. This made the Church their guarantor to a certain extent and any disputes that might arise out of them had to be submitted to the person who had appended his signature to the deed. This gratuitous jurisdiction spread widely during the twelfth and thirteenth centuries.

In addition to these real cases the ecclesiastical court also took cognizance of personal cases. The humblest tonsured clerk was in duty bound to deny the competence of any lay court and demand that his chattels be not seized. If he was caught red-handed the public justice could arrest him but was obliged to hand him over at once to an ecclesiastical court; an officer who failed to do so would have incurred excommunication on the spot. But the number of clerks was almost incredible. Just think of the many who had been tonsured but were married and, though they lived a worldly life, enjoyed the benefit of clergy. Think too of all the priests— they may well have accounted for 5 or 6 per cent of the adult population in the West. To these must be added those who were legally considered on a par with clerks, namely all crusaders, students, and such *miserabiles personae* as widows and orphans to whom the Church owed protection. Lastly, there were all the impostors who had the top of their head shaved to win people's confidence or keep out of reach of the police; it was no easy matter for public justice to get hold of them without causing a scandal.

In all these ways the clergy were distinguished by their privileged position apart from the rest of the Christian society; what is more, the exercise of divine and human justice gave them effective control over all the major activities of that society.

Further proof of this control over the vital forces of the West and their subjection to the Church is provided by the construction of cathedrals, abbeys and religious edifices of all sorts. Erected in their thousands and tens of thousands, they mobilized the labour, revenues and capital of tens of millions of men, who were perhaps drained of their energies and resources by the gigantic task.

It is difficult to draw up a balance sheet. On the one hand, the edifices, many of them extraordinarily beautiful, bear witness to an original civilization at its peak and to the technical progress that was at once their cause and their effect. On the other, billions of working hours and colossal sums of money were squandered on achievements that brought the community little *material* profit. It is worth recalling that in the West there were fewer than 200 persons to every church; in some districts of Hungary and Italy, fewer than 100. The ancient cathedral cities of York, Lincoln and Norwich had 140 churches for a total population of 20,000 people between the three. It has been calculated that at the end of the thirteenth century there were close on 350,000 places of worship for a total population of 70 million. This does not seem far fetched if we think of the thousands of monastic houses, almost a thousand cathedrals and several times as many great minsters and collegiate churches. Many of those buildings were very large; as a rule, large enough to assemble on important occasions all the inhabitants of the town or village except the young mothers, the nurslings and the aged. Amiens Cathedral, for example, covers a surface of about 83,000 square feet for some 10,000 inhabitants, of which only three quarters could be counted on. In the ancient parts of Toulouse and Cologne there are still a great many churches dating from the Middle Ages; so are there, with all the more reason, in Venice, Florence and Rome. And their height is sometimes hardly believable. The keystones under the towers of Seville Cathedral are 184 feet above the ground, those of the choir at Beauvais 157 feet; the tower at Strasbourg is 465 feet high, while that at Beauvais was higher than 500 feet before it collapsed.

Why did the Church demand such enormous efforts and how did it succeed in stimulating them? What were the immediate consequences for the everyday life of the population?

That temples consecrated to the deity employed rare materials, prompted the development of advanced techniques, and were the finest and noblest achievements of an entire civilization was nothing new. Proof of this is provided by Abu-Simbel, the Parthenon, Chichen-Itza and Angkor. But the cathedrals and churches of the West were not set aside for the exclusive use of the priests; the faithful were also permitted to enter them and approach the holy of holies. The huge workforce did not toil to give their brothers and sons merely a sight of the outside of the temple; the house of God was also the house of His people. It was open to all: not only for prayer but also for walking, eating and sleeping. People took their dogs there with them and argued in loud voices about matters both sacred and profane. In the towns churches often served for meetings of the guilds and the municipality. Lastly, on Sundays and the feasts of specially revered saints, which were

The Church was very active in the social field, chiefly in the matter of care for the poor, the sick and the orphaned. Above right: Two stretcher bearers carry a sick man to the Hôtel-Dieu in Paris; on the left, the reception of a novice who wants to devote her life to the service of the sick. The rules of the Hôtel-Dieu stipulate: 'Receive the sick like Christ in person... Treat each patient like the master of the house'.

The clergy often displayed great courage in their dealings with the lords, reminding them that justice should be tempered with mercy. Below: two monks intercede for a condemned man and obtain his pardon.

The clergy often withstood the demands of those in power, notably by granting asylum. Below: A peasant clasps a pillar of the church where he has taken refuge, while soldiers endeavour to remove him by force.

The erection of a church—with all the more reason of a cathedral—went on for several generations. Ulm Cathedral (right), whose foundation stone was laid in 1377 through the munificence of the rich burghers of the town, was only finished in the nineteenth century, differing from the original project.

Opposite page: on the portal of Saint-Etienne at Bourges Christ welcomes the faithful in the guise of a teacher. The tympanum is occupied by the Last Judgment, with the resurrection of the dead on the lowest register. In the middle, St Michael weighs their souls; at the top, Christ presides enthroned flanked by angels with the instruments of the Passion. The Virgin Mary (left) and St John (right) intercede for man.

Bishops and, as a special favour, the most generous donors were buried under the floor of the cathedral (below). It was believed that proximity to the holy relics ensured their salvation.

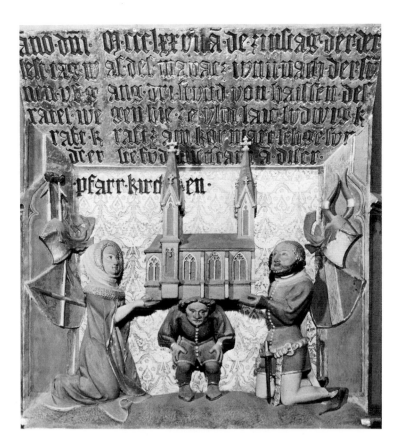

holidays of obligation, the most splendid and grandiose ceremonies provided at no charge pious, sanctifying spectacles that attracted the vast majority of the inhabitants of the surrounding countryside. Another church activity was the religious theatre, the paraliturgical cycles that developed into the famous mystery plays which were spread over several days and drew huge crowds especially at Christmas and in Holy Week. The relics preserved in the altars were visited constantly by pilgrims from the diocese and even farther afield, depending on how holy and famous they were. Churches sited on the great pilgrimage routes like those to Santiago de Compostela, Rome or the Holy Sepulchre, were enlivened by the hosts of pilgrims passing through. Those which lacked that advantage did their best to offer an attraction and persuade travellers and tourists to go out of their way to visit them; that is how Florence succeeded in receiving a good proportion of the people who travelled to Rome from Western Europe.

The great spiritual fervour that led to the erection of the cathedrals at a time when the West was going through a period of demographic and economic boom should not make us overlook the many uses to which they were put and the huge resources mobilized for their construction. Rich men gave freely for the repose of their souls because they had often made their money on the very fringe of the Ten Commandments; but they were also inspired by a spirit of emulation which urged them to want their cathedral to be bigger and more beautiful than that of the nearby town. They may have realized too that the crowds of visitors it attracted would increase their turnover. At Chartres the guilds obtained stained-glass windows in the deambulatory with their signature and image placed at the lowest possible level right under the eyes of visitors who were also possible customers. The poor and those of more limited means gave too, both out of interest and to make a show. The canons of the cathedral or collegiate church in course of construction, who directed the work and endeavoured to find the necessary funds, were expert at granting indulgences, making

collections, asking for donations large and small, and distributing alms-boxes for the benefit of their church. They cashed in on the coveted authorization for burial under the pavement close to the relics; they touched men's hearts by persuasive sermons and organized fruitful tours of the relics in the diocese and sometimes even throughout the whole of Western Europe. As a matter of fact, they also levied heavy taxes on their own prebends and revenues and never tired of asking other prelates and the bishop himself for gifts and donations.

The huge financial problem never found a perfect solution. Most cathedrals continued to be built for generations; very few were completed according to plan, and the majority of those caught in the depression of the fourteenth century, such as Siena, Beauvais, Toulouse and Cologne, were unfinished.

The technical and scientific problems were mastered better. The churches of the Merovingian and Carolingian periods had been erected in accordance with the Roman methods which had stood the test of time; the same is true of those built in Spain under the Visigoths and the Byzantine province of Italy. It was Ottonian art in West Germany, and particularly in the Rhineland; the Romanesque style; and later the Gothic; that introduced a number of new procedures, less in ground-plan than in elevation, which were employed in edifices of a different type. Side by side with the host of unskilled labourers who dug the foundations, evacuated the earth and transported the stones, workers of a higher category prepared the mortar, mixed the plaster, cut the stones and set them in place. The instruments most commonly used were trowel, level, plumb-line, saw and chisel; the latter made of very tough metal. Even brick churches needed well-dressed stones for the vault ribs and, of course, the sculptures. Improved techniques employed by blacksmiths meant that iron braces could be used to prevent the walls from diverging and ties used inside the walls to strengthen them, as in the Sainte-Chapelle in Paris.

But it was outside the walls, in correspondence with the pilasters which supported the vault, that

Above: cathedrals were used for religious services long before building work was finished. The magnitude of that work and the length of time it lasted were a heavy drain on the city's revenues. Beauvais and many other towns were crushed by the weight of their debts. This explains why few cathedrals were completed during the Middle Ages.

A miniature from *Fasciculus Temporum* (1474) confirms the huge size of the cathedrals and shows that of Cologne towering above the houses of the town (top left); note the crane set up to facilitate building operations. Very few plans are still extant, among them Michel Parler's for Strasbourg Cathedral (left). Many of those buildings are still incomplete; others were finished very differently from the initial project.

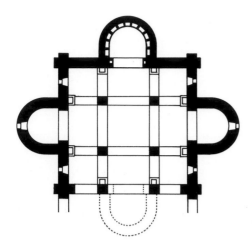
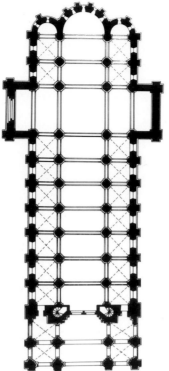
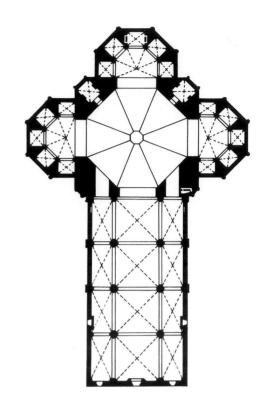

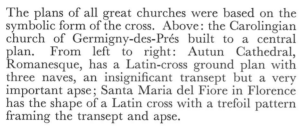
The plans of all great churches were based on the symbolic form of the cross. Above: the Carolingian church of Germigny-des-Prés built to a central plan. From left to right: Autun Cathedral, Romanesque, has a Latin-cross ground plan with three naves, an insignificant transept but a very important apse; Santa Maria del Fiore in Florence has the shape of a Latin cross with a trefoil pattern framing the transept and apse.

the twelfth century architects realized their greatest invention, namely the flying buttress with one or more arches. It enabled the vault to soar straight up scores of feet above ground level, while at the same time a great deal of the wall surface between the pilasters could be eliminated and replaced by large openings or vast areas of stained glass. The vault itself did not undergo any such revolution; domes supported by squinches or pendentives already existed at Byzantium, as did barrel vaults, groined vaults, which were formed by the intersection of two perpendicular barrel vaults, and pointed arches. Stressing and strengthening groined vaults with diagonal ribs between wall arches and cross springers, though undoubtedly an advance, was not a revolution. It must simply be borne in mind that these Gothic vaults owed their greater breadth chiefly to the perfection of the ribbing and that, being made of incombustible material, they have lasted longer than the timber roofing previously employed. Actually, because it had to withstand rain and snow, the roof above the vault was far more elaborate than in ancient times, while the base of the walls was protected from trickling water by the invention of the gargoyle which projected rain water outwards.

The excessive weight of Roman tiles would have caused them to slip down the steep roofs, so they were replaced with slates, small tiles or lead, the whole structure being supported by a splendid timber framework. Other innovations concerned ornamentation and architectural principles. In ornamentation relatively little use was made of ancient procedures. Mosaic, which had been employed very generally throughout the entire West until the tenth century, was subsequently neglected except in those parts of Italy that were in contact with Byzantium. During the Romanesque period most walls and vaults were covered with paintings, mainly frescoes, while much of the outside was painted in bright colours. Subsequently, monumental sculpture tended to oust all other forms of decoration. The art of bronze casting was already known in Italy and Germany, as witnessed by the doors of San Zeno at Verona and those at Mainz, Hildesheim and Novgorod, the latter brought from Magdeburg. But the most popular material was stone, chosen and cut with loving care. Cutting was very often done before it left the quarry for two reasons: first, transport was very expensive and it was more profitable to load a waggon with finished material;

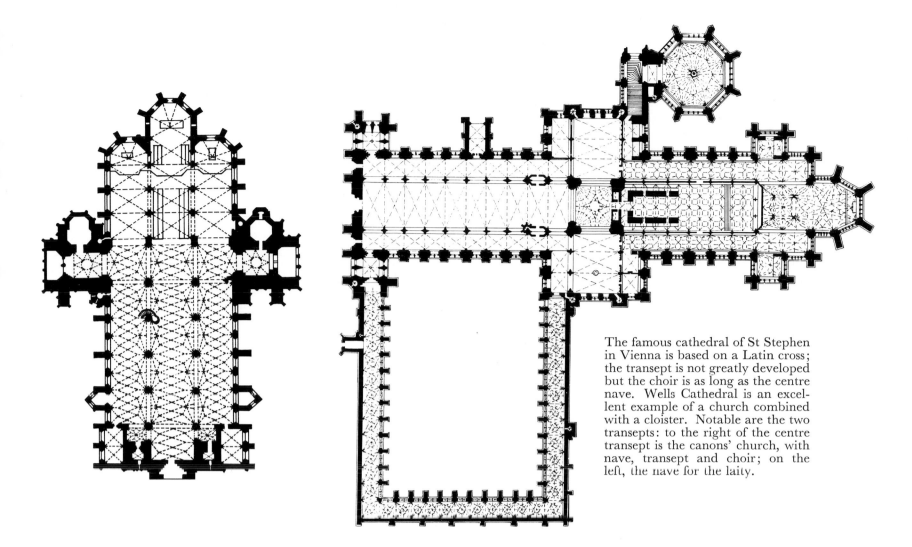

The famous cathedral of St Stephen in Vienna is based on a Latin cross; the transept is not greatly developed but the choir is as long as the centre nave. Wells Cathedral is an excellent example of a church combined with a cloister. Notable are the two transepts: to the right of the centre transept is the canons' church, with nave, transept and choir; on the left, the nave for the laity.

secondly, a sculpture carved in a stone identical with those which adjoined it found its proper place in the overall design. The Cluniac priories at Moissac, Toulouse, Autun, Vézelay, Conques, Beaulieu and Carennac have very fine portals with sculptured tympanum, lintle and sometimes window pier, arch stone and jambs. In the cloisters all the columns have capitals that display scenes seething with life. Gothic architecture incorporated robust column figures and a quantity of sculptured motifs that ended up by covering the entire facade and ultimately the side porches too. In the Flamboyant Gothic style the statues became more and more numerous but were 'additions' to the building rather than an essential part of it.

The second extremely original feature of Gothic architecture was the systematic use of vast areas of stained glass between pilasters shored up by the flying buttresses. Stained-glass windows had already been employed during the Carolingian period but the apertures were far too narrow to constitute an essential element of the decoration. A German monk called Theophilus, who lived in the twelfth century, has left us a very detailed description of the elaborate techniques applied in the production of glass and its

colouring. The window was first drawn on a cartoon and the wrought-iron framework set in place, then the details of the design were transferred in grisaille to pieces of glass of different colours and fixed by a second firing, lastly, the pieces of glass were secured with strips of lead inside the wrought-iron framework. The glass was very thick, full of air bubbles and coloured all through, but not evenly because the mineral colouring matter was not uniformly distributed in the mass; in those windows the refraction of the sun's rays and the contrasting colours produce an extraordinary glow.

More important than the techniques employed were the overall concepts which governed the layout of the cathedral and its ornamentation. Here various questions arise. Did the architects, or any one of them, possess the knowledge needed to plan in detail the execution of the project they were entrusted with? Were their plans constantly checked and corrected by the canons who had commissioned it? There is no reliable answer to the first question, for only two really medieval architects are known by name. They are the thirteenth-century Villard de Honnecourt, whose sketchbook is still existant, and Roriczer of Regensburg, who published a variety of handbooks at the end of the fifteenth century. (I have not forgotten Leon Battista Alberti, Piero della Francesca or other Italians, but their outlook is considered 'modern'.) Villard jotted down any detail he found interesting or possibly useful; he sketched a number of human and animal figures and a quantity of mechanical objects, both real and imaginary, that he thought of utilizing for building a church or furnishing it; he also proposed solutions of various practical problems of mechanics, trigonometry and geometry. The plans, cross-sections and elevations of different churches that he studied or built himself prove that no detail escaped his notice. Some thirteenth-century plans for Strasbourg cathedral that have been rediscovered bear witness to the extreme accuracy of the project. And a study of the Palatine Chapel at Aix-la-Chapelle and of Saint-Denis, Laach and Canterbury suffices to convince one that empirism was confined within an extremely strict geometrical scheme.

The ornamentation too, the sculptures and the stained-glass windows, was planned and ordered with no less rigour. The choice of subjects and their location were not left to the sculptor's fancy or the interest of the donors; it was the architect who decided, acting on the general instructions received from the chapter, the abbot or the bishop. Those instructions were often very detailed. Emile Mâle proved that only clerics and theologians could have arranged most of the compositions that have been preserved to our own day. Abbot Suger chose all the themes for the windows at Saint-Denis and wrote the inscriptions himself with an eye to making certain symbols more easily accessible to the congregation. The tapestries at Troyes and very many of the frescoes which adorn Italian churches were described in detail in the contracts concluded with the artists before their execution was taken in hand. In 787 the Council of Nicaea had insisted that 'the composition of the religious images is not left to the artists' inspiration; it rests on the principles laid down by the Catholic Church and religious tradition. The art alone appertains to the painter, the composition to

the fathers.' Thus a Gothic cathedral expresses the vision of the universe conceived by Roman orthodoxy; it is an open book in which even the illiterate could read and the ignorant learn.

A cathedral was a complex designed for the service of the God of the Christians; its chief function was liturgical, as demonstrated by C. Heitz, and its ruling principle was scholastic theology, as E. Panofsky has suggested. Its ornamentation crystallized the beliefs and cognitions of the faithful.

I have borrowed from Emile Mâle's book, which is still as topical as when he wrote it, the following passage which will help us to realize what an essential place the cathedral occupied in the life of the West: 'From a distance its transepts, spires and towers make it look like a great ship setting sail for a long voyage. The whole city can embark in the massive nave without the slightest difficulty. Let us approach closer. In the porch we first see Jesus Christ just as he appears to every human being who comes into the world. He is the key to life's riddle. Round about him is inscribed the answer to all our questions, and our own story [is set] side by side with that of the vast universe. Let us go inside. First of all the sublimity of the great vertical lines acts on the soul like a sacrament. Here too we find an image of the world. The cathedral, like a plain or a forest, has its own atmosphere, its perfume, its light, its chiaroscuro, its shadows. The great rose-window is like the sun. We have the feeling that we have already entered the heavenly Jerusalem, the city of the future. We delight in its deep peace. The cathedral was a total revelation [for medieval man]. It embodied all the arts—words, music, the living drama of the mysteries, the motionless drama of the statues. There a man confined within a social class or calling, dispersed and pulverized by life and by his daily toil, rediscovered the consciousness of the unity of his nature; there he recovered balance and harmony. The crowd assembled for the great festivals felt that it formed a living unity. The faithful were all mankind, the cathedral was the world, and the Divine Spirit filled both man and creation.'

270

This small portable altar, which is about 10 inches long, is embellished with splendidly chiselled sheets of gilded copper. The designs illustrate scenes from the legend of St Felix of Aquileia.

As a rule wood sculptures were painted in bright colours. Here Christ is mounted on an ass which children hauled through the streets of Steinen (Switzerland) during the Palm Sunday procession about 1200.

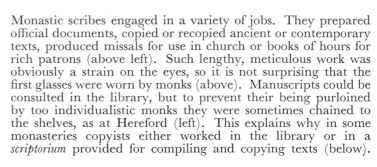

Monastic scribes engaged in a variety of jobs. They prepared official documents, copied or recopied ancient or contemporary texts, produced missals for use in church or books of hours for rich patrons (above left). Such lengthy, meticulous work was obviously a strain on the eyes, so it is not surprising that the first glasses were worn by monks (above). Manuscripts could be consulted in the library, but to prevent their being purloined by too individualistic monks they were sometimes chained to the shelves, as at Hereford (left). This explains why in some monasteries copyists either worked in the library or in a *scriptorium* provided for compiling and copying texts (below).

It was not only with pictures that cathedrals, minsters and, to a lesser extent, parish churches instructed the illiterate masses. For more than eight centuries the Church had a monopoly of culture and active education which enabled it to maintain its spiritual and intellectual preponderance over society.

During the Late Empire period, when the Christian Church first came into being, it aimed at imparting an instruction diametrically opposed to classical culture. Unable to disengage itself entirely from the liberal arts, it endeavoured to utilize the *trivium*, grammar, rhetoric and dialectic; and the *quadrivium*, arithmetic, geometry, music, astronomy; as well as history and the natural sciences, geography, zoology, medicine, botany, mineralogy; to explain the Bible and teach people to express their thoughts. That principle is mirrored in Saint Augustine's *De Doctrina christiana*, the basic charter of Christian culture and one of the books most read during the Middle Ages.

However, the victory of the Germans brought into the Romanized West an aristocracy of warriors and uneducated peasants, whose sole cultural tradition consisted of epic poems or songs exalting strength, glory and success. At that time the young Christianized Germans received an education at once physical, running, swimming, hunting and warlike sports, and moral, based on the stoic principles of prudence, justice, courage and self-control. The old-type school which had provided the training ground for Cassiodorus at the beginning of the sixth century and Pope Gregory the Great at its end, though still alive, was steadily declining. In any case, it was not suited to a certain type of pupil, namely the seekers after saintliness—the future monks, who were enrolled when 6 or 7 years old, learnt by heart stories from the Bible and maxims from the Book of Proverbs, and only after that were taught to read and write. Side by side with these monastic schools, the parish priests organized village schools where young laymen came for lessons. In principle they were expected to enter the priesthood in due course, but actually most of them, on attaining their majority, left the Church and married. Episcopal schools were also established in the circle of Caesareus of Arles and in Visigoth Spain; they were boarding schools of a sort where young clerks could receive instruction up to the age of 18, at which time they had to decide whether or not to continue and enter the priesthood. Lastly, preachers had the task of instructing the people by putting the major articles of faith within their reach.

The rule of Saint Basil and Saint Benedict, the letters of Saint Jerome and other documents give an idea of how those studious children lived. They were given special treatment involving better food, better sleeping quarters and a more agreeable temperature. Rebukes had to be less severe and the whip applied less frequently; prizes were awarded to encourage emulation. The children's good qualities did not go unrecognized: they were frank, unresentful and 'do not delight in womanly beauty'. Adolescents were watched over with greater care for fear of incontinence, both natural and homosexual. They all learnt the psalter by heart, just as the pupils of present-day koranic schools learn the Koran sura by sura; after that they practised reading under their breath without moving their lips, for that helped to understand the text better.

All in all, on examining the Carolingian period we discover three things. First, that the old-type school had definitively disappeared, though the subjects it had taught were not entirely lost. Secondly, that the only laymen who received any education—and it was moral rather than religious—were the young members of the aristocracy. Thirdly, that the clergy had a virtual monopoly of culture and teaching. Charlemagne and Louis the Pious insisted that the parish schools should take in lay children free of charge, and some Benedictine monasteries—for instance, that of Saint Gall—ran a day school at least for the young nobles. They taught reading, writing, singing and, where possible, the *trivium* and *quadrivium* of the Romans; but theology, not philosophy, was their ultimate aim. A considerable number of classical works saved by Irish and Italian copyists were preserved in the monastery libraries, where they were recopied or loaned out for recopying. And some great minds like Alcuin, Hrabanus Maurus and Einhard displayed a genuine culture. Unfortunately, that Carolingian Renaissance was shattered by the invasions of the tenth century. Normans, Saracens and Hungarians made the monasteries their chief targets, pillaging their treasures first and burning them, manuscripts and all, afterwards. Besides which, when the Benedictine monasteries withdrew from contact with the outside world after 817, the monastic schools became virtually inaccessible to all but the most powerful.

Only a few centres—Canterbury, York and Winchester in England; Reims, Chartres and Fleury in France; and particularly Regensburg and Saint Gall in Germany—continued to offer a small elite schooling based increasingly on Latin grammar as a result of the 'Ottonian Renaissance' which continued until the mid-eleventh century. Most twelfth-century masters and intellectuals were trained in those monastic and episcopal schools and stayed on to teach there. By that time Paris had won an international reputation for the monasteries of Notre-Dame, Saint-Victor, Saint-Germain-des-Prés, Saint-Maur and Sainte-Geneviève. At the end of the twelfth century the scattered masters and their pupils joined forces to create important teaching centres. They were all clerks and therefore subject to the Church, but their only occupation was teaching or listening to lectures. Those professionals enjoyed stipends (or benefices), rights and immunities and were grouped in what were called 'universities': those of Bologna, Salerno, Paris, Oxford, Cambridge, Naples, Toulouse, Salamanca and Rome sprang up in the space of a few decades. Prague, Heidelberg and Vienna did not become established until the second half of the fourteenth century. All those universities, founded by the pope or by sovereign princes with the pope's approval, shared three basic privileges. They were outside the jurisdiction of bishop or abbot and could appeal directly to the pope; they were also independent of the temporal authority and had their own regulations and police; lastly, they managed themselves, chose their teachers,

held a monopoly in the conferring of degrees and could go on strike. The influence of the papacy over the universities was very strong, and it was not long before the teaching staff was recruited from the orders most loyal to the Holy See, namely Dominicans and Franciscans.

In this way small autonomous enclaves sprang up in various towns in the West, some of them divided into several faculties, such as theology, law, medicine, arts with students grouped in 'nations' based on affinity of language or geographical origin that added up to a very considerable number. How were they lodged? Some were rich or had wealthy parents who could pay for a room for them, an apartment or a house and even servants to carry their books. But the majority were poor and needy; to cut the cost many of them lived together in large rented buildings governed by a 'principal'. Colleges were founded by rich and charitable persons. The Sorbonne in Paris, founded by Robert de Sorbon in 1256, was originally intended for poor masters of arts who wanted to obtain a doctor's degree in theology. The colleges of Harcourt and Navarre are less ancient. Oxford and Cambridge are still towns dotted with colleges that offer board, lodging, magnificent libraries, and tutors. Lessons were often given in the professor's own home, where space was limited and lighting inadequate. But when there was a numerous audience—and the teachers spared no efforts to attract students—classes were held out of doors. Place Maubert in Paris is believed to have got its name from the great German Dominican Albertus Magnus, later bishop of Regensburg, who once taught there. In winter, when the ground was too cold to sit on, it was covered with straw; this gave its name to the Rue du Fouarre in Paris, *fouarre* or *feurre*, being the old French word for straw. Dante translated it literally by *vico degli strami* in the passage about Siger de Brabant in his Paradiso (X. 134–6).

The master as a rule had his place on a dais behind a desk which bore the book he read and commented on to the seated students, who took notes. The general assembly of the faculties was held in the

onginneð · godspell · æft · matheus

Incipit euangeli um secundum mattheu

crister

soðlice

autem generatio

RATIOXPIERATCUM

ESSEDESPONSATA

MATEREIUSMARICUOSEPH

High education was dispensed in some monasteries and the universities. Left: the so-called chair of Albertus Magnus at Regensburg. Above: Merton College, Oxford, one of the oldest university buildings still standing; it dates from the end of the thirteenth century. On the opposite page: a lecture in a German university in the fourteenth century (right); William of Wykeham (1367–1404) lecturing in the open air at Oxford (far right).

capitular hall of some great monastery, like that of the Cistercians in Paris. Each faculty was a separate association; the most numerous was the Faculty of Arts, which provided instruction in the 'classics' and was the gateway to the others. At Paris in 1245 four 'nations', French, Picards, Normans and English, chose a head, whom they called Rector; not long after he was asked to administer the other three faculties as well.

University degrees differed little from those conferred at the present day, namely bachelor, master and doctor. Naturally, in order to teach it was essential to have a *licencia docendi*. Many of those who had received a degree from the Faculty of Arts endeavoured to continue in the study of disciplines that were already considered 'profitable' because of the openings they provided. Consequently, law and medicine were more popular than theology, though the latter was the noblest discipline of all. By and large, students had a reputation for being serious, hard-working and orderly. The poorest recopied their lecture notes and sold them to those who were better off, worked as water carriers or engaged in

other secondary activities; the most deserving were awarded scholarships. In principle, work was only done during the day for lack of lighting facilities, but it could also take up part of the night. Once, as Saint Louis was strolling in the streets of Paris, a student who was up before dawn emptied a chamber pot on his head; far from punishing the early riser, the saint rewarded his diligence with a money grant.

Of course, more is heard about the wild, pleasure-loving throng that amused themselves in the Pré-aux-Clercs by ragging their well-behaved fellows who went there to repeat their lessons; they were, as Robert de Sorbon said, 'more familiar with the rules of the game of dice than with those of logic'. They frequented the Law Courts, quarrelled with the peasants of Saint-Germain-des-Prés just as hotly as with the police, and took every possible advantage of their immunity from interference by the civil authorities. Philip Augustus saw them as braver than knights. 'These clerks', he said, 'who wear the tonsure and have neither helmet nor coat of mail rush into the fray brandishing a knife.' Needless to say, they did not take the oath of chastity and had no

use for continence in any shape or form. They spent their time eating and drinking—every student on receiving a master's degree was in duty bound to offer his teachers and class-mates a banquet—carousing in taverns, and cultivating a more or less admissible familiarity with pimps and prostitutes.

During the twelfth century Western Europe was the happy hunting ground of the goliards—impoverished non-conformist students with neither fixed residence nor means of subsistence, who wandered from one school or university to the next in the wake of a favourite professor, chanting the praises of wine, women and song and violently attacking the ordered society in which they lived. They were merciless in their censure of peasants as ignorant boors who lied and stole; of nobles, whose birth did not make up for their vices; of brutal soldiers, incapable of the tender love that clerks made so well and the ladies so greatly appreciated; above all, of the Church, grasping and simoniacal; of lazy, gluttonous, lewd monks and sincere friars who shunned natural pleasures; of the pope, the bishops and the entire ecclesiastical hierarchy. They pictured the pope as an all-

devouring lion flanked by a calf (the bishop) that cropped the grass before his flock. A lynx (the archdeacon) had a piercing eye to discover every prey, which a dog (the deacon) beat up towards the nets spread by the huntsman (the official principal). The stabilization of the universities in the thirteenth century led to the gradual disappearance of the goliards, but not of their ideas, which anticipated the libertine, rebellious attitudes of centuries to come and have their counterparts in our own day.

By and large, the establishment of the universities went hand in hand not only with the spread of scholasticism and the New Aristotelism whose leading spokesmen were Albertus Magnus and Thomas Aquinas, but also with the more rigorous unification of Western Christendom under the control of the Catholic Church. The intellectual trends that had quickened the ranks of the nobility were slowed down for the time being and the middle-class lay school was still hardly more than a dream. So the universities must be viewed as the centre of the vast movement which aimed at putting the Church in complete control of all western society.

In Paris university professors and students formed a community that was very jealous of its independence. Above: the seal of the university, with the Virgin between St Nicholas and St Catherine. Left: a bas-relief on the tomb of Pierre de Gougis (1440) shows the king's bailiffs apologizing to masters and students for having infringed the charter of the Sorbonne. In fact, masters and students were answerable first and foremost to the ecclesiastical authorities.

The question arises whether that control was really total or whether a more or less important part of that society put in doubt its unity within the bosom of Holy Mother Church. The fact is that all those who defied law and order also defied the Roman Catholic Church which vouched for it, and vice versa. They were excommunicated as a matter of course and their reaction took one of two forms. Either they created a schism that respected the Church's doctrine but not its traditional hierarchy; or, more typically, they adopted a heresy and founded a religion which, if not entirely new, at least propounded a doctrine that was clearly different. In addition to the schisms that preceded the definitive break with Byzantium and Eastern Christendom in 1054, another great schism (1378–1417) split the West first into two parts and then into three but was brought to a close by the Council of Constance and only reappeared sporadically for a decade in the mid-fifteenth century (1439–49). The outbreak of heresies in the very early Middle Ages was followed by two others—one from the eleventh century to the thirteenth which comprised the Patarines, the Waldensians and the Cathars; the second in the fifteenth century, when the Lollards and Hussites were the distant precursors of Luther and Calvin. This shows that heresy was not part of everyday life, though the crises were so violent that the Church was permanently in arms to prevent their revival.

It is worth recalling very briefly the lives of some of those heretics—for example, the Cathars, who thrived in some parts of Germany, Northern Italy, Provence and all Southern France from the Rhône to Albi, Toulouse and Foix. Their doctrine rested on an elementary Manichaeism brought from the Levant by the crusaders and merchants who had come in contact with the Bogomil sectaries of Bulgaria. Though some sources of information are far from reliable, we know a great deal about that doctrine and the practices it produced. Catharism was based on the fundamental belief that the universe is torn by the struggle between two principles: Good and Evil. Living in a world where Evil holds sway, man cannot resist it, so he cannot be held responsible for his actions. Consequently, the immense majority of Cathars could live free from the strict obligations and

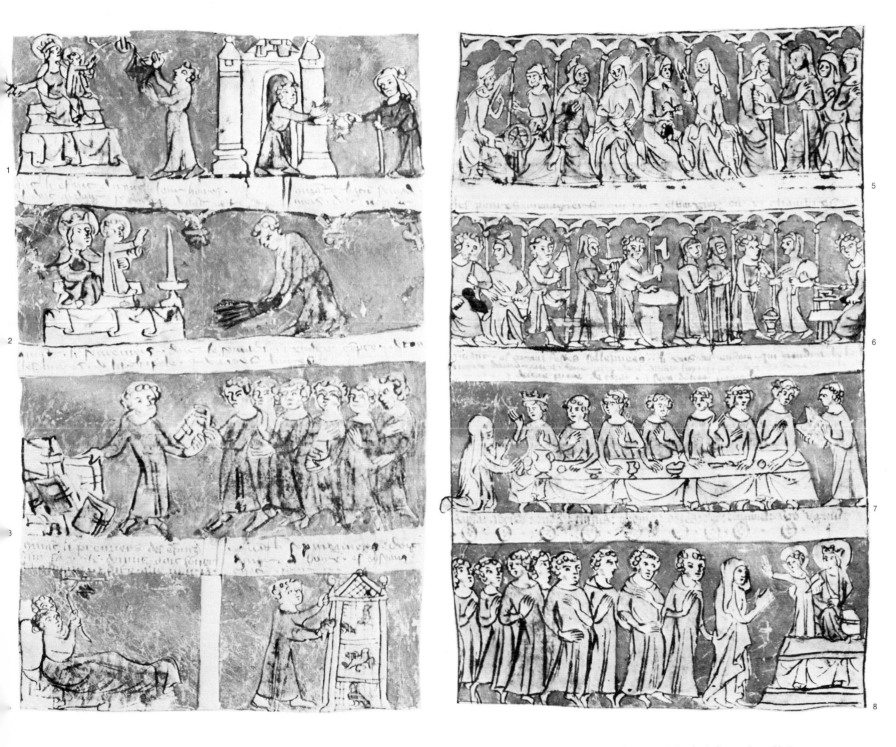

The life of the students of Ave Maria College in Paris is described in a fourteenth century manuscript. 1. The hebdomadary lights the lamp before the statue of the Virgin. 2. He sweeps the chapel on Saturday. 3. At the end of the week he hands over the library books, some chained, to his successor in the presence of five fellow students as witnesses. 4. Every morning the first awake must ring the bell and say a Hail Mary; the hebdomadary feeds the college gold finches. 5. & 6. The college performs a work of mercy by distributing alms to ten poor women and ten poor men. 7. A traditional play in which the chief characters are the Virgin (on the left) and the founders of the college. 8. The students go in procession to the Virgin's statue to receive the blessing of the Infant Jesus.

moral taboos that the Roman Church imposed on Christians. Hence their contempt for the Cross, the sacraments, the liturgy, churches, the Old Testament, but not for Jesus Christ or the Gospel. In any case, they led a free, untrammelled life which was probably very pleasant too.

This does not mean that they abolished marriage, or at least the durable union of two individuals of opposite sex who lived together and brought up a family; and occasionally there were even public confessions. But only a very small fraction of the believers endeavoured to combat Satan and devote themselves to the service of the good God, Light and the Spirit, against Matter and the forces of darkness. They were called the Perfect and could be both men and women. Dressed all in black, until the persecution forced them to wear the same garb as the rest of the population, they lived in chastity, poverty and abstinence. They refused all foods of animal origin because of their belief in a succession of future lives, but were not absolute vegetarians since, oddly enough, they ate fish. They neither told lies nor took oaths, and promised not to abandon the Cathar community or to fear death by fire, water or other means. To become perfect it was necessary to receive the *consolamentum* after laying on of hands by the Perfect who were present and reception of the Book, probably the New Testament. Non-perfect believers only received the *consolamentum* at the point of death; it confirmed the victory of Good over Evil and was a guarantee of salvation. Catharism can hardly be viewed as a socially revolutionary movement because it had adepts in every class, but it tended to disrupt western society and for that reason was stamped out so ruthlessly.

The fifteenth-century heresies that developed among Wycliffe's disciples in England and Hus's in Bohemia were far closer to the Catholic doctrine. It was only among the followers of Hus that two genuinely revolutionary sects were found: the Taborites and the Adamites. The former rejected purgatory and the real presence of Our Lord in the Eucharist; the latter wanted to make ready for the

end of the world and the reign of the Holy Spirit by destroying social classes, churches, villages, books.

Cathars, Lollards and Hussites were subjugated by the soldiery after the Church had mobilized the temporal power against them, and thereafter kept under strict control by the Inquisition, which spread rapidly through Western Europe early in the twelfth century and became an essential factor of daily life. Heretics and those who abetted them were seen as traitors to, and seeds of destruction of, the Christian society. They had to be hunted down, convinced of their crime by the bishop and handed over to the prince for burning. Their property and that of their declared friends was confiscated. Since the bishops were reluctant to apply these sanctions, in 1232 the pope put the matter in the hands of the Dominicans. As a result, they set up the Inquisition, which was to all intents and purposes outside the control of the Ordinary, and after 1252 was entitled to torture suspects in order to wring confessions from them. That terrible guardian of the faith also took up the cudgels against magic and sorcery, besides keeping unremitting watch on the non-Christian enclaves in the Christian West. In this last respect its chief quarries were the Moriscos (Mudejars), the Jews and the Marranos (recently converted Jews) in Spain.

There were virtually no Jews in the rural districts; most of them lived in urban communities that had been rich and prosperous from time immemorial. From the eleventh century the Christians began to mistrust them for three reasons. First, because their brethren in the Levant were thought to assist the Turks in persecuting pilgrims; secondly, because they did not take part in the great movement of purification which developed in the West at that time; thirdly, because they refused to recognize Christ's Divine nature. Christendom was going through a phase of active expansion and therefore had less need of their services, and what had begun as envy turned into hatred and ended in persecution. The first pogroms occurred in the Rhineland in 1096, just before the First Crusade, and soon a virulent anti-Semitism accentuated the gulf that had existed be-

To preserve the unity of the great Christian family, the Church refused to tolerate heresy. The defection of the Albigensians caused a particularly grave crisis in the late twelfth century and the early thirteenth. Right: the fortified cathedral at Albi proves that the Church had to withstand armed attack in the Languedoc. Bottom right: the Church preaches the crusade and wages war against the heretics.

The curriculum comprised the seven liberal arts personified in this picture below. Clockwise, starting at the top: grammar, rhetoric, dialectic, music, arithmetic, geometry and astronomy. They are arranged like the petals of a flower whose centre is philosophy, which unites and enlivens all knowledge.

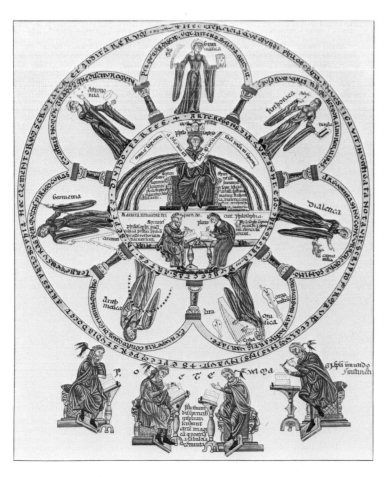

tween Jews and Christians since the early Middle Ages and that had been deepened by the pietistic revival among the Sephardic Jews in Spain and the Ashkenazic Jews in Germany. The result was that the western sovereigns confined the members of the despised race in certain sections of the towns, the future ghettos, and obliged them to wear a special badge and a conical hat. B. Blumenkranz has shown how Christian iconography typified the Jews as short, swarthy and bearded and insisted on their role in Christ's Passion as hateful and hated deicides. The situation of their communities went from bad to worse. They were tormented and finally expelled from England in 1144, from France in 1182 and again at the end of the thirteenth century and from the Rhineland (except Worms and Frankfurt) at the beginning of the fifteenth. After 1380 they were strictly controlled by the Inquisition and the royal authorities in Castile, and persecuted in Catalonia after 1390. Little by little most professions were closed to them including medicine and pharmacy; finally, they were driven back to pawnbroking and money-changing, until their competition became too

fierce, which helped to focus hate and envy on them. Little by little the Jews fled the West, taking refuge in the Slav countries or settling in certain German towns. Those in the South migrated to Spain, where their situation, though uncomfortable, was still acceptable and they were allowed to continue working as merchants, soldiers and peasants Though some popes relented belatedly—for example, Eugenius IV in 1436—the Church bears a heavy responsibility for a general intolerance that crystallized in sporadic persecutions and provided one of the starting points of modern anti-Semitism.

These various interventions on the part of the Church, of which we have examined only a few particularly typical examples, preserved the purity of the Christian society from within.

In this context we may find it easier to understand one of the factors of that extraordinarily complex phenomenon, the crusades, which united and partially pacified Christendom under the leadership of the Holy See in a common struggle against an external enemy, the non-Christian infidels. For several centuries—and not only from the capture of Jerusa-

From the end of the eleventh century the Jews were strictly controlled, when they were not persecuted. Christian iconography represents them bearded, wearing a pointed hat and guarding chests full of gold, an allusion to their activity as money-lenders which earned them envy, hatred and sometimes persecution.

In France the Templars, recognizable by the cross on their habit, were suspected of heresy and thrown into prison by Philip the Fair (opposite left). After a somewhat irregular trial the pope decreed the dissolution of the order.

The Church handed over to the secular arm those who were convicted of heresy. The king had them burnt, like the disciples of Amaury of Chartres (opposite far left). In the middle distance, the gibbet of Montfaucon with sixteen stone pillars linked by timber beams; in the middle, the tower of the Temple; to the left, the Bastille.

lem in 1099 to the loss of Saint Jean d'Acre in 1201—the Church strove to make the faithful and their princes conscious of the war that was being waged under its aegis in the sign of the Cross for the conquest or defence of the Holy Sepulchre. All possible means—sermons, exhortations, the granting of privileges—were employed to persuade them to take part, the former by paying a tax, the latter by lending assistance in that just and holy struggle. This concept of the crusade was still very much alive at the dawn of modern times, during the reign of Charles V, at the battle of Lepanto in 1571 and again at the siege of Vienna in 1683. Propaganda and the almost permanent enlistment of volunteers and mobilization of resources continued at least until the beginning of the fourteenth century. In addition, the pope and his best preachers made their voices heard in the general campaigns that the Church organized from time to time throughout the West. For example, Urban II spoke at Clermont in 1095 on behalf of the First Crusade and Saint Bernard at Vézelay in 1147 for the Second. It was these official appeals and, less frequently, those launched by popular preachers which mobilized the forces of the West and made the crusade a factor to be reckoned with in the daily life of the population.

The first name that comes to mind in this connection is that of Peter the Hermit and the long march he undertook through France and Germany accompanied by Walter the Penniless after the Council of Clermont in 1095. Chroniclers have obligingly left us pictures of that mass movement of craftsmen, merchants, farmhands, knights and barons, who left everything they possessed behind them and started off with their wives and children. Whenever they came in sight of a town or castle, they asked: 'Is that Jerusalem?' We still have the wording of the prayers and benediction in which the priests entreated the Lord to bless the pilgrims' cross as he had blessed Aaron's rod and not to abandon those who were on their way to fight for Christ but to send the Angel Gabriel to protect them. At the close of the ceremony the Cross was bestowed with the words: 'Receive this sign, image of the Passion and death of the Saviour of the world, in order that neither sin nor accident may befall thee on thy journey and thou mayst return happier and above all better to thy family.'

Other documents tell us of Saint Bernard's preaching at the very time when he was considered the most influential figure in all Christendom. The first meeting was held in the presence of Louis VII on a hill near Vézelay. A huge crowd listened to the inaugural speech, of which the text is still extant. The saint recalled the Turks' recent offensive against the Holy Land, the dreadful sins of the Christians, 'the din of arms, the perils, toils and strains of war, which are the penance imposed by God'. The lords and knights took the cross in their hundreds. Bernard went on to preach in the towns and villages of France and Germany, from Constance to Maestricht, and wrote fiery, pathetic letters to be read in all the Italian churches. The throng of Germans who pressed round him—though they could not quite understand his sermons in Latin—was so great that on one occasion he would have suffocated if he had not been rescued by the Emperor Conrad. The results were in keeping with the effort made. Bernard wrote to Pope Eugenius: 'The towns and castles are deserted; all one sees are widows and orphans whose husbands and fathers are still alive.'

If this is only a slight exaggeration of the facts, it is not always easy to interpret them. Certain political factors contributed to the initial success of the crusade, but they also made that success precarious and entailed the need to send out an incessant stream of reinforcements. The Christians had recaptured Southern Italy, Sicily and part of Spain from the Muslims and were accustomed to fighting the infidels with the Church's blessing. On the other hand, in the Eastern Mediterranean the Byzantine empire was threatened by the Seljuk Turks; it had enlisted 'Frankish' mercenaries in its defence and hoped to obtain assistance from the West at no cost by appealing to the sentiment of Christian solidarity. Lastly, after 1092 the Turks, Arabs, Egyptians and other Muslims in the Near East were at war with each other, and that anarchy undoubtedly favoured

Pilgrims were crusaders in a peaceful guise. Whole families (right) took up the pilgrim's staff, sewed on their clothes a badge indicating their destination (below), and began their journey invoking the protection of St James.

For Christian knights the crusade was a great collective adventure. The next two pages are occupied by a map of the Mediterranean showing the expeditions organized by St Louis (1244–1270). We can recognize Sicily, Cyprus, Jerusalem, the Nile delta, Carthage and other places.

spangne

aguemorte

roanne

noroc

de hou de matloc

noroc

sizille

marroch

chastel
de cartage

thunes

sirie

iherusalem

cypre

egipte

acrer

malduue

damiete

flum
denile

babiloune

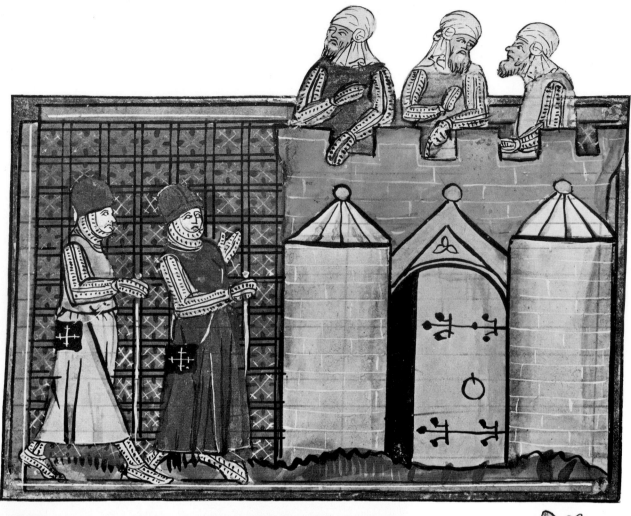

The protection of the great pilgrimages to the 'Holy Places' was entrusted to the Hospitallers and Templars. They policed the roads (left), welcomed and housed the pilgrims and guided them from one stage to the next. Pilgrims, and with all the more reason crusaders, saw themselves as soldiers of Christ (below left). The contradiction between warlike expeditions and the Christian ideal of peace caused no concern whatsoever in those days.

288

those first expeditions; subsequently, when Islam presented a united front, the outcome was rather more in doubt. But so huge an enterprise would have been impossible without the coincidence of purely political and religious considerations in addition to the demographic and social factors—the nascent population boom in the West, the fragmentation of agricultural property, the difficult division of knightly estates due to the right of primogeniture.

The pope may well have thought that the crusade, by mobilizing against the infidel the warlike forces of a Christendom whose spiritual head he was, would do still more than the Truce or Peace of God to pacify the western countryside. There was a hope that the common front against Islam might end the schism with Byzantium, and that the emperor of the East might even help the pope against Henry IV, the excommunicated emperor of the West. Thus the notion gradually crystallized of the 'holy' war in which the warrior blest by the clergy was a soldier of Christ, certain of salvation if he died on the field of honour, and the crusader protected by the Church was under the jurisdiction of the ecclesiastical court. Jerusalem became the focal point of the crusades, which was due less to commentaries on the Apocalypse and the idea of the heavenly Jerusalem than to the pilgrimages and the revivalist movements that drew the masses to the tomb of Christ. Those pilgrims, who hoped to earn their salvation, carried valuables of all sorts as offerings to the Holy Sepulchre and were a tempting prey for the brigandish Bedouin. It was to defend their goods, their lives and their liberty that they found it necessary to carry arms. It should also be said that the rapid occupation by the Turks of the Byzantine lands in Anatolia was another obstacle to the march of the innumerable pilgrims whose transportation was beyond the means of western shipping. As well as this, the fees charged for admission to the Holy City might have been put up. From the foregoing it is clear to see that the causes of the crusades were complex in the extreme.

What also is astonishing is that they lasted for over two centuries. This cannot be completely explained by the fear of the Turks and the enthusiasm of Christians in general, and particularly of the knights who were tempted by the prospect of earning riches and glory and the merchants who did very profitable business. But the long duration explains why they left so deep a mark on daily life in the West. The crusades were responsible for the fashion for silk stuffs, the spread of armorial bearings and the definitive formulation of heraldry; for the greater use of spices in the diet of the knightly class and the introduction of new products, for example the apricot; new building techniques, such as the barbican and the pointed arch; and new mental attitudes, Catharism, 'amour courtois', and the improved status of women. More important still was the mark they made on society. The countryside enjoyed relative peace; power was centralized in the monarch's hands owing to the absence of the turbulent vassals; there were fewer quarrels over successions and lands became easier to dispose of. The fighting class accumulated debts while mariners and merchants made enormous profits and discomfiture grew among the lords and still more among the clergy. While the capture of Constantinople in 1204 and the difficulty of living in peace with the orthodox Christians accentuated the schism, the papacy lost credit and prestige as a result of the incessant appeals for funds, and the false crusades launched not only against heretics and unbelievers in the West but also against its political enemies, chief among them the emperor.

The crusades coincided with the great period of prosperity that lasted from the eleventh to the thirteenth century. They were one of the most outstanding events in the whole history of the West. Being largely initiated and sustained by the Church as the guardian of Christendom, their decline was due no less to the Church's loss of control over society than to the gradual exhaustion caused by so disproportionate an effort. They were partly responsible for the exceptional dynamism of the urban population and in particular of the merchants and mariners of the Mediterranean seaboard, who in the last analysis were the chief beneficiaries.

TRADE AND COMMERCE

The orderly society of the eleventh century had no place for townsmen or for those who roamed the roads. There were already towns, of course, at least the Late Empire cities with their bishop, his small court and his officers. There were also roads, the old Roman roads from which branched off tracks used desultorily by carters, pedlars, pilgrims, knights and lords. But those people formed only a minute fraction of the population and had a stable home, or at least a solid link with the rural society. Economic conditions had already begun to change, but it was not until the end of the eleventh century, and more particularly the twelfth, that the revival of trade, the growth of the towns, the increase in traffic on the old roads and the making of new ones, brought about a far-reaching modification of traditional society and its way of life. New sorts of people, new associations, a new scenery appeared—burghers, patricians, merchants, seafarers; ward brotherhoods, craft guilds, communes, the urban fabric in general.

'In the beginning was the way.' There is more truth than parody in these words, which render the fundamental importance of the road. In fact, roads serve not only to pierce the isolation and form a link between self-sufficient, autonomous cells but also to convey ideas, techniques, goods and people.

Except in the regions east of the Rhine and north of the Danube never durably occupied by the Romans, the West inherited from the Roman Empire an amazing network of straight, paved roads that were the decisive factor in the choice of most routes and were utilized throughout the entire Middle Ages. Though their paving stones were extremely robust, they worked loose in the course of time, ending up by making the highway impassable except on the edges. Besides the *via lapide strata*, or briefly *strata* (from which our 'street' derives) there were the cobbled medieval roads whose stones were bonded with mortar; they were less straight than the Roman roads because they wound hither and thither in order to pass close to certain castles or abbeys, instead of leading directly from one town to the next, or from a town to a point fixed by nature and improved by

Siena in the fourteenth century (left) was typical of the medieval towns in close contact with the countryside. Flocks of sheep and trains of pack mules and asses were frequent sights. The streets were extremely lively and picturesque. Goods were sold in open booths; craftsmen plied their trade on the roadway; schoolteachers found object lessons in the motley scene. At Siena roofs piled up like beetling crags above the streets.

man, such as a mountain pass, a ford, a causeway, through marshland or over a bridge. At the very beginning of the Middle Ages roads could already be divided into various categories as they are today, depending on their local, regional, national or international interest. Ph. de Beaumanoir, in the thirteenth century, classified by width: footpaths (3 feet), tracks (8 feet), roads (15 feet), main roads (32 feet) and royal roads (54 feet).

On the latter, which were the most important, traffic was always intense. Their chief users were potentates, who were constantly on the move with part of their family and servants from one estate to another in order to consume the stocks of provisions accumulated as a result of rents paid in kind. They also used them to reach the court of the king, whether Merovingian, Capetian or Plantagenet, or emperor; to travel to Rome to intrigue or obtain a rich benefice, a crozier or a mitre; to attend the provincial synod; to launch a quick raid on an enemy; to lead a band of armed men to the feudal host; or to undertake a pilgrimage for the sake of their bodily health or the salvation of their soul. Many humbler folk—soldiers, messengers, pilgrims, merchants and, in the thirteenth century, mendicant friars—travelled for the same motives.

The majority went on foot; few employed wheeled vehicles, or at any rate horse-drawn carriages, because the roadway was so badly worn that a journey of any length was extremely uncomfortable. Only very short stretches—a matter of a few miles—were covered at the sluggish pace of a yoke of oxen, at which speed the jolts were bearable and heavy loads could be hauled from place to place. Most of the rich and powerful, those too who were reasonably well off, were mounted on asses, mules or horses. Saddle and pack animals were therefore in the majority, even for carrying goods. Shoeing, introduced in the early Middle Ages, protected them better and employed their strength to better effect. Saddle and stirrups improved the rider's seat and reduced fatigue; he wore spurs—at least one on the left heel—to urge on his mount. But even with the most rapid

means of transportation stages were very short: at most twenty miles or so a day.

A certain progress is observable between the tenth century and the thirteenth. Not, however, with regard to coping with hills and mountains, or the inclemency of the weather. In fact, the roads were not kept up properly by the lords, who had other uses for the tolls they collected; so when it rained or snowed, thick mud and deep potholes made them almost impassable. Consequently, the increase in speed must be ascribed to a general improvement in safety conditions and lodging facilities. Many new bridges were built, routes through marshes were more reliably marked; most important of all, the roads were better policed so that travellers did not have to be accompanied by a slow-moving armed escort and could keep going until sunset. At night, the roads continued as before to be the preserve of armed robbers and brigands. Another factor was the growing number of towns, villages and other halting places along roads which were better and better maintained by the local population. Actually, the spread of castles where travellers were warmly welcomed, of rest houses attached to monastic establishments, and of hospitable villages, tended to slow down rather than speed up communications because it was more advisable to do a safe stage of 6 miles between two abbeys one day and an equally safe stage of 15 miles to a third abbey the next day than to risk covering the whole distance of over 20 miles without a break.

The overall slowness of travel made the West incomparably vaster for the people who lived there during the Middle Ages than the entire globe is for their descendants today. True, the special messengers employed by the popes at Avignon covered over 50 miles a day, and the knights in Joan of Arc's circle did over 30 miles a day when really in a hurry. But ordinary travellers took almost a month from Bayonne to Ghent without leaving the borders of France, and 25 to 30 days from Venice to Bruges via Southern Germany.

Oddly enough, travel was faster by river and still more by sea. A ship doing 5 knots could cover more

Brattahlið
(Nanortalik)

Vinland
(America)

Terra nova

Bergen

Edinburgh

Dublin

London
Winchester

Brugge
Ieper

Bremen
Hamburg
Lübeck

Stockholm

Danzig

Reval
(Tallinn)
Novgorod

Riga

Moskva

Kiev

Astrakhan

Bokhara

Tana

Trebizond

Tabriz

Samarkand

Mosul

Baghdad

India

Paris
Troyes
Basel

Frankfurt
Leipzig

Nürnberg

Augsburg
Wien

Kraków

Bordeaux
Lyon

Milano
Venezia
Genova

Dubrovnik

Constantinople

Zaragoza
Barcelona

Firenze
Roma

Toledo
Valencia

Bari
Napoli

Thessaloniki

Damascus

Lisboa
Córdoba

Messina

Tunis

Tripolis

Alexandria

	Trade Routes
Sea Routes	
– – –	Venetians
–·–·–	Genoese
·········	Hanseatic
+++	Viking
○	Fair Towns
⊙	Banking Centres

Land and sea routes in the Middle Ages: The Northern peoples, notably the Vikings and Normans, were daring navigators. The former were the first to venture as far as North America. The Southerners, first of all the Venetians and Genoese, competed strenuously for control of trade in the Mediterranean. On land the major banking centres were located close to the ports south of the Alps and also at Barcelona, London and, especially, Bruges. North of the Alps the most important fairs were a great attraction for merchants. Trade routes linked East and West, the Mediterranean basin and the Baltic. At the end of the thirteenth century those from North to South traversed the Rhône Valley, Southern Germany and certain Alpine passes.

293

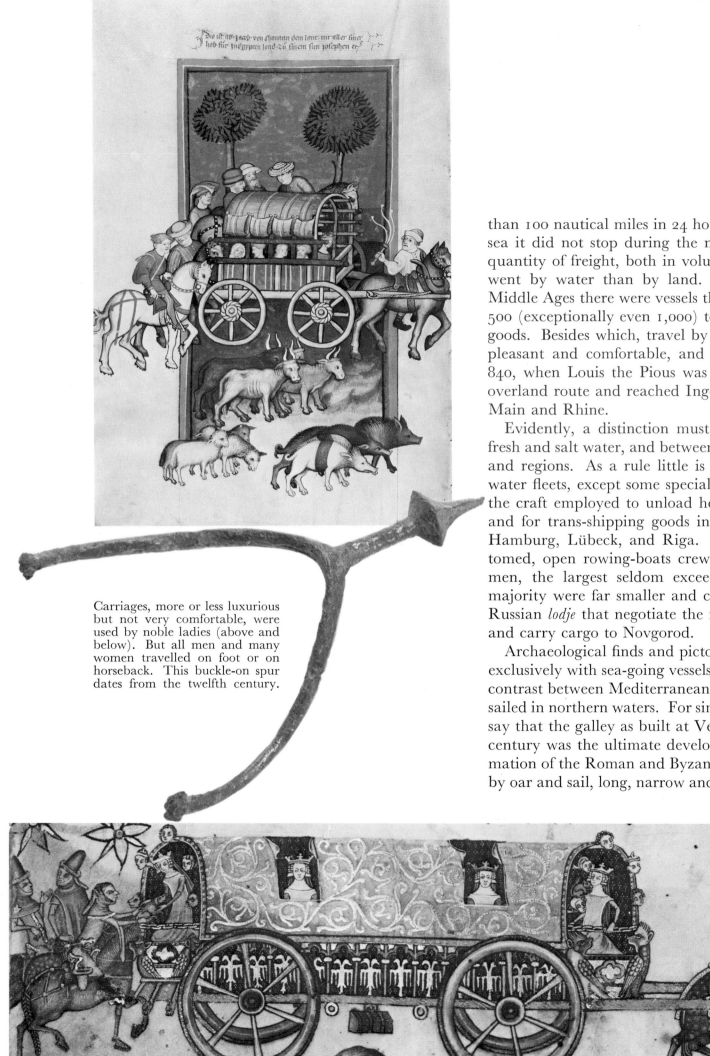

than 100 nautical miles in 24 hours because when at sea it did not stop during the night. A far greater quantity of freight, both in volume and in tonnage, went by water than by land. At the end of the Middle Ages there were vessels that could hold up to 500 (exceptionally even 1,000) tons of miscellaneous goods. Besides which, travel by water was far more pleasant and comfortable, and was even safer. In 840, when Louis the Pious was very ill, he left the overland route and reached Ingelheim by the rivers Main and Rhine.

Evidently, a distinction must be drawn between fresh and salt water, and between the various periods and regions. As a rule little is known about fresh-water fleets, except some special cases: for example, the craft employed to unload heavy sea-going ships and for trans-shipping goods in river ports such as Hamburg, Lübeck, and Riga. They were flat-bottomed, open rowing-boats crewed by three or four men, the largest seldom exceeding 12 tons. The majority were far smaller and comparable with the Russian *lodje* that negotiate the rapids of the Volhof and carry cargo to Novgorod.

Archaeological finds and pictorial documents deal exclusively with sea-going vessels. There is a striking contrast between Mediterranean ships and those that sailed in northern waters. For simplicity's sake I may say that the galley as built at Venice in the fifteenth century was the ultimate development and consummation of the Roman and Byzantine ship. Propelled by oar and sail, long, narrow and low in the water, it

Carriages, more or less luxurious but not very comfortable, were used by noble ladies (above and below). But all men and many women travelled on foot or on horseback. This buckle-on spur dates from the twelfth century.

was amazingly fast and easy to handle. And in addition to freight it could carry a certain number of passengers. But it required a very large crew: up to 200 oarsmen and a score of cross-bowmen selected by competition. This entailed carrying a very large quantity of provisions, and the total pay added up to a substantial sum because until the sixteenth century the crew members were all free men; but the galley could boast a very long range and offered considerable protection against the risks of the voyage. Many of these ships had 3 masts—a foremast with a small square sail; a mainmast up to 100 feet tall, supported by 12 shrouds on each side; and a mizzen-mast. In addition to this remarkable vessel, there were round-bowed sailing ships, descended from the ancient merchantmen; those built at Genoa were large enough to carry 1,000 tons of freight. Their bulwarks were enormously high and, as J. Heers has proved, the forecastle dominated the entire vessel like a fort. Though less fast and handy, they required a smaller crew and could compete with the big ships of the northern countries, some of whose features they had borrowed.

We know quite a lot about Saxon and Scandinavian ships through the splendid archaeological finds like those at Sutton Hoo in East Anglia and Nydam in Schleswig. Before the eighth century few had masts and most were propelled by thirty rowers. Prow and poop were designed along the same lines, so the ship could go astern at a stroke; there was no keel but simply a keelson, and a steering oar the size

Roadside inns, marked by very visible signs, offered accommodation for travellers and their beasts. There were separate dormitories for men and women (below). The hostelry in the fortified township of Pérouges (Ain) is still much as it was seven centuries ago (above).

of a sweep at one side. This must have made it impossible to hold a rectilinear course, and therefore the vessel was obliged to follow the coastline. The ship unearthed at Kvasund had one mast and a small sail. But the *drakkar* or dragon boat found at Gokstad displayed an immense advance over its predecessors. It dates from the ninth century and is a sort of whale-boat measuring 78 feet in length, with 32 oars and a displacement of 23 tons. Its keel gave it such stability that an exact replica built in 1893 had no difficulty in crossing the Atlantic. The Vikings could also make the crossing in a straight line and land in England, Iceland, Greenland and even North America. Subsequent improvements led to the construction in those northern waters of the first real sea-going freighters, namely the *kogge* and hooker of the Hanseatic merchants. The first had a bulging, rounded hull ideal for bearing down on the waves, a long keel that gave excellent stability and an ample spread of canvas that permitted sailing reasonably close to the wind with the aid of the robust rudder slung from the stern-post. The second had no fore-peak and the flat bottom allowed it to be run straight aground on the sandy shallows of the northern seas or to sail up the rivers. Being far rounder than the *kogge*, its burden was also greater and could exceed 500 tons; it only needed a small crew—30 or 40 seamen—and could therefore accommodate a large number of traders, pilgrims and clerks. It had an amazing turn of speed and, hugging the wind day and night, could cover between 80 and 180 nautical miles in 24 hours.

Ships were, as a rule, laid up in winter. At Bergen they were beached and roofed over. In some river ports they were sheltered if not from ice at least from breaking-up floes. In spring, when the thaw came, they were repainted and set sail accompanied by vocal and instrumental music and the blessing of the Church. The masters received no institutional training nor instruction in the art of navigation. In fact, that would have been quite impossible for they were unable to read. They put their trust in what they had learnt by experience and the oral informa-

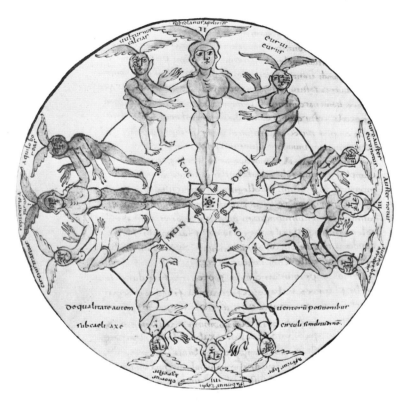

Navigation was governed by the winds, but the first compass cards were far from accurate. This one, which dates from the ninth century, gives the winds their Roman names: *Aquilo* for the North wind; *Eurus* and *Auster* for East and South; *Africus* and *Zephir* for South-west and West.

Opposite page: great improvements were made in sea-going vessels. The Viking drakkar (ninth century) was a big boat with some thirty oarsmen. In the fourteenth century the English had ships with fore and after castles, side rudder, top, bowsprit and square sail (right). The fifteenth century Catalan *nau* had a stern-slung rudder (far right).

tion received from their elders and contemporaries. Since dead reckoning was far from reliable and coastal navigation was a difficult matter, it appears probable that those master mariners were perfectly acquainted with every detail of the coast—reefs, capes, mountains, groups of trees, castles, towers, mills and, in particular, the splendid, soaring steeples intentionally erected away from the other buildings, as at Reval, to serve as easily identifiable landmarks. On occasion, seamarks were set up in particularly dangerous channels, such as those at Falsterbo, erected by Valdemar in 1225, and at Neuwerk, on an island in the River Elbe; they were indicated by light buoys or a beacon.

In daylight ships avoided running aground either by observing the changes in the colour of the water depending on the depth, or more usually by soundings; this involved casting the lead as far ahead as possible in order to have it directly under the bow when the vessel reached its point of fall. The lead had a small cavity greased with tallow, which collected samples of the seabed; by scrutinizing them a practised eye could discover the nature of the sample, which gave an indication as to where the ship was. In 1458 a Venetian master mariner said that in the Baltic ships were not navigated by chart or compass but exclusively by soundings. This was undoubtedly an exaggeration, but it pinpoints the difference in the methods required and employed in northern waters and the Mediterranean.

But whether North or South, it is difficult to insist too much on the excellence of those methods, however empirical, as of the quality of both equipment and personnel. These factors reduced navigational risks to the minimum. However, they could not be eliminated entirely, and since nearly all vessels were obliged to sail close to the same points and, except for the galleys, they were not easy to handle in wind and current, collisions were common. There was also danger from sandbanks; reefs, which might be exposed or not, depending on the tide in northern waters; early or permanent ice like that which isolated Stralsund from Prussia in 1410; and storms and hurricanes, like the one which damaged six vessels of the Elbing fleet in 1404 and another that battered the Danish fleet off Falsterbo for three days and nights in 1435.

These natural dangers were not all: far more fearsome were pillagers, pirates, corsairs and warships. When a vessel was driven on to the coast the wreck and survivors were plundered by the local inhabitants. In November 1432 Jacques Cœur, returning from his first voyage to the Levant, was cast away on the shores of Corsica. According to the report that has come down to us, 'while the crew and passengers reached land in a small boat and were endeavouring to take off those who were still on board the galley and save the cargo... [the islanders] arrived suddenly, fell upon them, assaulted them, stripped them of their clothes, hose, and even their shirt.' They locked them up, demanded a ransom for their freedom, and kept all their property.

If the spoilers took the advantage of their opportunity, it was the pirates that provided it. There is no point in dwelling upon the activities of the Slavs of the Narenta River in the Adriatic during the eleventh century, the Barbary pirates during the following period and those dreaded rovers of the Baltic, the *Vitalienbrüder*, at the end of the fourteenth. Undeclared wars gave corsairs a chance to intercept vessels which had escaped the fleets on the high seas. John of Salisbury and the Lord Mayor of London were captured by Paul Beneke of Danzig in 1473 when he seized the galley chartered for a voyage to England by Thomas Portinari, the Medici's agent at Bruges.

Overland travel was more risky still for the roads were infested by hordes of robber lords and knights, the *Raubritter*, brigands, outlaws and soldiers. These ruffians were not interested in devastation and destruction; what they wanted was to lay their hands on money and merchandise. Their numbers are an indication of the intensity of traffic on the roads.

Commercial activity varied greatly at different times and in different regions, not only in magnitude but also in methods. Before the tenth century trade was concentrated in the hands of Syrians, Levantines and Jews, who formed trading colonies and travelled from town to town. There were also a few thousand pedlars, who with little capital covered long distances on food carrying luxury articles for a limited class of privileged customers. They dealt in fine Syrian woollens, silks and cloth of gold from Byzantium, leather from Phoenicia and later from Cordova, gems, glassware, papyrus, slaves; they also provided their rich patrons with spices, dates, figs, almonds, Greek and Syrian wines and olive oil, which was in great demand in countries where the olive tree could not thrive. In fact, they dealt with all the produce of the Mediterranean lands or that which was transported from further afield via the Mediterranean to the fields and forests between the Loire and the Rhine. Western Europe had inherited from the Late Empire its poverty and its division into small rural nuclei, which were self-governing if not self-sufficient and between which trade was limited to this tiny trickle for the advantage of the rich and powerful.

It will, therefore, be readily understood that the irresistible Muslim conquest, which in less than a century (639-711) had overwhelmed the greater part of the Mediterranean basin, the centre of trade in ancient times, had extremely important consequences. According to some authors, it accentuated that region's rural character by cutting it off from the major trade routes; others say that on the contrary, it acted as an incentive to large-scale trade because it enabled the West to supply the Muslims with timber, iron, slaves, weapons and furs in exchange for the precious metal seized by the conquerors, delivered as tribute by Byzantium, or brought by caravan from Nubia and the Sudan. This precious metal was used by the West to purchase materials, purple, perfumes, spices and other luxury products from Byzantium.

A third group stresses the importance of relations with Scandinavia based, more or less, on the recent diggings which demonstrate dealings with Islam on the one hand—80,000 Arab coins discovered in Sweden, 40,000 of them on the island of Gotland alone—and with Western Europe on the other. Scandinavian steatite has been found in Germany and Rhenish

The Mediterranean towns grew and developed their facilities. This miniature shows a whole fleet at anchor in an extensive outer harbour. A port of this type was both a fortress and a starting point for warlike and commercial expeditions. We note the presence of the Hospitallers, recognizable by the Maltese Cross on their coat; they may have had a financial interest too.

From the confines of Europe merchants journeyed to Central Asia. The caravan depicted below started out from Sarai on the Volga with destination Cathay. The camels are loaded with merchandise; the escort are mounted on horseback. The crusades opened the door to trade between Muslims and Christians. Bottom: a treaty of peace and trade between the king of Tunis and the Christian kings of Sicily, France and Navarre concluded after the disastrous crusade in 1270.

glassware in Scandinavia. Actually, it remains to be proved that those treasures, which date from before 950, were not mainly the booty of pillagers, who left a hoards like the 800 English coins discovered in Finnish territory. Be this as it may, it is generally agreed that from the eleventh century trade in the West increased by leaps and bounds; this may have been due to the reaction following a period in which the economy had remained stagnant at a very low level, but in any case it was closely linked with the resurgent population boom.

The most important feature of this rebirth of trade was the fair, which developed out of the local market where the lord sold off his surplus produce, craftsmen perhaps offered their wares, and commodities were sometimes exchanged between one region and another. Some of these markets, which were active as early as the tenth century, became meeting places for merchants' caravans on certain fixed dates. As a rule a series of fairs held in the same region provided an opportunity for an almost permanent flow of trade. This was the case in Flanders, at Ypres, Lille, Bruges, Messines and Torhout, for wool and cloth; in England, at Winchester, Boston, Northampton, St Ives and Stamford, for wool; in France, at Le Lendit near Paris, and particularly in the Champagne region, Troyes, Provins, Lagny and Bar-sur-Aube, where the shrewd policy of the counts attracted Flemish and German merchants from the North, and Italian, Catalan and Provencal merchants from the South all the year round.

Those fairs lasted at least two or three weeks. It took the merchants a week to unpack their wares and set up their displays; then came several days of trading; lastly eight to ten days were spent in closing accounts, making payments and arranging clearing transactions. The Lendit fair was held in June, from the feast of Saint Barnaby to Midsummer Day; it was grafted on a religious festival commemorating the delivery of the relics to the abbey of Saint-Denis. As a preliminary, the merchants of Paris called on the abbot or prior or other representative of Saint-Denis early in May to discuss the site. The opening ceremony was presided over by the Archbishop of Paris in person, who came in procession from Notre-Dame to give the traders his blessing. Tents, booths and barrows were arranged regularly over a large area. The various specialities were kept together—here tools and implements, scythes, sickles, hatchets, axes; there foodstuffs; further on clothiers, linendrapers, those who specialized in hides, leather and furs, the great furriers who dressed the rich and noble, parchment-makers who supplied students and clerks, leather-workers, tanners, saddlers, cobblers, and so on. Drinking booths did a thriving trade; so did the tents that served both as wineshops and as offices for those rich money-lenders, the Lombards.

The organization of the fairs raised a number of problems. First of all, the people who attended them had to be granted safe-conducts to protect their persons, their wares and their money on the way there and back. The counts of Champagne had the safe-conducts issued for their fairs confirmed by all territorial princes, and from the beginning of the thirteenth century they bore the guarantee of the king of France. Accommodation had also to be found for the merchants—a section of Provins was called Germanstown. The Lombards were entitled to a special chamber and at Troyes, there were halls and houses specially reserved for the people of Montpellier, Lerida, Valencia, Barcelona, Geneva, Clermont, Ypres, Douai, Saint-Omer and the like. Those who came from the same town formed associations and after a time appointed consuls to settle their disputes and act as their local representatives.

The merchants' safety during the fair had to be assured and their business transactions checked. This was done by the 'wardens', who little by little assumed jurisdiction over affairs in litigation and later over contracts. In the thirteenth century a great many merchants appeared before them to append their signatures to agreements drafted by a host of notaries. Police duties were performed by bailiffs. There was also the problem of payments, for they were not settled on the spot. After the sales period accounts were checked and dealers who had sold more than they had bought received the difference, which was paid by those whose purchases exceeded their sales. But the fairs in the Champagne region gained so great a reputation that many of the recognizances signed throughout the year in all Western Europe, not only by merchants but by clerks and nobles too, were made payable there. In this way the Champagne fairs did duty as clearing houses for the whole Western World from the mid-thirteenth century to the early fourteenth. Also worth noting is that since all sorts of currencies were used in the transactions, the money-changers were kept very busy fixing exchange and interest rates. And it was from there that the most advanced banking methods of the day—those employed by the Sienese and Florentines first, by the Venetians and Genoese later—spread to the other great trading centres of Christendom.

This intense banking business pinpoints another feature of the revival of trade and commerce whose impact can still be felt to the present day: the use of coinage and other means of payment. It is almost certain that until the eleventh century there was very little coinage in circulation among the inhabitants of the West. I do not want to be misunderstood: gold was known even in the Slav and Scandinavian countries and silver was used in commercial transaction but not minted; it was weighed like any other merchandise—so much so that foreign coins were chopped up or melted down into ingots. In the countries that had been Romanized at an early date the landed aristocracy and the merchants with whom they did business continued to count and pay in gold *solidi*, but those coins grew smaller and smaller—the *tremissis* was one-third of a *solidus*—and their gold content became less and less until they were nearly half silver. Early in the ninth century they disappeared altogether, even in the West. There remained a silver coin, the denier, whose title was improved by Charlemagne; its value was quite considerable, being equal to almost a bushel and a half of oats or a dozen loaves of bread. There was no fractional coinage, except the obol, which was literally half a denier.

The inference is that the common people did not use coins to pay for their day-to-day purchases and must have employed a system of barter. Indeed, the term day-to-day purchases gives a wrong impression because peasant households were virtually self-sufficient. Therefore, the 'black' coins produced by the feudal lords, which were of very little value and circulated only on their own lands, may well have been better suited to the then economic situation.

Coins became indispensable as a medium of exchange when peasants reached a position where they were able to sell their surplus to people who needed it because their chief activity was not farming. At the same time the peasants were not obliged to buy articles produced by craftsmen or offered by traders. The merchants who had long employed in their transactions the gold dinar of Islam and the besant of Byzantium, which were the international currencies of that age, were also greatly in need of a stable silver coinage accepted throughout the West and not merely in the seigniory of the lord who minted it; their preoccupations were shared by the great territorial princes.

The first coins of this type were the silver *grosso* of Venice (late twelfth century) the English sterling or silver penny and, a little later, the *gros* of Saint Louis. Christian states in touch with the Muslims, such as Catalonia, Castile, Portugal and Sicily, began to strike gold coins again in the eleventh and twelfth centuries, but they did not become common until a stock of gold had been built up; this could only be done by trading because, except in Hungary, no gold was produced in the West. A start was made by Lucca, Florence, and Genoa with the florin, in the mid-thirteenth century, followed by Venice—with her ducat—in 1284. Their example was not copied by the monarchies until the next century, though actually Henry III of England and Saint Louis of France attempted to issue gold coins during the thirteenth.

As the use of coins spread gradually from town to country, revolutionizing the peasants' way of life, merchants were faced with new problems. The most important were the hazard of travelling with large sums of money, the trouble of having to employ different currencies in the different regions they passed through, and the difficulty of finding sufficient capital to finance their operations.

Bills of exchange, the use of which spread very rapidly during the fourteenth and fifteenth centuries, went a long way towards solving two of these problems. Let us take an actual example. A merchant or banker of Bruges, named Riccardo degli Alberti, wanted to send a sum of money to his agent at Barcelona, Brunaccio di Guido. He had no difficulty in doing business with one or more merchants of Bruges, among them Guglielmo Barberi who needed some ready money to pay for goods; sheets for shipment to his agent at Barcelona, Francesco di Marco Datini. So Barberi borrowed the money from Riccardo and instructed Datini to settle the debt with Brunaccio di Guido. The transaction involved exchanging Flemish currency against Catalan, a commercial operation, a transfer of funds, a credit, and probably a profit for the person who opened it; it involved the difference in exchange rates between Bruges and Barcelona, and a time factor, at least that required for the bill to reach Barcelona plus the time required to honour it.

As for the problem of finding capital, various methods were adopted simultaneously before the invention of loans disguised in the shape of bills of exchange. Some merchants came from families which had made a fortune in the service of feudal lords; either as stewards entrusted with the task of purveying rare and costly products, whose sons after evading serfdom or being emancipated continued trading on their own account; or as peasants who, having put away money by hard work, good luck, a fine family or an inheritance, made money-changing first a part-time and later a full-time activity; or even, as in Venice, as big landowners who invested the profits from their estates in overseas trade. Others had some capital of their own as descendants of the very small merchant class of previous centuries. But the majority, even when they had enough capital to set up in business, were forced to seek out people with 'fresh' money in order to develop it fully.

A procedure already applied in Venice in the tenth century spread later on a vast scale through the entire West, namely the *accomandita* or limited partnership. This is how it worked: a merchant about to start out on a sea voyage persuaded someone to become a sleeping partner by putting up a sum of money to be employed in the venture; on his return the sum was repaid and the profits were split up between the partners, three-quarters to the capital and one-quarter to the work. If the active partner put up one-third of the capital he took half the profit: a quarter for his capital and a quarter for his work. Needless to say, a merchant could form several partnerships with different sleeping partners and so increase his profits; he could also invest in other ventures where he was the sleeping partner.

Since business involving transport on land was, in principle, less risky, partnerships lasted as a rule for more than one venture. Some were agreements concluded for several years by several persons, who often belonged to the same family, sat at the same table, and put their capital into a common fund, which was divided into a certain number of shares. The profits were divided up in proportion to the number of shares held and the partners were jointly responsible. Their number enabled them to accompany their goods in transit, settle in various important trading centres, besides offering other advantages. In addition to its capital the 'company' could have the use of sums deposited in consideration of a fixed rate of interest by people who were not shareholders. At the end of the thirteenth century the great Italian companies established branches with joint responsiblity. Some developed into huge concerns: at the beginning of the fourteenth century the Bardi of Florence had 25 subsidiaries, the Peruzzi 16. The former had a share capital of close on 150,000 florins and the annual turnover came near to 900,000 florins. To obtain an idea of what this figure meant, it need only be remembered that the pope purchased the lordship of Avignon for 80,000 florins.

To cross a bridge (above), travel on a road or enter a town (below) entailed payment of a toll to the local lord. Duties levied on merchandise were fixed by a detailed tariff.

Those companies were ruined by the general recession that occurred in the fourteenth century and by the principle of joint responsibility which made each subsidiary answerable for all the others. The new generation which grew up at the end of that century and during the fifteenth—it included the Datini and the Medici—had more solid foundations. Most of their subsidiaries were self-governing and could go bankrupt without ruining the rest. The partner who had a majority holding in all of them acted as general manager either personally or through a deputy. The well-balanced Datini complex, with branches at Prato, Florence, Genoa, Pisa, Avignon, Barcelona, Valencia and Majorca, and a host of agents at Bruges, London, Paris, Venice, Milan earned over 20 per cent profit a year. The founder, who had started from nothing, possessed 70,000 florins in land and investments when he died.

A new merchant learned his business as a young man travelling from one big fair to another; then he settled down and seldom left his headquarters. His days and nights were spent reading and writing letters—over 150,000 have been preserved for the Datini complex alone—sending his agents in the various centres orders to buy and sell, keeping his books in order or checking them. He had dozens—the Bardi hundreds—of assistants, managers and factors, thoroughly trained and chosen with the greatest care.

France could boast at least one great merchant of this type—Jacques Cœur (1395–1456). But he preferred to take part in a great many ventures of all sorts rather than set up a highly organized establishment of his own. In Germany there were both great merchants who operated through small companies, like Hildebrant Veckinchusen in the early fifteenth century and most of the major northern traders, and large-scale concerns which flourished chiefly in the Rhineland and still more in the South. The big Ravensburg company, active from 1380 to 1530, had 13 'antennae' and a host of agents; at the end of the fifteenth century it had a capital of 157,000 florins, and the chief shareholder, Lutfrid

Fairs held at regular intervals attracted, traders, buyers and idlers. The Lendit Fair near Saint-Denis (Ile-de-France) was opened by the bishop of Paris, who went there in person to give his blessing. Awnings stretched on timber frames served as booths and taverns.

Opposite page: currency differed enormously in geographical origin, weight and content of precious metal. This led to a great many money-changers setting up shop in the places most frequented by foreigners, such as Bruges and Antwerp, where Quintin Matsys may have painted this money-changer and his wife. Here are a few coins in actual size: 1. silver denier, Charlemagne (ninth century); 2. *trifollaro*, Sicily, Roger I (1072–1101); 3. penny, England, Henry II (1154–1189); 4. gold *ambrosino*, Milan, first republic (1250–1310); 5. *gros tournois*, France, Louis IX, from 1266; 6. rose noble, England, Edward I (1276–1307); 7. *grossus* of 20 deniers, Trient, about 1300; 8. *thaler*, Berne, 1494.

1

2

4

5

3

6

7

8

Muntprat of Constance, died in 1447 worth 53,550 florins. The Diesbach-Watt company lasted from 1420 to about 1460; in 1436 one of the founders, the Bernese Nicholas de Diesbach, had a fortune of 70,000 florins. The Frankfurt firm of Blum did over 300,000 florins worth of business in the two years 1491–3. Jakob Fugger, who set up the firm of that name on his own, became the richest man in the world; his personal fortune cannot be reckoned exactly, but it was somewhere between two and three million florins.

Those great merchants and all the others who operated less successfully along the same lines brought about, by their mentality and their way of life, a radical change in the tradition-bound medieval society. They bought from the nobles the surplus produced on the latters' home farms and collected in payment of feudal dues—wheat from the East German Junkers, wool from the English gentry, wine from Aquitaine, and the like. Sometimes they borrowed money from them, but more often granted them loans at least sufficient to purchase all the luxury wares the merchants themselves supplied. As surety they were given pieces of jewelry, monopoly contracts, the right to collect manorial revenues, even tracts of land. And the lands, acquired through forfeiture or purchase, in which they invested their capital for prestige reasons or because it was less at risk, gave them part of the power which the nobles lost in the process. The peasants derived very little advantage from the change of owners. Indeed, the new arrivals were perhaps greedier for gain and more intent on managing their lands as a business proposition, investing money in them to increase their yield and producing commodities for which there was a ready, lucrative market.

Sometimes the merchants and nobles were mutually incompatible and treated each other with contempt. The Florentines held mock-tourneys in which the antagonists were mounted face to tail on hogs. Sumptuary laws that favoured the nobles tended to forbid the rich merchants to wear certain luxury materials. But there were merchants who lived as the nobles did, performed their service on horseback with a sword at their side, owned castles and estates, and finished by marrying their heirs to noblewomen or succeeded in entering the nobility themselves.

As regards the Church, merchants were in a difficult position because they had no recognized place in the orderly society. Indeed, Thomas Aquinas says that 'trade as such has a rather disreputable character' for it involved a love of wealth and profit and also because it enabled money to beget money, through the interest on loans which was usury and therefore an abomination. But by degrees the Church came to accept that the risks and losses a merchant incurred through delayed payments justified his receiving interest, and also that he had the right to demand a just price for his work and the services he rendered the community. In the fifteenth century ideas had changed to the point where it was accepted that large-scale trade did not run counter to God's will.

What is more, many clerics had no compunction in lending money at interest or investing it in trade. The Cistercians and Templars, for example, became wool merchants and bankers respectively. The Knights of the Teutonic Order established an important trading concern with offices at Königsberg, Marienburg and Bruges; their factors travelled as far afield as Novgorod the Great. Conversely, many merchants ended their days as monks in the odour of sanctity following in the footsteps of Saint Omobono of Cremona, Saint Bernardo Tolomei of Siena and the merchant's son Saint Francis of Assisi. As a matter of fact, most of them kept on their books an account in the name of 'The Lord God' for donations to charity, which they hoped would earn a pardon for the liberties they took with the Church's doctrine and the ban on usury. Some, like Francesco di Marco Datini, were led by the fear of hell to leave all their worldly goods to the poor.

But even when the merchants were reconciled with the Church and accepted as members of the traditional society, they still remained problem children and trouble makers. Those rational organizers had a methodical mentality which forced them to calculate, reckon, foresee, and find a reasonable explanation for everything. They insisted on their children receiving a very different education from that imparted in the schools and universities controlled by the clergy. Notably, the ability to do sums and write a swift, legible hand, besides precise notions of geography and cartography. In place of the ancient compendiums with their half-digested verbiage, they insisted on handbooks which presented in a practical form a synopsis of everything they needed to know which witnessed their instinct for concrete facts and figures and precisely measured time. This new mentality also made its mark on the painting and architecture those merchants subsidized and inspired. Traditional painters had concentrated exclusively on religious subjects represented in a flat, conventional manner; the new generation adopted new themes, such as portraits of merchants realistically represented in correct perspective in their homes and counting-houses. The merchants' impact on architecture, as on politics, government and society as a whole, must be viewed in the setting that was theirs *par excellence*, namely the medieval town.

TOWNS AND TOWN LIFE

During the Late Empire, in the third and fourth centuries, the West was dotted with towns. Twelve hundred years later, in the fifteenth, it was no less urbanized but in the interval the appearance of the towns had changed beyond recognition, though some still occupied the same site.

The change set in under the Emperor Aurelian (A.D. 270–5). The Roman city, wide open to the countryside, fenced itself round with a belt of ramparts that were often hastily thrown up with stones taken from ruined buildings. In that way only the heart of the town was protected; the suburbs, depopulated by the demographic deflation and the departure of the big landed proprietors for their estates, were left to the tender mercies of the Barbarians. That is what gave the town the aspect it presented during and after the great invasions—a small urban core surrounded by a turreted wall. With the exception of Rome (3,150 acres), Milan (1,000 acres), Trier (700 acres), Mainz, Nîmes, Merida, Toulouse and Cologne (about 250 acres), most towns had an area of less than 125 acres.

The Church condemned usury and for a long time money business was monopolized by the Jews, who were not subject to the rules of Christianity. The miniature on the right shows Jews granting a loan, the amount of which is entered in a book. Behind are articles left as surety.

Opposite page: in the late fifteenth century rich burghers took an interest in the arts, particularly in painting because it enabled them to leave their likeness to posterity. Here a citizen of Ghent has come to see his favourite painter, who is busy on a portrait of his wife. We can recognize the same man in the pictures on the wall; he appears four times in all, engaged in different activities.

But those small fortified towns could boast many new buildings of a new type—the churches. As a rule, one of them was a cathedral, for the priest of the city was a bishop. He was often chosen from among the leading local families and had the task of sustaining and stimulating the fervour of his flock by organizing processions, promoting the cult of relics, founding monasteries within the walls, setting up schools, and instructing the clergy and laity. The bishop had broad estates from which he could bring part of his stocks and revenues into the city. He and the members of his circle patronized the local craftsmen, who went in for better-class work—fine materials, jewelry and pottery—rather than those employed in the rural workshops, the merchants who came from distant parts and the Jewish communities of the vicinity. The inhabitants of the surrounding rural area came to the city to receive the sacraments and revere the relics as well as to sell their surplus produce and buy the few articles they could not do without. Poor people settled there in the hope of finding sustenance, particularly when there was a famine. The count, who was the highest local dignitary, passed through occasionally to administer justice. The king himself sometimes stopped there with his court and was welcomed with songs and processions.

The Merovingian town was far from dead, but it had lost many of its inhabitants, and fields and gardens appeared here and there on the site of ruined buildings inside the walls. It is also true that it lived largely on the countryside, where in fact the rich and powerful had taken refuge and the Germans had often settled because they did not feel at home cooped up in a town, never having been accustomed to living in that way. The Goths and Vandals, more amenable to the urban way of life, disappeared more rapidly.

In Western Europe by the seventh or eighth century the town had almost entirely lost its political power over the surrounding countryside and was indeed penetrated through and through by rural influences. What strikes us most is its rampart, its monumental aspect and the intense religious activity of which it was the centre. Particularly when it stood in the heart of a rich, fertile land, suburbs began to spring up around the walls, along the roads and in the shadow of the monasteries. Paris, whose population was probably never less than 20,000 people, had not by any means shrunk to only the Ile de la Cité. Its rampart enclosed a church and served as its foundations; on the left bank of the Seine the churches and ancient monuments were surrounded by dwelling houses.

In the days of the first Carolingians, when peace was better kept, ramparts were less useful and the city centre became too cramped for the growing population. It was the time when new towns and villages grew up around a palace or an ancient villa, as in the case of Aix-la-Chapelle and Frankfurt; a stronghold or *castrum*, such as Douai, Ghent, Nimwegen, Utrecht, Basle, Bonn; a monastery, Saint-Denis, Saint Gall, Fulda, Reichenau, Saint-Riquier; a large estate or even a seaport, Quentovicus, Duurstede. But it was chiefly in the eighth and ninth centuries that new settlements, whose inhabitants were not occupied exclusively in working the land, developed alongside the old episcopal cities, monasteries and strongholds. The *vik, portus* or *burgus*, enclosed initially by a palisade and later by a wall established in the immediate vicinity of a traditional trade centre, along a road, at a crossroads or a river junction, was a useful addition to the medieval city. Its inhabitants engaged in new activities connected with consumption: bakers, butchers, coopers, innkeepers; transport: carters, porters, mercers, drapers; or production: wheelwrights, blacksmiths, tanners, weavers of flax or wool.

Even in Italy, where five towns out of six were of Roman origin and the seat of a bishop, their function gradually changed and with it the composition of their population and their very substance. Pavia, Milan and Bergamo were no less flourishing trade centres in the ninth and tenth centuries than the towns situated between the Loire and the Rhine, though less involved in the domanial system.

Nowhere better than at Carcassonne can we get an idea of what a fortified town looked like in the Middle Ages. The double wall encloses the church of Saint-Nazaire and an impregnable castle. Few other towns had such strong defences. The Narbonne Gate and the Treasure Tower are two of the most efficient fortifications left us by the late thirteenth century.

Except for the 'cities' where a bishop had his seat, it was not always an easy matter during the Middle Ages to distinguish a town from a mere village. To be considered truly urban, built-up areas had to display certain characteristics. They did not differ radically from the country because they comprised fields, orchards, gardens, barns and stables, and many of their inhabitants still engaged in rural pursuits. Nor was the wall that encircled them an exclusive feature, for there were also fortified villages; but it separated them from the open country, defended them against attack, filtered the people who entered through the main gate and the goods that had to pass the toll-house, and forced the dwelling houses to jostle and crowd each other, particularly when population and economy were booming, to add new storeys, invade the bridges and press around the churches. Nor can

we take as a criterion a minimum number of inhabitants, say 2,000, as we do today, for some medieval towns counted only a few hundred people. However, other modern standards may be applied. Townspeople were distinguished from the peasantry by their occupations, mentality and way of life. They followed a trade or craft at home; spent most of their working hours inside the built-up area, like the urban clergy and nobility and the purveyors of food and drink; or had their residence, family or home there, as in the case of travelling merchants. The fact of having a market and being the seat of administrative, judicial, religious, military and political function, enhanced the town's domination over the country and stressed their difference. Lastly, a more or less comprehensive urban 'law', involving legal and political privileges, distinguished the most active

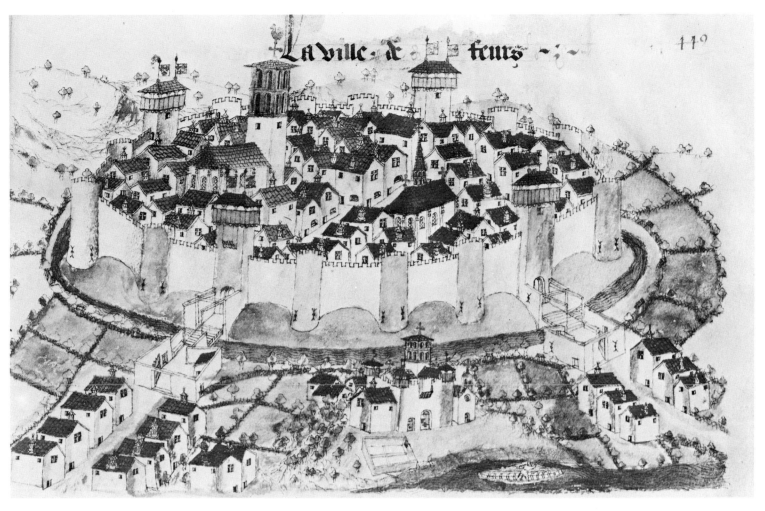

This miniature represents the town of Feurs in the Forez district: a typical picture of a small fortified town. The houses crowd round the church and the lord's castle. The whole is protected by a wall strengthened with towers; the gates are preceded by drawbridges. Outside the walls are gardens and a monastery; the few houses which line the roads are the nuclei of future suburbs.

and in many districts by far the most numerous section of the population from the peasantry.

Some medieval towns have been preserved until the present day, but we can form a still better idea of how their inhabitants saw them from miniatures, prints, paintings and seals: namely, as a mass of towers and steeples enclosed by a mighty wall. Outside the walls, houses lined the roads, built closer together the nearer they were to the gates; then came the river or a moat, the latter fed as a rule by a diversion from the river, and which powered a number of mills. Towns were seldom far from a watercourse but the many that were situated on the edge of a cliff found it difficult if not impossible to add a moat to their defences. The wall was often of huge size and encrusted with turrets and bastions. Two good examples are Avila, on the bare plateau of Castile, whose wall was a mile and a half in length, 40 feet high and had 88 massive towers, and Avignon, one of the largest towns in Christendom, besides being its capital in the fourteenth century, whose walls, almost two miles six furlongs in length, harboured some 30,000 people. The gates—there were rarely more than four—were framed by a massive bastion similar to but larger than the one that protected a castle gate. It would be a mistake, however, to presume that walls and towers served a merely defensive purpose; they were equally important as symbols of the town's power over the country and as an expression of urban aesthetics. The number and shape of the towers varied for no practical reason, while the gates became more numerous and ornamental at the very time when the introduction of artillery made them more vulnerable.

311

On passing through the gate, it was easy to lose sight of the town as a panorama unless a turret was climbed, from which it appeared as a sea of roofs pierced by towers here and there. The streets were narrow and winding, lined by bulging or corbelled houses that left only a slender ribbon of sky. Workshops and stalls encroached on the ill-paved street, which was usually muddy, littered with straw and refuse, with a gutter running down the middle. Now and again a small open space with a cross or fountain in the middle marked the junction of two or three streets or added dignity to the facade of some rich merchant's mansion, *hôtel*, or *palazzo*. Even the most important religious edifices were hemmed in by houses and, when viewed from so close up, were liable to overwhelm with their dizzy height.

At last the main square was reached. Called variously *plaza mayor*, *piazza maggiore*, this was the typical feature of the Western town and the point where several streets converged, each inhabited by members of a different craft who embellished their houses with handsome wrought-iron signs. In Florence those streets are still named after the great corporations, *arti maggiori*, formerly settled there— Por Santa Maria (silk weavers), Calimala (cloth finishers), Pelliceria (furriers). The vast square, wide open to the sky, was lined with the fine houses of the rich, dominated by the Town Hall, *Hôtel de Ville*, *Palazzo Comunale*, or *Rathaus*, and its clock tower, *beffroi*, *campanile*, *Turm*, counterpart of the feudal keep and symbol of independence and power. The Town Hall was often the town's handsomest lay building and served for many purposes: meetings, sales, gatherings, shelter; its cellars were utilized for storing archives or as prisons. Besides the spacious esplanade where the burghers held their meetings and the militia assembled when the tocsin sounded, the square usually also contained a covered market (*marché, mercato, Kaufhalle*) where most craftsmen and retailers could display their wares grouped by specialities as in the nearby streets. At Breslau, for example, on the *Grosse Ring* the impressive drapers' hall stood side by side with the building that housed the linen-weavers, leather-workers and bakers. The gibbet rose close by the large and small balances, while the fish market separated the *Grosse Ring* from the *Salzring*. At Lübeck the arrangement was the same but the church of Our Lady also stood in the huge square. The union of lay and religious buildings was not always so harmonious. Some very fine collegiate churches, and in particular the cathedral, were more usually erected on a separate square.

When a town had a dual or multiple origin, this was mirrored in its topography, characterized by two or more nuclei. Toulouse, for instance, has two— Bourg-Saint-Sernin and the city with its lively Capitole Square, whereas the cathedral of Saint-Etienne is situated on the periphery. Cracow also has two: Wawel with the cathedral and castle overlooks a commercial town of some importance centred round the draper's hall; between them is a more recently built up space. Lübeck originally had three or even four small nuclei—the castle, the cathedral, and the centre where the merchants and craftsmen lived. Brunswick and Hildesheim had five; each was girded by its own rampart until the common wall embraced them all without altering the peculiar character of each. At Metz the cathedral is surrounded by the old town where the clergy and patricians lived a quiet life in houses that were less tightly packed. In some places the various nuclei never blended. At Provins, for example, the upper and lower towns are separated by a steep houseless slope; at Limoges the city and castle have stayed apart. In the simplest, most harmonious case, as at Aix-la-Chapelle, Bruges and Florence, the town developed concentrically round about a unique or unified nucleus—the Palace, the episcopal or comital *castrum* or the *portus*. But the first rampart of a town in full growth prevented the houses from spreading. Hence a phase of pause and 'compression' preceded the construction of a second rampart, which relaxed the pressure for a time. If growth continued this second rampart was followed by a third and a fourth. At the beginning of the fourteenth century Florence was already at its sixth, Vienna at its fourth.

Most Western towns have an ample square that serves as gathering place for the citizens. The town hall, usually the handsomest of the lay buildings, faces on to it. Above left: the Palazzo Communale of Volterra, the oldest in Tuscany. In Italian towns the leading citizens, who were often of noble descent, crowned their houses with a tall tower. San Gimignano (above right) had seventy-three; the thirteen that still stand today form a unique ensemble.

Avila remained in the hands of the Muslims from 714 to the eleventh century. After it was retaken by the Christians its old Roman walls were restored and a ring wall was erected a mile and a half long with eighty-eight towers that still dominate the bare plateau of Old Castile. At its highest point stands the cathedral, whose fortified apse (mid-twelfth century) is integrated in the city wall.

The wall of Aigues-Mortes forms a rectangle, whose long sides measure 690 and 542 yards and short sides 329 and 294 yards respectively. It has 20 towers and 10 gates. The streets of the town are angled to prevent their being ravaged by the mistral.

Bram, in the Aude district, is a circular town built round a church. This is rather unusual since most new towns in France were built to a rectangular plan reminiscent of the Roman colonies for military reasons.

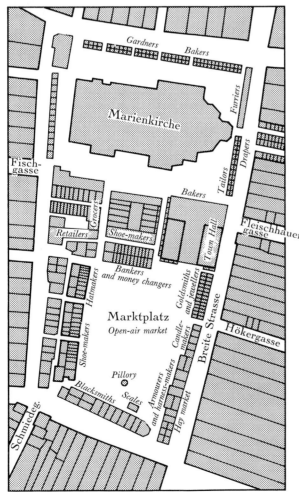

The market place was the centre of the town's commercial activities. At Breslau (below right) it contains not only the town hall but also an impressive drapers' hall and a building for all the other crafts (goldsmiths, bakers, shoemakers *et al.*). At Lübeck (left) the layout was similar, but the square also contained the red-brick church of Our Lady.

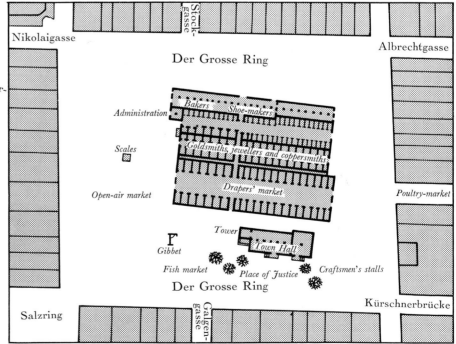

In less than a century and a half Ghent built five:
in 1163, 1213, 1254, 1269 and 1299. Some towns
erected in a single effort at a later date were laid out
on a rational chequer-board plan that took into
account their future requirements and even their
population; examples that spring to mind are the
new Carcassonne, Aigues-Mortes, Grenade-sur-Ga-
ronne and other fortified new towns of South-West
France, and the new quarters of some German towns.

Medieval towns never spread over a very large
area. Even Ghent covered barely 1,500 acres—
slightly more than Venice, or Paris including the
suburbs outside the walls. Cologne and a very few
others exceeded 1,000 acres. But the population
density was sometimes extremely high, though it
never reached that of the Polish *grod*, where in the
early Middle Ages the inhabitants were apparently
crowded together at the rate of 400, 500 or even 800
to the acre—6 times as many as in Paris today.
Southern towns like Albi and Genoa had over
250 inhabitants to the acre lodged in multi-storeyed
houses, each room of which sheltered a large family.
A population of that magnitude must be considered
very large, particularly in view of the economic con
ditions of the time. To crowd together 200,000
people in less than 1,500 acres seems impossible, yet
Paris must have done so. Genoa had 100,000 inhabitants packed into 275 acres, the same number as
Florence, Venice, Naples and Milan. Ghent with
50,000, London with 40,000 and Cologne with
30,000 must also be counted among the big medieval
towns. Those amazingly cramped conditions, rendered still worse by the fact that the religious communities owned large gardens inside the walls, were
partly responsible for a number of calamities. Fire
spread rapidly through a town built of wood. Hygiene
was non-existent and epidemics reaped victims
by the hundred. To make matters worse, the fixed
population was increased all the year round by a
host of pilgrims, tourists, merchants, and peasants
from the surrounding countryside.

The streets, their width reduced by booths and
barrows, were filled from dawn to dusk. The wives

Fire was the greatest hazard in wartime as in peace. In 1405 a
great fire broke out in Berne. The chronicler shows women and
children fleeing for their lives, while the men fight the flames.
The town was almost totally destroyed.

and children of the poor, who were miserably housed,
spent their time there playing games, chatting with
the neighbours, making a few purchases and admir-
ing the permanent spectacle offered by the shopkeepers, the nobles and clerics who were their customers,
and all the motley throng. Here the furrier showed
his finest furs, white and black lamb, squirrel,
marten, ermine; there the grocer offered drugs, a
real 'smell of paradise', tincture of roses to assist the
digestion, electuaries and syrups; further on the
draper, apothecary and goldsmith had their booths.
At every turn an innkeeper invited guests to enter
his den and sit on the reeds which covered the
beaten-earth floor; he served salt herring with his
wine and beer to give a thirst. A man could strike
up an acquaintance with the idlers, knaves, lazy
students and sharpers who gathered there, always

The narrow streets were paved; the houses were built of brick or half-timbered. Tailors, furriers, barbers and other craftsmen plied their trade in full view of the passers-by.

On the public squares fountains supplied running water for man and beast. Some were surmounted by an allegorical figure or legendary hero and added a touch of colour to the lively traffic round about. Right: the fountain of the Ogre in Berne.

Business transactions involved a certain amount of mutual trust born of small talk and bargaining. Even a small purchase was a big event for there was far less ready money than there is today.

316

Seated in front of his booth, this Spanish apothecary boasts the merits of his products to a motley crowd in which Christians mingle with Moors. During the Middle Ages Islam had a decisive influence on the preparation and distribution of remedies in the West.

ready to play dice or any other game calculated to relieve the unwary of the few coins in his purse. On leaving, after the visitor's pet vice was miserably satisfied, be it wine, women or play, he was swallowed up by the milling crowds that filled the street.

Ambrogio Lorenzetti described the intense animation prevailing there in a famous fresco. It shows us, besides the merchants, tradesmen and artisans whose booths and workshops were open to the street, schoolboys at their books, women carrying clothes baskets on their head or infants in their arms, carriers and their mules loaded with wool, sacks, etcetera, and a goatherd driving a dozen animals followed by his dog. We miss the swine routing in the mud and refuse, so frequent under more northerly skies that the burghers of Nuremberg had to wear pattens to avoid soiling their shoes. Carts and coaches could only with difficulty negotiate those narrow, crowded streets, in which litters and men on horseback— nobles, patricians, merchants back from an inspection

or a journey proceeded more easily. Very frequently a vast throng was attracted and all traffic brought to a standstill by a procession: clerics promenading relics to give thanks to God, call down His blessing on the town, or celebrate a feast day; members of a guild or of a parish or local confraternity with their leaders in their Sunday clothes honouring their patron saint by carrying his statue through the streets.

On less frequent occasions, but all the more popular for that, the townspeople gathered around the pillory, the scaffold or the gibbet to see a condemned man tortured or executed. The crowd displayed the same passion and cruelty as in the recent past, showering insults and even blows on the unfortunate creature who was about to die; the more powerful he had been the more pleased they were. When Philip the Fair's all-powerful favourite Enguerrand de Marigny was hanged in 1316 the atmosphere was very like that when some French 'collaborators' were lynched at the end of the Second World War. It was the same when the Armagnacs were beheaded by their Burgundian conquerors and vice versa.

The streets and squares also provided other spectacles, less disgusting but just as popular: mountebanks, bear baiters, jugglers, preachers storming at the vices of this world, miracle plays and satirical farces. There was also singing, dancing and the distribution of food to celebrate some happy occurrence. Since those occasions were public holidays, we can easily envisage the huge number of locals and people from the surrounding countryside that thronged the public squares.

At night the city gates were shut and guarded, the streets dark and deserted. Though the watch went the rounds at regular intervals, it was inadvisable to go abroad at a late hour without an armed escort carrying torches, for the many robbers who haunted the churchyards and thieves' kitchens did their evil deeds under cover of darkness, cutting purses, hamstrings and throats. No medieval town of any importance ever succeeded in getting rid of those dregs of humanity who rounded off their nightly gains during the day by mendicity, touching charitable hearts with a display of fake infirmities. M. Defourneaux quotes an order by the king of France against beggars of both sexes who 'pretend to be weak in their limbs, carrying sticks without any need, and feign epilepsy, bleeding sores, scabs and itches by applying plastered rags, painting with saffron, flour, blood and other false colours, also carrying iron in their hands, rags on their head and other muddy, nasty, dirty, slimy and abominable dressings even in church, and falling down in the biggest, busiest thoroughfares and the grandest company and gathering they can find, such as a general procession, discharging through their mouth and nostrils blood made of mulberries, vermilion or other dyes, all this to extort undeservedly alms that are owing to God's true poor.' The larger the town, the greater was the chance of alms (and thefts) and the more it abounded with beggars both real and sham. The number of those professional vagabonds was so great that whole-

sale expulsions were necessary from time to time. This accounts for the 'caymans' deported from Paris and put to work at Melun and elsewhere and the careful checks by German burghers aimed at removing 'strange' paupers who might compete with 'their own' native breed, disturb the charity/poverty balance, and spark off riots jointly with the most miserable proletarians.

Its outer appearance and the way of life of the people who lived within its walls were not a town's sole distinctive features. As I have already mentioned, it was also characterized by the legal status of the inhabitants and the 'law' that distinguished them from the countrypeople and the members of the traditional orderly society. Townsmen were in a minority in a world administered by the lord of the manor; they lived on land which belonged to him and engaged in rural activities for which they paid him fees; some were craftsmen or traders, in which case they were charged rents, tolls and duties. They appeared before his court, bore the brunt of his wars, and felt all the more isolated because they formed a close-knit, dynamic nucleus whose solidarity was stressed by the rampart that crowded them together while at the same time protecting their wealth. The ties that bound them were strengthened by their equality before the law, in other words by the personal freedom they all enjoyed, whatever their origin, whether vagabonds, runaway serfs, officials or any others; and by the mutual oath—a current usage when concluding an alliance, coalition or contract— that pledged all the *jurati* of the 'commune', all those who lived in the urban area.

To safeguard its freedom, ensure its independence and self-government, the commune had to obtain the lord's consent. In such former Roman cities as Cologne, Worms, Cambrai, Laon, the lord was a bishop. Although he had little in the way of brute strength, he was quite determined not to surrender the authority he still wielded in what was still his seat. This led to conflicts that were brought to an end either by the granting of a franchise or charter after lengthy discussions, or by violent fighting in which

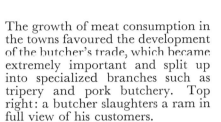

The growth of meat consumption in the towns favoured the development of the butcher's trade, which became extremely important and split up into specialized branches such as tripery and pork butchery. Top right: a butcher slaughters a ram in full view of his customers.

New crafts began by borrowing the tools of those which already existed and later modified them to suit their needs. Here we see a cleaver (left) and a meat hook (right) dating from the fifteenth century. These implements have changed very little throughout the centuries.

Below: sea and fresh-water fish was sold fresh, salted, smoked and dried. It replaced meat chiefly during Lent and Advent.

Travelling merchants called on their customers in town and country to offer their wares and spread news of public and private interest. Bottom right: a merchant offers an assortment of belts and knick-knacks to an elegant lady who carries a little dog on her right arm.

The urban way of life first appeared towards the twelfth century. Depending on the season, it was made up of processions, parades and solemn ceremonies. On festive occasions the houses were decorated and the streets strewn with flowers (below), while the people drank and made merry.

the bishop was sometimes victorious as at Cambrai in 1077 or, more frequently, defeated and expelled as at Worms, Cologne and others, or reduced to a mere figurehead as in the Italian cities.

Lay lords who lived as a rule outside the town and visited it only occasionally, like the count of Flanders at Bruges, the count of Champagne at Provins and the duke of Burgundy at Dijon, were readier to grant franchises for a consideration; the sovereign did so more readily still. Philip Augustus had thirty-nine 'good' cities; by the thirteenth century the king-emperor of Germany reigned over some fifty imperial cities *(Reichsstädte)*, among them Lübeck, Aix-la-Chapelle, Dortmund, Wetzlar, Goslar, Nuremberg, Regensburg, Frankfurt and Augsburg, and seven (or nine) almost independent 'Free Cities', the former episcopal sees of Cologne, Mainz, Worms, Spires, Strasbourg, Basle and Constance. The kings of England and Castile also granted charters to some of

their towns, but with less ample privileges. Some non-sovereign princes did the same, chief among them the German *Fürsten*, who granted special rights to almost 3,000 towns.

Once the existence of their 'commune', their constituent assembly, and their right to manage some of their interests had been recognized, many of those towns went no further than to obtain the right to collect certain taxes, exercise justice at the lowest level, and levy certain duties. Though they influenced the rural world around them by spreading the use of coinage on the local market, they remained largely dependant on the territorial lord. The latter continued to insist on certain dues such as mortmain, *marchetum*, and the wine tax, and sometimes on jurisdiction at the lowest level. Payment of quit-rents and poll-taxes, the provision of supplies for the army and quotas of armed men, and attendance at the lord's court continued as before. A smaller number of towns adopted a pseudo-feudal status which made them, in effect, collective vassals who furnished soldiers for the army and the cavalcade (Poitiers), gave aid in the three customary cases (Abbeville) or did homage in the person of the mayor or a certain number of their burghers (Châteauneuf-de-Tours). Some paid the poll-tax *(Reichssteuer)* but in that case were represented in the Diet of the Empire *(Reichstag)* in the same way as the *Fürsten*.

As a collective lord, the city had its keep—the clock tower—its wall, its seal, its armed guard, its court and its absolute domination of the surrounding country. Some of those cities became virtually independent, refusing to swear allegiance to anyone (Strasbourg, Basle), engaging in their own foreign policy with total liberty to form leagues and alliances, administering an extensive peasant *contado* as the basis of their power (Florence, Siena etcetera).

Every Western city, however unimportant, had its deliberative assembly and its administrative body— the Town Council—which was sometimes divided into a number of mutually independent committees for dealing with certain matters. As a rule the councillors were few in number—usually twelve in Ger-

Most highway robbers, like these who are depicted attacking a wayfarer (below), ended their days swinging from a gibbet.

The townspeople were summoned to witness executions which they went to out of both fear and curiosity. Below: the market place in Paris swarms with people for the death of Amerigot Marchès, a famous brigand of gentle birth. He was beheaded with a sword; axes, like the one at left preserved at Sion, were also used.

many and Southern France, sometimes twenty-four, as at Freiburg im Breisgau, Mainz and Strasbourg. They were elected or co-opted or designated by lot; they had one or more leaders (mayor, burgomaster), who officiated at the same time or one after the other and were assisted by a staff of clerks, bailiffs and notaries which could total several hundred persons (200 at Lübeck and Frankfurt). Their functions depended on the charter granted the town. Italian magistrates were on a par with the members of a sovereign council; those in England and France were restricted in their action by a strong centralized monarchy or a powerful local lord; the German councillors, instead, could decide for themselves in most matters.

Even after difficulties with the lay lords had been solved, there still remained the possibility of conflict with the Church—particularly in legal matters. In fact, it was a moot question whether the ecclesiastical courts had jurisdiction over all the property held by the clergy either personally or collectively and whether their lands should pay taxes to the commune. Moreover, the burghers wanted their sons to receive a less religious and more practical education. In 1252 Lübeck was granted permission to open a 'secondary' school; its example was followed by Breslau (1266), Wismar (1269), Freiburg im Breisgau and Vienna. Universities were opened under municipal supervision at Erfurt in 1379, at Cologne in 1388, and at Rostock jointly with the Duchy of Mecklenburg. The Church did not abandon its rights or the monopoly of education, but permitted the Town Council to appoint a School inspector to watch over the teaching staff. In the field of social assistance the Church was gradually ousted by the town, which founded or administered hospitals, organized supplies and even fed the poor. Lastly, the town, like any other lord, could act as a patron and propose candidates for election as parish priests —Lübeck enjoyed that privilege from 1188 or 1226 at the latest—and as administrator of the community purse it could help to finance the erection of great churches like those at Ulm and Strasbourg.

Inside its walls and within its urban district, the Town Council gradually concentrated in its own hands all the powers not explicitly reserved to the prince. For example, the city police issued regulations concerning the carrying of arms, unauthorized gatherings, the safety of the streets by night, and the observation of the curfew. In towns built largely of timber, fire was apt to spread very rapidly and cause a catastrophe, so chimney sweeping was carefully controlled and voluntary fire-fighting units were numerous and well trained. Hygiene and morality were two of the major preoccupations of the severe, punctilious German burghers; both came into play in connection with syphilis, which increased at the end of the fifteenth century. Games of chance, intemperance in eating and drinking, and too luxurious apparel were strictly forbidden or precisely regulated by the sumptuary laws which flourished in Germany and Italy after the middle of the fourteenth century.

Military expenses were numerous and heavy. The burghers were liable for military service, on horseback if 'patricians'; it was possible, however, to send a substitute if his name was drawn by lot for the call-up because otherwise the burgher would be forced to relinquish his normal activities. So, if the guard at walls and gates, and even the night-watch, were often led by burghers, expeditions abroad and defence against attack from without were mostly entrusted to mercenaries who were needy lesser nobles. The military chief, who bore the title of Captain, was usually a nobleman, and was better paid than any other official. The men under his orders were few in number—at Nuremberg twenty-seven in 1377, a peaceful year, and eighty-seven in 1388, a war year. But if we add the cost of grooms to care for the indispensable horses, farriers, wheelwrights for the vehicles, blacksmiths and armourers, gunners, bombardiers and cannon founders, as well as that of arms and equipment, we can readily understand that military expenditure was the biggest item in the budget of a German town. It accounted for 82 per cent of Cologne's in 1379, a peaceful year!

The commune was defined as a body corporate by the possession of a seal marked with some characteristic feature. Above left: the seal of Saint-Omer represents the members of the town council. Above right: that of Middleburg (Netherlands) displays the clock tower and the town wall.

The civic authorities took the oath on the square in front of the town hall in the presence of the citizenry. Here they are seen at Basle when it joined the Swiss Confederation on 13 July 1501.

Regular revenue was very small for the excellent reason that the rich burghers who held the reins of local government hardly taxed themselves at all. Income tax was 'regressive', declining from 1 per cent for people who were merely well off to 0.4 per cent for the very wealthy; on the other hand, the poor were exempt entirely. I may add that domanial revenues depended on the poll-tax for the urban district, which was usually quite small, while indirect taxes on beverages and goods in transit were levied only with great difficulty before the fourteenth century and were so numerous and diverse that it is impossible to form any idea of their importance. On the other hand, the erection of a central market (*Kaufhaus*) or of separate markets for cloth, fish, salt and the like, where merchants—particularly those who came from outside the town—had to store their goods or sell them, ensured more regular receipts. The minting of coins—Lübeck, for instance, acquired the right to do so in 1226—was another source of revenue.

All these receipts barely sufficed to balance the ordinary expenditure. Whenever an extraordinary outlay had to be met the best way was to obtain a loan from the rich burghers, who were easier to approach than the Jews or Lombards, in return for certain guarantees, usually short-dated life or perpetual annuities. In 1351 the entire consolidated debt of the city of Cologne was founded on 30,920 marks of 10 per cent life annuities. At Venice there were no taxes but the citizens were asked for 'voluntary' contributions which could hardly be refused; they bore interest and were repayable, in theory, by the *Cassa dei Imprestedi*. We still have the accounts for many towns in England, France, Germany and Italy for that period. They show that not one had a regular, equitable fiscal system. And very often the responsible officials displayed a mean, narrow mentality that prevented them from looking beyond the details and visualizing a system at once simple and effective. Even at Florence and in the Florentine part of Tuscany, where a gigantic *Catasto* was established in 1427 listing all personal and landed property

323

The towns in the South of France were administered by a college of 'consuls'. At Toulouse the town council or 'chapter', dates back to 1152; its twelve members were called 'capitouls'. Left: a miniature in the official chronicle of the town shows the *capitouls* in 1369 wearing long red-and-black particoloured robes with their escutcheons slung from the roof over them.

The herald of the free independent city of Strasbourg is still preserved as an automaton on the organ in the cathedral.

and all the dependants of each head of a household, there is not the slightest trace of an equitable direct tax. In 1442 Cosimo de Medici replaced the *catasto* with an *arbitrio* and later with other taxes.

It must be admitted that the town councils and the magistrates they appointed had a particularly delicate task because they were answerable not only to the more or less important fraction of the urban population that had elected them but also to the whole body of taxpayers. There is no point in detailing the major influences exerted on them and the chronological order of their appearance in the course of the social history of Western Europe. It is worth recalling, however, that by and large their evolution was the same in Northern Italy and in Tuscany. During a first phase—in the eleventh and twelfth centuries—the nobles joined forces against the local lord, who was sometimes the bishop, to wrest power from him and elect their own consuls. But it was not

long before they were so rent by factions that they had to call in a *podestà* from another part of the country. In the thirteenth century the new moneyed aristocracy, the 'people' *(popolo grasso)*, organized in craft guilds *(arti)* through which they dominated the artisans and the lower classes *(popolo minuto)*, seized power and governed in the person of the *capitano del popolo*. Finally, the discontent of the lower classes, so long held in check by the rich middle class, was exploited by a strong man who succeeded in having himself elected *capitano* or *podestà* for life, first of one city and later of several. The title sometimes became hereditary and lordship over a single city led to the establishment of a principality, namely a group of towns under the same lord.

In Flanders the course of events was slightly different. During the twelfth and thirteenth centuries power was concentrated in the hands of the 'patricians', who ruled over the common people. They were organized in close-knit clans whose power was enhanced by intermarriage. Ownership of the urban area and of large estates beyond the walls enabled them little by little to give up the trade in which they had made their fortune, take over the farm of duties and managements, adopt the way of life of the nobility, do military service on horseback, take part in tourneys, and have themselves addressed as sir.

In Germany too, where the nobility deserted the towns at an early date, a patrician class became economically and socially predominant. They acquired and granted fiefs, monopolized administrative functions, led the Town Council *(Rat)*, and had the sole right to appoint canons to certain chapters and colleges. They lived in houses surmounted by a tower, travelled on horseback, armed and spurred, with a large retinue, and in general vied with the real nobles who had immigrated from the country, officials, knights and ennobled squires. Some patricians were related to the nobility by marriage; others never succeeded in advancing beyond the unenviable status of prospective noblemen.

During the thirteenth century the Flemish and German patricians, like the nobles in Italy, witnessed the rise of a new class of wealthy men supported by the craft guilds of which they were the leaders. In some places that mean, lower-middle class with a narrow, protectionist outlook ousted the patricians from the local government without winning over the common people. In Flanders its victory was short-lived for in the fourteenth century the people often upheld a tribune or a demagogic patrician against it and so enabled the territorial lord to regain possession of the towns. In Germany the master craftsmen, who were no less narrow-minded and whose one idea was to check competition and share profits among themselves, gained the upper hand only at a later date and then only in the Centre and South—at Magdeburg (1330), Cologne (1396), Mainz, Spires, Memmingen, and in Swabia, Alsace and Switzerland. In some cities, such as Constance, Vienna and Strasbourg, a balanced situation arose. In others, such as Hamburg and Lubeck in Northern Germany, Breslau, Nuremberg, Regensburg and Leipzig, the patriciate remained very active, rich, powerful and open to new families; this enabled it to keep the reins of important trade and the local government despite violent attacks not only by the master craftsmen but also by the numerous needy proletariat which formed the lowest stratum of the urban society. This aspect of the situation is not unlike that of Florence and other Italian cities when faced by the poor workers in revolt, such as the Ciompi in 1378 under the leadership of the wool carder di Lando.

To form an idea of how people lived behind the walls of a town it is not enough to consider only the churchmen and territorial princes who from within or without upheld their traditional rights or endeavoured to impose them. Another factor of major importance was the often fierce rivalry of the aristocracy, comprising nobles and patricians, the rich merchants, the artisans whether well-off or not, and the unprivileged workers. From the very start the merchants formed the most dynamic element of the new town together with a few seigniorial officials and landed proprietors; but even in great commercial centres like Venice and Lubeck, only a tiny minority

Rich burghers erected magnificent residences for reasons of prestige and to embellish the town of their birth. Few are as perfect as Jacques Cœur's 'palace' at Bourges, which combines harmoniously the office wing with a splendid mansion that foreshadows the Renaissance.

Monasteries and some lay lords made an important contribution to the spread and improvement of techniques. The urban revival led to a multiplication of crafts, old and new: coppersmiths, clock makers, organ builders, sculptors, inn-keepers. Top right: Each craft became independent and had its own guild, by-laws and traditions. Unfortunately, very few medieval implements have been preserved. Here we have a nail, a hammer head, and a fifteenth century anvil.

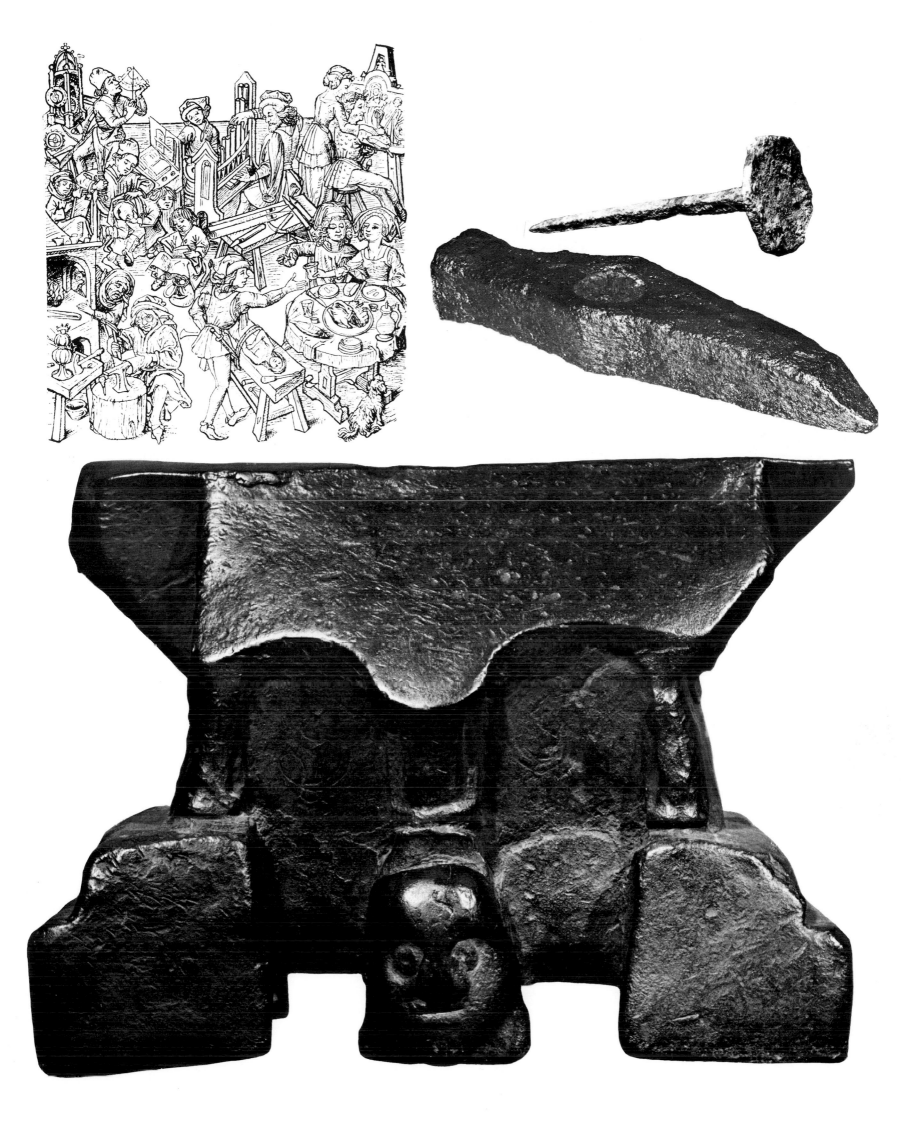

Opposite page: *The Holy Family*, by Jean Bourdichon, is really a picture of a fifteenth century joiner and his family. The child makes himself useful gathering up chips and shavings, while the mother spins and the craftsman smoothes a plank with a large plane. His tools lie on the bench in front of him; some are still practically identical with those in use today.

Working precious metals demanded a sure hand. Left, the master, seated on a bench, watches his apprentice at work and is generous with advice. He was authorized to use the rod, but his wife was not supposed to do so however quick-tempered she might be.

were engaged in large-scale trade. In the towns the artisan class was unquestionably the most numerous, as the peasantry was in the country. It worked for local consumption or the export trade and was either theoretically free or restrained by the fetters of a corporate organization. In both cases it was hampered by a number of general regulations issued by the municipal or seigniorial authority concerning the purchase of raw materials, the sale of finished products and their quality.

Hardly anything is known about the free workers, though they probably formed the majority of the population in a great many towns and cities, in some of which, such as Lyons, Bordeaux and Narbonne, the strict corporate regime never flourished. If we are to believe Etienne Boileau's *Livre des Métiers* (Book of Crafts), Paris at the end of the thirteenth century had only 101 sworn guilds, compared with over 300 mentioned in the poll-tax records. But it is a well-known fact that the inquiry made by the *Prévôt* of Paris is full of important omissions: for instance, the water sellers, the butchers and the furriers were 'forgotten' in the final summary. Some German regulations explicitly mention workers and masters who were 'outside the guild' but engaged in

the same activities as the regular members. This means that the situation varied widely.

The position of the corporations, namely the associations of artisans who plied the same craft and undertook by oath to obey the by-laws and respect the authority of the sworn experts in charge of them, seems to have grown steadily stronger up to the fourteenth century. The origin of those 'guilds' is obscure and their link with the Roman *collegia* purely conjectural. On the other hand, in many cases though not in all, there is no denying the part played by the 'brotherhoods'—mutual-aid associations whose members shared a veneration for the same saint and met more or less regularly at the same table for a banquet or drinking bout, or in the street for a procession in honour of their patron. Those brotherhoods sprang up in an urban ward, among a group of immigrants, or even in a rural parish; but the only ones of which much is known are those formed by members of the same craft under the protection of the saint revered as their patron—for instance, Saint Blasius for the masons, and Saint Eligius for the goldsmiths. Here is an example: at the end of the thirteenth century the Parisian goldsmiths undertook to care for such of their colleagues

as 'fell into poverty or sickness' and teach their orphans a trade. They also gave alms to the poor inmates of the Hôtel-Dieu (the hospital) on their major feast day so that all and sundry could rejoice on that occasion and appreciate their liberality. Their common fund was kept up by 'God's penny', levied on all sales at the rate of one *denier* per *livre*— about 0.45 per cent; the total profit made by the one workshop open for that purpose on holy days; and perhaps by a contribution from the masters who did not pay an entrance fee. The by-laws of many guilds both German and Italian provided for Sunday meetings to strengthen the bonds between the members, banquets to welcome new arrivals around a barrel of beer offered by the candidate, Requiem Masses for members recently deceased, and weekday meetings *(Morgensprachen)* to discuss their problems.

In many cases, as at Tiel and Valenciennes in the mid-eleventh century, the brotherhood preceded the corporation. Many of the earliest by-laws still extant deal exclusively with the craft guild, notably at Mainz and Saint-Omer; in Paris at the end of the thirteenth century those of several guilds make no mention whatever of a brotherhood. Be that as it may, the coalitions of artisans engaged in the same craft were controlled from the very start, and increasingly as time went on, by the authorities, both lay and ecclesiastical, who distrusted any organization that did not conform to the order established by God. To cope with competition from nearby towns and to put their members on the same footing, what had been open-ended gatherings were transformed into strictly hierarchized associations whose ultimate function was to control and regulate production. In the end the right to engage freely in a craft was reserved to the masters *(prud'hommes)*, namely the heads of workshops, who were enrolled by their peers after proving their capacity, by producing a

Like other corporate bodies, the guilds had their funds, their seals and their emblems. The drapers of the *arte della lana* of the Calimala in Florence had the task of finishing cloth imported from Flanders for sale. Below: their blazon on a background of fleurs-de-lis, the emblem of the city. The Paris water sellers were so powerful that their provost treated the king's representative on equal terms. Like that of the provost, their seal was a boat (right) which later became the emblem of Paris.

Before becoming a master, a journeyman had to prove his skill by producing a 'masterpiece'. This was carefully supervised to make sure that it was really a personal job. It involved a considerable outlay which eliminated the poorer workers. Opposite page: two candidate joiners working under the watchful eye of an elder.

'masterpiece', their honesty, and their easy circumstances; they had to possess sufficient capital to be able to pay fines for breaches of the rules. They were received into the guild in the presence of numerous witnesses; the ceremony involved taking an oath and, in many cases, offering a copious banquet. It became increasingly the custom to demand an entrance fee, which grew steadily larger.

A master had a number of assistants *(valets, Knechte)* and journeymen *(compagnons, Gesellen)*, who had the necessary technical skill but not the financial resources needed for opening a workshop, and therefore had to find employment with a master either for a single job or for a term of years. This entailed a temporary loss of freedom—hence the terms '*valet*' and '*sergent*'—but gave them a certain security during the dead season. Before obtaining promotion to the

higher category they had to save enough to pay for the raw materials for their masterpiece, the banquet and the entrance fee. A good marriage was a help for it either doubled a man's earning capacity, if the wife worked too, or brought a pretty dowry if, for instance, she was a master's widow. A master's sons had little difficulty in following in their father's footsteps.

Except for the size of his workshop or his financial situation, there was, in theory at least, no limit to the number of journeymen a master could employ; but he seldom had more than two or three apprentices *(Lehrlinge)* in addition to his own children. As a rule an apprentice was bound by a contract signed by his father or guardian. The time spent under the master depended on the difficulty of the trade in question but usually ranged from ten to twelve years. In Paris at the end of the thirteenth century apprenticeship lasted from two to four years in four trades, from five to seven years in nine, from eight to ten years in thirty-one and twelve years in three others. The master received a certain sum for keeping and training the apprentice until he could pay his own way; he also had the advantage of cheap labour, could hire the boy out and collect his wages, or even transfer or sell him to a colleague. During the first few years the apprentice acted as a type of domestic servant, running errands and walking the children; he could even be beaten by the master's wife. Later he learned his craft and was declared 'apt' after a fixed period or on passing an examination, or when he was capable of earning enough to provide for his wants.

Most workshops were rather small and also did duty as shops for selling the articles produced there. To save time the journeymen and apprentices had dinner with the master and his family; this gave the workers' mutual relationships an archaic, family character. There was little in the way of division of labour within a given craft and a journeyman was entrusted with the whole manufacturing process from the raw material to the finished article. On the other hand, demarcation was carried to extremes be-

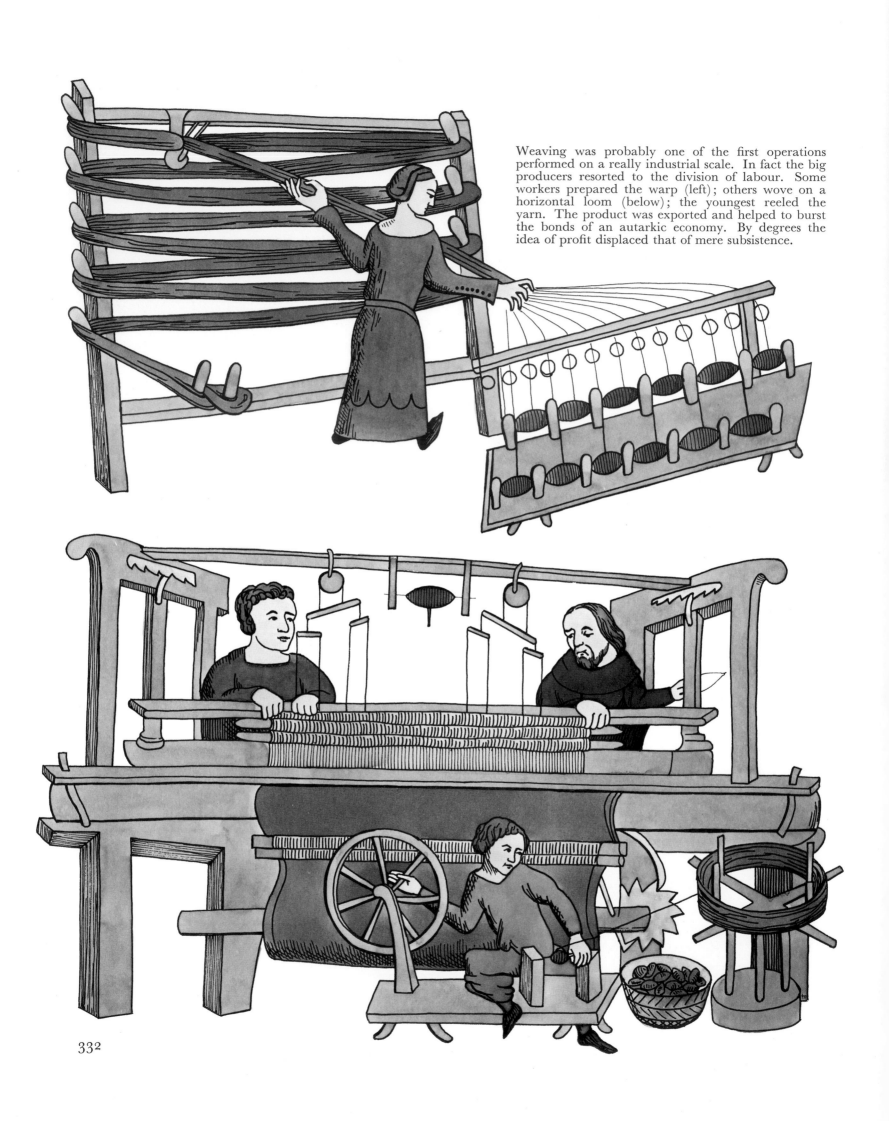

Weaving was probably one of the first operations performed on a really industrial scale. In fact the big producers resorted to the division of labour. Some workers prepared the warp (left); others wove on a horizontal loom (below); the youngest reeled the yarn. The product was exported and helped to burst the bonds of an autarkic economy. By degrees the idea of profit displaced that of mere subsistence.

Untreated cloth was bleached or dyed in big vats. Heat was required for reds and yellows; blue derived from pastel needed slow oxidation.

Embroidered work (above right) was much used; gold, silver and silk threads were employed to design motifs borrowed from legend or nature or religion.

There were no ready-made clothes. Tailors, working singly or in groups, dressed the nobility and the wealthy middle class. Articles of clothing were often worn by several people one after the other until absolutely threadbare. This explains the many old-clothes dealers.

tween one craft and another. At Frankfurt on Main iron workers were divided into over fifty trades. At Nuremberg the metal-working trades made up more than a quarter of the total. This exaggerated specialization may have ensured good quality but it certainly restricted output.

Quality was a very important matter: it was supervised by sworn experts elected by the masters or appointed by the municipal or manorial authority. They demanded that raw materials should be genuine and the job done openly; so night work was barred because it might give the product a certain clandestine character besides requiring costly lighting. Heavy punishments, ranging from fines to imprisonment, the pillory and even banishment, were stipulated for counterfeiting. The working day began at sunrise and ended when the candles were lit. It is easy to understand that under these circumstances in winter work lasted at the most from 8 a.m. to 5 p.m. On the other hand, the long hours worked in summer were partly made up for by Sundays—work stopped at noon on Saturdays—the many holidays of obligation, Masses for the souls of fellow guildsmen, funerals, and ceremonies for the patron saint.

It would be interesting to investigate the net monthly or yearly wages, but unfortunately that is out of the question. At Lyons at the beginning of the fifteenth century a labourer was paid 1 *sou tournois*, the price of 8 pounds of bread, for a day's work. This added up to less than 240 *sous* a year or under 6 pounds of bread a day. We have already seen that, if life at subsistence level was more or less assured in normal times, the slightest accident led to insecurity and distress. Lodging presented a less serious problem, even in a town like Paris where rents were very high. R. Cazelles has recently calculated that a journeyman spent only 8 per cent of his wages on rent, a master mason only 5 per cent. There remains the question of independent workers, who were not subject to the strict rules of the corporations but to the hard laws of competition. The problem was the same in Paris, Cologne or anywhere else. Those who did not succeed in finding an employer at the beginning of the day had either to accept a very low wage for an unskilled job or risk fasting.

It is possible to form a good idea of the artisans' way of life and its impact on the urban society by studying the specialized group of the cloth makers and the complex operations required in the only important industry in the Western World at that time. Let us concentrate on Flanders, where the situation is well known. It should be recalled at the start that most of the untreated wool used as raw material came from England. There producers and packers had sorted it into three grades—good, medium and poor. When the bales were opened the fibres were checked again and classed according to quality by female sorters *(elisseresses)*, then beaten with rods on a wicker hurdle to make them supple, scoured to remove the wool-fat that made them too rigid, and lubricated with a pure, light grease, sometimes with an olive-oil base, to make them soft and springy. They were next combed with an iron comb to remove the last burrs or carded with natural or iron teazles attached to a board to tease out the knots and disentangle the fibres. From the carder *(carderesse)* the wool passed on to the spinner *(fileresse)*, who wound the fibres round a distaff or spindles to form threads that the winder *(dévideresse)* combined in hanks. The introduction of the spinning wheel at the end of the twelfth century was a great improvement. Until then thread had always been produced manually by housewives both in town and country; though badly paid, it was a chance to earn a little extra money at home.

The thread was woven in a weaver's shop on a horizontal wooden loom. This was a relatively costly piece of equipment but the only one that could produce good-quality cloth. For the weaving process, the warpers prepared the warp of 1,000 to 3,000 threads on flexible rods called heddles. This had the same length as the finished piece of cloth—up to 56 ells. Next, other workers formed the weft by passing the shuttle alternately over and under the heddles. The fabric obtained by this process was freed from excess grease with clay, rinsed and tram-

In the thirteenth century Ypres produced tens of thousands of pieces of cloth adding up to several thousand miles of cloth a year. The great hall where it was stored and sold is the biggest civic building erected during the Middle Ages. Its 433-foot façade makes it almost as long as Cluny Minster, the largest of all medieval churches.

pled several times by the fullers; fulling mills were employed from the thirteenth century. When dry the cloth had shrunk and thickened. It was 'felted' while still damp by successively beating or rubbing it from the top downwards between progressively sharper teazles. After this it was wetted several times, smeared with butter or other fat, and fulled for three days. Lastly, it was 'stretched' lengthwise and cross-wise while still damp and cut in order to smooth the velvety finish on its two faces.

The process I have just described produced white cloth, but most cloth was coloured. That required the intervention of the dyer, who seldom treated wool before weaving for fear of producing a mottled fabric. The dyeing process was usually applied after the first cutting. The cloth was put in a copper tub with a strong, hot mordant—alum, pine ash or slaked lime—which removed the grease and prepared the cloth to fix the dyestuff. The latter was either vegetable, yellow weld, madder; or animal, the bright red kermes oak 'berry', or cochineal. Dyeing with woad (pastel) did not require alum: ordinary ash was enough. But it involved long soaking in hot water in wooden tubs and exposure to the air.

Flemish cloth differed greatly depending on the quality of the wool, the thread, the warp and the dye. The qualities ranged from *tiretaine* (shoddy, made of old wool), through *blanchet* (rather coarse), *burel* (plain), *saie* (combed but with uncarded weft), *camelin* (combed), *estanfort* (strong) to *écarlate* (fine, close woven and luxurious). The colours included apple blossom, perker (peach) blossom, light leaf green, blood red, watered effect and mixed. The many different operations—some thirty in all—took at least a month and involved numerous journeys from one workplace to another.

What is especially striking are the differences in social standing among the various workers and producers—the unskilled housewife who sorted, combed, carded and span; the weaver who selected the threads and manufactured the cloth with the help of semi-skilled assistants, whom he paid at the rate fixed by the town; the fuller or dyer who employed cheap, robust labour to trample and handle the heavy pieces of cloth—their length ranged from 65 to 100 feet—and have their fingernails blued by the dye-stuffs. Lastly, capping them all, the merchant draper who ordered the cloth, supplied the raw materials—wool, alum, and the like—and sold the product. Those entrepreneurs formed a wealthy, exclusive oligarchy, and several of those who thrived in the mid-thirteenth century are known to us by name. Beneath them were the master weaver, who had to haggle over the price if he was to safeguard his narrow profit margin, and the master dyer, who could juggle with the fixed rates of pay. Lastly, came the mass of workers, either protected like the journeymen or paid—usually underpaid—by the job. Those 'blue nails' seem to have been real proletarians.

This picture may not have been true of all the cities of the West, but it was the one most frequently found in the fourteenth and fifteenth centuries, and not merely where cloth manufacture was the only

industry. The situation was typical in Italy but was not unknown in Germany: rich men engaged in international trade continued to amass wealth. In 1418 Constance could boast 137 burghers with over 200 pounds (Heller) each, the average being 5,413; by 1454 their number had fallen to 123, but the average had risen to 6,377 pounds. At Rostock 24.4 per cent of the population paid less than 8 schillings in 1378, 34.4 per cent in 1409, 46.2 per cent in 1430, 37.8 per cent 1454, 48.3 per cent in 1473. Of the 4,485 households in Augsburg, 66 per cent paid no taxes at all because they were considered too poor to do so. Differences of the same order can be observed among masters of the same craft. At Basle in 1429, 15 blacksmiths had less than 10 guilders; 77 had between 10 and 150; 78 had between 150 and 200; 2 had over 2,000. At Görlitz in 1443, 23 weavers had less than 10 Marks; 75 had between 10 and 100; 39 had between 100 and 500.

The corporations endeavoured to remedy the situation by hunting down 'black' labour, banning peasant workers in the vicinity, limiting the number of guildsmen, restricting the size of the workshops, rigorously defining the scope of related crafts, and prohibiting the introduction of newly-qualified apprentices who might take work away from the less well-off masters to the advantage of those rich enough to buy expensive machinery. Besides the steps taken to react against those who were more fortunate than their fellows, the corporations imposed checks on the recruitment of apprentices, who had to certify that they were of honourable, free, German birth. Apprenticeship fees and terms increased. To become a master, a journeyman had to own property in the town, pay for the freedom of the city, and have the means to pay the cost of his masterpiece and the purchase of a workshop.

But the cure was worse than the evil. For one thing, many small masters continued to own their workshop and tools, but were forced to sell their workforce to the entrepreneur who granted them a loan; they also had to buy their raw materials from him at a higher price and sell him all their output.

The well-off masters became entrepreneurs and melted into the class of capitalist merchants. At Augsburg, of the seven richest taxpayers four had risen from the ranks of the master weavers, including Jakob Fugger, the richest of them all. This led to the organization of workshops manned by salaried workers—factories of a sort, which supplied woollens, silks and fustian (Strasbourg, Cologne, Saint-Gall), metals and metalwork, paper, glass, and printed books. These activities, like those of the great merchants, developed outside the too-narrow framework of the corporations.

On the other hand, journeymen found it very difficult to become masters if their fathers had not been masters before them. This was the case of twenty out of thirty journeymen carpenters at Erfurt between 1481 and 1498. Those who lived in the same town—in different towns too—formed 'brotherhoods' of the same craft. Travelling through Germany, they helped each other to find work and endeavoured by boycotts and riots to improve conditions of work and pay. They insisted on having their own *Trinkstube*, where they met to drink and deliberate, and Monday off *(guter Montag)* every week or twice a month to take a bath and talk things over; otherwise, working as they did in summer up to 16 hours a day, they never had a chance to do so. In 1407 close on 4,000 journeymen cobblers went on strike throughout the Upper Rhine region and in 1470 there was a general strike of journeymen furriers both there and in Alsace, which showed their independence.

The dependant, salaried workers and their families who formed the urban proletariat continued to multiply. They comprised not only the people directly employed by the merchants—porters, dockers, packers, measurers, weighers, crane handlers—who at Cologne with their wives and children made up 4 per cent of the total population, and large numbers of boatmen and lightermen, but also life journeymen, free workers, labourers, miners, gardeners, bailiffs, small shopkeepers, municipal employees, domestic servants, jugglers, prostitutes, beggars, syphilitics, neurotics, the blind, and the families of common criminals. There were sudden fluctuations in the price of cereals, while animal foodstuffs and raw materials in general became more and more expensive. As a result even when wages increased they never kept in step. At Halle in 1474 some workers demanded an increase of almost 100 per cent.

The foregoing paragraphs reflect the situation in Germany, but it was far from being exclusive to that country. There was a great increase in social tensions in the towns of Western Europe at the end of the Middle Ages. Their impact was very serious not only on the economic and occupational planes but also in local government and politics. We have seen that in some places several generations of the wealthy class kept power in their hands with the help of the common people *(popolo minuto)* but did not hesitate to turn against their supporters when they felt that the roots of their wealth and power were in danger.

The development of trade and the rise of a new type of town were perhaps the most significant events of the last centuries of the Middle Ages. True, peasants still made up between 60 and 90 per cent of the Western population; the nobility and clergy still owned enormous estates, enjoyed the highest rank and dignity, and occupied the highest offices in the territorial principalities. In England and France the towns were still held in check; in Germany they were closely controlled and 'retrieved' at the end of the fifteenth century; while the Italian cities surrendered their liberties to new lords, many of whom they had set up themselves.

Meanwhile merchants, burghers and townsmen in general had introduced, and brought into common use coined money and disposable funds that were easy to invest—on condition a taste for risk existed, paid for labour, earned profits and generated wealth. The middle class that had sprung up in the thirteenth century was ground to dust in the fourteenth and fifteenth, and the favourable conditions for a class struggle, first evolved in the towns, gradually spread to the countryside as a result of the economic crises. This led to the definitive destruction of the orderly society willed by God.

CONCLUSION

Living as we do in the closing decades of the twentieth century, we cannot help considering the Middle Ages as entirely alien to our mentality. A sketch, however rapid, of the everyday life of the society of that period will make it easier for us to understand.

It focuses our attention on structures of such long duration that some hark back to classical Antiquity, while others, more numerous, link the Middle Ages with our own modern world. The most striking and at the same time most elementary example is offered by the innumerable details of rural life, cereal husbandry and domestic livestock breeding. The cooking of a pig, the tales told at the fireside on winter evenings, the dwellings typical of the various regions and the materials employed to build them, the shoeing and harnessing of horses and oxen, the invention of the wheelbarrow, the seasons of the year and the great religious festivals, the constant contact with soil, plants and animals, formed the very essence of daily life for tens of millions of people in the West until the Second World War, if not later. The aristocracy still have their armorial bearings, sometimes their hunts and castles, even their tradition as professional soldiers. The doctrine and hierarchy of the Church, its influence on education and politics, are still very much the same. And the great changes in the aspect of the towns, still dotted with a quantity of medieval buildings, date back a few decades, at most a century; the same is true of the revolution that has taken place in transport and communications.

But it is not enough to observe these instances of a continuity at once deep-seated and occult. We must also consider the many things that existed during the Middle Ages and have been gradually lost since then. Nature was more vigorous and pervasive: the people's diet was less balanced, their clothing less varied, their lifespan far shorter. Men's judgment had lost the clarity of Graeco-Roman Antiquity and had not yet discovered the rationalism of Descartes. The ordered society willed by God, in which those who worked fed those who fought and those who prayed, was not easily open to change.

INDEX

BIBLIOGRAPHY

GENERAL WORKS

BAGLEY, J. J.   *Life in Medieval England*, New York & London, 1962

BERTRAND, SIMONE   *La tapisserie de Bayeux et la manière de vivre au XIe siècle*, Paris, 1966

BRAUDEL, FERNAND   *Civilisation matérielle et capitalisme*, Paris, 1967

CANTOR, NORMAN F.   *Medieval History*, New York, 1963

DEFFOURNEAUX, MARCELIN   *La vie quotidienne au temps de Jeanne d'Arc*, Paris, 1952

DELORT, ROBERT   *Introduction aux sciences auxiliaires de l'histoire*, Paris, 1969

DELORT, ROBERT, LA RONCIÈRE, CHARLES M. DE and ROUCHE, MICHEL   *L'Europe au Moyen Age. Documents expliqués*, 3 vol., Paris, 1969-1971

DUBY, GEORGES and MANDROU, ROBERT   *Histoire de la civilisation française*, Paris, 1968 (2e édition)

EVANS, JOAN   *Life in Medieval France*, London, 1925 — *Flowering of the Middle Ages*, New York, 1966

FARAL, EDMOND   *La vie quotidienne au temps de saint Louis*, Paris, 1938

FOERSTER, ROLF HELLMUT   *Das Leben in der Gotik*, Munich, 1969

FOSSIER, ROBERT   *Histoire sociale de l'Occident médiéval*, Paris, 1970

HASSALL, W. O.   *How They Lived (55-1485)*, Oxford, 1962

HAUCOURT, GENEVIÈVE D'   *La vie au Moyen Age*, Paris, 1944

HEER, FRIEDRICH   *Mittelalter*, Zürich, 1964

HUIZINGA, J.   *Le déclin du Moyen Age* (translated from the Dutch, original edition: Leyde, 1919), Paris, 1967

HUSA, VACLAV, PETRAN, JOSEF and SUBRTOVA, ALENA   *Hommes et métiers dans l'art du XIIe au XVIIe siècle en Europe centrale*, Prague, 1967 (Librarie Gründ, Paris, 1969)

KENDALL, P. M.   *The Yorkist Age, daily life during the War of the Roses*, London, 1962

LANGLOIS, CHARLES-VICTOR   *La vie en France au Moyen Age du XIIe au milieu du XIVe siècle*, 4 vol., 1926-1928, Paris

LE GOFF, JACQUES   *Civilisation de l'Occident médiéval*, Paris, 1964

POSTAN, M. M.   *The Medieval Economy and Society*, London, 1972

QUENELL, M. and G. H. B.   *A History of Everyday Things in England* (v.I.; 1066-1499), London, 1953

SALZMAN, L. F.   *English Life in the Middle Ages*, London & Oxford, 1926

SCHULTZ, ALWIN   *Deutches Leben im 14. und 15. Jahrhundert*, Vienna, 1891

STENTON, D. M.   *English Society in the Middle Ages*, Harmondsworth, 1952

WRIGHT, T. L.   *A History of Domestic Manners and Sentiments in England during the Middle Ages*, London, 1862

THE PHYSICAL CONDITIONS OF EVERYDAY LIFE

BARATIER, EDOUARD   *La démographie provençale du XIIIe au XVIe siècle*, Paris, 1961

BERESFORD, MAURICE W. and SAINT-JOSEPH, J. K.   *Medieval England. An aerial survey*, Cambridge, 1958

BOUCHER, FRANÇOIS   *Histoire du costume en Occident de l'Antiquité à nos jours*, Paris, 1965

BRIDBURY, A. R.   *Economic Growth: England in the later Middle Ages*, London, 1962

CUNNINGTON, C. W. and P.   *A Handbook of English Medieval Costumes*, London, 1952

DRUMMOND, J. C. and WILBRAHAM, A.   *The Englishman's Food: A history of five centuries of English diet*, London 1957

EVANS, J.   *Dress in Medieval France*, Oxford, 1952

FURNIVALL, F. J.   (ed.)   *Early English Meals and Manners*, London, 1868

GOTTSCHALK, F.   *Histoire de l'alimentation et de la gastronomie*, 2 vol., Paris, 1948

GUILLAUME, PIERRE and POUSSOU, JEAN-PIERRE,   *Démographie historique*, Paris, 1968

HIGOUNET, CHARLES   *Les Forêts de l'Europe occidentale du Ve siècle à l'an mil* (XIII. Settimana di Studio del Centro italiano di Studi sull'Alto Medio Evo), Spolete, 1965

LATOUCHE, ROBERT   *Les origines de l'économie occidentale (IVe-XIe siècle)*, Paris, 1956

LE ROY LADURIE, EMMANUEL   *Histoire du climat depuis l'an mil*, Paris, 1967

PIRENNE, H.   *Histoire économique de l'Occident médiéval*, Bruges, 1951

PISETZKY, ROSITA LEVI   *Storia del costume in Italia*, Rome, 1964

RUSSEL, J. C.   *Late ancient and medieval population*, Philadelphia, 1958

SERENI, EMILIO   *Storia del paesaggio agrario italiano*, Bari, 1957

TALBOT, W. H.; HAMMOND, E. H.   *The Medical Practitioners in Medieval England*, London, 1965

WHITE, LYNN   *Medieval Technology and Social Change*, Oxford, 1962

WOOD, M.   *The English Medieval House*, London, 1965

MENTALITY AND SOCIAL LIFE

CHAMPEAUX, GÉRARD DE and STERCKX, DOM SÉBASTIEN   *Introduction au monde des symboles* (Ed. Zodiaque), Saint-Léger-Vauban, 1966

DAVY, MARIE-MADELEINE   *Invitation à la symbolique romane (XIIe siècle)*, Paris, 1964

DENHOLM-YOUNG, N.   *History and Heraldry*, Oxford, 1965

GILSON, E. H.   *History of Christian Philosophy in the Middle Ages*, London, 1955

HEER, FRIEDRICH   *Aufgang Europas. Eine Studie zu den Zusammenhängen zwischen politischer Religiosität, Frömmigkeitsstil und dem Werden Europas im 12. Jahrhundert*, Vienna, s.d.

RICHE, PIERRE   *De l'éducation antique à l'éducation chevaleresque*, Paris, 1968

ROUX, JEAN-PAUL   *Les explorateurs au Moyen Age*, Paris, 1961

WULF, M. DE   *Histoire de la philosophie médiévale*, Louvain, 1934-1936

I WORK FOR ALL: The Life of the Peasantry

ABEL, WILHELM   *Geschichte der deutschen Landwirtschaft*, Stuttgart, 1962

AULT, W. O.   *Openfield Husbandry and the Village Community*, Philadelphia, 1965

BERESFORD, MAURICE W.   *The Lost Villages of England*, London, 1954

BLOCH, MARC   *Les caractères originaux de l'histoire rurale française*, 2 vol., 2nd ed., 1952-1956, Paris

DELÉAGE, ANDRÉ *La vie rurale en Bourgogne jusqu'au début du XIᵉ siècle*, 3 vol., Mâcon, 1941

DUBY, GEORGES *Rural Life and Economy in the Medieval West*, London, 1968

(Various Authors) *English Rural Life in the Middle Ages*, Oxford, 1965

FINN, R. W. *The Domesday Inquest*, London, 1961

FOSSIER, ROBERT *La terre et les hommes en Picardie*, Paris, 1968

FRANZ, GÜNTHER *Geschichte des deutschen Bauernstandes*, Stuttgart, 1970

HILTON, R. H. *A Medieval Society*, London, 1968

LENNARD, R. *Rural England (1086-1135)*, Oxford, 1959

LÜTGE, FRIEDRICH *Geschichte der deutschen Agrarverfassung*, Stuttgart, 1963

MODZELIWSKI, K. *L'archéologie du village médiéval*, Louvain, 1967

SLICHER VAN BATH, B.-H. *The Agrarian History of Western Europe (A.D. 500-1850)*, London, 1966

TITOW, J. Z. *English Rural Society*, London, 1969

I FIGHT FOR ALL: The Warrior

ANDERSON, WILLIAM *Castles of Europe*, London, 1970

BARLOW, F. *The Feudal Kingdom of England (1092-1216)*, London, 1967

BLOCH, M. *Feudal Society*, (English Translation) 1967

BOUTRUCHE, ROBERT *Seigneurie et féodalité*, 2 vol., Paris, 1959 & 1970

GANSHOF, FRANÇOIS-LOUIS *Qu'est-ce que la féodalité?*, Neuchâtel and Brussels, 1947

GAUTIER, L. *La chevalerie*, Paris, 1959

HEWITT, H. J. *The organization of war under Edward III (1338-1362)*, Manchester & New York, 1966

MARROU, H. I. *Les troubadours*, Paris, 1971

MATHEW, G. *The Court of Richard II*, London, 1966

SANDERS, I. J. *English Baronies*, Oxford, 1960

SCHULTZ, ALWIN *Das höfische Leben zur Zeit der Minnesinger*, 2 vol., Leipzig, 1879-1880

STENTON, F. M. *English Feudalism*, London, 1943

VERRIEST, LÉON *Le régime seigneurial dans le comté de Hainaut du XIᵉ siècle à la Révolution*, Louvain, 1917 (New Edition, 1956)

I PRAY FOR ALL: The Seekers for Perfection

BARLOW, F. *The English Church (1000-1066)*, London, 1963

CHARLTON, K. *Education in Renaissance England*, Toronto, 1965

CRANAGE, D. H. S. *The Home of the Monk*, Cambridge, 1926

CROSSLEY, F. H. *The English Abbey*, London, 1962

DUBY, GEORGES *Adolescence de la chrétienté occidentale*, Geneva, 1969

DUFT, JOHANNES *Studien zum Sankt Galler Klosterplan*, St Gallen, 1962

EVANS, JOAN *Monastic Life at Cluny, 910-1157*, London, 1931

GIMPEL, JEAN *Les bâtisseurs de cathédrales*, Paris, 1966

GRUNDMANN, H. *Vom Ursprung der Universität im Mittelalter*, Berlin, 1957

HALL, D. J. *English Medieval Pilgrimages*, London, 1965

KNOWLES, D. *The Monastic Order in England*, Cambridge, 1963

KNOWLES, M. C. (Dom David) *The Religious Orders in England*, Cambridge, 1950 & 1959

LE GOFF, JACQUES *Les intellectuels au Moyen Age*, Paris, 1960

MAAS, W. *Les moines défricheurs*, Moulins, 1954

MÂLE, EMILE *L'Art religieux de la fin du Moyen Age en France*, Paris, 1922
— *L'Art religieux du XIIIᵉ siècle en France*, Paris, 1925
— *L'Art religieux du XIIᵉ siècle en France*, Paris, 1938

PACAULT MARCEL *Les ordres monastiques et religieux au Moyen Age*, Paris, 1970

PANOFSKY, ERWIN *Abbot Suger on the Abbey Church of St-Denis and its Art Treasures*, Princeton and London, 1946

SMITH, A. L. *Church and State in the Middle Ages*, Oxford, 1931

ULLMANN, W. *The Growth of Papal Government in the Middle Ages*, London, 1955

TRADE AND COMMERCE

BERESFORD, M. *New Towns of the Middle Ages*, London, 1967

The Cambridge Economic History of Europe, Vols II & III, Cambridge

COORNAERT, E. *Les corporations en France avant 1789*, Paris, 1941

CARUS-WILSON, E. M. *Medieval Merchant Venturers*, London, 1954

GUTKIND, ERWIN ANTON *International History of City Development*, 5 vol., New York, 1970

HEYD, W. VON *Histoire du commerce du Levant au Moyen Age*, Leipzig, 1885-1886

LE GOFF, JACQUES *Marchands et banquiers au Moyen Age*, Paris, 1969

LEWIS, A. R. *The Northern Seas: Shipping and Commerce in Northern Europe (A.D. 300-1100)*, Princeton, 1958

LOPEZ, R. S. and RAYMOND, I. W. *Medieval Trade in the Mediterranean World*, London & New York, 1955

LUCAS-DUBRETON, JEAN *La vie quotidienne à Florence*, Paris, 1958

MELIS, FEDERIGO *Aspetti della vita economica medievale*, Siena, 1962

MERRIEN, JEAN *La vie quotidienne des marins au Moyen Age*, Paris, 1969

MUNDY, J. H. and RIESENBERG, P. *The Medieval Town*, Princeton, 1958

ORIGO, IRIS M. *The Merchant of Prato*, London, 1957

PIRENNE, H. *Les villes du Moyen Age*, Brussels, 1927

POERK, G. DE *La draperie médiévale en Flandre et en Artois, technique et terminologie*, 3 vol., Bruges, 1951

RENOUARD, YVES *Les hommes d'affaires italiens du Moyen Age*, Paris, 1949

ROOVER, R. DE *The Medici Bank: its organization, management, operations and decline*, London & New York, 1948

SALZMAN, L. F. *English Trade in the Middle Ages*, Oxford, 1931
— *English Industries of the Middle Ages*, (New Edition) London, 1964
— *English Trade in the Middle Ages*, (New Edition) London, 1964

WOLFF, PHILIPPE *Histoire générale du travail. L'âge de l'artisanat (Vᵉ-XVIIIᵉ siècle)*, Paris, 1960

ACKNOWLEDGEMENTS

The author and the publishers wish to thank the following institutions
and individuals for help in illustrating this book:

Aachen – Museen der Stadt.
Autun – Bibliothèque Municipale,
    Photo G. Varlez.

Barcelona – Photo Mas.
Basel – Aktion Bauernhausforschung in der
    Schweiz.
Basel – Historisches Museum, Photo Peter
    Heman.
Basel – Universitätsbibliothek.
Berlin – Helmut Peter Buchen.
Berlin – Preussischer Kulturbesitz: Kunst-
    bibliothek, Kupferstichkabinett, Staatsbi-
    bliothek.
Bern – Burgerbibliothek.
Besançon – Bibliothèque Municipale, Photo
    Jean Bévalot.
Bonn – Rheinisches Nationalmuseum.
Boston – Museum of Fine Arts: Helen and
    Alice Colburn Fund.
Boulogne – Bibliothèque Municipale, Photo
    Jack Audinet.
Braubach – Deutsche Burgenvereinigung e. V.,
    Photo Karl Müller.
Bruges – Musée Communal, Photo A.C.L.,
    Bruxelles.
Bruxelles – A.C.L., Bruxelles.
Bruxelles – Bibliothèque Royale de Belgique.
Bruxelles – Musée Instrumental, Photo Johan
    van Dyck, Antwerpen.
Bruxelles – Musées Royaux d'Art et d'Histoire,
    Photo A.C.L.
Burgo de Osma – Cathedral Archives.
Burgweinting – Photo Wilkin Spitta.

Cambridge – Cambridge University Collec-
    tion of Aerial Photographs.
Cambridge – Trinity College.
Carpentras – Bibliothèque Municipale.
Chantilly – Musée Condé, Photo Giraudon,
    Paris.
Chexbres – Photo Max F. Chiffelle.
Compiègne – Musée Vivenel, Photo Hutin.
Crissier – Werner Hertig Collection.

Darmstadt – Hessisches Landesmuseum.

Dijon – Bibliothèque Municipale,
    Photo R. Rémy.
Dinan – Château de la Duchesse Anne.
Douai – Bibliothèque Municipale (Gallois),
    Photo Giraudon, Paris.
Dublin – Photo Françoise Henry, Archives of
    the Department of Archeology, University
    College.
Dublin – National Library of Ireland.
Dublin – National Museum.
Durham – Cathedral, Dean and Chapter of
    Durham.

Elne – Photo J. Dieuzaide, Zodiaque.
Evreux – Archives de l'Eure, Photo B. Curé.
Essen – Münsterschatz, Photo Joseph A.
    Slominski, Essen.

Firenze – Photo Alinari.
Firenze – Biblioteca Medicea, Laurenziana,
    Photo G. B. Pineider.
Firenze – Photo Scala.

Gent – Musée Archéologique de la Byloke,
    Foto Claerhaout.
Gent – Rijksuniversiteit, Centrale Bibliotheek,
    Photo De Wulf Evergem.
Gerona – Cathedral Treasury.
Glasgow – Library of the University.
Göttingen – Niedersächsische Staats- und Uni-
    versitätsbibliothek.
Grenoble – Bibliothèque Municipale, Photo
    Piccardy, Grenoble.

Heidelberg – Canis-Foto.
Heidelberg – Universitätsbibliothek.
Hereford – Cathedral Treasury, Dean of the
    Hereford Cathedral.
Hohenheim – Universität,
    Photo Gunther Franz.

København – Nationalmuseet.
Köln – Schnütgen Museum, Photo Rheinisches
    Bildarchiv, Kölnisches Stadtmuseum.

Laon – Bibliothèque Municipale.
Lausanne – Bibliothèque Cantonale et Univer-
    sitaire.
Lausanne – Musée Cantonal d'archéologie et
    d'histoire, Cabinet des Médailles.
Leinfelden b. Stuttgart – Museum der Ver-
    einigten Altenburger und Stralsunder Spiel-
    kartenfabriken.
Liège – Musée Diocésain.
London – Photo A. F. Kersting.
London – Aerofilms Library.
London – British Museum.
London – George Weidenfeld & Nicolson, Ltd.
London – Inner Temple Library, London,
    Photo Preussicher Kulturbesitz, Kunstbiblio-
    thek, Berlin.
London – London Museum.
London – Montacute House (Somerset), Photo
    Ronald Sheridan.
London – National Gallery.
London – Public Record Office.
London – Science Museum.
London – Photo Ronald Sheridan.
London – Thames and Hudson, Ltd Publishers
London – The British Tourist Authority.
London – Tower, Department of the Environ-
    ment, Crown Copyright.
Lourdes – Photo Pierre Chambon, Edition
    Yan.
Lucca – Biblioteca Statale, Photo Guido San-
    soni.
Luzern – Historisches Museum, Photo Peter
    Ammon.
Luzern – Schweizerisches Museum für Brot
    und Gebäck.
Luzern – Zentralbibliothek, Photo Schweizeri-
    sches Landesmuseum, Zürich.

Madrid – Biblioteca Nacional.
Madrid – El Escorial, Photo Mas, Barcelona
    and Henri Stierlin, Genève.
Mainz – Mittelrheinisches Landesmuseum.
Mantova – Biblioteca Communale, Photo Gio-
    vetti.
Marburg – Bildarchiv Foto.
Metz – Trésor de la Cathédrale, Archives
    photographiques, Paris.
Milano – Biblioteca Ambrosiana.

Montpellier – Bibliothèque de la Faculté de Médecine, Photo Claude O'Sughrue.
Moscow – Lenin Library.
Moscow – Library of the Academy of Sciences, Thames and Hudson Ltd, Publishers, London.
München Alte Pinakothek, Photo Blauel Kunst-Dias.
München – Altes Rathaus, Fremdenverkehrsamt, Foto Otto Angermayer.
München – Bayerisches Nationalmuseum.
München – Bayerische Staatsbibliothek, Bildarchiv Foto Marburg and Hirmer Fotoarchiv, München.

Nancy – Musée Lorrain.
New York – The Metropolitan Museum of Art, The Cloisters Collection, Robert Lehmann Collection, The Collection of Irwin Untermeyer.
New York The Pierpont Morgan Library.
Norwich – Photo Jarrold Colour Publications.
Nürnberg Germanisches Nationalmuseum.

Offenbach am Main – Deutsches Ledermuseum.
Oslo – Vikingskipshuset (Viking Museum), Photo Staatsbibliothek — Bildarchiv Berlin.
Oxford – Bodleian Library.
Oxford – Christ Church Library.
Oxford – Corpus Christi College.
Oxford – Thomas-Photos.

Paris – Archives de l'Assistance Publique.
Paris – Archives photographiques.
Paris – Archives Nationales, Photo Giraudon, Lauros-Giraudon and Société Française du Microfilm.
Paris – Photo Baron A. de Wismes (p.p.), C.A.L.
Paris – Bibliothèque de l'Arsenal, Photo Giraudon and Bibliothèque Nationale.
Paris – Bibliothèque Nationale, Photo Giraudon, Archives photographiques, Patrick Guilbert, Bibliothèque Cantonale et Universitaire Lausanne and Skira, Genève.
Paris – Photo J. F. Bulloz.

Paris – Photo Robert Durandaud.
Paris – Photo Ecole des Beaux-Arts, Bulloz and Giraudon.
Paris – Photo Giraudon.
Paris – Institut Géographique National.
Paris – Photo Jean Roubier.
Paris – Musée de Cluny, Clichés des Musées Nationaux, Roger-Viollet and Archives photographiques.
Paris – Musée du Louvre, Clichés des Musées Nationaux and Bulloz.
Paris – Musée des Arts Décoratifs.
Paris – Photo-Hachette.
Paris – Photothèque Française.
Paris – Photo Roger-Viollet.
Pierry (Marne) – Château de la Marquetterie, Photo Champagne Taittinger, Reims.
Praha – Cathedral Treasury, Photo Joseph Ehm.
Praha – Knihovna Národniho Muzea, Photo Antonín Bláha.

Roma – Appartamenti Borgia, Vaticano, Photo Alinari, Firenze.
Roma – Biblioteca Apostolica Vaticana.
Rotterdam – Maritiem Museum " Prins Hendrik ".
Rouen – Archives de la Seine-Maritime.
Rouen – Bibliothèque Municipale, Photo " Paris-Normandie ".
Rouen – Musée des Beaux-Arts, Photo-Ellebé.

Saint-Germain-en-Laye Musée, Photo Giraudon.
Salzburg – Abtei St Hildegard, Rüdesheim, Eibingen, Photo Otto Müller Verlag.
Sankt Gallen – Stadtbibliothek (Vadiana).
Sankt Gallen – Stiftsbibliothek.
Santiago de Compostela – Biblioteca Catolica, Photo Lauros-Giraudon, Paris.
Sélestat – Bibliothèque, Photo Bibliothèque Cantonale et Universitaire, Lausanne.
Siena – Monte dei Paschi (Archivio Datini di Prato), Photo Federigo Melis, Firenze.
Siena – Palazzo Pubblico, Photo Scala, Firenze
Sion – Eglise de Valère, Photo Klopfenstein, Adelboden.
Sion – Musée cantonal de Valère.

Soest – Foto Streil.
Solinge-Ohligs – Photo Armin Alfermann, Landesverkehrsverband Rheinland e. V., Bad Godesberg.
Stockholm – Historiska Museum
Stockholm – Kungliga Biblioteket.
Strasbourg – Musée de l'Oeuvre Notre-Dame, Photo Musées de la ville de Strasbourg (Josef Franz), Service d'architecture de l'Oeuvre Notre-Dame and Archives photographiques, Paris.

Toulouse – Archives municipales, Photo Giraudon, Paris.
Toulouse – Reportage photographique YAN.
Tournai – Photo Jules Messiaen.

Überlingen – Rathaus (Bodensee), Photo Siegfried Lautenwasser.

Varberg – Varbergs Museum (Sverige).
Venezia – Biblioteca del Seminario Patriarcale, Photo Osvaldo Böhm.
Venezia – Biblioteca Marciana, Foto Toso.
Vich (Barcelona) – Museo Episcopal, Photo Mas, Barcelona.

Wien – Heeresgeschichtliches Museum, Photo Erwin Meyer.
Wien – Kunsthistorisches Museum, Photo Erwin Meyer.
Wien – Österreichische Nationalbibliothek, Bildarchiv Foto Marburg and Akademische Druck- und Verlagsanstalt, Graz.
Wien – Österreichisches Staatsarchiv, Photo Ernst Zimmermann, Rheinfelden.
Wilhelmshaven – Niedersächsische Landesstelle für Marschen- und Wurtenforschung.

York – Dean and chapter of York Minster, Photo W. J. Green.
Ypres – Archives Communales.

Zürich – Zentralbibliothek, Photo Paul Scheidegger.
Zürich – Schweizerisches Landesmuseum.

This book is edited and produced by
EDITA S.A., Lausanne
Printed in Italy and bound in Switzerland

Printed in Italy